Books are to be returned
the last date be

D0513521

GREENER MARKETING
A Responsible Approach to Business

edited by
Martin Charter

GREENER

MARKETING

A responsible approach to business

Edited by
Martin Charter

Greenleaf **Publishing** 1992

Published by Greenleaf Publishing
Greenleaf Publishing is an imprint of
Interleaf Productions Limited
Sidney Street, Sheffield S1 3QF
England

Typeset by Interleaf Productions Limited
and
Printed on environmentally friendly, acid-free paper
from managed forests
by The Cromwell Press, Melksham, Wiltshire

British Library Cataloguing in Publication Data

Greener Marketing: Responsible Approach to
Business
I. Charter, Martin
658.8

ISBN 1-874719-00-4

CONTENTS

Part III: Case Histories

ACKNOWLEDGEMENTS

Greener Marketing is one of a number of projects that have been created by KPH Marketing to encourage debate over issues related to business and the environment. *Greener Marketing* was developed from an original booklet produced by KPH Marketing in 1990.

The production of the book has been a team effort. Martin Charter was responsible for developing the concept of the book, editing and writing the Introduction, and chapters on 'Emerging Concepts', 'Greening Marketing Strategy', 'Greener People' and jointly writing the chapter on 'Greener Logistics'. Cerian Moss has been responsible for the coordination of contributors and the development of the case history section, and has provided invaluable assistance in editing. Andrew Fyfe has provided continual enthusiasm, and support on editing and computers. Stephen Charter is also thanked for his input into the project, especially on the 'Greener Logistics' chapter.

We would like to thank the contributors for their insight and hard work, often in difficult circumstances. Gratitude also goes to the suppliers of case history material for giving a practical perspective. Those not mentioned elsewhere include: Dr Chris Tuppen (BT); Paul Chapman and Richard Robson (ICI); Mark Campanale (Merlin Jupiter Tarbutt); Simon Bradford (Countrywide Holidays); Helmut Lusser (Sutton Borough Council); Lucy Mayer and Maryanne Hawes (Hampshire County Council).

Thanks also to the members of the Board of our parent company, Kiveton Park Holdings, for their interest and support in the book; to Pauline Climpson of Interleaf Productions Limited for the coordination of the project; and to Dean Bargh for his detailed editorial work.

FOREWORD

Sir Anthony Cleaver
Chairman, IBM (UK) Ltd

Over the last three or four years interest in the relationship between business and the environment has grown significantly. From an issue only espoused by extremists, environmental concern has moved to the forefront, with our leading newspapers devoting pages specifically to the environment week after week. It is now clear that this is no passing fad but a major issue to be considered by every serious business-person.

One indication of this growing awareness has been the birth of a number of organisations specifically concerned with the business/environment relationship. I have had the good fortune to be associated with two of these—Business in the Environment (BIE) and The Advisory Committee on Business and the Environment (ACBE). BIE was set up by Business in the Community to promote awareness of environmental issues among business-people and to develop practical approaches to sustainable development in the UK. More recently, in 1991, ACBE was established as a joint initiative by the Secretaries of State for the Environment and for Trade and Industry, seeking to provide industry with a way of communicating with government on environmental matters. Today there are many other organisations involved in this same area.

What we all share is the conviction that, while it may well be true that many of today's environmental problems are the result of industry's action, it is also true that in most cases only industry can provide the solution. And secondly, that although there remain areas of scientific uncertainty, there are many others where the issues are clear and it is now time for action, not just talk!

Today it is probably true that most large organisations do understand the issues and many are addressing the problems in a practical way. However, many organisations, both large and small, have yet to understand just what is at stake. It is to them, in particular, that this book is addressed. Parts I and II lay out first the strategic implications for business of environmental issues and then the practical implications that flow from them. In Part III, many of these issues are explored more specifically through a series of case histories based on the actual experience of a number of British and overseas companies.

There can be few company directors who would find nothing new in these case histories. Having had the good fortune to lead a company, IBM UK, that has had an environmental policy statement for over twenty years and has recently published its own set of environmental objectives for the nineties, I can certainly say that a number of areas addressed here are ones on which we had focused insufficiently. While the issues of product development, packaging, distribution and pricing are all important, for me the areas of greatest significance are those of communications and the impact on employees.

I suspect there are times when all of us who have become involved with the environment feel that the issues are simply too big to comprehend. The value of a book such as this is that it remains essentially practical throughout. Time after time there are examples of practical steps that could be taken by almost any organisation to further the cause. I hope that company after company will consider the examples given here and widen their own range of initiatives in building a better future for our successors.

INTRODUCTION

Martin Charter
Director, KPH Marketing

The world that we have made as a result of the level of thinking we have done so far creates problems we cannot solve at the same level at which we created them.

Carl Jung

Environmental excellence is an essential ingredient for the long-term business survival.

E.F. Schumacher

Corporations that think they can drag their heels on environmental problems should be advised: society won't tolerate it.

E.S. Woolard, Chairman, Du Pont

Every one of us will have to face the challenges of the environment in some way during the decade of the 90s.

Tony Cleaver, Chairman, IBM UK Ltd

The New Agenda

The last three decades have seen a progressive increase in worldwide environmental consciousness. This has been driven by a number of factors from increased media coverage to rising evidence of environmental problems such as the depletion of the ozone layer, acidification of rivers and forest degradation, the rise of pressure group activity, tougher legislation and major industrial disasters. Concern has moved from the local scale to a national and increasingly global scale.

A number of companies, notably those in the oil, automotive, chemicals and nuclear industries, are conscious that if they aim to be in business in the long term then they will have to invest in a greener future. These companies are also increasingly aware and concerned about their poor environmental image, and are ever more sensitive to pressure group activity and new environmental legislation. In response, innovative companies are now taking the lead in a movement towards environmental excellence as an integral part of Total Quality Management.

The rate of environmental degradation has intensified. The nineteenth century brought the first large-scale pollution as companies geared themselves to produce goods as fast as possible, with virtual disregard for human or environmental well-being. Nations battled for industrial supremacy using raw materials and creating pollution at a staggering rate. As countries became economically stronger, competition also grew. More efficient production methods were employed, and few, if any, companies gave a thought to the impact they were having on their surroundings. With the increase in water pollution from chemical works, and air pollution from the iron and steel industry, towns and cities began to pay the price for high industrial productivity.

The first real stirrings of the environmental movement developed in the sixties, a major influence being the publication of Rachel Carson's *Silent Spring*.[1] This book examined, for the first time, the use of pesticides and the potential long-term human and environmental health risks associated with the widespread application of agrochemicals.

The seventies saw a resurgence of environmental concern. In 1972 the historic United Nations Conference on the Human Environment took place in Stockholm, leading to the creation of the United Nations Environment Programme (UNEP). In 1972 the 'Limits to Growth Report' to the Club of Rome projected a catastrophic future if growth continued at the same rate, and many groups called for 'zero growth'.

A number of major companies started to respond to the challenge. In 1971 IBM had become one of the first companies to establish a formal corporate environmental policy, and 1974 saw the Control of Pollution Act in the UK and the creation of a comprehensive regime to tackle waste, water and noise pollution. That year also saw the establishment of the US Environmental Protection Agency and the subsequent tightening of US environmental legislation. In 1978, the first major environmental labelling scheme, the Blue Angel, was born in Germany, followed in the eighties by others in Canada, Japan, and Sweden.

The downturn in economic activity in the seventies led to less production and energy demands, and a substantial reduction in sulphur dioxide and other emissions. However, there were no major improvements in the standards of environmental protection.

In 1980 the first Earth Day was initiated, and the International Union for the Conservation of Nature and Natural Resources (IUCN) published their 'World Conservation Strategy'. The first World Industry Conference on Environmental Management (WICEM I) was held in 1984, with over 500 top industrialists debating environmental issues and business. As a result of WICEM, one of its sponsors, the International Chamber of Commerce (ICC) established a trans-industry clearing house for environmental management information, the International Environmental Bureau (IEB). Greener business trends were continuing to develop in Germany, and in 1984 the German Environmentalist Business Management Association (BAUM) was formed as a professional forum designed to examine the practical implications of profitable environmentally responsible business.

In 1987 The United Nations World Commission on Environment and Development recognised that zero growth was no longer a viable option if the needs and aspirations of the industrialising nations were to be fulfilled. As a result, 1987 saw the publication of *Our Common Future* (The Brundtland Report)[2] which concluded that economic growth had a role to play in improving the standards in the less industrialised world and also in reducing environmental destruction. It suggested that growth had to be of a different order, and had to move the world away from viewing the environment as an unlimited resource to be exploited by each incumbent generation. The concept of modern Sustainable Development was born.

The latter part of the eighties saw a number of environmental issues coming together. The unprecedented number of major environmental disasters in the seventies and eighties caught the public's attention and concern: Three Mile Island, Bhopal, Exxon Valdez, Seveso, Flixborough, and Chernobyl. In September 1987 the countries that signed the Montreal Protocol agreed to cut chlorofluorocarbon (CFC) emissions by half by the end of the century. The green revolution started in earnest in the UK in 1987 with the Great Storm and the widespread death of seals in the North Sea from an unknown disease. Further impetus was added in 1988 with the British Antarctic Survey's discovery of the depletion in the ozone layer over the Antarctic. Mrs Thatcher's subsequent speech to the Royal Society on the depth of the environmental problems facing the present and future generations then legitimised the debate among many non-environmentalists.

This was followed by the publication in the UK of *The Green Consumer Guide* in 1988,[3] and *The Green Consumer's Supermarket Shopping Guide* in 1989,[4] which gave consumers the first real opportunity to look into the background of companies that manufactured so-called 'green' products. The first phase of Greener Marketing then moved into gear, driven by a host of conferences and proposed exhibitions. Suddenly, there was a rush of excitement, with the word 'green' being daubed in every conceivable place. In the month of June 1983, the word 'green' was used 3,617 times in newspapers and magazines; in 1989 this figure had risen to 30,777. Similarly, the term 'environmentally friendly' was used once in June 1985, and thirty times a day in June 1989.[5]

With a lack of legislation and guidelines, many companies looked to exploit this new opportunity with greener-sounding public relations and advertising, rather than by developing strategies based on thorough research and action. A number of companies were well positioned for the change in consumer attitudes, and many saw it as an opportunity for short-term profit. Many claims were made, causing considerable consumer confusion. This 'greenwash', as some termed it, led to an increase in pressure group initiatives such as Friends of the Earth's 'Green Con of the Year Award' introduced in 1989 and *Green Magazine*'s 'Green Gremlins Award'. The Advertising Standards Authority (ASA) summed up the ethics of some of the first-wave green advertisers: 'Some advertisers seem to be paying more attention to making sure that their wares are perceived as sitting on the right side of the green fence rather than checking the factual accuracy of their claims.'

With the increasing recognition of the impact of green issues on UK business, in late 1989 The Environment Council launched the Business and Environment programme, which had achieved 700 members by 1991. This was followed by a number of environmental initiatives around the UK, such as the Business in the Community's Environment Target Team, the Department of Trade and Industry (DTI) Environmental Enquiry Service, and the Confederation of British Industry's Environment Unit. Smaller groups also developed, including Technology, Research, Enterprise and the Environment (TREE), Solent Industry Environment Association (SIENA) and the Coventry Pollution Panel (CPP).

Recession and issues of global security have diverted and diluted media interest in environmental issues, but underlying concerns appear to be strengthening with the recognition that business has been responsible for much of the increase in environmental problems. Over recent years environmental impacts have intensified, faster than many business people have realised.

There are four broad features of the changing global environmental problems:

- A cumulative effect. The sea has been viewed as a dumping ground for toxic waste. The accumulation of pollutants in the

North Sea now poses a major threat to the marine environment.

- A long-term effect. There are thousands of landfill sites which have been described as 'toxic time-bombs' because of their capacity to produce methane and other pollutants and to leach and contaminate ground waters.

- A long-range effect. Emissions of sulphur dioxide and nitrous oxide from fossil fuel burning are accumulating in the upper atmosphere. They are trans-boundary, can travel considerable distances, and are capable of undergoing complex chemical reactions, causing acid rain, and creating problems of forest die-back and acidification of lakes and rivers.

- A fundamental effect. The production and use of chlorofluoro-carbons (CFCs), and their subsequent discharge into the atmo-sphere, has led to a depletion in the ozone layer, especially over the Antarctic, and more recently over the Arctic and continental Europe. In parallel, the discharge of CFCs and the burning of fossil fuels appears to be leading to global warming, with potentially catastrophic implications.

April 1990 saw the second Earth Day, and the United Nations con-ference 'Action for a Common Future' in Bergen in May 1990 called for better communication of environment and business issues. Novem-ber 1990 saw the outbreak of The Gulf War of 1990–91, one of the worst recorded environmental catastrophes, with untold destruction to flora and fauna. Apart from the huge toll on human life, the media displayed images of blackened skies resulting from hundreds of burn-ing oil wells, and of oil-laden seabirds caught up in massive slicks.

The Second World Industry Conference on Environmental Manage-ment (WICEM II), was organised in Rotterdam in April 1991, this time with over 700 major industrialists participating. The event heralded the launch of the International Chamber of Commerce's Business Charter for Sustainable Development, which by January 1992 had over 900 corporate signatories.

The year also saw the launch of the Business Council for Sustainable Development (BCSD), who have worked closely with the International Chamber of Commerce (ICC) on the proposals for the United Nations Conference on Environment and Development (UNCED) in Rio de Janeiro—the 'Earth Summit'—in June 1992. The central debate for many leading companies is starting to focus on Sustainable Develop-ment, and its practical implications for business. Many of the ramifications will go to the heart of the organisation and will have major implications for the way in which business operates into the next century.

Opportunities and Threats

Environmental constraints are becoming more and more pressing every day. Today's boardroom can ill afford to ignore factors such as tougher legislation, pressure group activity, media interest and increased public concern. One of management's biggest hurdles is reconciling the dilemma of satisfying Stakeholder needs and profitability against the reality of deteriorating natural resources and environmental quality. In many circles, sensitivity to the social, economic and environmental context in which the firm operates is being recognised as simply good business, and certainly a prerequisite for the lasting legitimacy and survival of the firm.

Companies should begin to prepare for the greener 1990s by re-examining the social and environmental impacts of their activities, notably corporate and marketing strategy and manufacturing processes. This is likely to mean re-evaluating product portfolios, as consumers switch to buying corporate responses and not just products.

It will become essential to understand companies' environmental status. There will be tougher European legislation, with stricter penalties for pollution and waste and a likely movement towards voluntary, and then compulsory, undertaking of Environmental Audits, with greater pressure exerted to disclose corporate environmental information.

This increasing complexity is presenting business with an ever greater number of opportunities and threats. Pressures are coming from a number of directions, and studies are indicating that there is increasing concern from a variety of Stakeholder groups, ranging from customers to investors, legislators and employees.[6] The pressures will create opportunities for the development of new greener consumer products, and environmental technology and services (see Fig. 1).

Many industries and companies are well aware of the shifting position, and a number of these organisations and industries are transforming threats into opportunities. ICI have been perceived as being socially responsible, yet environmentally irresponsible, and both Greenpeace and Friends of the Earth have hounded ICI over issues such as production of CFCs and ozone depletion, and water pollution and health concerns. The company is responding to the green challenge, with environmental responsibility being incorporated into staff performance through the development of an innovative employee awareness

EC Pollution Control Market			
Country	**1990** ECU m	**1995** ECU m	**Growth %pa**
Denmark	767	1,077	7.0
Germany	16,851	21,559	5.1
Netherlands	2,525	3,275	5.3
Belgium/Luxembourg	929	1,389	8.4
France	7,572	11,120	8.0
Ireland	294	439	8.3
Italy	4,889	7,423	8.7
UK	8,101	13,432	10.6
Greece	290	562	14.1
Portugal	400	755	13.5
Spain	1,602	2,919	12.7
Market Segment	**1990** ECU m	**1995** ECU m	**Growth %pa**
Air Pollution Control	9,584	12,683	5.8
Water/Waste Water Treatment	12,739	21,162	10.7
Contaminated Land Reclamation	1,023	2,319	17.8
Waste Management	20,874	27,786	5.9
Total	44,220	63,950	7.7

Source: ECOTEC

Figure 1

and training programme. It is also starting to examine opportunities in the greener marketplace with developments such as a biodegradable plastic, 'Biopol', a water-based paint, 'Aquabase', and a meat substitute, 'Quorn'.

Several other chemical companies are also acting proactively: BASF intend to sell their incineration know-how; Union Carbide have patented a novel process for mobile incineration, particularly applicable to the clean-up of hazardous waste sites; and Air Products have targeted the environmental sector in which to contribute 30% of their growth by 1996.[7]

However, Greener Marketing is not just about cadmium-free batteries and unbleached nappies, it is about a philosophy for business. The Body Shop had been a successful business before the existence of the green consumer became acknowledged. Its approach is based on a deeply held set of personal values which make sound business sense. Anita Roddick, the founder of The Body Shop, sums it up: 'Our products reflect our philosophy. They are formulated with care and respect. Respect for other cultures, the past, the natural world, our customers. It's a partnership of profits with principles.'[8]

The International Dimension

Environmental issues are now a global concern for business, especially for those companies operating internationally. In 1993 we will see the realisation of the Single European Market, with a greater harmonisation of standards across a variety of areas. Environmental legislation will be driven by the European Community, with Germany and The Netherlands continuing to lobby for stricter regulations to match their tough national standards. Environmental laws in Germany required the chemical industry to spend DM8bn in 1991, 60% more than any of their competitors.[9] The introduction of the 'environmentally aware' EFTA countries into the European Community, and many East European countries by the end of the decade, will present a new set of greener opportunities for proactive companies.

The EFTA countries tend to be more environmentally advanced, as many have had to face up to environmental problems for many years. Scandinavian banks are investing in environmental technology joint ventures with Poland in an attempt to tackle trans-boundary pollution problems at source. Over the last ten years, Austrian companies have increased the amount invested in environmental protection by 13% per annum,[10] with the country spending 1.9% of GNP on environmental protection, more than any other country in the world.[11] In Switzerland, a national information campaign on waste has been launched by the Federal Office for the Environment, Forests and Countryside (OFEFP); the campaign will focus on individual responsibility for waste, and will encourage consumers to buy high-quality goods with a long lifespan, and products made from recycled materials.[12]

With the fall of the Berlin Wall, there has been increased consciousness of the environmental problems of central and eastern Europe. The huge environmental problems in many of these countries provide major opportunities for companies in the pollution control and environmental services business. In a report on the pollution control market in Eastern Europe in 1991, Frost and Sullivan predicted that the fastest growing market segments are likely to be waste management, followed by air pollution and water pollution control, especially waste water treatment plant and equipment.[13]

At present, the prime barriers to development are the shortages of money and technology in the countries. Short-term opportunities will depend on international funding mechanisms and joint-venture agreements, but in the longer term growth will be driven by domestic legislative reforms.

The US has been driven by tough environmental legislation through the Environmental Protection Agency, with green consumerism being a relatively new phenomenon. California may provide indications—as it does in many areas—of the future direction of environmental legislation. The proposed Environmental Quality Act of 1990 linked a diversity of environmental issues to one main theme. 'Big Green', as it became known, included measures to combat global warming and control pesticide use, to establish an oil spill clean-up fund and provide protection for California's redwood forests. 'Big Green' was defeated for a number of reasons: voters felt that environmentalists were moving the green agenda too fast, the bill was too sweeping and complex, and also the timber, pesticide, agricultural and car interests spent US$35 million on lobbying.[14]

Japanese companies are closely examining environmental opportunities at home and abroad. The Japanese Ministry of International Trade and Industry (MITI) now require Japanese companies operating abroad to comply with stringent domestic anti-pollution legislation. Previously, Japanese companies had been required to comply with the host country's anti-pollution laws, but the new regulations are based on those in Japan. MITI are also considering whether to subsidise or award low-interest loans to companies which sell pollution control equipment to industrialising countries, or which are involved in technology transfers for protecting the environment.[15]

The less industrialised countries are facing tremendous problems associated with attempting to balance much-needed economic growth with the conservation of natural resources. It is in many of these countries, in native tropical rainforests and river systems, that most of the earth's biodiversity exists. Yet these countries also face increasing population pressures and poverty, and have few resources to put into the protection of their environment. The transfer of appropriate technology from north to south may be one way of attempting to increase the productivity of these countries and combat these problems, but not if such technology is bought with exports that exploit natural resources. Similarly, if such countries do manage to develop and generate higher disposable incomes, this will generate a tremendous increase in global consumption. For instance, if all individuals in such countries were able to buy refrigerators, CFC production would rise considerably, with consequent problems relating to the depletion of the ozone layer. If the West wishes to curb environmental degradation, then real sacrifices on the part of industrialised countries may be needed to alleviate the effects of industrialisation in less developed countries. Attempting to introduce Sustainable Development into these economies will be one of the greatest challenges for both business and the environmental movement.

The indications are that the next generation worldwide is likely to be more educated and concerned about environmental matters. The mid-1990s will see a considerable reduction in the number of younger people across Europe. This will mean that the next generation is likely to be more demanding of corporate behaviour, with environmental and social irresponsibility increasingly frowned upon. Research[16] across Europe is suggesting that concern for the environment is now becoming integrated into children's thinking. This is being driven by media interest and increasing input from the education system, with environmental issues being incorporated into a wide range of different syllabuses.

The Responsibility of Major Companies

Why should business incorporate social, ethical and ecological aspects into day-to-day decision making? How can business identify and make the most of the opportunities, and minimise the threats? These are just two of the difficult and complex questions that are being asked, and which have led the Manchester Business School to establish the International Institute of Social Responsibility to examine some of the implications of management in a complex and changing world.

Multinationals bear a considerable moral and economic responsibility for their past, present and future actions. Larger firms such as IBM and 3M state that being green is good business and that they, as corporate citizens, have a wider responsibility to the communities within which they operate. In response, a number of companies are starting to invest in environment and industry initiatives. British Airways completed a major environmental review[17] that indicated that they produced 1% of the UK's carbon dioxide emissions, and hence that they are major contributors to global warming. As a major worldwide industry, tourism is coming under increasing scrutiny from greener consumers, pressure groups and legislators, and to fill the information gap British Airways are investing £500,000 in the development of a Green Tourism Unit at Oxford Polytechnic.

Some commentators are suggesting that the large firms leading the movement towards the development of greener enterprises can afford to do so, something their smaller counterparts cannot. Others are also arguing that large companies are using greening as a tool to squeeze out small competitors. So, should larger companies be supporting smaller enterprises and encouraging symbiotic relationships?

In March 1991 Michael Heseltine, the UK Secretary for the Environment, established a group of twenty-five senior business people under the heading of the Advisory Committee on Business and the Environment (ACBE). The role of the group is to advise the Government on environmental issues from the business perspective. In November 1991 the group made its first set of recommendations, which covered energy efficiency targets for each industry sector, increases in petrol tax, incentives for diesel cars, higher Vehicle Excise for large cars, cuts in VAT on fuel-saving equipment, and minimum efficiency standards for household appliances. The group also indicated that many major companies are likely to put suppliers under increasing pressure to conform to new greener standards. Several large companies are now putting down formal challenges to suppliers with the objective of moving them voluntarily towards new standards through a more cooperative approach.

But, are the benefits of greening and the acceptance of responsible practices trickling down to small and medium-sized companies? The UK's business profile is highly skewed in the direction of smaller companies, with 74% of companies having less than ten employees.[18] A recent study indicated that 85% of smaller companies felt they produced no pollution, and only 10% of smaller companies had conducted Environmental Audits.[19] Small and medium-sized companies are often less well placed to deal with environmental pressures; it is often difficult for them to find the financial resources and staff needed to meet the challenge; and consultants are often too expensive.

However, a number of initiatives are being established to help address this problem. In December 1991 the Confederation of British Industry (CBI) announced the development of the Environment Business Forum designed to encourage collaboration between large and small companies in the provision of information and expertise on green issues. In January 1992 a Green Business Network was launched by Nottingham Polytechnic, aimed at small to medium-sized companies with the objective of increasing environmental awareness among local businesses.[20] Leicester City Council—Leicester being the first 'Environment City'—are providing subsidised environmental consultancy services to companies in the city,[21] and Eastleigh Borough Council and BP established The Green Business Service to work with local companies on improving environmental awareness and understanding.

The Green Revolution

Markets appear to be moving through an initial phase of immaturity and irresponsibility, and a number of industrialists and environmentalists are now acknowledging the benefits of cooperation and partnership rather than confrontation. Bryn Jones, former chairman of Greenpeace and founder of Ark, summed up the need for a new vision: 'Because our problems are caused by industry and the solutions must be found by industry, environmentalists have got to roll their sleeves up and get stuck into working with industry.'[22]

Consumers are also becoming more aware of the issues, although many are still confused by the complexities of the problems. Ogilvy & Mather indicated in a recent survey that consumers are becoming apathetic to green advertising.[23] This point is strengthened by research from Saatchi & Saatchi, which discovered that the simple advertising of green products is no longer good enough.[24] The consumer wants to see the whole company taking responsibility for the environment.

Legislation appears to be catching up with consumer demands. The UK's Trade Descriptions Act is likely to be amended to incorporate regulations covering environmental claims as a result of the debate over environmental labelling. Suggestions by the House of Commons Environment Committee to incorporate full product information and re-use and recycling information into product packaging have not yet been fully accepted by the Department of Trade and Industry (DTI). However, the Government is likely to take the EC route on eco-labelling, with the first labels appearing in the Autumn of 1992.[25]

Apart from assessing the 'environmental friendliness' of products, there are increasing calls to assess the greenness of companies. The lack of standards covering Environmental Audits in the UK is being addressed through three bodies that were established in 1991: The Association of Environmental Consultancies (AEC), the Institute of Environmental Auditors (IEA), and the Institute of Environmental Assessment (IEA). The prime drive to improved standards is the publication of the Environmental Management System BS7750 by the British Standards Institute (BSI), and the EC's Eco-Audit regulation expected at the end of 1992.

The UK appears to be lagging behind its European competitors on environmental policy development. This lack of proactivity is supported by two surveys[26] conducted by Touche Ross in 1990 and 1991.

In 1990, every company interviewed in Germany had a written environmental policy, and in The Netherlands the figure was 50%. In comparison, many UK companies had included their environmental policy within health and safety policies or 'good citizen' statements. The 1991 Touche Ross survey indicated that over 50% of European companies surveyed had an environmental policy, rising to 75% of companies in Sweden, Switzerland, Poland and Hungary.

Despite the publicity over Environmental Audits as a precursor to policy development, the UK still appears to be slow in adopting this approach. A study by David Bellamy Associates in November 1991[27] supported research undertaken by Cranfield in 1990,[28] and indicated that Environmental Auditing is still a relatively new area for UK companies. Only 22% of companies in the sample of 176 organisations had conducted an audit, although 39% expressed interest in completing one in the future. In reality, the figure of 22% is likely to be lower, as a number of those that claimed to have conducted audits had completed them internally with no independent verification.

The first stage of the green revolution has seen the development of 'friendly' followed by 'friendlier' products, but it will be progressively more difficult for a company or product to claim to be entirely green, as awareness grows and attitudes deepen. Greater demands will come from an ever more critical and informed 'environmentally conscious' marketplace, which will increasingly reject absolute claims. The second phase of the green revolution may see a movement towards a deeper ecological viewpoint, where there is increasing emphasis on conservation, and increasing debate not just about consuming differently but about consuming less. Fundamentally, 'less is more'.

The Evolution of Marketing

Marketing in its traditional sense is a corporate philosophy concerned with products and markets. It has evolved over the last thirty years, rising to pre-eminence in the eighties.

> Marketing is the whole business seen from its final result, that is from the customers' point of view.
>
> *Peter Drucker*

> Marketing is the management process for identifying, anticipating and satisfying customer requirements profitably.
>
> *The Chartered Institute of Marketing*

The concept of marketing has evolved through several stages:

- **Production:** product standardisation and mass production, with marketing restricted to distribution
- **Sales:** increasing competition leading to the need for advertising and personal selling
- **Marketing:** focus on researching pre-purchase attitudes and meeting consumer preferences
- **Broadened marketing:** extending the concept to service and non-profit organisations and all client relationships
- **Generic marketing:** includes all Stakeholders, not just customers, in order to work effectively within increasingly polarised markets

The heightened environmental and social concern of the sixties and seventies saw the emergence of a number of variations on the traditional marketing concept including 'the human concept',[29] 'the intelligent consumption concept',[30] the 'ecological imperative concept',[31] the 'ecological marketing concept'[32] and the 'societal marketing concept'.[33]

The last two provide a useful example of how environmental and social issues entered marketing. The ecological marketing concept concerned all marketing activities that:

- Have helped to cause environmental problems
- May provide a remedy for environmental problems

It concerned the positive and negative aspects of marketing activities of pollution, energy depletion and non-energy resource depletion. The prime focus of the approach was on recycling, and the re-use of existing resources.

A broader concept of societal marketing was also developed. Kotler described it as:

A management orientation which holds that the key task of the organisation is to determine the needs and wants of the target markets and to adapt the organisation to delivering the desired satisfactions more effectively and efficiently than its competitors in a way that preserves or enhances the consumers' and society's well-being.[34]

The underlying principles of the societal marketing concept are:

- Consumers' wants do not always coincide with their long-run interests or society's long-run interests
- Consumers will increasingly favour organisations which show a concern for meeting their wants, long-run interests, and society's long-run interests

- The organisation's task is to serve target markets in a way that produces not only want satisfaction, but long-run individual and social benefit as the key to attracting and holding customers

The eighties saw a prolonged period of economic growth, and can be said to have been 'The golden age of marketing'. However, the eighties obsession with immediate satisfaction led to an over-concentration on short-term payback, with less attention to longer-term development. This has left many marketing directors being asked to achieve more, in an ever more competitive marketplace.

The recession of the early 1990s has seen a variety of questions being asked: How long can the new strategy be given to work? What resources is the marketing director given to check its efficiency? and, What is the role of green, social and ethical issues in the marketing strategy? In some quarters, the role of marketing in its traditional sense is being questioned, and this has led some companies to remove layers of middle management, leaving flatter organisation structures with greater accountability and speed of response.[35]

Greener Marketing

The 1991 British Social Attitudes report[36] indicates that the UK, like many countries, is experiencing a cultural shift with concern for environmental issues permeating society more widely. There is evidence of an increasingly global perspective, especially among younger adults and children, with greater concern about the destruction of the rainforests, pollution and ozone depletion. Fifty per cent of those interviewed in the survey thought that damage to the environment was the biggest single problem facing Europe in the next twenty years.

Considerable change is emerging in traditional consumption patterns, with a growth in the greener and social criteria used to make personal buying decisions. This is being accelerated by an number of books and publications aimed at the green or new consumer. Additional pressures are also coming from major companies, with suppliers being asked to provide greener alternatives, and to provide more information on the 'friendliness' of companies' policies, processes and systems. Manufacturers and retailers who recognise these underlying changes and offer a greener choice may provide opportunities for differentiation through organisational factors, as consumers, employees and investors increasingly seek to direct their efforts in positive ways, and companies look to ensure that inputs are cleaner and greener.

Individuals will not just buy brands, but instead will buy entire company philosophies and policies, as illustrated by the success of The

Body Shop. People will not only vote politically on environmental, social and ethical issues, but will increasingly vote through the market with their purchase, investment and employment decisions. If products or organisations directly support a greener project or stimulate development in less developed countries, will people feel they have greater impact by supporting those organisations than by giving money to an environmental cause or group? The challenge for business is to recognise this as an opportunity.

Greener Marketing is a holistic and responsible strategic management process that identifies, anticipates, satisfies and fulfils Stakeholder needs, for a reasonable reward, that does not adversely affect human or natural environmental well-being.

The late 1980s has seen the first phase of the greening, which has been concerned primarily with short-term public relations and promotional aspects rather than a deeper strategic response. The new demands of the 1990s will move companies away from traditional functional organisational concepts to a greater emphasis on holistic management and systemic thinking,[37] with increasing recognition of the wider Stakeholder relationships. The second stage of the green revolution will see progressive companies taking a wider view of their activities, recognising that responsibility extends outside the factory gates or the high street shop front, and into the next generation. A number of legislative developments are pointing the way forward. The UK Environmental Protection Act has established a 'Duty of Care' with respect to waste, which means that companies are legally responsible for disposal of waste by contractors from April 1992.

At some point all products may have built-in ecological and social benefits, so from a narrow viewpoint Greener Marketing may be a transitional concept. Taking a wider perspective, Greener Marketing is a philosophy for business, recognising that the enterprise has a responsibility to each Stakeholder, each with their own set of needs and concerns. As environmental awareness and education grows worldwide, there are likely to be mounting pressures on organisations to become greener. This inevitable process will affect markets and products both indirectly and directly, with pressures arising from a number of directions.

Greener Marketing implies that corporate, marketing and environmental strategies are inextricably linked. The product must reflect the values of the firm, but first has to function and be of the appropriate quality and price. The environmental and social attributes of the product or service are unlikely to sell the product by themselves. Generic attributes, such as the production process, the corporate stance on the environment and the benefits of the purchase will need to be illustrated. The key prerequisite is to assess the total effect of the product from cradle to grave through techniques such as Life Cycle Analysis (LCA). A precursor to any movement towards the greening of the product portfolio will be to generate a clearer picture of the firm's environmental position through the undertaking of an Environmental Audit (EA) of existing facilities and systems, and Environmental Impact Assessments (EIA) on the development of new facilities.

The Greener Marketing approach will be recognised as being increasingly integral to a movement towards Total Quality Management. Companies will need to understand their environmental impact clearly, and have policies in place to ensure that they are driving change, rather than reacting to pressures. Stakeholders, whether as customers, employees or investors, will increasingly expect the company's approaches to be reflected in greener products and processes. The challenge will mean that greener companies will need to be more open, with greater dialogue and participation encouraged amongst all Stakeholders, notably customers and employees.

Sustainable Development will become a key concept for business, with the practical implications becoming an increasingly important debating point, especially in relation to issues concerning less developed countries. If companies do not accept the challenges of a greener world, opportunities will be lost and the environmental problems will loom ever larger.

The aim of this book is to develop discussion about a strategic response to green and environmental issues. The book is split into three parts. Part I examines the strategic implications of Greener Marketing, Part II the practical implications of Greener Marketing, and Part III is a case history section. Chapter 1 of Part I examines the key environmental problems facing business, and responses being taken by a selection of industry sectors. Chapter 2 examines a number of key concepts that business should be addressing as a result of the greening process. Chapter 3 discusses some of the major underlying strategic issues that companies are facing in an ever greener world. Chapter 4 examines some of the responses functional areas are taking to green pressures.

Part II starts with Chapter 5 which illustrates some key pointers for the development of a Greener Marketing strategy, before examining specific elements within a Greener Marketing mix. Chapter 6 examines some of the major areas for consideration in the greening of products. Chapter 7 suggests some of the environmental opportunities and threats that companies will face in the area of packaging. Chapter 8 examines the role that logistics has to play in the greening process. Chapter 9 examines the key issues which companies will need to consider in relation to the greening of pricing. Chapter 10 illustrates the need to develop integrated communications programmes aimed at all Stakeholders, with particular reference to consumers. Chapter 11 examines a key success factor in greening, the involvement and commitment of employees. Part III is a case history section which illustrates twenty unique approaches that companies have taken to the challenges of Greener Marketing.

We wish every success to those far-sighted companies embarking on the complex process of Greener Marketing. Companies that recognise the underlying trends and develop conscious holistic approaches will be those that prosper into the next millennium.

Martin Charter
Alton, Hampshire
UK
May 1992

References

1. R. Carson, *Silent Spring* (Harmondsworth: Penguin, 1963).
2. World Commission on Environment and Development, *Our Common Future* ('The Brundtland Report'; London: Oxford University Press, 1987).
3. J. Elkington and J. Hailes, *The Green Consumer Guide: High Street Shopping for a Better Environment* (London: Victor Gollancz, 1988).
4. J. Elkington and J. Hailes, *The Green Consumer's Supermarket Shopping Guide* (London: Victor Gollancz, 1989).
5. 'Green about Green', *Marketing Magazine*, 14 September 1990.
6. M. Charter, *Graduates: Fewer and Greener* (Alton: KPH Marketing, 1990), and M. Charter, *The Greener Employee* (Alton: KPH Marketing, 1990).
7. T. Steer and R. Hardman, *The James Capel Green Book* (London: James Capel, 1990).
8. The Body Shop Promotional Literature, 1990.
9. Christopher Parkes, 'Not so Miraculous', *Financial Times*, 14 January 1992.
10. 'Private Companies Contribute More to Environment', *Presse*, 24 November 1991.
11. '1.9% of GNP is Spent on Environmental Measures', *Presse*, 23 December 1991.
12. 'Campaign to Reduce Waste Launched', *Journal de Genève*, 19 November 1991.
13. 'Pollution Control to be Strong Market', *Water Engineering & Management*, November 1991.
14. P. Carson and J. Moulden, *Green is Gold* (Toronto: Harper Business, 1991).

15. 'Companies Operating Abroad Must Meet New "Green" Rules', *Nikkei Weekly*, 29 June 1991.
16. 'Attitudes towards CPP's amongst Younger People', *Educational Project Resources*, March 1991.
17. British Airways and Technica, 'British Airways Environmental Review: Heathrow and Worldwide Flying Operations' (February 1991).
18. Department of Employment, *Census of Employment* (London: HMSO, 1984).
19. Cranfield Management School, 'How Green are Small Companies?' (October 1990).
20. Larry Elliot, 'Heseltine Tells Firms not to Miss the Green Boat', *The Guardian*, 11 November 1991.
21. Ian Hamilton Fazey and John Hunt, 'Keeping One Step Ahead of the Pack', *Financial Times*, 13 November 1991.
22. 'Screaming Green Murder', *The Director*, May 1990.
23. A. Rawsthorn and K. Zagor, 'Gunning for "Green Con" Commercial', *Financial Times*, 21 June 1991.
24. 'Gunning for "Green Con" Commercial', *Financial Times*.
25. 'DTI Criticised for Delaying Trades Description Act Changes', *Environment Business*, 20 November 1991.
26. Touche Ross European Services, 'European Management Attitudes to Environmental Issues' (March 1990), and DRT International/Touche Ross, 'Managers' Attitudes to the Environment' (June 1991).
27. David Bellamy Associates, 'Industry Goes Green' (November 1991).
28. Cranfield Management School, 'How Green are Small Companies?'
29. L.M. Dawson, 'The Human Concept: New Philosophy for Business', *Business Horizons*, December 1969.
30. J.T. Rotle and L. Benson, 'Intelligent Consumption: An Attractive Alternative to the Marketing Concept', *MSU Business Topics*, Winter 1974.
31. G. Risk, 'Criteria for a Theory of Responsible Consumption', *Journal of Marketing*, April 1973.
32. K. Hennison and T. Kinnear, *Ecological Marketing* (New Jersey: Prentice Hall, 1976).
33. P. Kotler, *Marketing Management, Analysis, Planning and Control* (6th edn; New York: Prentice Hall International, 1988).
34. Kotler, *Marketing Management, Analysis, Planning and Control*.
35. Linda McMurdo, 'A New Discipline', *Marketing Week*, 6 December 1991.
36. R. Jowel, 'British Social Attitudes Report (8th Report)' (Aldershot: Gower Publishing Company, December 1991).
37. E. Callenbach, F. Capra and S. Marburg, *The Elmwood Guide for Eco-Auditing and Ecologically Conscious Management* (Berkeley, CA: The Elmwood Institute, 1990).

PART I

THE STRATEGIC IMPLICATIONS OF GREENER MARKETING

Chapter 1

ENVIRONMENTAL ISSUES
AS THEY AFFECT BUSINESS

Nigel Fisher

Project Manager, Bioscan (UK) Ltd[1]

Introduction

Environmental awareness has grown considerably in recent years. Many people have heard of the major environmental issues, such as the greenhouse effect, the ozone hole, and deforestation. But how many people realise that every day they make decisions which will have environmental effects? For example, driving a car probably contributes to global warming, buying a hamburger in a foam container may further expand the ozone hole, and purchasing a teak table could encourage more deforestation in the tropics.

On an individual level, the impacts of each decision are very small. For industries and businesses, however, the aggregate effects of decisions can be much greater. Indirect effects come from the choice of resources and products that a company uses, but the selection of production systems also directly affects the environment, through the degree to which the system pollutes.

Environmental issues have already led to, and will continue to lead to, legislation and regulation which will ultimately affect the operation of world markets. Many businesses have responded by increasing their environmental awareness, taking the initiative and staying ahead of legislation. This trend is set to continue.

The first part of this chapter is designed to introduce some of the major environmental issues. The second part discusses the relevance and implications of these issues to selected industrial sectors. These subjects are presented from an environmental viewpoint which may be unfamiliar to some of those working in industry and commerce. This different perspective should be useful, if only to see what influences consumers and policy makers. For those readers who already have an understanding of the environment, it is hoped that this will be a useful summary of current issues.

Pollution

What is Pollution?

Pollution has been defined as 'something present in the wrong place, at the wrong time, and in the wrong quantity'.[2] This may be rather imprecise, but it conveys the basic fact that it is not necessarily the pollutant itself which is the problem but the quantity of it in relation to the environment's ability to cope with it. Many substances which we regard as 'pollutants' occur naturally in much greater quantities than those created by human activity, but it is possible that human activity generates them faster than environmental systems can deal with them. Unwanted and potentially harmful changes are the result.

Atmospheric Pollution and Acid Rain

The late twentieth century has seen a massive increase in the quantities of sulphur dioxide (SO_2), nitrogen oxides (NO_x), and hydrocarbon compounds emitted into the atmosphere. The main sources of these pollutants have been power stations, industrial plants, and motor vehicles. Man-made emissions of SO_2 and NO_x are now approximately equal to all natural emissions.[3]

These pollutants can form acidic compounds, which are deposited directly from the air ('dry deposition') or by rainfall ('wet deposition'). The latter is also known as 'acid rain'. These compounds can be deposited thousands of miles from their point of origin. British power stations have been implicated in the acidification of Swedish lakes, and Eastern European industries in the death of German forests.

Air pollutants, such as those emitted by motor vehicles, can directly affect human health. SO_2, NO_x and ozone (O_3) can cause breathing difficulties, and many hydrocarbons are carcinogenic. Lead pollution has been linked with impaired brain function in children—emissions from vehicles using leaded petrol are a major source. However, the levels of lead measured in the blood of people in Britain have been falling since the mid 1970s[4] in part because of the introduction of unleaded petrol.

The Greenhouse Effect and Global Warming

The greenhouse effect is caused by a complex mixture of compounds in the atmosphere: carbon dioxide (CO_2); nitrogen oxides (NO_x); methane (CH_4); chlorofluorocarbons (CFCs) and water vapour (H_2O).

These allow short-wave radiation (ultra-violet and visible light) from the sun to reach the surface of the earth, but prevent the escape from the atmosphere of the longer-wave (infra-red) radiation emitted at the earth's surface. This leads to an accumulation of heat in the atmosphere, as in a greenhouse. Without the greenhouse effect, the earth would be cold and barren, but the temperature balance is the critical factor. This century has seen a large increase in the quantities of 'greenhouse gases' in the atmosphere. CO_2 is released whenever fossil fuels are burnt and forests are cut down; CH_4 is released from paddy fields and from animal wastes, and CFCs have been widely used in industry. Other pollutants such as ammonia (NH_3) and carbon monoxide (CO) have indirect effects which can increase the levels of CFCs and CH_4. The main man-made sources of CO are the burning of fossil fuels, deforestation, and oxidation of methane; NH_3 is released by the reduction of nitrogen fertiliser and from animal wastes.[5]

The response of the world's climate to the increased levels of greenhouse gases has been predicted using computer models. Most models suggest that global temperatures will increase by between 1.5–4.5°C by the middle of the twenty-first century. The uncertainty is due to inadequate knowledge of the operation of the world's complex climatic systems.

An increase in global temperatures could lead to a rise in sea levels (as ice caps melt and ocean waters expand on heating) and to possibly permanent shifts in weather patterns. These effects could lead to flooding of low-lying coasts (such as eastern England, the Netherlands and Bangladesh), and to declines in agricultural productivity in major food-producing areas (such as the Great Plains of the USA). Changes in annual rainfall or temperatures might benefit some areas. In contrast, some tropical islands (such as the Maldives) could be completely inundated by rising sea levels. In 1988 the Toronto Conference called for a reduction in global emissions of greenhouse gases by 50% over the period 2030–2050, and set a target of reducing CO_2 emissions by 20% of 1988 levels by 2005. The UK Government has said that by 2005 it will have returned CO_2 emissions to 1990 levels if other countries have done the same. Measures to reduce levels of CO_2 include reafforestation, and greater fuel economy and efficiency.

The Ozone Hole

Ozone (O_3) in the upper atmosphere has the effect of absorbing incoming ultra-violet radiation (UVR). This is a beneficial effect for life at the surface of the earth as exposure to large doses of UVR is harmful to most organisms.

Since the late 1980s there has been increasing concern that 'holes' have been occurring in the ozone layer over the polar regions, and that thinning of this layer has been occurring over the whole globe.

It is thought that the main cause of ozone depletion has been the release into the atmosphere of chlorofluorocarbons (CFCs). These decompose to release chlorine (Cl), which reacts with ozone to form other compounds which do not absorb UVR. CFCs have been used since the 1930s as propellants for aerosols, as refrigerants, and as industrial solvents. It has been predicted that every 1% decrease in ozone in the upper atmosphere will lead to a 1% increase in fatal skin cancer around the world[6]—the incidence of skin cancer in Australia has increased fivefold in the last fifty years. It has been suggested that rising levels of UVR could also have detrimental effects on plankton, which could be disastrous for the food chain in oceans and seas all over the world.

The main international convention on this issue is the Montreal Protocol of 1987, which set targets for reductions in the use of substances which deplete the ozone layer. Many industries have responded to this issue by finding substitutes for CFCs. Products such as non-aerosol sprays, and safe disposal schemes for refrigerants, are now more widespread than only a few years ago.

Fresh Water Pollution
Water is an essential resource and the quality of water is one of the most important indicators of the quality of the wider environment. Water pollution affects aquatic habitats and species, and can be a health hazard for humans. It reduces the degree to which the water can be used for industrial, agricultural and domestic purposes.

In Britain, until recently, the main concern was pollution of watercourses by industry. Environmental controls have led to a reduction in this sort of pollution, and have led to notable events such as the return of salmon to the Thames. Reductions in water quality are now being caused by agriculture and sewage treatment works, and pollution, through both industry and agriculture, has resulted in an overall decrease in water quality in many rivers and streams. Survey work undertaken by the National Rivers Authority showed an overall decrease in river water quality from 1980 to 1985. The survey for 1985 to 1990, the results of which were leaked to Friends of the Earth, showed that nearly 4,000 miles of waterway had deteriorated since the last survey.

Elsewhere in Europe the situation is similar. Heavy metal pollution (mostly from industry) in the Rhine in Germany and France has decreased from a peak in 1980, but nitrate pollution (mostly from agriculture) has increased.[7]

In developing countries the main problem is more basic: 46% of populations in less developed countries (LDCs) had no access to safe drinking water in 1985.[8] Public health problems, such as the 1991 cholera epidemic in Peru, are often the result.

In developed countries, water has been undervalued as a resource, and as a result water is often used at levels which in the longer term cannot be sustained. It is likely that in the future water will become more expensive, and that efficiency of use and recycling will have to increase. This, and the likely introduction of a policy of 'the polluter pays', will mean that those industries which take a lead in adopting non-polluting technologies and water-efficient production systems will be at an economic advantage.

In the UK proposals include widespread water metering and the need for water companies to commit greater resources to the prevention of leakages from mains.

Marine Pollution

Marine pollution incidents, such as the Torrey Canyon and Exxon Valdez oil spills, raise concern about the effects on the marine environment. However, the greatest problems are the result of long-term processes, such as the discharge of effluents and waste.

Discharges from the various nuclear installations on the west coast of the UK have led to the Irish Sea being the most radioactive sea in the world.

In 1988 the UK discharged 8.5m tonnes of sewage sludge into the seas around Britain,[9] some of which returned to pollute beaches. The UK Government has committed itself to ending the dumping of sewage sludge at sea by 1998, which should help to improve the water quality around Britain's coasts.

Electromagnetic Pollution

There is increasing interest in the potentially harmful effects of electromagnetic radiation (EMR) on humans. The last fifty years have seen a large increase in the extent and strength of EMR at frequencies which may effect humans. The main sources of these fields are electricity transmission systems, TV/radio transmitters, and microwave generators. At locations close to communications and navigation equipment and near power lines, EMR is several times higher than natural background levels.

EMR can have effects on the brain and other tissues, and it is known to raise body temperature.[10] Although a direct effect has not been proven, EMR has been linked with increased levels of cancer in people exposed to high levels, and it is thought to increase susceptibility to genetic disorders and stress.[11]

In most countries, safety standards do not take sufficient account of these possible effects. EMR is generally not recognised as a pollutant, but this is likely to change in the future

Noise Pollution

Noise is the most ubiquitous of environmental pollutants. Although it does not cause global environmental change, it is possibly one of the most significant factors affecting quality of life. The major source of this pollutant is transport. An estimated 15% of the world's population is regularly exposed to noise louder than that recommended as the maximum long-term exposure level.[12]

Resource Use and Abuse

Waste, Efficiency, Re-usability, and Recycling

Waste production continues to grow in most countries, and is one of the major environmental impacts of the modern consumer-oriented society.

While consumption of resources has dramatically increased, the efficiency of resource use has in many areas decreased. In the UK, only 19% of aluminium was recycled in 1987, compared with 32% in 1971. For steel, the figures were 36% in 1987, and 44.6% in 1976. Some countries are more committed to re-use than others: for example, in 1984 Hong Kong recycled 67% of its waste paper (UK, 29%), and in 1980 Finland recycled or re-used 15% of its plastics (UK, nil). The USA recycled 10% of its glass in 1985, compared with a figure of 53% in New Zealand in 1980.[13]

This failure to re-use and recycle is a waste of resources, creating unnecessary environmental impacts. New raw materials and energy are consumed while existing resources are incinerated or landfilled. Disposal of material has become increasingly difficult as the quantities have increased and suitable disposal sites become more scarce and more costly. Municipal disposal of material in the UK increased from 16 million tonnes in 1977 to 26 million tonnes in 1985.[14]

Hazardous waste is a major problem. Incineration is a recognised method of disposal, but the construction of incinerators is politically controversial. Many countries lack the technology to be able to deal with their hazardous waste, and have to ship it elsewhere. The UK is developing into an international treatment centre for hazardous waste, with imports increasing more than tenfold during the 1980s.[15] Because safe disposal is expensive, some hazardous waste is shipped around the world and dumped illegally. This has become a serious problem in some West African countries.

The United Nations is attempting to negotiate a treaty to prevent illegal dumping. The 1990 Environmental Protection Act set out the legislative framework for waste treatment in the UK.

Land Degradation

Agricultural practices are a major cause of land degradation in both developing and industrialised countries. Irrigation schemes in many countries (e.g. Pakistan, Iraq, Australia, and the USA) have led to saline soils; intensified agricultural methods have led to soil erosion; and extension of agriculture into marginal areas has contributed to desertification. Although these are often perceived to be 'third-world' problems, industrialised countries also suffer great losses of land to these processes.[16] Such degradation has other indirect detrimental effects, such as a reduced capacity to retain water, sedimentation of water courses, and impacts on habitats and species.

Industrial pollution of land is sometimes chronic, resulting in the land being unsafe for any use unless major restoration work is undertaken. An estimated 45,700 hectares of land in England was derelict in 1982, an area larger than the whole of Merseyside.[17] Eastern Europe experiences major environmental problems over enormous areas of contaminated land.

Widespread contamination of agricultural land is being caused by atmospheric pollution. Studies in the UK have shown that soils are being contaminated with heavy metals and hydrocarbons by deposition from the atmosphere. The sources of these pollutants are probably road vehicles, industry and the concentration of toxic substances through the application of inorganic fertiliser.[18]

Land degradation represents a reduction in the resources available to a growing global population.

Loss of Habitats and Species Diversity

Diversity, Gene Pools, and Stability

The destruction of natural and semi-natural habitat through deforestation, development, pollution, and other processes is occurring throughout the world. Human modification of the environment has always happened, but the speed and extent of change is faster than it has ever been.

The destruction of habitats is a loss not only to the species which live in them: as well as the aesthetic and spiritual value of a rich natural environment, humanity benefits from the diversity of habitats in several ways, and is likely to suffer if overall diversity decreases. There is increasing concern that these changes will reduce global biodiversity and lead to greater environmental instability.

Biodiversity is the variety and variability of plant and animal species. This diversity occurs on three levels: variation within a species; the variety of species within a habitat; and the variety of habitats on the planet. This diversity has two sorts of value to humans: use value and existence value.[19]

Use value is the economic value resulting from the exploitation of biological diversity, including direct uses such as the development of genetic resources for improved plant breeding, or for new pharmaceuticals. Many modern drugs are based on tropical plant extracts. The destruction of tropical rainforests is likely to lead to the extinction of many useful plant species which are presently unknown to science. This is a reduction in the 'gene pool' available for human use in the future.

Existence value is the intrinsic value of a diverse environment including aesthetic and spiritual benefits. This has some economic value through the generation of earnings from tourism or scientific research. Some species and habitats also have an existence value because they are indicators of environmental quality. Bird species are often regarded as environmental indicators: the increase in the population of peregrine falcons in Britain since the late 1960s has been an indication of the reduction in use of persistent toxic pesticides such as DDT.

Developed countries are to some extent relatively effective in conserving their remaining biodiversity. However, most such countries are in temperate areas, where natural diversity is relatively limited. The most diverse natural habitats are generally found in tropical and equatorial regions, including tropical rainforests, mangroves and coral reefs. However, these habitats are often under threat from various pressures such as mining or deforestation and clearance for agriculture, and most tropical countries do not have the necessary finances to protect these biological resources adequately.[20]

At present we have a situation where global biodiversity is being reduced because there is currently insufficient perceived economic benefit in protecting it. Issues to be addressed include the rights of less developed countries to be paid for new products and innovations based on 'their' genetic resources. For example, deforestation might be reduced if pharmaceutical companies paid substantial sums for genetic material from tropical rainforests. Such payments would provide an economic rationale for the preservation of biodiversity.

Environmental Stability

Natural systems act as environmental 'buffers', but their capacity to ameliorate environmental pressures is often reduced by human disturbance. Ecosystems are often less stable after they have been disturbed by human activity. Habitat disturbance often leads to greater soil erosion and sedimentation of watercourses. Susceptibility to 'natural' disasters such as hurricanes and landslides increases when the ability of ecosystems to absorb impacts is reduced by human interference: mud slides in the Philippines, which killed many people during 1991, were directly linked with deforestation.

The disturbance of ecosystems also has indirect effects. For example, deforestation and the ploughing up of grasslands contribute to the greenhouse effect by releasing carbon into the atmosphere.

Awareness of these problems has led to calls for more appropriate development of natural areas and for industry and agriculture to adopt sustainable methods of resource use.

Population

Population Pressures and Development

Global population is expected to increase from an estimated 4,450 million in 1980 to 6,251 million in 2000.[21] Most of this increase is expected in the less developed countries (LDCs), where birth rates are high and family sizes large. Environmental pressures in these countries are increasing, including major global problems such as deforestation and desertification, and it is often suggested that population increase in LDCs is the major global environmental threat.

However, the root causes of such problems are the consumption and production patterns of the industrialised world, the 'export' of these patterns to the LDCs, and the poverty of the populations of LDCs, rather than the increase in population itself. The average rate of population increase in LDCs has been falling since 1960.[22]

The main consumers of resources, and generators of pollution, are the rich industrialised countries. Developed countries, with less than 25% of the world's population, consume 60% of total global energy production[23] and twenty-one countries account for 85% of all man-made emissions.[24] The populations of the rich countries are more of an environmental threat than the expanding populations of less developed countries.

However, the massive indebtedness of most LDCs contributes to poverty, and leads to a vicious cycle of dependence, further poverty, and environmental damage. Poverty forces people to 'mine' their resources (i.e. exploit for short-term gain in an unsustainable way) out of necessity. Ninety per cent of deforestation in LDCs is undertaken for agriculture, often by the poorest inhabitants in order to feed their families.[25]

Environmental degradation has been encouraged by the rich countries' demand for low-priced resources and commodities. For example, forests in southeast Asia have been exploited to supply Japan's consumption of tropical hardwoods, and mineral extraction and refining to supply industries in other countries causes deforestation, river pollution, and habitat loss in South America and southeast Asia.

In order to meet their foreign debt requirements, LDCs are under pressure to produce resources cheaply for sale to the richer countries, which inhibits them from applying environmental controls. LDCs have often been put in a position by major international institutions, such as the World Bank, where they are often constrained to follow the same unsustainable development path as that of the industrialised countries—the same countries that are now becoming so concerned about the global environment. This situation has led to calls for financial institutions in rich industrialised countries to forego the money owed by LDCs, and in return to insist on environmental protection, such as investment in afforestation.

Sustainability of development is the latest theme for the developing world. This is the idea that in the long term, consumption should be based on the sustainable use of resources. This idea is also being increasingly applied to the industrialised world. The World Bank is now beginning to show signs of greater environmental awareness through the development of its Green Fund.

Summary

This chapter so far has covered some of today's major environmental issues. Industrialisation, urbanisation, and the extension of agriculture have all caused increased environmental pressures. These have been due to consumption patterns which are unsustainable in the long term.

The ways in which resources are consumed determine the extent to which pollution and waste are generated and the degree to which the resources can be re-used and recycled. The effects of single actions and decisions concerning consumption and production may be relatively minor, but the cumulative results can be measured on a global scale.

As our understanding of environmental problems increases, so does our understanding of the need for action to prevent the causes of these problems. governments, organisations and individuals are beginning to find responses which will reduce the environmental impacts which they make. Sustainable Development is becoming widely accepted as the goal which must be achieved.

The rest of this chapter looks at the way in which environmental issues relate to specific industrial sectors, and the ways in which these industries are responding.

Environmental Issues and Industry: General Issues

Pressure on industries is increasing as public awareness rises and legislation and policies on environmental subjects tightens. In the Netherlands the Government's 200-point National Environmental Policy (NEP) aims to reduce all pollution and waste by 70% by 2010. In Britain the 1990 Environmental Protection Act covered a range of environmental issues, including waste management, litter and genetic engineering, and allows for the bringing into effect of EC environmental policy and other international agreements to which the UK is a party.

The following sections describe some of the major environmental issues relevant to a selection of industrial sectors. However, it is important to remember that all industries cause environmental effects through their use of land, electricity, timber, transport, etc. These issues are also important to customers, as they will bear the costs of using less damaging alternatives.

Environmental concerns affect industry at various scales. On the local scale, issues relating to specific sites are likely to predominate. Examples such as emissions into watercourses or the building of new units on greenfield sites are common concerns in Britain. On a regional or national level, the issues may be the loss of important habitats, such as impacts on Sites of Special Scientific Interest (SSSIs) in the UK. Issues which will affect industry worldwide include those which lead to global environmental change, such as the greenhouse effect.

The response of industry will depend on the scale at which the impacts occur. Global problems may require changes in the whole production pattern of an industry. Local problems may be easier to solve on a site-by-site basis.

Industrial Sectors

The Electricity Supply Industry

The production of electricity is a major source of pollution and environmental damage. Power stations are a major source of atmospheric pollutants and the construction of stations consumes land and massive quantities of building materials. The extraction and transport of coal, oil, gas and uranium have significant environmental costs. Electricity transmission generates electromagnetic pollution.

Most electricity is generated using fossil fuels (oil, coal and gas) which produce large quantities of greenhouse gases and compounds which are known to lead to acid rain.

The EC Large Combustion Plants Directive requires a 60% reduction of SO_2 emissions from such plants by 2003 and the reduction of 30% of NO_x emissions by 1998. The greater fuel efficiency of Combined Cycle Gas Turbines is one reason why increasing interest is being shown in the UK in the use of gas in power stations.

Combined heat and power (CHP) plants are increasing in importance in Britain, and currently supply about 3% of UK electricity. These are smaller power plants which utilise the heat as well as the electricity generated. These account for 45% of electricity in Denmark, and could account for 25% of electricity generated in the UK in 2020. Their smaller scale makes them more flexible than larger stations, and their greater efficiency means that CO_2 emissions are lower.[26]

Electricity generation from nuclear fission produces much smaller amounts of atmospheric emissions than conventional power stations, and in this context can be regarded as 'clean'. However, nuclear power is comparatively expensive. The environmental arguments against nuclear power include the potential for major environmental impacts through a nuclear accident. Although safety standards in the nuclear industry are generally high, the potential for environmental problems is very great. The Chernobyl accident, although unlikely in modern nuclear power stations, demonstrated what can happen when a nuclear reactor goes wrong.

Nuclear power also creates major disposal problems—particularly for high-level nuclear waste. This will continue to be an environmental hazard for thousands of years. The transport of nuclear material, including waste for disposal, around the world increases the risk of accidents. Nuclear power is also involved in the proliferation of nuclear arsenals around the world, through the provision of material suitable for use in weapons.

Against these concerns must be weighed the fact that, under present projections of production and consumption, nuclear power may have to supply 20% of energy requirements in 2030.[27] If nuclear energy is to be rejected on environmental grounds, alternatives, including greater energy efficiency, will have to be developed rapidly.

Research into nuclear fusion (which promises virtually unlimited energy supplies and fewer problems with radioactive waste) is progressing through the Joint European Torus (JET) project. However, the contribution of fusion to future energy provision is not yet certain.

'Renewable' energy sources are those which take advantage of natural energy systems, including hydroelectricity, wave power, solar power, wind generators, tidal power, geothermal energy, and biofuels (e.g. wood, fuel-alcohol, and biological gas generation). Despite the variety of possibilities, renewable energy sources have generally received much smaller amounts of government investment than conventional and nuclear electricity generation.

These systems are not completely free of environmental effects, but they are generally less environmentally damaging than conventional systems. Exceptions to this include the environmental problems often caused by major hydroelectric power (HEP) schemes.

Some large HEP schemes cause major environmental impacts, both directly, through their construction and the flooding of large areas, and indirectly. Indirect effects can include damage to downstream ecosystems and habitats. A well-known example is Aswan High Dam which has altered the flooding regime of the lower Nile (affecting agriculture) and reduced nutrient flows into the Mediterranean Sea (damaging the marine ecosystem and reducing commercial fish stocks). Large reservoirs behind dams can lead to earthquakes because of the increased pressure on the earth's crust caused by the weight of water.

Large water projects such as these supply electricity and water for industrial and agricultural development, and this is usually the economic justification for their construction. However, such projects have been questioned on conventional financial grounds, as well as for environmental reasons, and sometimes the real reason for building large dams has been their supposed 'prestige' value. HEP projects currently under way which have been opposed for environmental reasons include the James Bay Project in Canada, and the Narmada Dam in India.

It has been estimated that renewables could supply quantities of energy equivalent to 25% of current consumption levels by 2025.[28]

However, increased demand for energy in the future could offset these gains unless efficiency of energy use and energy conservation are improved. Existing measures, such as better insulation, could reduce electricity consumption by 25% in the UK, but more determined policy and legislation is required to achieve this goal. With this in mind, the British Government launched a £10 million advertising campaign in November 1991 in an attempt to encourage greater energy efficiency in the home.

The Chemicals Industry

The chemicals industry produces some very toxic substances for use in industry. Occasionally these are released into the wider environment and the results can be devastating, as illustrated by the incidents at Bhopal (where a gas emission killed and injured thousands of people) and at Basle (where chemicals polluted the Rhine from Switzerland to the North Sea).

These occasional incidents are not the only environmental problems. The production of chemicals usually involves large amounts of electricity, and thereby contributes to the greenhouse effect and other problems. The products of the industry (fertilisers, CFCs, pesticides, petrol, etc.) often become major pollutants.

The disposal of unwanted chemicals is a serious problem, and one which is sometimes 'solved' by illegal dumping in LDCs and countries where environmental controls are less strict or more easily evaded. The export of pollution, in this and other ways, is a serious problem. Many companies in the chemicals industry have taken a lead in areas such as Environmental Auditing of sites and operations in order to ensure that impacts are minimised. Proposals for integrated chemicals installations in the EC are subject to environmental assessments under the terms of directive 85/387/EEC.

Transport

The motor vehicle has brought social benefits in terms of individual freedom to travel, and the accessibility of many areas has been increased as a result. However, the expansion of the use of motor vehicles has been one of the biggest environmental problems of the twentieth century.

The internal combustion engine is one of the major sources of atmospheric pollutants. The construction of roads uses massive quantities of building materials and destroys natural and semi-natural habitats. The construction of vehicles consumes vast amounts of metals and plastics and energy. The expansion in the use of vehicles has led to major congestion problems in many countries, with average speeds falling correspondingly. On average, over 300,000 people a year are killed throughout the world due to road transport:[29] a global environmental problem.

Technological advances have led to some improvements in the environmental record of the internal combustion engine. Diesel engines emit smaller quantities of greenhouse gases than petrol engines (although they emit other toxic compounds). Interest continues in the development of electric and water-hydrogen power. In Brazil biofuels (sugar-alcohol) have been used for many years, with the significant benefit of being a renewable resource. The technology now exists to recycle the modern car completely[30] and some manufacturers are researching into designing for easier recycling.

Some environmental 'solutions' must be carefully examined to ensure that they are used only where appropriate. A good example of this is the catalytic converter for vehicle exhausts. When operating properly, these can reduce harmful emissions. However, for this to occur, the ambient air temperature must be suitably warm (as in California). Tests have suggested that in cool climates (such as northwest Europe), catalytic converters operate inefficiently, resulting in higher emissions and higher fuel consumption. This is a good example of the complexity of many environmental problems, and the need for solutions appropriate to each case.

Legislative changes, which are likely in many countries, include punitive taxes on the use of fossil fuels and stricter controls on emissions from vehicles. Despite these improvements, the greatest environmental progress would be made by a reduction in the number and use of vehicles. Support is required for public transport, which suffers from unfair competition with the private vehicle because the greater environmental costs of the latter are usually not taken into account.

Farming and Fishing Industries

In industrialised countries the agricultural industry has become a major source of environmental pollution. Problems include increased water pollution by nitrates and air pollution by ammonia (both from use of fertilisers). The use of pesticides and growth hormones has led to increased levels of toxins and synthetic residues in foodstuffs.

Increased use of agricultural chemicals has been implicated in health problems in farm workers. Health issues in the UK have included BSE and salmonella in farm animals, both of which have been associated with 'industrial' farming techniques.

Interest in organic farming (agriculture using humane animal husbandry and without the use of synthetic inputs such as artificial inorganic fertiliser) has grown with concern over the environmental effects of industrial agriculture. Organic farming aims to maximise long-term output by maintaining natural resources.

As mentioned previously, agricultural practices are a major cause of land degradation in both developing and industrialised countries. Additional environmental effects include a massive rise in the last twenty years in methane emissions caused by increased areas of paddy fields and increased numbers of farm animals,[31] and the loss of tropical rainforest to agriculture. These processes have contributed to the greenhouse effect.

The major environmental concerns relating to the fishing industry include over-fishing of stocks, and detrimental effects on non-target species. Fisheries in many areas are now depleted due to unsustainable fishing in the past. In some places (e.g. the North Sea), the problem is worsened by pollution, which reduces fish populations' ability to recover.

Drift-net fishing in the Pacific has led to the death of massive numbers of dolphin and other non-target species trapped in the nets, and has motivated the United Nations General Assembly to consider a ban on drift nets. In Scotland, fish farming has polluted lochs through the use of pesticides and the increased levels of organic material in the water.

The development by some major food processing companies of products such as 'dolphin-friendly tuna' (caught without the use of drift nets) and 'free-range meat' is a response to some of these issues.

The Packaging and Plastics Industry
The packaging and plastics industries are major users and producers of some of the more persistent pollutants. Many plastics in use at the moment are not biodegradable, and unless they are re-used or recycled have to be disposed of by incineration (which involves the release of toxic compounds) or buried. The use of CFCs to produce expanded foam for packaging has been a factor in the creation of the ozone hole.

From an environmental perspective, the 'over-packaging' of goods for marketing or aesthetic reasons is a waste of resources, and there are increasing pressures to reduce, re-use and recycle materials.

The Electronics and Computer Industry
Even the high-tech and seemingly clean electronics industry creates some environmental problems. Some of the major computer companies have undertaken Environmental Audits in order to assess their

environmental record. One of the ideas being developed is the replacement of CFCs (used as solvents in the production of circuitry) with water-based solvents.

Other possibilities for reducing the environmental impact of the industry include a move towards 'environmentally friendlier' packaging (reducing the use of non-recyclable plastics), and the development of greater energy efficiency of individual computers and the environments in which they are used. The wasteful disposal of computers is being reduced by the development of recycling schemes, whereby users can return their old computers to the manufacturer when they buy new systems.

The Waste Management Industry

Waste recovery is likely to develop further as regulation and public pressure increase. Glass, metals, paper and plastics are the main areas in which there is most interest, although rates of recycling in some countries have fallen during the 1980s. Recycling of plastics is difficult at the moment because of the need to separate different types, but as the technology improves, the potential for recycling will increase. What is required is legislation to make recycling more economically viable and to discourage the production of waste which cannot easily be re-used or recycled.

The handling of waste presents opportunities for those who can develop and operate the best technology. 'Recycling, re-manufacturing and re-consumption . . . will become the hallmarks of industrial activity in the twenty-first century'.[32]

The Construction Industry

The construction industry has major environmental effects through its massive consumption of resources.

It is estimated that the production of building materials, construction, and the uses to which buildings are put, accounts for 50% of UK energy consumption. Concrete manufacture is a major source of carbon emissions. The construction industry is also a major user of CFCs (in refrigeration and air conditioning equipment), and tropical hardwood products. These factors contribute to acid rain, the greenhouse effect and global warming. Improvements in the environmental standards of the construction industry would be a major step forward.

In the UK, a number of major construction companies have formed the Construction Industry Research and Information Association Environment Forum, to promote and research into environmental aspects of the industry. The Building Research Establishment has established guidelines for increasing energy efficiency and reducing the use of environmentally damaging materials in building design. However, some countries have taken much greater steps in this area: the UK has now reached the energy efficiency standards set by the Swedish Government in the 1930s.

Summary

Industry currently faces a wide range of environmental problems and issues. Many industries and individual producers have begun to seek solutions based on new means of production, the development of alternative materials and resources, and the minimisation of waste and pollution. However, it is important that the solutions which are proposed are appropriate in terms of the scale and location of the problem with which they are concerned.

Increasing environmental awareness and current and future legislation is likely to promote environmental issues further, and will present opportunities for those who can devise appropriate products, technologies and solutions.

Conclusion

This chapter has introduced some of the major global environmental problems and issues. Public awareness of these issues has risen markedly in the last few years, and governments and regulatory bodies have responded, and will continue to respond, with new and more stringent controls on the causes of environmental damage.

A number of responses are required at an international level in order to tackle global environmental problems. These include:

- Adoption of alternative measures of economic growth which take into account environmental costs
- Introduction of more favourable trading arrangements for LDCs
- Increases in the efficiency of resource use
- Greater funding for research
- Development of appropriate alternative energy sources
- 'Environmental taxes' to penalise pollution and environmental damage
- Tighter controls on the emission and disposal of all pollutants
- Action to prevent deforestation and encourage reafforestation

- Measures to increase environmental awareness
- Greater international cooperation

Social and technological innovation will be required in order to implement such proposals, and their effects could radically alter the business environment.

Such changes will present industry and commerce with new challenges and opportunities. These will not be limited to targeting products or information at the green consumer. Companies will benefit from developing new business opportunities, and expansion of the environmental industry will provide the impetus for technological development. The environmental record of employers will become an increasingly important factor in their ability to attract employees and customers. The company which ignores the new environmental realities will miss these opportunities and will suffer in the long term.

Sustainable Development must become the long-term goal for modern society. The response of industry will largely determine the degree to which this is achieved.

References

1. The views expressed in this article are those of the author and not necessarily those of Bioscan (UK) Ltd.
2. M.W. Holdgate, *International Symposium on Identification and Measurement of Environmental Pollutants: The Need for Environmental Monitoring* (Ottawa, Canada, 1979).
3. United Nations Environment Programme (UNEP), *Environmental Data Report* (Oxford: Basil Blackwell, 1989).
4. UNEP, *Environmental Data Report*.
5. UNEP, *Environmental Data Report*.
6. UNEP, *Environmental Data Report*.
7. UNEP, *Environmental Data Report*.
8. UNEP, *Environmental Data Report*.
9. R. Oake, 'Sewage Sludge Disposal', in T. Burke, N. Robins and A. Trisoglio (eds.), *Environment Strategy Europe 1991 including WICEM II Official Report* (London: Camden Publishing, 1991).
10. S.F. Cleary, 'Biological Effects of Radiofrequency Radiation: An Overview', in G. Franceschetti, O.P. Gandhi and M. Grandolfo (eds.), *Electromagnetic Interaction* (New York: Plenum Press, 1989).
11. S. Szmigielski and J. Gil, 'Electromagnetic Fields and Neoplasms', in Franceschetti *et al.* (eds.), *Electromagnetic Interaction*.
12. UNEP, *Environmental Data Report*.
13. UNEP, *Environmental Data Report*.
14. UNEP, *Environmental Data Report*.

15. UNEP, *Environmental Data Report*.
16. A.S. Goudie, *The Human Impact on the Natural Environment* (Oxford: Basil Blackwell, 1990).
17. Environmental Advisory Unit (EAU), *Transforming our Waste Land: The Way Forward* (London: HMSO, 1986).
18. UNEP, *Environmental Data Report*.
19. A. Bennett, 'Introduction', in Overseas Development Administration, *Biological Diversity and Developing Countries: Issues and Options* (London: ODA, 1991).
20. Bennett, 'Introduction', in ODA, *Biological Diversity*.
21. L. Brown, 'State of the World', in The Conservation Trust, *Business and the Environmental Challenge* (London: The Conservation Trust, 1991).
22. UNEP, *Environmental Data Report*.
23. S.R. Hatcher, 'Energy and Population', in Burke *et al.*, *Environment Strategy Europe 1991*.
24. UNEP, *Environmental Data Report*.
25. R. Sandbrook, *The World Environment: Key Environmental Issues (4)* (British Gas, 1991).
26. D. Green, 'Combined Heat and Power', in Burke *et al.*, *Environment Strategy Europe 1991*.
27. Hatcher, 'Energy and Population'.
28. D. Elliott, *Renewable Energy: Key Environmental Issues (13)* (British Gas, 1991).
29. UNEP, *Environmental Data Report*.
30. G. Willburn, 'Total Car Recycling', in Burke *et al.*, *Environment Strategy Europe 1991*.
31. UNEP, *Environmental Data Report*.
32. Burke *et al.*, *Environment Strategy Europe 1991*.

Chapter 2

EMERGING CONCEPTS IN A GREENER WORLD

Martin Charter
Director, KPH Marketing

Introduction

The dawning of the environmental age is leading to the emergence of many new concepts for business, some of which are being discussed at the highest level. The speed of change is posing considerable difficulties for management, especially for those companies operating multi-nationally and in multi-product markets. There are huge gaps in the awareness and understanding of environmental issues, ranging from those companies who believe that they have no effect on the environment, through to those companies who are conducting audits to determine their position on global warming and those that are setting corporate objectives to reduce carbon dioxide emissions, ahead of international agreements.

This chapter discusses seven key emerging concepts:

- Sustainable Development
- Corporate Social Responsibility
- Stakeholder analysis
- Total Quality Management
- Greener consumption
- Environmental Auditing
- Life Cycle Analysis

Sustainable Development

Sustainable Development is not only a necessity for the environment, it is also good business.

Torvild Aakvaag, President of Norsk Hydro a.s.

The eighties have seen Sustainable Development arise as the central theme in the debate over the future of economic development. In 1987 The United Nations World Commission on Environment and Development recognised that zero growth was no longer a viable goal, especially if the needs of developing countries were to be met.

Sustainable Development involves devising a social and economic system that is designed to ensure that a variety of objectives are sustained, such as growth in real income, increases in educational standards, improvements in health, and the advancement of the 'quality of life'. The underlying theme is that future generations should be compensated if there is any reduction in the bank of resources brought about by the actions of present generations,[1] but that reductions should be avoided if possible. David Pearce in *Blueprint for a Green Economy*[2] suggests three broad strategies to achieve Sustainable Development:

- **Value the environment:** to substantially increase the value attached to the natural, cultural and built environment

- **Extend the time horizon:** to extend concern, not only to short- to medium-term horizons of five to ten years, but to the longer-term future, to be inherited by our grandchildren and beyond

- **Equity:** to place emphasis on providing for the needs of the least advantaged in society ('intragenerational equity') and also the fair treatment of future generations ('intergenerational equity')

Sustainable Development can be described as:

> ... development that meets the needs of the present without compromising the ability of future generations to meet their own needs. It contains within it two key concepts:
> —the concept of 'needs', in particular the essential needs of the world's poor, to which overriding priority should be given; and the idea of limitations imposed by the state of technology and social organisation on the environment's ability to meet present and future needs[3]

Sustainable Development suggests that individual well-being should be increased over time, or, from a wider perspective, it suggests that a set of 'development indicators' should rise over time. Business controls most of the technological and productive capacity needed to initiate, develop and launch cleaner and more environmentally benign processes and products, and therefore has a responsibility to the next generation to move towards the required changes to maintain and enhance the 'quality of life'.

Commitment to Sustainable Development will mean a move towards a more responsible and more thoughtful approach throughout the organisation. Changes will mean that organisations will need to learn to manage differently and organise operations in a more integrated manner—'systemic management'.[4] This will require a transformation in the way many companies do business, from the mechanistic to an ecological world view. It will place both a moral and economic obligation on all firms to investigate renewable and sustainable alternatives. The fossil-fuel-based economy is under threat; if present consumption levels continue it is predicted that there are only forty-five years of oil left![5]

The needs of the market economy and of nature are interrelated, and future economic growth will have to be in a different form. Economic sustainability must be based on a sound ecological platform, as in the longer term there is no economy unless there is a planet worth living on. Therefore, those companies planning to be in business in 10, 20, 50, 250 years' time will need to plan for a greener world, as natural resources will run out sooner rather than later if present levels of consumption continue.

A number of initiatives are being taken by industry to address the relationship between Sustainable Development and industry. Following the WICEM II conference in Rotterdam in March 1991, the International Chamber of Commerce (ICC) launched the Business Charter for Sustainable Development which has sixteen guiding principles (see Fig. 1). By May 1992 it had achieved over 900 signatories worldwide.

In 1991 the Business Council for Sustainable Development (BCSD) was established, with members drawn from a number of worldwide companies. Much of its activity is focusing on the United Nations Conference on Environment and Development (UNCED) in Rio de Janeiro—the 'Earth Summit'—in June 1992.

The United Nations gave a mandate to the BCSD for the UNCED conference, which includes:

- Providing a clear understanding of environmentally Sustainable Development, and providing a business perspective on ways to progress towards this goal on a global basis

- Challenging business to self-examine its performance with reference to environmentally sound and Sustainable Development

- Encouraging business to develop goals and actions for Sustainable Development—within existing market conditions and in the context of future international agreements, governmental policies and fiscal measures

Business Charter for Sustainable Development

1. **Corporate policy.** To recognise environmental management as among the highest corporate priorities and as a key determinant to Sustainable Development; to establish policies, programmes and practices for conducting operations in an environmentally sound manner.

2. **Integrated management.** To integrate these policies, programmes and practices fully into each business as an essential element of management in all its functions.

3. **Process of improvement.** To continue to improve corporate policies, programmes and environmental performance, taking into account technical developments, scientific understanding, consumer needs and community expectations, with legal regulations as a starting point; and to apply the same environmental criteria internationally.

4. **Employee education.** To educate, train and motivate employees to conduct their activities in an environmentally responsible manner.

5. **Prior assessment.** To assess environmental impacts before starting a new activity or project and before decommissioning a facility or leaving a site.

6. **Products and services.** To develop and provide products and services that have no undue environmental impact and are safe in their intended use, that are efficient in their consumption of energy and natural resources, and that can be recycled, re-used, or disposed of safely.

7. **Customer advice.** To advise, and where relevant, educate, customers, distributors and the public in the safe use, transport, storage and disposal of products provided; and to apply similar consideration to provision of services.

8. **Facilities and operations.** To develop, design and operate facilities and conduct activities taking into consideration the efficient use of energy and materials, the sustainable use of renewable resources, the minimisation of adverse environmental impact and waste generation, and the safe and responsible disposal of residual wastes.

9. **Research.** To conduct or support research on the environmental impacts of raw materials, products, processes, emissions and wastes associated with the enterprise and on the means of minimising such adverse impacts.

10. **Precautionary approach.** To modify the manufacture, marketing or use of products or services or the conduct of activities, consistent with scientific and technical understanding, to prevent serious or irreversible environmental degradation.

11. **Contractors and suppliers.** To promote the adoption of these principles by contractors acting on behalf of the enterprise, encouraging and, where appropriate, requiring improvements in the practices to make them consistent with those of the enterprise; and to encourage the wider adoption of these principles by suppliers.

12. **Emergency preparedness.** To develop and maintain, where significant hazards exist, emergency preparedness plans in conjunction with emergency services, relevant authorities and local community, recognising potential trans-boundary impacts.

13. **Transfer of technology.** To contribute to the transfer of environmentally sound technology and management methods throughout the industrial and public sectors.

14. **Contributing to the common effort.** To contribute to the development of public policy and to business, governmental and intergovernmental programmes and educational initiatives that will enhance environmental awareness and protection.

15. **Openness to concerns.** To foster openness and dialogue with employees and the public, anticipating and responding to their concerns about the potential hazards and impacts of operations, products, wastes or services, including those of trans-boundary or global significance.

16. **Compliance and reporting.** To measure environmental performance; to conduct regular Environmental Audits and assessments of compliance with company requirements, legal requirements and these principles; and periodically to provide appropriate information to the Board of Directors, shareholders, employees, the authorities and the public.

Source: International Chamber of Commerce

Figure 1

- Stimulating analysis and wide discussion on the major public policies that concern business in the worldwide progress towards Sustainable Development

Leading companies worldwide are starting to examine their position on Sustainable Development. European Community member states are starting to recognise that the commitment in the Treaty of Rome to 'continuous and balanced expansion' and an 'accelerated raising of the standard of living' is no longer acceptable. There are increasing calls for sustainable and non-inflationary growth that respects the environment rather than continued unlimited growth (see Fig. 1).

Corporate Social Responsibility

There has been a considerable movement away from the unrestricted free market concept typified by Milton Friedman's famous statement,

> There is one and only one social responsibility of business—to use its resources and engage in activities to increase its profits.

Corporate Social Responsibility refers to the concept that business has a wider responsibility to all the communities within which it operates. At present, Corporate Social Responsibility tends to be quite narrowly defined. Research conducted as part of the study, 'The Rewards of Virtue'[6] found that Corporate Social Responsibility is usually defined in two ways. The most common view is that Corporate Social Responsibility refers to a company's interaction with the immediate community, or community relations.

An emerging, yet far from typical, view is that Corporate Social Responsibility means sensitivity to all of the company's Stakeholder groups. The difference between the two views centres on the definition of 'community'. The first narrowly defines the 'community' as the immediate micro-environment, while the second sees each Stakeholder as part of a more global community. The benefit of the holistic perspective is its strategic value.

Implicit in the definition of Corporate Social Responsibility are strong relationships between the company and its Stakeholders. Shelley Taylor, head of Shelley Taylor and Associates, commented in 'The Rewards of Virtue' survey: 'Intrinsic to the discussion of Corporate Social Responsibility is the idea that a company exists solely as a collection of its various corporate constituents or Stakeholders. An organisation is only as strong as the relationships it has with these groups.'[7]

An important element of Corporate Social Responsibility is the recognition of the issues of concern for each Stakeholder. Developing

What Level of Importance do Potential Employees Attach to the Following Company Policies with Regards to Social Responsibility?

Policies	Level of importance (%)	
	Graduates	Managers
Personal policies	83	92
Environmental policies	76	82
Community concern	63	61
Industrial democracy	60	63
Connections with oppressive regimes	56	59
Marketing policy	53	84
'Third-world' involvement	49	53
Military sales	47	40
Size and influence	44	55
Political links	43	38
Nuclear power	42	37
Secrecy	33	56

Source: M. Charter, *Graduates: Fewer and Greener* (Alton: KPH Marketing, 1990), and M. Charter, *The Greener Employee* (Alton: KPH Marketing, 1990)

Figure 2

this understanding relies on a two-way dialogue—active listening and responding. Also important are the broad or global issues which affect business and society: issues such as the environment and ethics. Corporate Social Responsibility is becoming a catalyst for considerable organisational development. Although much of the recent development in this area has stemmed from increasing environmental awareness, the issues are likely to change, and only a socially responsible company will be in a position to anticipate and respond to these changes.

Two surveys in the UK in 1990[8] indicated that considerable importance is attached to a socially responsible corporate image by existing and potential managers (see Fig. 2). But there is a considerable lack of understanding of the practicalities of the concept. Forty-one per cent of the sample of 101 middle managers selected from the UK's largest companies did not know what guidelines to expect from a socially responsible company. Of those that responded to the survey, single issues were mentioned most often, with 20% mentioning employee care policies and 13% mentioning community relations. This indicates a rather narrow view of Corporate Social Responsibility and a potential lack of holistic and systemic understanding amongst the UK's middle management.

When asked about specific corporate policies, there was clear concern over individual elements of Corporate Social Responsibility, notably the treatment of employees and the environment.

The debate is now widening to embrace the role of business, ethics and morality in the marketplace. Progressive companies should be conducting Corporate Social Responsibility audits, to assess their position before difficult questions are asked.

A Corporate Social Responsibility audit is likely to operate at three levels:[9]

1. **Policy**
   - Are there written policies for each area of social responsibility?
   - Do they reflect current thinking/knowledge?
   - Do people within the relevant parts of the organisation know that the policies exist and roughly what they say?

2. **Systems and standards for measuring performance in each area**
   - Do the systems exist?
   - Do they measure the right things?
   - Do they work? Are they used?
   - Are the standards high enough? (i.e. will they be overtaken by legislation?) Can we seize competitive advantage by adopting higher standards? How do our standards compare with best practice elsewhere?
   - Are the standards clearly understandable and precise enough to be measured accurately, year on year?

3. **Recording and analysing performance**
   - Current
   - Versus previous years
   - Versus targets set

A number of companies have had to examine their position on the wider issues of Corporate Social Responsibility.

For example, for many years, Barclays in South Africa offered positions to black Africans, Coloureds and Asians with university degrees, who could not find employment elsewhere, and actively recruited and trained those without education. This programme led to Barclays being the first bank in South Africa to have black cashiers and black managers and to be known there as the anti-apartheid bank. In 1986, the bank withdrew from South Africa for commercial reasons. One of

these was the fifteen-year campaign against the bank by the National
Union of Students in the UK. This resulted in inconvenience to the
bank's customers and vandalism against Barclays property. Over the
same period, Barclays saw its market share in the important student
sector reduce by over 50%. Since pulling out of South Africa, the
bank's share of the student market has fully recovered.

A number of publications and surveys are indicating that Stakeholders and, notably, consumers are concerned with a wider set of
social and environmental issues. The success of *The Green Consumer
Guide*[10] and *The Greener Consumer's Supermarket Shopping Guide*[11] indicated
that people are actively seeking greener companies and products. A
particularly interesting organisation is New Consumer which was established as a non profit making research body aimed at examining corporate activity across a broad range of social issues.

In 1991 New Consumer launched two books that examined companies' philosophies and products across a range of criteria from disclosure of information and animal testing to involvement with military
sales and gambling. *Changing Corporate Values*[12] and *Shopping for a Better
World*[13] were developed from research originally undertaken in the US
by the Council on Economic Priorities (CEP). The success of these
publications indicates that certain groups of consumers are now
actively seeking the facts behind the gloss.

Dragon International carried out a major worldwide survey in 1990
to examine whether consumers were translating statements of good
intent into hard purchasing decisions. The research was undertaken by
Diagnostics Social and Market Research, and produced the following
findings:[14]

- Consumers are interested in corporate behaviour, beyond the
  areas that affect them directly.

- Consumers understand commercial motives, and do not expect
  companies to be altruistic, but want to see companies making a
  contribution to society.

- Well-regarded corporate behaviour worked in favour of the
  company. Consumers would be attracted by companies and
  products which helped them to feel good and relieved guilt.

- New factors, such as environmental performance and community involvement are being taken into account, along with product quality, safety and innovation.

- The link between consumer purchasing decisions and corporate
  reputation will increase significantly in the future. This could

happen rapidly, judging by the speed with which 'green' criteria have moved onto the agenda.

- Companies can gain competitive advantage by being seen to be innovative in areas like the environment, fair trading, employee welfare, community involvement and ethical marketing.

This research was supported by Mintel's 'Second Green Consumer Report' which was conducted, in May 1991, among a sample of 1,336 adults.

When asked what would make people stop buying, the top three answers were as follows:

- Any environmental issue   70%
- Any ethical issue   60%
- Any animal issue   60%

These results indicate that consumers have a wider social and environmental agenda on which they are buying, and this has implications for a range of corporate activities, from branding strategy to corporate and brand coordination, reputation of management and monitoring. It suggests that investing in a socially and environmentally responsible reputation makes sound commercial sense.

The Stakeholder Concept

A Stakeholder can be defined as a person or group that can influence the commercial existence, viability and direction of the firm. Stakeholder influences on the firm should be prioritised, depending on the particular business issues facing the company and the manager.

Companies will need to accept that their overall performance is dependent on a number of Stakeholders, with each of these groups being interdependent and interconnected. For example, an employee might also be an investor, a customer and a member of a local pressure group. The priorities attached to the influence of Stakeholders will depend on a number of factors ranging from the level of environmental awareness to job function, organisational status, size of company and industry sector.

The Greener Employee survey[15] illustrated the perceived importance of customers and employees in environmental policy development (see Fig. 3).

The Stakeholder concept suggests that the operation of the firm is dependent on a number of interacting groups, the sum of which is greater than the individual parts. Companies should be looking to

Perceived Importance of Stakeholder Influence on Environmental Policy Development	
	%
Customers	75
Employees	70
Suppliers	55
Government	48
Media	46
Pressure Groups	30
Trade Unions	18

Source: M. Charter, *The Greener Employee* (Alton: KPH Marketing, 1990)

Figure 3

encourage greater participation and the development of stronger relationships with all Stakeholders.

Stakeholders are now calling for greater corporate disclosure of social and environmental information, but in the past companies have been unwilling to 'open up' for competitive reasons. The EC movement towards Environmental Auditing, the implementation of the EC directive on Freedom of Access to Environmental Information and a private members bill on corporate disclosure in the UK[16] indicate a trend towards greater openness, as environmental and social responsibility becomes more of a competitive issue.

In 1990, a survey of 200 international companies' annual reports was undertaken in twenty-eight countries, based on those published during the year ending December 1987. It found a wide variation in the information that firms revealed about environment, employees and energy usage. Only twenty-six of the annual reports (13%) gave environmental protection statements. The lowest level of detail was found in the Japanese reports, most of which did not disclose any voluntary information, and only three of the forty North American reports (7%) mentioned what action they had taken to protect the environment. By contrast, 21% of the European reports made some mention of environmental protection. German reports gave the most detail, with 40% making a clearly defined statement on the environment, including the costs of measures undertaken. Of the fifteen UK Company Groups in the sample, two (13%) gave environmental protection statements.[17]

A separate survey conducted in 1991 by Company Reporting, using a sample of 670 annual reports, found that only 3% highlighted environmental information, and it concluded that the majority of disclosure is so low that is virtually meaningless. In 1991 the Campaign for Freedom of Information analysed twenty large companies that had been convicted of safety or environmental offences in the financial years since 1989. None of the companies revealed the information in their annual reports.[18]

The first step is to recognise both internal and external Stakeholder interests and influences in environmental policy development, and then to work with groups to achieve objectives and tackle problems. Consensus building approaches, pioneered in the US, are often useful for resolving the dilemmas involved in environmental issues, and may change perceptions of the problem. They narrow the scope for disagreement, and clarify the differences between the parties. Specific obstacles to agreement can then be identified, and constructive solutions negotiated. This requires skill and perseverance, and is concerned as much with how things are done (the procedures) as with what issues are being tackled (the content), and with feelings as much as thoughts. It is wise to build confidence in the methods by approaching lesser issues first (see Fig. 4).

Figure 5 examines Stakeholder relationships with regard to the understanding of the corporate environmental performance of a car manufacturer.

We now examine, in greater detail, the potential interests of various Stakeholders in corporate environmental performance.

Parent Company
The holding company will need to know about its subsidiaries' environmental actions, with a view to determining the impact on the balance sheet and the profit and loss account. If acquisitions, mergers or disposals are considered, then the environmental performance of companies will have to be assessed in relation to liability, insurance and the potential impact on the buying and selling price. A survey by Touche Ross in 1990[19] indicated that 80% of Belgian companies considered environmental performance of potential merger and acquisition partners, compared to 90% in the US and 18% in the UK. If a group of companies has one bad environmental performer it may lead the spotlight onto the performance of associate companies.

The Board of Directors
Companies will be put under increasing legislative and public pressure to conform to stricter environmental standards. Directors are likely to become criminally liable for environmental negligence. The environment will become an important aspect of competitive advantage, and will need to be addressed through thorough corporate planning. The

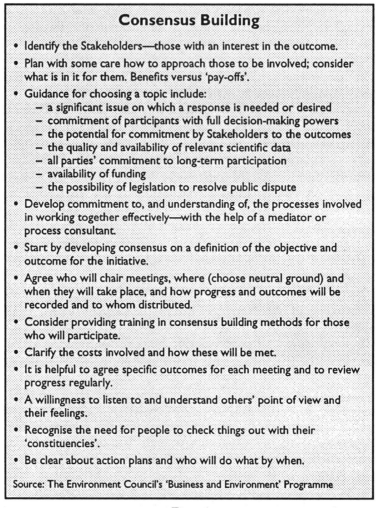

Consensus Building

- Identify the Stakeholders—those with an interest in the outcome.
- Plan with some care how to approach those to be involved; consider what is in it for them. Benefits versus 'pay-offs'.
- Guidance for choosing a topic include:
  - a significant issue on which a response is needed or desired
  - commitment of participants with full decision-making powers
  - the potential for commitment by Stakeholders to the outcomes
  - the quality and availability of relevant scientific data
  - all parties' commitment to long-term participation
  - availability of funding
  - the possibility of legislation to resolve public dispute
- Develop commitment to, and understanding of, the processes involved in working together effectively—with the help of a mediator or process consultant.
- Start by developing consensus on a definition of the objective and outcome for the initiative.
- Agree who will chair meetings, where (choose neutral ground) and when they will take place, and how progress and outcomes will be recorded and to whom distributed.
- Consider providing training in consensus building methods for those who will participate.
- Clarify the costs involved and how these will be met.
- It is helpful to agree specific outcomes for each meeting and to review progress regularly.
- A willingness to listen to and understand others' point of view and their feelings.
- Recognise the need for people to check things out with their 'constituencies'.
- Be clear about action plans and who will do what by when.

Source: The Environment Council's 'Business and Environment' Programme

Figure 4

greening process is likely to have significant implications for resource allocation, and may mean that companies will need to evaluate core values and mission statements closely. The directors, as the stewards of the company, are likely to be increasingly questioned about corporate social and environmental performance by a wide range of different Stakeholders. Organisations will need to have board-level responsibility for environmental matters, with the Chief Executive openly stating the company's commitment to environmental matters through a policy statement, quantified objectives and a well-structured policy.

Stakeholders and their Potential Interest in the Environmental Positioning of a Car Manufacturer

Stakeholder groups	Why do they need to know about the company's environmental impact?
Parent company	– Corporate environmental performance, profitability
The board of directors	– Corporate environmental performance, profitability
Senior management	– Personnel issues/training

Employees	– Long-term security:
	  – personal
	  – company

Customers	– Buy companies' approach, not just products

The community	– Impact on:
	  – life and well-being
	  – the local environment

Legislators	– Legislative compliance
Investors	– Long-term profitability
Suppliers	– Cradle-to-grave analysis

Dealers	– Sell:
	  – products
	  – corporate image

Pressure groups	– Campaign publicity
Competitors	– Edge to marketing/competitive positioning
The media	– Corporate image
Trade unions	– Protecting employees
Trade associations	– Setting industry standards
Professional bodies	– Professional standards
Pensioners	– Community affairs
Academia	– Research

Figure 5

Senior Management

Senior management in different functions will need to be aware of their area's environmental performance and impact. Certain key areas may start to have environmental responsibility and performance criteria built into job descriptions. There will also be the need for greater cooperation and the development of more effective internal and external information systems and communication channels.

Employees

Employees will become more interested in the company's corporate environmental performance and image. If the company is taking positive environmental steps, then this may lead to greater commitment and motivation, and conversely if the company is acting irresponsibly, problems with morale and recruitment may develop. There may be increased questioning of the destination of the company's pension fund monies, the quality of the working environment and health and safety issues. Employees should be involved in the development and implementation of the company's environmental policy, and they should be kept informed of new developments and initiatives. There may also be a growth in 'eco-consciousness' groups that act as internal pressure groups with the aim of influencing management to 'green up'.

The greenest consumers tend to be women, and especially young women and those with teenagers or young children. With demographic changes, women will have to be attracted back into the workforce to fill the gaps produced by fewer young people. Women returners are unlikely to leave their green attitudes at home, so will dissonance set in if the company's behaviour is at odds with individual values?

Customers

Customers will increasingly buy not just the product, but the company's response to environmental issues. The 1991 Touche Ross survey[20] indicated that just under half of the companies surveyed had adapted products to meet customer demand, and of these, 70% had altered existing products and just over half had introduced new products. Customers may be more likely to switch brands if a company performs environmentally irresponsibly. A survey of US consumers in June 1990 showed that 70% of consumers had switched brands over environmental concerns on at least one occasion.

The Community

The company's local community is likely to supply both past, existing and prospective employees, customers, investors and suppliers, and as such is an important Stakeholder. A company's record on pollution and industrial accidents will become an important factor in good community relations, and positive alliances should be established with local schools and pressure groups. Local authorities are also likely to be interested in the environmental performance of the firm. For example, if the firm wishes to expand or set up new facilities, Environmental Impact Assessments (EIA) may be required (see Fig. 6). There are also likely to be increasing calls for disclosure of corporate environmental

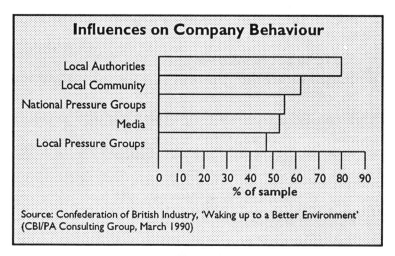

Figure 6

information as awareness grows through the public registers, established through the Environmental Protection Act.

Legislators

The EC and national governments are likely to exert increasing environmental pressure through legislation such as the Environmental Protection Act in the UK; with the implementation of Integrated Pollution Control (IPC); through Her Majesty's Inspectorate of Pollution (HMIP), the National Rivers Authority (NRA), and local authorities. There may be an eventual move to an integrated UK or EC Environmental Protection Agency which deals with all environmental media.

Through the Environmental Protection Act, local authorities will have responsibility for air emissions and through the EC Directive on Environmental Impact Assessment they already have responsibility for the planning implications of certain developments. There will also be interest in the environmental education and health needs of the communities they represent whether it be at a county, district, city or town level.

The EC is likely to have a growing influence in Europe through the legislative process. Particular pressure is likely to be felt through proposals on packaging, Environmental Auditing and eco-labelling. In June 1991 there were eighty-seven EC environmental proposals in the 'policy pipeline', that complemented the 450-plus environmental laws already enacted.

A report[21] conducted in June 1991 by Environmental Policy Consultants analysed the planned environmental policies of the European Commission. It observed that there were:

- Nine proposals formally adopted by June 1991
- Twenty-six published proposals currently under formal consideration
- Twenty-seven proposals being drafted that were awaiting feedback from the Commission, and
- Thirty-four proposals under consideration by the Commission for possible legislative enactment

The implementation of these proposals will have major impacts upon British business, namely:

- **Very substantial cost implications,** undoubtedly running into billions. For example, the proposal on reducing sulphur in gas oils will, alone, cost British refineries some $430 million.
- **Corporate strategies will have to be re-written,** for example, in the light of the eco-labelling proposal's adoption of cradle-to-grave analysis.
- **Significant managerial changes,** for example, the Eco-Auditing proposal on total environmental management systems.

The most significant trends in EC environmental policy are:

- The continuing development of environmental policy with new standards set in the light of new scientific knowledge: the Directive on dangerous substances has just been extended for the eleventh time
- Tighter controls across more sectors: it is not just the chemical sector that is in the front line
- Increasing use of fiscal incentives, for example, on packaging

There are also likely to be increasing calls for wider-scale international agreements and possibly legislation. There is also likely to be an increase in accords such as the Montreal Protocol on the reduction in the production of CFCs and the North Sea agreement on the elimination the dumping of toxic waste.[22]

Investors
Private and corporate investors are starting to examine companies' environmental profiles to assess the long-term profitability of firms

against the potential environmental risks associated with the company or the industry. Research by Shelley Taylor and Associates in 1991[23] found that 10% of the UK equity market is being screened according to some social and environmental criteria. These investors are primarily institutions and include pension funds, as well as funds managed by insurance companies and other asset management companies. Other research, by Dewe Rogerson in 1991,[24] indicated that two-thirds of the sample of eighty fund managers thought that environmental issues were a significant factor for UK business. However, they considered that only 20% of UK companies had a coherent environmental policy. A number of fund managers are now starting to incorporate environmental aspects into stock selection criteria, and the stockbroker James Capel have developed a Green Index to monitor the performance of greener companies. This has indicated that in many cases greener companies are performing better than non-green companies.

Personal investors are also increasingly investing in ethical and green unit trusts. Despite the interest, these funds account for a very small percentage of the total unit trust market and less than 1% of the total UK equity market. 'The Rewards of Virtue' survey calculated that green and ethical unit trusts totalled £330 million in twenty-six different funds in January 1991.[25] A separate survey by Mintel in May 1991[26] indicated that 45% of the sample of 1,336 adults would avoid using services of a financial service institution on ethical grounds. This rose to 56% amongst 15–34 year-olds.

Suppliers

Suppliers' environmental performance will be scrutinised more closely to ensure that purchases are cleaner and greener, and that processes used are friendlier from cradle to grave. A survey by Touche Ross in 1991[27] indicated that 60% of the UK's larger companies consider their suppliers' environmental performance, and have asked them to change their practices or guarantee environmental performance, compared to 40% across Europe. Conversely, a survey by David Bellamy Associates[28] indicated that only 28% of the sample of 176 UK companies had made green purchase choices, and that policies were not comprehensive.

Companies will look to design-out potential environmental problems at source, rather than relying on 'end-of-pipe' technological fixes. Some companies are already setting stricter standards through 'supplier challenges', and are undertaking Environmental Audits throughout the supply chain that require more information about the impacts of products and processes. A number of companies will look to select suppliers, not just on the BS5750 quality standard, but also on BS7750, the new BSI Environmental Management System.

Corporate buyers and specifiers are also likely to become more aware of green issues as employees become more educated, and companies invest in training. There is also likely to be an increasing call for more information on environmental performance of materials, as well as policies and processes. For example, in 1992 The Engineering Council are launching a green code for their 300,000 members covering environmental responsibility within the engineering profession.

Pressure Groups

The UK membership of environmental groups is continuing to rise; notably, the membership of Greenpeace and Friends of the Earth (FoE) has increased by over 700% and 600% respectively from 1985 to 1990. The emerging influence of the pressure groups was strongly felt by the aerosol industry in 1988 with the FoE campaign over CFCs, which led to a fundamental market re-structuring in 1989.[29]

The number and interests of pressure groups are both likely to grow. They are also likely to become more proactive, sophisticated, and professional in their approaches. National and local pressure groups will be interested in the overall environmental performance of the firm, and in specific areas of interest, e.g. rainforests, beaches, etc. There are likely to be more calls for greater corporate openness through 'Right to Know' legislation, with companies involved in certain sensitive areas, such as nuclear and animal testing, finding themselves facing increasingly hostile action. The area of animal testing is drawing considerable attention, and this will be a continuing issue with the movement towards vegetarianism, especially amongst younger women. The emergence of pressure group activity outside pure environmental areas is indicating that broader green issues are permeating through society.

Environmental groups may be increasingly prepared to use the power of the law, or even go beyond it. Greenpeace recently found that Albright and Wilson's Whitehaven factory had surpassed discharge levels permitted by the National Rivers Authority (NRA). The company were taken to court and fined £2,000 and were ordered to pay £20,000 costs to Greenpeace.[30] New more radical groups may form— Earth First, a US based group with 200 UK members, are committed to use non-violent eco-sabotage, as they believe that things will not change through the established political channels.[31] Pressure groups may increasingly make alliances with other Stakeholder groups. For example, a recent shareholder action campaign was orchestrated by Friends of the Earth (FoE) and Norwich Union against Fisons over the destruction of Sites of Special Scientific Interest (SSSIs) for peat extraction.

Other groups may also play the role of pressure groups if they feel added weight can be put towards an argument. For example, recently the General Synod of the Church of England called for a boycott of Nestlé's brands because of the company's involvement in marketing powdered milk products in less developed countries. Companies will be advised to set up a two-way dialogue and involve pressure groups in the planning of projects on a local, national and international level.

Competitors

Companies will look to develop competitive advantage based on environmental matters, and this will mean that understanding competitors' green performance will be increasingly important. There may be opportunities for the development of cooperative strategies that cover common environmental issues affecting firms in an industry, or cross-industry. Innovative companies may take initiatives to drive up standards in the industry. Examples are Norsk Hydro's publication of its Environmental Audit, British Airways' investment in the establishment of a Green Tourism Unit at Oxford Polytechnic, and BMW's establishment of car dismantling and recycling plants.

The Media

International, national and local media will be interested in companies' good and bad environmental performance, and should be kept informed of developments. If any environmental problems are publicised, the company should react quickly with a response from the Chief Executive, the Managing Director or the Environmental Director. The media should have a contact point for environmental issues, and they should be aware of activities happening throughout the company or group. Directors and senior management should be briefed in media relations and an open dialogue should be developed and encouraged.

Trade Unions

The UK trade union movement have not been particularly proactive in incorporating environmental matters into employee–management negotiations, compared to their colleagues in continental Europe. The situation appears to be changing, as a number of trade unions are starting to incorporate green matters, such as Environmental Auditing and training, into collective bargaining. As part of the increased priority attached to green issues, the Trades Union Congress (TUC) have published *The Greening of the Workplace,* a handbook designed to assist trade unionists with issues relating to environmental policy formulation.

Trade Associations

Trade associations are representatives of industries, and as such are taking a greater interest in corporate environmental performance. They are represented on government advisory groups, with information being fed through to and from members, and with a number of industry-specific initiatives being taken. For example, signing of the Chemical Industries Association 'Responsible Care' programme has become a prerequisite of association membership. The 1991 Touche Ross survey[32] found that about half of the companies surveyed were involved in external environmental committees, especially those in chemical and pharmaceutical sectors, with two-thirds of UK companies being involved. The reasons for participation included lobbying for changes in legislation, developing new and improved standards, self-protection and improving public relations (see Fig. 7).

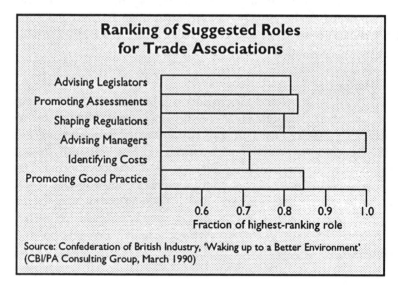

Figure 7

Professional Bodies

Professional organisations are slowly developing positions on environmental matters and sponsoring research into the implications of green issues for the professions. A survey amongst professional associations in the UK by the University of Stirling indicated that 27% had an environmental policy, and 35% indicated that they had a Code of Practice, but these rarely had any environmental perspective.[33]

In 1990 The Chartered Association of Certified Accountants (ACCA) commissioned Professor Rob Gray, then at the University of East Anglia, to examine the implications of the environmental agenda for accountants. He produced a 200-page report which indicated that the profession had a considerable role to play in the widening of the debate.[34]

Non-Regulatory Bodies

There has been a rapid growth in 'business and environment' organisations worldwide, such as the International Network of Environmentalist Management (INEM), the Global Environmental Management Initiative (GEMI) in the US, and the Business Council for Sustainable Development; and, in the UK, the Environment Council's 'Business and Environment' programme, and Business in the Community's Environment Target team. Peer group pressure is also going to be an important factor in corporate environmental performance amongst corporate membership organisations.

Codes of conduct and standards are likely to increase. The BSI Environmental Management System BS7750 is likely to be launched in 1993, and will be the first in the world. The Valdez Principles were developed, in the US, by the Coalition for Environmentally Responsible Economies (CERES) in the wake of the Exxon Valdez disaster, with the key objective being to create a voluntary mechanism that monitors business, consistent with a long-term commitment to Sustainable Development. The International Chamber of Commerce (ICC) have set down guidelines for the undertaking of Environmental Audits, and have developed the Business Charter for Sustainable Development, with sixteen key principles.

Academia

There is growing academic interest in the research, educational, and training implications of environmental and social aspects of business. An example is the establishment of the Information Technology Centre for Educational Research, Development and Training in Environmental Sciences (IT CERES) at the University of Southampton, which specialises in the use of information technology in environmental education and training. IT CERES is linked to eight other European universities, and has conducted projects for a number of major companies and institutions, including work for the United Nations on Geographical Information Systems (GIS).

Business schools worldwide appear to be slow to adapt to the changing student and industry requirements, with a lack of environmental courses and course modules. Recent research[35] has indicated that there is strong pressure from students, lecturers and industry to develop greener courses, but in many cases Business School management appear to be lagging behind the change.

Summary

Stakeholder analysis indicates the complex set of relationships and perspectives that organisations face. The key will be to recognise and understand separate Stakeholder interests, concerns and needs, and to develop positions on the issues based on thorough research, and then proactively to establish two-way dialogue with separate groups.

Total Quality Management and Environmental Excellence

Total Quality Management (TQM) is a concept that has dominated Japanese and US companies in the eighties and early nineties. European businesses are also now starting to adopt the principles and realise the benefits.

TQM is, however, not a new concept—its roots lie in quality control, which was developed in America in the fifties by Dr Edward Deming. Quality is easily recognised and is, by its very nature, desirable in a product, process or mental approach. It is something, however, that cannot be strictly defined or measured. The desire for quality is a fundamental feature that lies behind the growing dissatisfaction with the attitudes of the eighties that were so often centred on quantity rather than quality. TQM's fundamental assumption is that if we desire an improved quality of life, then we must have improved quality of products and improved quality of management processes.

Although the origins of TQM lie in statistical analysis of quality control, Deming laid great emphasis on the human aspects of management—in particular the customer and supplier relationships that are essential to long-term success. TQM influences the product and production system through a set of guiding principles that aid management decision making. It is a philosophy that drives management towards a zero-defect goal—something that is not easily achieved. However it thrives through the realisation that every step towards that goal is a movement that will produce a positive result. It has brought about a management movement that continually strives to improve product quality, to cut out expensive 'end-of-line' testing and prevent rejection or correction of faulty goods.

With the development of the Stakeholder concept and the realisation that society and the environment are the 'consumers' of corporate waste, environmental excellence has become integral to the TQM programmes of large corporations such as IBM, Tioxide and 3M. Greener Marketing and TQM are philosophies that imply each other's existence; they are largely interdependent and they are both about getting it right first time—although from an environmental perspective Zero Impact Management (ZIM) is not possible because every company or product has an environmental impact. Greener Marketing, however, brings in a wider context for management decision making that goes beyond the product and production process and brings in environmental and social considerations, and looks at the full range of Stakeholder relationships that are not necessarily implicit in the TQM approach.

The key to the success of TQM and Greener Marketing is without a doubt the way in which they are implemented—there are no short cuts available, so the approach cannot be superficial. They can, and should, run in parallel, as both approaches seek to treat the cause of problems directly, and not the symptoms. Implementation is where Greener Marketing, like TQM, emphasises the human element in management. If the manager is positive and proactive, it is easy to see the benefits of both approaches and therefore implementation becomes a matter of common sense—not necessarily always easy, but always self-justifying and making good business sense.

Sir Anthony Cleaver of IBM identifies the following factors as integral to TQM:

- Management commitment
- Training and awareness raising
- Accurate information gathering
- Assessing failure
- Concentration on prevention rather than cure

3M launched its 'Pollution Prevention Pays' (3Ps) programme in 1975, realising the direct link between environmental excellence, TQM and competitive advantage. It utilised employee initiatives to create and implement pollution prevention solutions. The company established a corporate quality department in 1980 and then went on to market their expertise through seminars and training workshops. The corporation's European quality improvement team now includes their European quality manager, the Vice President for Europe, a regional Vice President, and the directors of manufacturing, human resources, logistics, sales and marketing. A quality improvement plan is included in each subsidiary's annual review, with senior management involved in agree-ing plans, setting targets and recording progress against the plan.

The benefits from the 3M approach can be seen in improved raw material yields through reduced waste. Supplier management has been tightened and, inevitably, the environmental performance of suppliers has come under scrutiny. Customer satisfaction has also risen with the improvements in product quality that are fundamental to the pro-gramme. Quality improvements have become more difficult to achieve, as the 'easy' solutions of pollution prevention have been taken up, but this has strengthened the drive for environmental excellence through product innovation by designing-in pollution prevention.

The success of the programme has put the company in a strong market position and there appears to be no weakening in the resolve to implement the programme; in fact it has been re-emphasised through the introduction of the 'Pollution Prevention Plus' which aims to cut air pollutants by 90% by the year 2000.[36]

The differences between TQM and Greener Marketing lie in the emphasis of their benefits. The problem for business is to balance the achievement of corporate objectives against deteriorating environmen-tal quality. TQM places its emphasis on the corporate body while Greener Marketing's emphasis is on its relationships with Stakeholder groups. Greener Marketing includes TQM's emphasis on the internal communication of the environmental and quality policy, but goes beyond TQM in the recognition of a wider set of Stakeholder needs.

Greener Consumption

Fundamental to the greening process is the acceptance that both organisations and individuals have a major role to play in social and environmental change and transformation. The emergence of the 'green consumer' is well documented, but major organisations are now starting to recognise their role as responsible corporate citizens, and some are starting to add the green screen to purchase decisions as a movement towards environmental excellence and Total Quality Management (TQM).

Greener Organisations

Both private and public sector organisations are starting to exercise greater influence over greener buying. A number of local authorities have started to implement environmentally friendlier purchasing poli-cies. This has been illustrated through several local authorities banning the purchase of peat products after pressure from Norwich Union and a number of pressure groups over the destruction of Sites of Special Scientific Interest (SSSIs) for peat extraction. Local authorities are screening pension fund monies against green and ethical criteria, and by the spring of 1991 £3.5bn of pension fund monies had been invested through the UK Environmental Investors Code.[37]

Central Government have recently published an 'Environmental Action Guide' aimed at building and purchasing managers. This is one of the results of the 1990 White Paper on the Environment. The objective is to ensure that green issues are incorporated into all purchasing, building and land decisions made by the Government.

Companies may be involved in supplying greener consumer products or services, but the greener company is also likely to display a range of other characteristics (see Fig. 8).

The purchasing of materials provides an opportunity for organisations to exercise an environmental commitment, through working with suppliers to reduce and minimise environmental impact from cradle to grave. Leading companies such as IBM, British Telecom, B&Q and Gateway are starting to select new suppliers on environmental performance, and put pressure on existing suppliers to change processes, to reduce or eliminate the use of CFCs, and to improve energy efficiency (see the chapters relating to these companies in Part III).

Characteristics of a Greener Company

- Leadership through environmental excellence
- Openness
- Flexibility
- Holistic/systemic vision
- People-oriented
- Sensitive
- Participative
- Good community relations
- Emphasis on self-learning
- Good communication systems
- Ethical
- Quality conscious
- Coordinated
- Integrated
- Collaborative
- Partnership

Figure 8

Greener Consumers

According to a recent survey, 85% of the industrialised world's citizens believe that the environment is the number one issue.[38] Opposition to perceived irresponsible environmental behaviour has grown, and there has been a growth in boycotting, and, more disturbingly, eco-terrorism. The new greener consumer does not just look at the price of the product, but also asks, 'Is there an environmental or moral issue involved?'

In the US, a consultancy, Yankelovich Clancy Shulman, completes an annual survey of Fortune 500 companies that identifies, measures and tracks consumer values and behaviour. The research has identified the emergence of a new consumer—the 'Neotraditional' consumer—who bases purchasing decisions on a solid foundation of values, constructed from both the traditional and the new. Neotraditional consumers seek goods that are straightforward, honest and reliable, and respond to the need for emotional fulfilment.[39]

If a more holistic perspective is taken, personal consumption subdivides into three broad categories: products or services; savings or investment; and employment. There are indications that across the spectrum people are investing energy in positive greener directions. Greener consumers will look to direct themselves towards greener products and organisations. The challenge for business is to provide the option and the benefits.

Greener consumption goes through a number of phases. The environmental consciousness of the consumer is high when cognitive, affective and conative reactions are relatively consistent:[40]

- **The Cognitive dimension:** the subjective knowledge of the ecological consequences of consumption.

- **The Affective dimension:** the opinions about the ecological consequences of consumption patterns.

- **The Conative dimension:** behavioural intentions, which reflect the willingness of the consumer to participate actively in solving environmental problems.

When Gallup undertook research into consumer attitudes back in 1989, environmental consciousness or general awareness of ecological change—the cognitive dimension—stood at an estimated 54%, as illustrated in Figure 9. The unprompted level of concern can be attributed mainly to the emergence of green consumerism, media interest and pressure group activity.

```
┌─────────────────────────────────────────────────────────────┐
│              Worst Aspects of Living in Britain               │
│                     Sample: 924 adults                        │
│                                                               │
│                                    All    16–24 year olds     │
│                                    (%)         (%)            │
│   Pollution to the environment      54         51             │
│   Litter                            36         30             │
│   Disappearance of the countryside  30         31             │
│   Disappearance of community spirit 27         19             │
│   Traffic congestion                26         21             │
│   Graffiti                          20         17             │
│   Derelict and empty buildings      17         19             │
│   Disappearance of wildlife         16         20             │
│   Standard of living compared to other countries  15   17     │
│   Public transport                  11         14             │
│                                                               │
│   Source: Gallup, March 1989                                  │
└─────────────────────────────────────────────────────────────┘
```

Figure 9

As a result of increased concern and activity, consumers became more aware; but how far were their emotions and opinions changed by the prospect of ecological damage?—the affective dimension. Studies in Britain have shown that the problem of environmental pollution is broken down into specific aspects, when applied to the individual. 'Green Issues: Evolution to Revolution'[41] highlighted the issues shown in Figure 10 when questioning individuals on their personal feelings towards the environment.

```
┌─────────────────────────────────────────────────────────────┐
│            Prioritisation of Environmental Problems           │
│                                                               │
│    Most urgent        Pollution                               │
│         │             Traffic, smell, litter                  │
│         │             (atmosphere, chemicals, rain)           │
│         │                                                     │
│         │             Waste (disposal of)                     │
│         │                                                     │
│         │             Power                                   │
│         │             Non-renewable sources                   │
│         │                                                     │
│         │             Deforestation                           │
│    Least urgent       (Noise)                                 │
│                                                               │
│  Source: C. Haines and O. Murphy, 'Green Issues: Evolution to Revolution' (Market │
│  Research Society, 1989 Conference Papers)                    │
└─────────────────────────────────────────────────────────────┘
```

Figure 10

There are indications that there has been a behavioural change among some groups—the conative dimension. The consensus is that the greener consumer, in one form or another, represents an estimated 60% of the population.[42] In 1990 MORI undertook a survey of 3,040 adults which indicated that green consumerism was prevalent in many areas (see Fig. 11).

Figure 12 indicates that, although students and mothers with teenagers are actively seeking to change their lifestyles, most individuals feel only guilty or slightly concerned at best about the environment.

The greener product should have at least the same benefits as the product it aims to replace. It should not be more expensive if it does not provide significant added benefits to the consumer, and it should avoid the perception of the cliched imagery[43] of early greener products. Green consumerism can be described as the use of individual consumer power to promote less environmentally damaging consumption as promoted by *The Green Consumer Guide*[44] and *Shopping for a Better World*[45]. A wider view may include the buying of products or services against a set of social and ethical criteria, such as excluding companies that are involved in animal testing, or in nuclear and military sales. Its emergence may:

- Provide an incentive to businesses to 'clean up their act'
- Put pressure on retailers to meet demand for environmentally friendlier products
- Empower individuals to accept personal responsibility for their own choices
- Encourage individuals to assess the company and all its activities, not just its products
- Improve the state of the environment and quality of life through the cumulative impact on green consumerism

The above illustrates slightly modified market behaviour. However, a more radical, darker-green perspective might be as follows:

Green consumerism means a great deal more than simply changing over from an earth-bashing product to a slightly more environmentally sensitive one. It means questioning both the nature and the volume of our consumption.[46]

Environmental Auditing

There will be a growth in demand for Environmental Audits as individuals switch to buying not just products, but also companies'

Green Consumerism

Which, if any, of these things do you do, or have you done in the last twelve months, as a result of concern for the environment?

	Total				Green Consumerists*			
	1989 %	1990 %	1991 %	89–91 ±%	1989 %	1990 %	1991 %	89–91 ±%
Buy ozone-friendly aerosols or try to avoid buying aerosols	75	73	71	–4	94	92	91	–3
Buy products which come in recycled packaging	27	41	55	+28	41	58	74	+33
Buy products made from recycled material	n/a	40	52	–	n/a	58	72	–
Buy household, domestic, or toiletry products that have not been tested on animals	n/a	43	51	–	n/a	59	70	–
Buy free-range eggs or chickens	n/a	44	46	–	n/a	53	58	–
Keep down the amount of electricity and fuel your household uses	32	44	44	+12	37	51	55	+18
Regularly use a bottle bank	33	39	39	+6	39	49	49	+10
Avoid using chemical fertilisers or pesticides in your garden	34	41	38	+4	46	52	49	+3
Buy environmentally friendly phosphate-free detergents or household cleaners	33	38	37	+4	51	55	56	+5
Send your own waste paper to be recycled	30	31	36	+6	34	37	43	+9
Buy products which come in bio-degradable packaging	16	26	34	+18	28	43	53	+25
Buy food products which are organically grown	29	25	28	–1	41	33	41	0
Avoid using the services or products of a company which you consider has a poor environmental record	15	23	19	+4	22	33	31	+9
Keep down the amount you use your car	n/a	19	19	–	n/a	23	25	–
Buy low-energy light bulbs for home	n/a	n/a	16	–	n/a	n/a	22	–
Buy a fridge/freezer with reduced CFCs	n/a	n/a	12	–	n/a	n/a	16	–
Avoid buying chlorine-bleached nappies	7	13	10	+3	10	19	15	+5
Have a catalytic converter fitted to your car	n/a	9	7	–	n/a	12	9	–
Any of these	92	93	92	0	99	99	100	+1
Average number done	3.6	5.6	6.1	+2.5	4.7	7.3	8.3	+3.6

Base: All

Source: MORI

* 'Green consumerists' are defined here as: people who have said that over the last year or two they have selected one product over another because of its environmentally friendly packaging formulation or advertising.

Figure 11

Hypothesised Differentiation by Life-Stage

Age/Life-stage	Apathy/Disinterest	Guilt	Concern
			Some Activity
10 years+ School			
Adolescents			
Students			
Young Male Workers			
Young Women			
Young Mothers			
Mothers with Teenagers			
'Empty Nesters'			
Embarrassed Capitalists			
Retired			

Source: C. Haines and O. Murphy, 'Green Issues: Evolution to Revolution' (Market Research Society, 1989 Conference papers)

Figure 12

processes, policies and philosophies. Pressures will also come from tougher EC environmental legislation as companies seek to understand their environmental position clearly.

Environmental Auditing has been in operation in the US and the Netherlands since the seventies. But in the UK, Environmental Auditing is a relatively new discipline outside the sensitive sectors of oil and chemicals, and in many cases audits have evolved out of health and safety assessments. The lack of professional standards covering Environmental Audits in the UK is being addressed through the development of three organisations established in 1991: The Association of Environmental Consultancies (AEC), the Institute of Environmental Auditors (IEA), and the Institute of Environmental Assessment (IEA). The prime drive to regulate auditing is the publication by the British Standards Institute (BSI) of the Environmental Management System BS7750, and the EC's Eco-Audit regulation expected at the end of 1992.

The International Chamber of Commerce define Environmental Audits as follows:

> An Environmental Audit is a management tool comprising a systematic, documented, periodic and objective evaluation of how well environmental organisation, management, and equipment are performing with the aim of helping to safeguard the environment by:
>
> 1. facilitating management control of environmental practices;
> 2. assessing compliance with company policies, which would include meeting regulatory requirements.[47]

The rise of 'greenspeak' has led to a considerable confusion of terms. An Environmental Audit is not the same as an Environmental Impact Assessment (EIA). An Environmental Audit relates to an existing project or facility while an EIA relates to a proposed facility or project and sets out to establish what will happen to the physical and qualitative environment if a new project proceeds.

The purpose of the audit should be to determine what the organisation has done, is doing, and will need to do in relation to the environment. Environmental Audits can broadly be defined as managerial or technical. Companies should clearly define what they are trying to achieve before they embark on an environmental review or audit. The particular type of audit will also depend on the purpose. For example, BP define different types of Environmental Audits for separate purposes: compliance audits examine performance with regard to environmental legislation; site audits examine all environment-related aspects of the site; activity audits scrutinise cross-functional operations such as transport; issue analyses explore the company's involvement in critical environmental problems, such as global warming or rainforest depletion; corporate audits examine the total impact of individual businesses; supplier audits do the same for suppliers; and acquisitions audits ensure that there are no hidden environmental problems or liabilities in companies that are being purchased.

Environmental Auditing covers various meanings from a desk study, based on data supplied by the commissioning organisation, to a detailed examination, involving interviews with key personnel and independent measuring of all the parameters. Essentially, the aim is to build up a picture of the business from an environmental point of view. However, the audit should not be seen in isolation, but rather as an important element of an integrated approach to corporate strategy and environmental management. The auditing should be seen as part of an overall Environmental Information System (EIS), which in turn should be seen as part of the Management Information System (MIS), and structured according to operational, tactical and strategic planning needs. The option for the company is to develop an EIS that is integrated into separate functional information systems, or to organise a specialist system.[48]

Many companies with a number of subsidiaries or outlets are likely to be confronted by a series of dilemmas: Which subsidiaries or outlets should we audit? On what basis do we decide to audit subsidiaries or outlets? and, How do we coordinate our activities? The first task is to identify those business areas with the biggest environmental risk, and focus the audit there. The next task is to assess the position of the company with reference to its minimum statutory responsibilities before considering the wider environmental context. However, proactive greener companies will look at environmental excellence as the philosophy, and will exceed legal requirements.

Risk analysis may form an essential part of the audit:

- What would be the extent of the damage if some defined event took place?
- What is the likelihood of the event happening?
- What would be the cost of taking steps to make the event less likely to happen or to reduce or eliminate the adverse impact if it did?

Companies that are planning to launch greener products must conduct Environmental Audits, as the knock-on effects of getting it wrong can be traumatic. For example, Fort Sterling conducted a rigorous auditing programme to ensure that the environmental positioning of products and processes were closely coordinated. The company formed an audit team to identify key areas which would have greatest impact—effluent control, raw materials, transport, internal waste, neighbourhood relations, packaging and employee relations. The company's new greener product requirements have meant substantial changes to operations, especially production processes.

However, some organisations are starting to take a wider and deeper view of the Environmental Audit. A more all-embracing approach has been developed by the Elmwood Institute in the US, based on ideas originating in Germany. The Elmwood Institute see the Environmental Audit essentially as a reactive and defensive tool, typified by the compliance audit. Eco-audits are seen as a more proactive, creative and holistic approach. The purpose of an eco-audit is to minimise a company's environmental impact, and to make the operation more ecologically sound.

The Elmwood Institute base eco-audits on deeper environmental considerations. They believe there are two ways in which individuals view the environment. These are:

- The Shallow-Rooted Ecologists who care primarily for the human race and treat nature as a resource to be utilised. For example, the rainforests must not be destroyed as they may hold the key to the development of new medicinal drugs.

- The Deep-Rooted Ecologists who see humanity as one species among many and who have no greater right to life than any other. They do not think of humankind as the sole element of value, but as one of many.

The Elmwood Institute favour the second view and define an eco-audit as follows:

> An eco-audit is an examination and review of a company's operations from the view of deep ecology. It is motivated by a shift in values and in corporate culture from domination to partnership, from the ideology of economic growth to that of ecological sustainability. It involves a corresponding shift from mechanistic to systemic thinking, and, accordingly, a new style of management known as systemic management. The result of the eco-audit is an action plan for minimising the company's environmental impact, and making its operations more ecologically sound.[49]

The environmental impact of the firm is unlikely to change unless there is a radical shift in corporate culture, with a movement towards viewing the world as a living system. The undertaking of an eco-audit is still a relatively new concept, but there have been some experiments in environmentally advanced Switzerland and Germany.

The benefit of all forms of green audit is to generate a clear picture of relative environmental internal strengths, weaknesses, and external opportunities and threats. The audit is only the first step. Objectives should be set, a policy established, and actions identified and progressively implemented and monitored. Employees should then be encouraged to own the policy. For example, The Body Shop and IBM give incentives to the workforce to join environmental organisations through employee volunteering. The benefits of proactive policy development will include reduced costs, improved energy efficiency, effective crisis management procedures, protection against potential fines, identification of possible new market opportunities, and, ultimately, competitive advantage.

Life Cycle Analysis

Life Cycle Analysis (LCA) is a relatively new discipline developed in the 1970s, the first applications being in the packaging industry. LCA is essentially a diagnostic tool, which is used to make a judgement about the total environmental impact of a product or production process from cradle to grave. Informed decisions will need to be made about the environmental effects of a production process, given the best available scientific knowledge and understanding of intricate ecological processes.

The three stages in LCA are: a life cycle inventory; environmental evaluation; and then an environmental improvement plan. These can pose complex managerial problems (see Fig. 13).

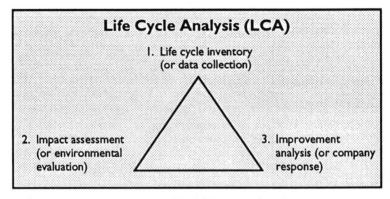

Figure 13

In building an inventory, the initial task is to define the system, i.e. what is to be analysed and what is not. The validity of the LCA will depend on the quality and range of data collected. The first stage is to gather relevant information about a product or activity by undertaking an inventory of all the principal stages in the life cycle of the product or process. The inputs are measured in terms of energy and resources consumed at every stage in the life cycle, and the outputs measured in the form of emissions or discharges to the atmosphere, water and land. It is important to recognise that there will be limitations to the way in which the data can be interpreted or used. A consensus on recycling and by-products is crucial, as there is no obvious way to partition energy and material flows where waste is recycled. Another issue is the extent to which data can be harmonised and made available to other researchers through database networks, to permit greater consistency between studies, and improve comparative analysis.

The second stage is to interpret the environmental problems associated with the product or process in a way that reflects their relative environmental significance. For instance, oil spills can be very damaging to marine life. But how damaging is this when compared to pesticide run-off, or discharges of raw sewage, or heavy metals compounds? We need to know the answers to these questions so that we can set priorities. In order to judge the importance of a system's impacts on the environment, an expert evaluation must be made of the inventory results in the light of an understanding of the relative significance of different environmental problems.

Landbank, an environmental consultancy, has established an independent panel of scientific and environmental experts—in conjunction with a number of European universities—whose task will be to make informed and authoritative judgements about pollutants or environmentally damaging activities associated with industries. An environmental points system will be developed to reflect the relative importance of each pollutant. These weighted judgements will then be applied to the individual product or activity to give a 'reading' indicating the total environmental impact of the product or activity, and also to highlight areas of particular environmental concern.

The environmental points reading will give the company or industry a basis to plan its response—the third stage of the process. A strategy will need to be developed to improve the environmental performance of a company's products and/or production processes—or any other activity identified as a cause for concern such as resource conservation, a reduction in pollution and waste, and energy saving.[50]

The current uses for LCA are:

- To define the present environmental burden of a product or package
- To support environmental claims and eco-labelling schemes
- To identify where improvement might be made
- To guide environmental improvement and development work

The benefits of LCA are:

- LCA is a comparative tool: it allows the environmental burdens associated with particular systems to be analysed.
- LCA is an inclusive tool: all inputs and emissions are listed and totalled. It is inclusive because it integrates:
  - all components of a system
  - all inputs to, and all emissions from, the system

- all inputs and emissions over the whole life cycle
- the effects of all constituent processes in the life cycle
- all issues, i.e. source reduction, re-use and recycling

The prime value of LCA is that it expands the total debate over the environmental impacts of products, processes and packaging, away from single issue criteria, such as solid waste and recycling.[51]

The use of LCA will be driven by the growing trend towards regulation and increasing scrutiny of products. Within the EC, the 1985 Directive on beverage containers was a stimulus for a number of LCAs, with a number completed by materials suppliers who were nervous at losing out to competitors. IBM request that LCA is completed on each of their products to determine whether fewer, or smaller quantities of, toxic materials can be substituted.[52]

The Netherlands may provide an example for future green requirements, as they are examining the environmental impact of product life cycles very closely, and may eventually ban disposables or planned obsolescence. The Netherlands' comprehensive National Environmental Policy (NEP) plan has objectives including:[53]

- Integrating Product Life Cycle (PLC) management that closes resource loops to reduce emissions and waste

- Increasing energy efficiency

- Improving product quality to reduce toxic waste and to lengthen the usefulness of resources

The introduction of the European eco-labelling scheme in Autumn 1992 is likely to focus interest on LCAs. While early eco-labelling schemes, such as West Germany's Blue Angel programme, were initially based on single criteria, most are now taking into account all the major environmental impacts across a product's life cycle. The impending EC scheme may require some form of LCA to be carried out for many of its product award areas. There will be an increased need for LCAs as products become more 'transparent', as the awareness of the full environmental impact of products grows, and as more is known about the individual elements and impacts of products. A major problem may be the present lack of information on the environmental performance of materials.

The proposed eco-labelling scheme will require companies to examine inputs and outputs from cradle to grave. An illustration is provided by a flowchart showing the life cycle of a washing machine, which outlines the typical issues and areas of consideration (see Fig. 14).

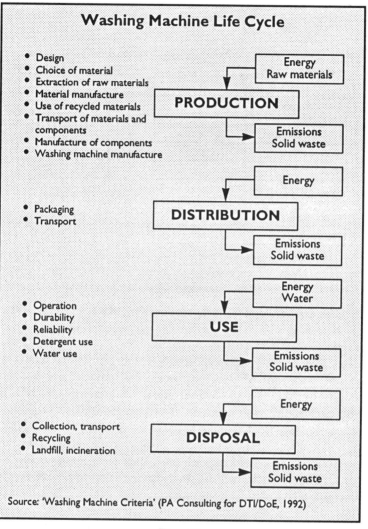

Figure 14

The EC have also produced a matrix that is intended as a framework for developing product group criteria for the European ecolabelling scheme to be launched in Autumn 1992 (see Fig. 15).

Conclusions

The nineties will see business people needing to take a more systemic and holistic view of the environmental performance of their opera-

Indicative Assessment Matrix

Environ-mental fields \ Product Life cycle	Pre-Production	Production	Distri-bution (inc. packaging)	Utilisation	Disposal
Waste relevance					
Soil pollution and degradation					
Water contamination					
Air contamination					
Noise					
Consumption of energy					
Consumption of natural resources					
Effects on eco-systems					

Source: European Communities

Figure 15

tions. New terminology is likely to develop, which business will need to grasp if it is not to be caught out in an ever more competitive marketplace.

Sustainable Development will mean that organisations will need to take greater account of their environmental impacts, not just in the present, but in the past and in the future. The development of a more holistic philosophy of Corporate Social Responsibility suggests that organisations will need to take account of a wider set of social and environmental issues, and will need to consider the relationships with a wider group of Stakeholders, each with their own interests and set of priorities. Organisations will increasingly see environmental excellence as prerequisite for Total Quality Management (TQM), and individuals and organisations will realise that they can influence the market by purchasing environmentally friendlier products from greener organisations. With increasing concern over the greenness of companies and products, there will be increasing use of Environmental Audits to determine corporate impacts, and Life Cycle Analysis (LCA) to determine the environmental effects of products and packaging. The key for organisations is to understand these new concepts and to implement proactive programmes to gain competitive advantage.

References

1. D. Pearce, A. Markandya and E.B. Barbier, *Blueprint for a Green Economy* (London: Earthscan, 1989).

2. Pearce *et al.*, *Blueprint for a Green Economy*.

3. World Commission on Environment and Development, *Our Common Future* ('The Brundtland Report'; London: Oxford University Press, 1987).

4. E. Callenbach, F. Capra and S. Marburg, *The Elmwood Guide to Eco-Auditing and Ecologically Conscious Management* (Berkeley, CA: The Elmwood Institute, 1990).

5. The Department of Energy, Statistics Department, 1989.

6. Shelley Taylor and Associates, 'The Rewards of Virtue' (June 1991).

7. Shelley Taylor and Associates, 'The Rewards of Virtue'.

8. M. Charter, *Graduates: Fewer and Greener* (Alton: KPH Marketing, 1990), and M. Charter, *The Greener Employee* (Alton: KPH Marketing, 1990).

9. D. Clutterbuck and D. Snow, *Working with the Community* (London: Weidenfeld and Nicolson, 1990).

10. J. Elkington and J. Hailes, *The Green Consumer Guide: High Street Shopping for a Better Environment* (London: Victor Gollancz, 1988).

11. J. Elkington and J. Hailes, *The Green Consumer's Supermarket Shopping Guide* (London: Victor Gollancz, 1989).

12. R. Adams, J. Carruthers and S. Hamil, *Changing Corporate Values* (London: Kogan Page, 1991).

13. R. Adams, J. Carruthers and C. Fisher, *Shopping for a Better World* (London: Kogan Page, 1991).

14. Laura Mazur, 'On the Front Line', *Marketing Business*, 3 September 1991.

15. Charter, *The Greener Employee*.

16. Andrew Jack, 'Green Tinge to Company Books', *Financial Times*, 15 January 1992.

17. C. Roberts, 'International Trends in Social and Employee Reporting' (Glasgow University, 1990).

18. 'Green Tinge to Company Books', *Financial Times*.

19. Touche Ross European Services, 'European Management Attitudes to Environmental Issues' (March 1990).

20. DRT International/Touche Ross, 'Managers' Attitudes to the Environment' (June 1991).

21. Environmental Policy Consultants, 'Anticipating the Future: EC Environmental Policy Agenda' (June 1991).

22. Department of the Environment, 'UK Guidance Notes on the Ministerial Declaration: 3rd International Conference on the Protection of the North Sea' (July 1990).

23. Shelley Taylor and Associates, 'The Rewards of Virtue'.

24. 'Green Issues Sway Fund Managers', *The Ethical Investor*, Summer 1991.

25. Shelley Taylor and Associates, 'The Rewards of Virtue'.

26. Mintel, 'The Second Green Consumer Report' (May 1991).

27. DRT/Touche Ross, 'Managers' Attitudes to the Environment'.

28. David Bellamy Associates, 'Industry Goes Green' (November 1991).

29. F. Cairncross, *Costing the Earth* (London: Economist Books, 1991).

30. 'Greenpeace Launches Campaign against Industry', *Water Services*, November 1991.

31. 'Earth First', *The Independent*, 5 December 1991.
32. DRT/Touche Ross, 'Managers' Attitudes to the Environment'.
33. M. Osborne and K. Sankey, 'Towards Environmental Competence: Phase 3—Professional Bodies' (University of Stirling/Scottish Environmental Education Council, November 1991).
34. R.H. Gray, *The Greening of Accountancy: The Profession after Pearce* (London: ACCA, 1990).
35. D. Hart and D. Smith, 'Business Education and the Environment: Ramshackle or Innovative?' (Liverpool Business School, 1991), and A.-C. Peckham, 'Towards Environmental Competence in Scotland: Phase 2—Industry and Commerce' (The Peckham Partnership, 1991).
36. N. Robins, *The Quality Route to the Environment* (London: Business International, 1990).
37. 'Green Investor Guide Worth £3.5bn so far', *The Ethical Investor*, Spring 1991.
38. P. Carson and J. Moulden, *Green is Gold* (Toronto: Harper Business, 1991).
39. Carson and Moulden, *Green is Gold*.
40. M. Seidler, *Environmental Arguments as Marketing Strategy: The Marketing Responses in West Germany and the U.K.* (1990).
41. C. Haines, and O. Murphy, 'Green Issues: Evolution to Revolution' (Market Research Society, 1989 Conference Papers).
42. Mintel, 'The Second Green Consumer Report'.
43. Haines and Murphy, 'Green Issues: Evolution to Revolution'.
44. Elkington and Hailes, *The Green Consumer Guide*.
45. Adams *et al.*, *Shopping for a Better World*.
46. J. Button, *How To Be Green* (London: Century Hutchinson, 1989).
47. International Chamber of Commerce, 'Environmental Auditing' (1989).
48. M. Charter and W. Wehrmeyer, 'Environmental Information Systems', (unpublished paper, February 1992).
49. Callenbach *et al.*, *The Elmwood Guide to Eco-Auditing and Ecologically Conscious Management*.
50. C. Charlton, 'Life Cycle Assessment: Making Sense of Environmental Complexities', *CBI Environmental Newsletter*, November 1991.
51. P.R. White, 'Experience of Life Cycle Analysis' (PIRA Seminar on Eco Labelling and Life Cycle Analysis, 22 October 1991).
53. Carson and Moulden, *Green is Gold*.
54. 'Life Cycle Analysis: An Environmental Management Tool for the 1990s' (ENDS Report, September 1990).

Chapter 3

STRATEGIC ISSUES

Walter Wehrmeyer

Research Fellow, The Durrell Institute, University of Kent, Canterbury

Introduction

Since the late 1960s, the public's attitude towards corporate environmental protection has changed substantially: it has shifted from the extremes of perceiving big business as the 'dirty man', towards a perspective where industry might be the only saviour from environmental catastrophe. This chapter will suggest that both these views are misconceived.

The 'dirty man' scenario emphasises the apparent contradictions between economy and ecology, and tends to neglect those areas where they coincide; the 'saviour' scenario considers the benefits of sustainable economic growth. Over the centuries, society at large has valued economics above ecology, and it is foreseeable that this way of viewing the world is unlikely to be sustainable.

This chapter will not attempt to deny the difficulties that firms may have in minimising their contribution to environmental problems. Instead, the problems may be separated into two different sets of issues:

1. **Green Facts.** These realities add a whole new (and profitable) dimension to firms, their operation and long-term prospects

2. **Underlying Issues.** These are the undercurrents of the rise in environmentalism

Green Facts are issues which give companies a rationale for 'turning green'; they open up new markets, save money and create new opportunities. An example of a green fact is that pollution control will increase and that the market for environmental technology is growing at about 8–12% per annum, depending on which market segment is examined. In many cases, Green Facts can be 'actioned' with relative ease.

On the other hand, **Underlying Issues** require shifts in corporate strategy. They stem from large-scale and long-term changes in societal values and beliefs. The shift from the 'green consumer' to the 'ethical consumer', and changes in the pattern of work and employment are examples. These are aspects of a general and overall shift in traditional values. Because these issues change very slowly, they are easily mistaken for 'Green Facts'.

Cooperation and Competition between the Environment and Business

There are two issues which crystallise the debate between business and environmentalists, namely issues of economic growth and Environmental Quality Management; the former represents the 'dirty man' perspective, and the latter the 'saviour'. As we shall see however, both may be misconceived.

The literature about growth, its perils and its blessings, is vast but inconclusive. The opponents to growth argue that it is a hollow concept and that we are addicted to a notion which, ultimately, must fail, as stated by the Law of Entropy, because we are on a planet with limited resources. The proponents or defenders of growth argue that the limits to the earth are expandable by means of technology and, after all, the growing world population has to be fed, housed and cared for, along with provision of the other necessities—and that a zero-growth economy would easily mean that the rich stay rich and the poor stay put.

The concept of **sustainable growth**—first presented in The Brundtland Report, 1987[1]—has changed the dichotomy of these arguments fundamentally. It suggests that it is possible to reconcile the two positions, arguing that growth can continue, but it has **'to ensure that humanity meets the needs of the present without compromising the ability of future generations to meet their own needs'**. Interestingly, this concept provides a compromise for environmentalists favouring no growth and growth-orientated business people.

Another new concept for business is that of Environmental Quality Management (EQM), which is similar to Total Quality Management (TQM). TQM indicates a company's commitment to absolute quality in all aspects of corporate activity. The aim is Zero Defect Management (ZDM) in all products and activities.

Using the same logic, EQM would indicate the firm's absolute commitment to reduce its impact on the environment to nil in all products and activities. Thus, the goal here would be Zero Impact Management

(ZIM). However, this interpretation of EQM is misconceived. Strictly speaking, companies do **want** to make an impact upon the natural environment by means of producing a marketable product. Firms strive to change their natural and social environment and, apart from exclusively service-orientated companies, most compete with each other to do just this. For example, a construction firm seeks to change the environment by building houses.

Thus, the view that a company should strive for a zero impact on the environment is misleading. Firms should strive for a **less harmful** effect on their environment—a goal which is largely outside the traditional performance measures.

The point is that TQM can be judged by existing business performance measures, whereas EQM changes the goals of business. It requires a new set of plans and corporate goals which will fundamentally alter the traditional framework of business.

In summary, it may be misleading to imply that all is harmonious between economy and ecology. There are tensions and trade-offs between them, which could be resolved by open dialogue—as in the case of the growth debate—and which have so far found an uneasy alliance with TQM.

Tightrope Management versus Prescribed Management

The whole environmental question is perhaps better viewed as a management of tensions; there is nothing new for managers in this approach, as the successful balancing of conflicting interests both within and outside the firm has always been crucial for corporate success. This balancing act permeates all levels and functions of the firm, and sets a pattern which becomes increasingly important as more and more expectations are introduced.

In order to contrast this balancing act with the traditional model of Prescribed Management, it will be referred to as **Tightrope Management**. Contentious issues are placed at opposite ends of a pole with which the manager is balancing his or her path along a tightrope. The more the manager leans towards one side the more difficult it is to balance and to concentrate on the way ahead.

For example, if the economy gets preference and ecological matters are neglected, balance becomes difficult—the situation we have faced for a long time and which has brought about the environmental problems we face today. The solution can be found in attempting to find a **balance between both issues, at the same time, by placing them** so that the relative weight of each is equal for that particular person and context (see Fig. 1).

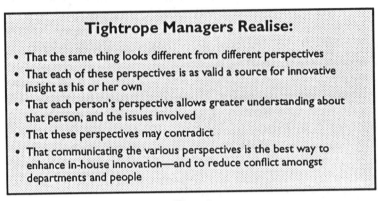

Figure 1

The alternative, **Prescribed Management**, rests on the assumption that the world is stable. Thus, decisions are taken as if nothing in the future will change. In this scenario, the manager has not been allowed to use his or her judgement in individual situations, as inherent conflicts of interest are not perceived as areas of contention.

Tightrope Management acknowledges the pluralistic nature of activities, and attempts to manage perceived dichotomies. Further, it allows the firm to incorporate environmental issues without oversimplifying them. **Tightrope Management** seeks a 'joint venture' between environmentalists and business, where each side contributes to the mutual benefit of the other (see Fig. 2).

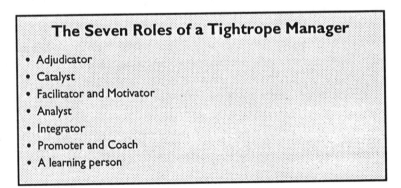

Figure 2

The Added Dimension of Environmental Issues for Business

Environmental issues will mean fundamental changes in approach for business. To highlight this point, some areas of corporate life will be analysed to show the impact of Green Facts and the Underlying Issues.

Economics

The economics of turning green have often been clouded by prejudice rather than realism. The larger part of our society's annual growth results from exploiting our environmental resources. The Organisation for Economic Cooperation and Development (OECD) has estimated that the costs of environmental degradation in industrialised countries amount to 3–4% of GNP. The German Ministry of the Environment estimated a figure of roughly 6%, stating that this could be a bench-mark for all industrialised countries.[2]

Since the rate of real growth is smaller than this figure, this suggests we are living dangerously off our reserves, and that we are still far from the position where growth rates even compensate for environmental destruction, as the Sustainable Development principle requires (if growth can compensate for environmental destruction). There are five cogent reasons why turning green has economic advantages for companies:

1. Given that pollution legislation is becoming tougher, the clean-up of pollution is becoming more expensive than the prevention of the pollution. Moreover, the process of cleaning up may present as yet unknown problems in the future when clean-up activities are likely to be more expensive than anticipated. This is particularly true for pollutants that react with the environment or other pollutants—'the chemical cocktail effect'. In addition, forthcoming European Community environmental legislation will make such negligence a criminal offence. Managers administering such a policy could be held personally responsible, and could be subject to fines or periods of imprisonment.

2. The US Superfund legislation made firms liable for clean-up costs related to activities which took place more than forty years ago. This indicates that firms will not be able to escape liability in the future unless they stick to the Best Available Technology (BAT) of the day.

3. Producing less waste from a given amount of inputs will allow greater resources for production and increased efficiency. Such a cost saving on raw materials may lead to increased profit.

4. Minimising waste inevitably means less costs for waste disposal. Given the dwindling landfill reserves in the world, this point will be even more important in the future, when waste disposal costs are likely to rise sharply. In the short to medium term there may also be increasing markets for waste products.

5. Insurance premiums are lower for companies which produce in a less dangerous way, or which use less dangerous substances.

As these points suggest, the very definition of what constitutes costs and benefits will be subject to significant changes. The reason for this is simply that our economic performance measures—discounted cash flow analysis, payback period comparisons and so on—are largely inappropriate for these new definitions. What we now see as more realistic measures will inevitably change our yardsticks, which subsequently will also alter our way of thinking about the finished goods and their production processes.

In summary, the costs of not turning green are beginning to show, not only in terms of stagnating market shares of those who do not follow the trend, but in real comparative cost disadvantages. At the same time, the present definition of costs and benefits and the appropriateness of purely economic and accountancy-based calculations attract increasingly strong criticism. In this respect, firms have to abandon the profit motive as the **sole** guideline of plans and activities. Companies must be run as if they are responsible world citizens.

Finance

Environmental issues affect businesses in two distinct yet related ways: one is the way a firm spends its money, the other is the extent and quality of access to financial markets for borrowing.

'Put your money where your mouth is', has been the call of green consumerism, and the same call has begun to be heard in corporate accounting and purchasing departments. Increasingly, questions are being asked about the destination of the pension fund investments, and whether they have been screened for their ethical implications, and if companies have made donations to environmental groups. This range of questions will also be applicable to subsidiaries and other related companies.

Furthermore, the sources of funds are being screened to determine where the monies originated, and what the other business connections of the lender are, and so on. At the same time, companies are doing more research into suppliers' backgrounds; finding out what their environmental track records are; and generally, how environmentally risky is the supply from a particular organisation. There are sound reasons for doing so, as an environmental accident in the supplier's firm will affect the production schedules and reputation of the receiver.

This approach is not merely affecting the day-to-day activities of the firm, it also affects corporate image, and the firm's reputation for quality among other things. Therefore, suppliers are increasingly coming under scrutiny from their customers regarding input factors, their toxicity, how dangerous the production process is, and so on. Trade unions have also become interested in 'greening the workplace' because of the health and safety and other social issues involved.

The second issue is the risk assessment of a firm. Companies with a high potential for environmental accidents will find that their cost of capital will be higher than others because banks take into account the physical risk in lending policies. The same will happen with mergers and acquisitions, and Environmental Audits have become standard procedure for many corporations, such as the Hanson Trust and Monsanto. Both these firms were caught out by buying firms which appeared good buys, only to find that they had not accounted for the cost of environmental clean-ups.

The financial significance of environmental issues is even more crucial, as cheaper (or at least comparatively cheaper) capital is crucial for technological developments, and thus competitiveness. Since financial institutions have begun to take environmental assessments into account for the risk ratings of loan applicants, it has become important to achieve and maintain a high level of corporate environmental performance.

Legislation

The essential role of legislative regulation in environmental matters is undisputed. This role will increase dramatically in the next two to five years, for a variety of reasons:

- Awareness by the general public of environmental issues and of environmental pressure groups will continue to increase, and governments may take legislative action as a response.

- Competitors who have the environmental edge may press for stricter limits; perhaps not directly, but via industry pressure groups, or simply because this is an edge such firms may exploit.

- International trends, such as the Single Market harmonisation, will mean that companies will have to compete EC-wide on a common level of regulation. This inevitably puts firms that are currently under stricter regulations in a better position, as they can both exert pressures to tighten controls over less stringent firms and enjoy a technological and competitive advantage.

International considerations will have to take into account cultural differences. Countries such as Germany and The Netherlands have, over the last few years, moved more strongly towards recognition of environmental issues compared to other EC member states. It is obvious that these countries will wish to maintain their higher environmental standard when legislation is harmonised in 1992. In Germany, the depth of the environmental debate is greater, and so too is the awareness of the need to transform traditional business practices.

Thus, instead of a futile attempt to beat off the inevitable regulations, companies should try to cooperate with firms to buy in or jointly research the environmental technology which may soon become standard.

Generally, the UK environmental legislative process is increasingly driven by European Community policy. The pace and amount of planned EC legislation is growing, ranging from the classical areas of soil, water, air, waste and nature conservation to the more recent topics of Environmental Auditing, assessment and labelling.

The fact that environmental regulation is being increasingly harmonised across the European market and that it is expanding into more lateral areas, means that the classical 'yardstick approach' to environmental law is no longer appropriate. Previously, legal limits defined what was good and what was bad. Being in compliance with the law today is no longer enough—tomorrow may bring yet more changes. There is likely to be an increase in lobbying in Brussels, as companies and industry bodies seek to influence the legislative process, and in some instances to slow legislative development.

Environmental law is also becoming more complex as the number of regulations mushroom and as new issues are added, such as:

- The introduction of **no-fault liability**, which means paying for environmental restoration even if the company was not negligent or at fault.
- BATNEEC (Best Available Technology Not Entailing Excessive Costs): a concept originating in the EC which effectively links pollution and emission standards to the least polluting

technology, which in most cases means regular technological upgrading for business.

- IPC (Integrated Pollution Control) regards a company as an entire emission unit, and the limits of that unit have to be acceptable, as opposed to considering single pollutants.

- Environmental Audits will be required as a result of the EC Eco-Audit Directive in late 1992, initially on a voluntary basis.

- EIA (Environmental Impact Assessment) will be required for an increasing number of development proposals and planning applications.

- Eco-labelling: an independent body, in most cases, assesses a product according to environmental standards, and, if satisfactory, the body issues a label which can then be used for advertising and general recognition of that product. An EC scheme will be in operation from Autumn 1992.

All of these changes indicate that merely satisfying legal limits is no longer sufficient, and corporate planning will become an even more formidable task. Firms will have to take up environmental matters in a proactive way. Legal limits will need to be seen as indicators of the direction that standards are taking, rather than justification for action or inaction.

Social and Community Affairs

The Stakeholder concept indicates that the sole corporate goal of maximising the wealth of a firm's shareholders falls far short of the needs and necessities of today's corporations. For example, local community Stakeholders must be made aware of the activities and potential dangers of a site. This is not only paramount in case of an accident, but also necessary to keep friendly relations with the local community. Few things cause greater anxiety than having incomplete knowledge of potential dangers of a facility.

The general lesson to be learned from the Stakeholder concept is that, in many areas, companies have to cooperate rather than compete. It is crucial to develop trust-based relations with Stakeholders, because only by taking perceived threatening issues seriously and trying to learn from them can a firm keep up within an ever-changing world.

An example is provided by Norsk Hydro, who, having completed an Environmental Audit of all activities, sent a copy of it to every person and organisation in the vicinity of relevant sites. By doing so, the company managed to clarify many doubts about Norsk Hydro's activities and developed better relations with informed and understanding local authority planners. The recommendation which seems to emerge is that if there is nothing to hide, disclose as much as possible without giving away competitive advantages; if there is something to hide, discontinue the activity.

This example highlights the recognition that people are knowledgeable and ethical human beings, and this concept supersedes the conventional view of humans as consumers. This is another aspect of the shift in consumer awareness, whereby the green consumer is '**shopping for a better world**'. This movement tries to shift producers towards a more environmentally friendly option and it has been remarkably successful, with significant growth in markets for green consumer products.

The 'new consumer' is typically educated, urban, often married with double income, mostly with no or few children, and generally he or she is in the financial position to afford better-quality products. This person is not only concerned about the environmental impact of products, but also about issues in less developed countries, discrimination against women, minorities or the disabled, and about animal welfare. Thus, green consumerism is shifting and broadening towards ethical consumerism **without** losing its power.

As a result, companies have to follow this trend by being honest and credible in the information disseminated about the products, making a **real** effort towards taking up ethical issues, trying to build up a trusted and trusting relation between the firm and the Stakeholders; and, generally, being cooperative with the pressure groups and not discriminating against them.

A good anecdotal example of this is Albright & Wilson, who, while at a recent graduate recruitment round, were accused of being environmentally destructive. Instead of denying the validity of the claim, the company offered these graduates a job **to improve the company's environmental performance**. The firm may well have found some highly motivated and committed employees.

Technology

Technology will play an ever-important role in the development of strategies for the environmental agenda. Modernisation usually results in less emissions, which is why the EC bodies put such an emphasis on the BATNEEC approach.

Moreover, technology binds the company to the use of certain input factors, thus if one wants to reduce the environmental impact of a firm, a change in technology seems an obvious route. This acts as an incentive for funding improvements in energy efficiency and also for attempts to use less environmentally damaging input factors.

There are two major benefits of using or developing cleaner, greener technology. First, the use of this technology often results in massive cost savings: for example, payback periods of less than a year for an efficient lighting system in offices is not unusual. Secondly, the firm may be able to sell its solution to other companies and thus develop another business opportunity. For instance, Technocell, an innovative pulp mill firm in south Germany, could not expand their operations as the pollution emitted by the available technology was too high. Instead they developed a pulping process without using chlorine but resulting in 100% whiteness, and they have discovered that by avoiding chlorines in their bleaching process they could expand their operations. Subsequently, selling the technology has itself proved to be much more profitable than actually using it.

The firm could only convert the threat into an opportunity by committing itself firmly to a long-term strategy and by deliberately putting aside short-term profits. This provides one example of how putting long-term profits before short-term gain can improve a firm's performance.

This is true for Japanese firms, for many German ones and for most of those firms which were 'In Search of Excellence'.[3] The attitude of many British firms who are more concerned with quarterly profits than with long-term strategy may turn out to be a costly one.

Wider Aspects of Environmental Issues

Firms may like to think that Green Facts and Underlying Issues can be incorporated into their operations without strategy changes, but this is unlikely to be the case. The environmental debate will force a fundamental change of business philosophy. This change is crucial if the world collectively wants to enjoy a sustainable living standard.

Respecting the natural environment has important repercussions for all spheres of business, and some of these 'wider aspects' have already been mentioned. To give an example: by trying to minimise resource usages, it becomes apparent that traditional performance measures of profit are inappropriate for an assessment of the relative success of these efforts. The new definition of what is good business sense, which includes ideas of corporate social and environmental responsibility, implies a fundamental shift in performance indicators.

In fact, this shift is part of a wider change in society, where more free time and larger disposable incomes have affected work and career attitudes towards a stronger emphasis of 'quality of working life' and 'quality of life' as criteria of success and personal welfare.

Interestingly, many corporations are already following this shift in the Underlying Issues. Not only are firms more committed to flexibility, but longer-term value statements are also being incorporated into organisational decision making. Corporate mission statements are changing companies' functional and operational objectives as these statements are turned into plans, guidelines and operational principles.

Corporate culture is changing and reinforcing moves in the right direction. This process can happen in different ways. For some companies the process is a top down one, where change is initiated by management. For others, the change in attitude moves from staff to management. In most cases, wherever the change is initiated, a participative management style will be the best method of stimulating ideas and drawing up a clear corporate policy.

The advent of environmental issues entails a new way of viewing the world. Many of the problems companies and society face today are the result of past solutions to problems: solutions which were based on different values and ideas of what was good business practice. Therefore, new values have to be taken into account in this new type of analysis.

To give an example: we face unprecedented traffic and car transport problems because we think it is 'good' (i.e. practical, sensible etc.) to drive a one-ton car to the local supermarket for ten kilograms of shopping goods—40% of the weight of which is packaging. Further, it is generally thought of as being 'better' to own a big car than a small car, although it costs more, pollutes more and wastes more energy. In the future we may well view these values with scorn.

If businesses are to succeed in a world of uncertainty, lifestyles will have to be taken into account as much as the changing framework within which these daily activities take place. This may require a change in direction.

Scenario Planning for the Environment

Much will have to be changed with regard to planning and forecasting. In a world, where, as Charles Handy has put it, **'change is not what it used to be'**,[4] the traditional method of planning by extrapolating the past into the future has become unreliable. When past data is unsuitable for predicting future plans, what is left is to use the future to guide our activities today. Scenario planning is much easier than it sounds, and this approach has already been applied in many spheres of business. It means finding answers to the following questions:

What are the firm's core competencies?

- What are the key features of the business?
- What are those areas of expertise with which the company makes the largest and most reliable profits?
- What are the strengths and what are the weaknesses of the firm?

Where does the firm visualise its future?

- What are the desired future scenarios which are worth working for?
- What are those futures which are deemed undesirable for the firm?
- Which of the desirable scenarios need substantial efforts, and which of them will inevitably be achieved?
- What are the potential opportunities and threats in each of them scenarios?

What can be done **today** to work towards the desirable future scenarios?

- What are the activities that have to be ceased today which would otherwise hamper the achievement of the desired scenarios?
- Which activities are useful in achieving more than one scenario? Which activity hampers the facilitation of any or all desired scenarios?
- Which of the corporate strengths and weaknesses does the firm intend to foster or remedy, in order to achieve the scenarios?
- Which areas of expertise and investment are to be enhanced and developed, and from which does the firm plan to divest?

Here, the key is the full development of the intended scenarios, where the development and preparation of several scenarios provide the necessary flexibility. It is crucial, and indeed potentially very profitable, not to confine the analysis to a compartmental one, but rather to work towards a systemic understanding of the problem.

This analysis of a wider picture is fundamental to the holistic world-view suggested by Theodore Levitt,[5] where the global view of the problem, including the setting in which the problem is placed, may result in new solutions. The crucial questions then will not be whether a firm can produce and market a better heater, but how a firm can sell 'warm houses' in a way which offers the most appropriate solutions to the consumer. Likewise, does a firm produce a 'better car' or a 'better solution for individual transport', which entails a much larger range of alternatives? Holistic management (see Figs. 3 and 4) is one expression of this new analysis, and it is crucial that a firm develops knowledge about its core competencies today and in the future.

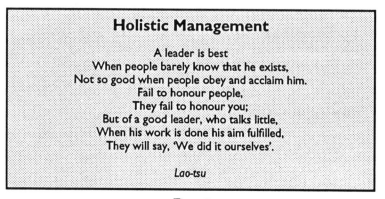

Holistic Management

A leader is best
When people barely know that he exists,
Not so good when people obey and acclaim him.
Fail to honour people,
They fail to honour you;
But of a good leader, who talks little,
When his work is done his aim fulfilled,
They will say, 'We did it ourselves'.

Lao-tsu

Figure 3

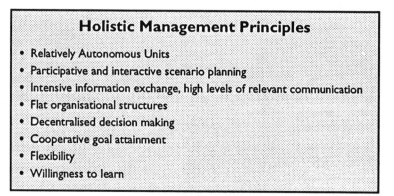

Holistic Management Principles

- Relatively Autonomous Units
- Participative and interactive scenario planning
- Intensive information exchange, high levels of relevant communication
- Flat organisational structures
- Decentralised decision making
- Cooperative goal attainment
- Flexibility
- Willingness to learn

Figure 4

'Seeing the wider picture' is a major step forward, as it unfreezes current thinking and practice. Mercedes' recent involvement in rail transport systems, Volkswagen's research move into solar-driven cars, or Opel's emerging involvement in local authorities' planning to find attractive urban travel and transport arrangements, are all examples of how the German car industry has used precisely this 'wider thinking' after realising—through scenario planning—that their traditional business was leading to a dead end.

The fact that past data is often insufficient and too specific makes it even more necessary to avoid planning based on extrapolation of the past. For example, emission data is often not available, because many companies considered pollution to be 'not in my back yard'. The environmental movement has brought home the message that there is only one world, thus there is nothing outside the 'communal back yard'. A compartmental analysis may exclude part of that back yard which may change the whole outcome of the analysis.

This type of analysis has gained much more credibility since it became obvious that rigid corporate structures will have more and more difficulties finding a market environment which suits their needs. In a chaotic marketplace, monolithic structures with hierarchical or autocratic management styles will find it difficult to exploit their traditional strengths.

Conclusions

Environmental issues will fundamentally alter business practice, just as the microchip altered office practice. The management function has to shift from **Prescribed Management** towards **Tightrope Management** if firms are to keep up with the changing circumstances. Environmental issues are but one facet in the larger picture, which calls for **Corporate Social Responsibility**. This concept embodies a more holistic approach towards management as it recognises the ethical implications, the environmental concern, the social dimension and the human face of modern corporate enterprises.

Companies are not seen to be exclusively in existence to maximise the wealth of their owners; they have a social function and a place in society. After all, who wants to work for a company which only exists to maximise the wealth of the owners? Companies perform a service for their social and political environment and they have to reduce the impact they inevitably make on the natural environment.

The implicit message from the Underlying Issues scenario is that people want to perform a useful function for their social, economic, political and natural environment that has meaning to themselves and their peer group. Companies that fail to recognise this will fail in other areas as well—they will fail to attract high-quality and highly motivated staff, fail to gain access to cheap capital as the firm is seen as a risky investment, fail to grasp the economic common sense of reducing waste and energy usage, fail to cash in on new and exciting opportunities which emerge because values and needs are changing, and fail to recognise that a new, holistic analysis is needed in a changed and changing world.

The differences between reactive firms who focus on the Green Facts, and the more far-sighted firms who acknowledge the Underlying Issues, are visible already. It seems that corporate interest in the environment has shifted from 'green is good business' towards a longer-term view of 'good business is green business'. The equation of good equals green is, however, not necessarily universally true for all companies. **Tightrope Management** will help to find the right balance between environmental aspects and economics.

Management will shift from engineering clearly defined tasks in a clearly structured world to a balancing act of facilitating core competencies within a holistically viewed system, taking account of a set of contingencies. This will mean much more than employing an environmentally trained person in the marketing department for instance. It will be the best way forward for management in a world which looks increasingly uncertain and unsustainable.

References

1. World Commission on Environment and Development, *Our Common Future* ('The Brundtland Report'; London: Oxford University Press, 1987), p. 8.
2. D.W. Pearce and J.-P. Barde (eds.), *Valuing the Environment: Six Case Studies* (London: Earthscan, 1991).
3. T.J. Peters and R.H. Waterman, *In Search of Excellence: Lessons from America's Best-Run Companies* (New York: Harper & Row, 1982).
4. C. Handy, *The Age of Unreason* (London: Hutchinson, 1989).
5. T. Levitt, 'Marketing Myopia', *Harvard Business Review*, September–October 1965, pp. 26-44, 173-81.

Chapter 4

THE CORPORATE RESPONSE

Peter James

Ashbridge Management Research Group

Introduction

Business is responding in very different ways to the environmental shaping of production and markets. Some companies are ignoring it, particularly in the small business sector.[1] Another set of companies have confined their response to **impact amelioration**, which can be summarised as reasonable compliance with environmental legislation, investments in high-return energy efficiency and other environment-related measures, and improved public relations. Some—especially those which have experienced environment-related disasters or have been under pressure from the green movement—have moved beyond this to a position of **corporate responsibility**. This involves a recognition that business objectives should go beyond the pursuit of profit and incorporate a concern for communities and the natural environment. Such companies set environmental standards which go beyond those required by legislation, incorporate environmental concerns into their mainstream activities and have policies of product stewardship (that is, an acknowledgement of responsibility for products from cradle to grave). These companies are the principal subject of this chapter and most of this book.

A few pioneers have moved even further to a fourth stage of **clean design**. The hallmark of this stage is using the environment as a fundamental source of competitive advantage, reflected in the radical redesign of processes and reformulation of products to achieve low environmental impacts. The success of such strategies depends upon a high level of environmental consciousness among both employees and customers, which is zealously fostered by the enterprise. As environment-based threats and opportunities increase in the 1990s, more and more companies will try to make this transition.

Despite the fact that Britain is the home of one fourth-stage organisation, The Body Shop, most British companies have been slower than their European or American competitors in responding to environmental issues. Volkswagen's Director of Environmental Affairs, Ulrich Steger, recently made a composite judgement about national governmental and business responses to environmental issues. He placed Britain with Spain in the lowest category of 'latecomers', behind a middle grouping of France and Italy and a front-runner group of Germany, Austria, Switzerland, the Netherlands and the Scandinavian nations.[2]

His judgement is confirmed by a government-backed study of Britain's poor performance in pollution control markets, which found that under a third of British companies considered the environment to be an opportunity, almost half were oblivious of impending environmental legislation (which would almost certainly affect them), and two-thirds had no form of environmental training.[3]

However, there are some bright spots in this dismal scene. As in the area of quality, multinational companies are introducing higher standards while their British competitors are increasingly recognising that they must play by German or Californian environmental rules if they are to survive in international markets. Directors are also becoming uncomfortably aware of their potential personal liability for a growing number of environmental problems. For these reasons (and others), environment-related spending has been relatively unaffected by recession. Leading retailers too have been notable for stressing environmental issues, with consequent effects on their own suppliers. Recent years have also seen the development of an infrastructure of consultancies, standards bodies and other sources of assistance for companies wanting to improve their environmental performance. Above all, the case histories and other examples from this and other chapters demonstrate that, once British companies recognise the nature and significance of the environmental challenge, they can take effective action.

The Clean Corporation

Effective corporate responses to environmental pressures are those which **strengthen competitive advantage by minimising environmental impacts and risks and maximising public acceptability.** This requires change in the attitudes and behaviour of individuals and in the structure and functioning of the organisation itself.[4] Success therefore requires generic skills in the management of change.[5] However, environment-shaped change has several distinctive aspects. Its aims go beyond conventional business objectives and it requires a fundamental re-examination of individual values and thought processes. Its practice often involves actions which are counter-intuitive to the conventional business mind, as when chemical manufacturers replace satisfactory products with ones which appear less efficient and more costly, or electrical utilities take measures to reduce the demand for their products. Finally, the contentiousness of environmental issues means that a large component of environment-related change is about improving the political skills which are needed to influence environmental groups, politicians and regulators.

The most effective responses are those which make the company **CLEANER**, that is which develop:

- Coherence
- Leadership
- Enthusiasm
- Awareness
- New processes and products
- Efficiency
- Review

Coherence

Environmental management is difficult. It must deal with a multiplicity of interactions between the company and the natural environment through actions that will often cut across traditional functional boundaries and hierarchies. It therefore requires a clear sense of direction, sustained and mutually reinforcing changes in all areas of a business, and its permeation with positive environmental values.

The capstone is a statement of environmental policy. The fact that only half of leading British companies had developed such a policy by 1991 indicates how far UK business has to travel.[6] After surveying many of the policy statements which do exist, the Institute of Business Ethics[7] identified six key criteria for judging their effectiveness:

- The policy should be **comprehensive**, that is, it should deal with all aspects of a company's impact on the environment, its use of resources as well as its emissions, product as well as process impacts, short-term as well as long-term effects.

- The policy should be more than just a statement; there should be programmes to implement the approach and goals which can be **measured**.

- The policy should be easily **communicated**, that is, it should be available in a convenient and comprehensible form. It should also be transparent, in that as much information as possible on the goals, targets and procedures generated is available, not just within the company, but to outside audiences.

- The policy should be **implemented**, that is, there should be specific rules, guidelines and responsibilities allocated appropriately to different functions and sites, and the necessary machinery to manage implementation should be installed.

- The policy should be the result of a **process**, that is, the workforce and management at all levels should be involved in the preparation as well as the implementation of the company's policy.

- The policy must be **led**, that is, there must be a single clear focus in the company not just to report to, but also to provide inspiration and innovation.

One key policy issue is that of common environmental standards between different subsidiaries and different countries. For multinational companies, common standards run counter to policies of business decentralisation, and increase costs by requiring all units to conform to the world's most stringent environmental regimes, which are usually to be found in California or Germany. In the case of less developed countries, they also make the company vulnerable to charges that they are acting as environmental imperialists by imposing western standards on poor countries.

However, not to impose common standards endangers cohesion and exposes companies to charges of hypocrisy and lack of concern from environmentalists and communities in countries with less stringent regimes. This danger is increasing as radical consumer groups and environmentalists try to make holding companies more publicly visible.[8] Teesiders were outraged when they discovered in the late 1980s that ICI was operating its local plants to less stringent standards than its German operations. The accident at Union Carbide's Bhopal plant made that corporation vulnerable to charges that it was exploiting less developed countries by operating to lower safety standards than in the West. As a result, many environmentally sensitive companies have decided that all their new plants, and all environment-related activities, must conform to best international practice.[9]

Leadership
Environment-based change is like any other: it involves abandoning the comfort of the known for the uncertainty and fear of the unknown. It therefore requires champions who can inspire their col-

leagues and subordinates with a vision of the future and persuade them that its achievement is both necessary and desirable.

Such leadership is required at all levels. However, that of top management is especially critical, for it is action at this level which not only motivates the middle- and lower-tier levels of the organisation but also ensures coherence.

By general consent, it was the vision and commitment of Du Pont Chairman Edgar Woolard which galvanised that company into taking environmental issues more seriously—as with their decision to phase out CFC manufacture—and has won it a reputation as a leader in corporate environmental management. In contrast, many observers attributed ICI's slowness in tackling environmental issues during the 1980s (relative to its American and German competitors) to the absence of such leadership. A *Financial Times* correspondent noted that ICI's Chairman, Sir Denys Henderson, a marketing man with little science background,

> seems less than comfortable when talking about the details of waste problems. One ICI manager said 'He would much rather be talking about how ICI can raise its image amongst shareholders and customers than engage in a dialogue with environmental groups.' His German counterparts, particularly Mr Hermann Strenger, at Bayer, and Mr Hans Albers, at BASF, are happy to enter into animated conversations on the environment—even if they spend most of their time complaining about the undue pressures they say environmental legislation puts on their companies.[10]

Board-level representation for environmental matters is also important. Volkswagen demonstrated how seriously it took environmental issues when it appointed Ulrich Steger, a politician and business academic, as a Main Board Director with environmental affairs as his sole responsibility. Steger's job description could fairly be summarised as one of hastening Volkswagen's progression from a stage of corporate responsibility to one of clean design—a transition which will involve persuading his colleagues of the inevitability of speed restrictions on German autobahns.[11] Unfortunately, few British companies have made a director explicitly responsible for environmental affairs, and those which have have usually combined it with responsibility for health and safety.

The cynicism of middle and junior managers is one of the principal impediments to any kind of organisational change. This is a particularly serious problem when, as with the natural environment, the changes require a great deal of time and effort to understand and implement. Experience suggests that the best way to gain commitment is a high level of involvement in the shaping of policies, linking environmental performance to individual and collective rewards and sanctions, and a

considerable amount of well-focused training and support from specialist advisers in an environment unit.

Enthusiasm

Ultimately, the spark of leadership is useless without the tinder of
enthusiasm for environment-related actions among all the workforce.
This can readily be achieved because the desired change is ultimately a
response to growing social concern about environmental issues. Hence
many employees, especially those who are young and well educated, will
already accept the basic rationale for change, and indeed be pressing
for it. Many companies have been pleasantly surprised by the extent of
the enthusiasm and commitment which their environmental policies
have unleashed. Indeed, it is not too far-fetched to see channelled
environmental enthusiasm as a centripetal counter to the centrifugal
forces of status and functional differentials in companies of the future.

One means of generating and maintaining enthusiasm is by maximising the ability of employees to shape the direction and implementation
of environmental policies. Environmental suggestion schemes have
been effective, with one survey finding that 80% of companies with
such a scheme had changed their processes or products as a result.[12]
Recycling schemes also provide a tangible means of linking individual
actions to strategic goals, of fostering a positive feeling that change is
possible, and of raising consciousness about the scale and nature of
waste generation. Support for, and encouragement of employee
involvement in, community and environmental organisations also generates goodwill and commitment (although most companies are wary
of too close an involvement with campaigning groups such as
Greenpeace).

Awareness

Enthusiasm is fostered by an understanding of the reasons why change
is necessary. As previous chapters have shown, concepts such as greening and Sustainable Development require business to:

- Recognise its **interdependence** with the natural environment
- Recognise that it has **obligations** to the biosphere and society,
  as well as to shareholders

It is therefore important that there is a widespread understanding of
the ecological theories which underlie the first point and the social
theories (particularly those of the green movement and other radical
groups) which underlie the second. Some companies have sought to
achieve this through internal communications programmes, training

and increased contact with informed outsiders, but most have only begun the process of re-examining their core values and assumptions.

It is important to stress that awareness is not synonymous with approval. There are clearly major philosophical and political differences between the green movement and business which may never be bridged. However, a number of large companies, particularly those in Germany and the USA, have recognised a need to comprehend political environmentalism so that they can either counter its arguments more effectively or engage in more fruitful dialogue with its organisational manifestations.

The increased complexity of the environmental debate is also creating new opportunities for alliances between business-orientated environmentalists and 'environmentally aware' business. The aluminium industry is convinced that the recyclability of aluminium is a critical competitive weapon against plastic, steel, paper and other packaging materials, and has therefore established close relationships with environmental groups to develop a recycling infrastructure. And British agrochemical manufacturers established an alliance with Friends of the Earth and other pressure groups to press government for reform of pesticide approvals procedures.

New Processes and Products

As the costs of pollution control and waste management mount, so it becomes more desirable to prevent rather than treat pollution and waste. 3M claims that its innovative 'Pollution Prevention Pays' programme has saved the company around $500m, and a number of studies have shown that there is enormous scope for similar measures in other companies.[13]

To date, most pollution prevention measures have been modifications to existing activities. However, the greatest pay-offs come when environmental factors are integrated into the design of new products and processes. This is particularly true for complex manufacturing processes which have had various pollution control measures 'bolted on' in an incremental manner. Fundamental redesign to create inherently clean technology can often reduce environmental impacts while improving economic performance.

The tightening of environmental legislation and the rise of the green consumer are also creating enormous opportunities for new, more environmentally benign products. The Body Shop is a particularly successful example of a company targeting its products to the green consumer. Over time, products which can be produced by clean technology will be substituted for those which cannot. Products based on chlorine-based processes are already being phased out of the chemical and paper industries on environmental grounds and may eventually almost disappear. And the aluminium industry, whose products are light and can easily be recycled at a reasonable cost, is using these advantages to win market share in packaging and car components—sectors which are increasingly shaped by government measures to increase recyclability and fuel efficiency.

Efficiency

Waste is not only an environmental problem, but also a sign of business inefficiency, for it is a failure to convert inputs into saleable outputs. It is also far more costly than most managers realise. Many companies appreciate that payments for waste disposal and excessive energy use form part of the 'cost of waste', but far fewer add in such categories as defects, residues, write-offs or shrinkage. Very few take account of the direct and opportunity costs of the management time spent on dealing with these problems, or recognise that reducing waste can often provide an increase in capacity. According to waste management consultants, Orr & Boyd, when such calculations are made it can be seen that British manufacturers alone are losing some £6bn per annum, with some individual companies having total waste costs which are higher than labour costs and net profits.[14]

Review

The contemporary business environment is complex and dynamic. Strategy theorists emphasise the need for regular monitoring of changes in the environment, and the interaction of these with the internal environment of the company, and the implementation of strategic plans. As the relationship between business and the natural environment rises up the strategic agenda, so regular and structured examination of this relationship becomes more vital.

Surveys indicate that only around half of large British companies undertake any kind of environmental review.[15] Many of the half have conducted only fairly basic Environmental Audits of their sites. However, effective environmental review, while incorporating Environmental Auditing, is far broader in scope.[16] As we have seen in Chapter 2, sophisticated environmental managers such as BP conduct different kinds of analyses for different purposes. But perhaps most important, and rarest of all, are company-wide strategic reviews that consider not only environment-related threats, but also environment-related business opportunities.

Environmentalists believe that audits should generally be published. Most companies have disagreed. One exception is Norsk Hydro, which published the results of an audit of first its Norwegian operations and then its British subsidiary, and was pleasantly surprised at the generally favourable reaction. In the long run, the problem may be resolved by a similar distinction to the one that exists between management and financial accounting: on the one hand, internal audits are undertaken in-house and are designed to assist management; and on the other, an external audit is conducted by an external agency with the aim of satisfying external Stakeholders of the company's probity.

British Airways is one company which has conducted and publicised a fundamental review of its environmental policies and actions. Its consultants, Technica, found that, while 'general awareness and expressed intentions are high, the present understanding by senior management of the commitment required for implementation of the environmental policy is low'.[17] In particular, while there was widespread support for ad hoc environmental initiatives, there was much less realisation of the need for regular examination of the environmental impacts of all activities. This was reflected in poor performance in areas such as infringement of noise limits, control of hazardous substances and waste management and recycling.

The Board's response to the report was the development of new mechanisms to ensure that environmental considerations permeated the company. An environmental council has been established with a membership of most executive directors and senior environmental managers. The council determines detailed environmental targets for the company's 200 line managers and receives reports on performance, which are summarised in an annual review.

This kind of formal reporting mechanism up to board level is still rare outside the chemical and energy industries. Linkage between Environmental Auditing and corporate governance is also hampered by a lack of mutual understanding between general managers and the environmental scientists and technologists who are undertaking the reviews. I recently heard the results of an environmental review of a building company I was working with. The tone of the presentation was largely negative, focusing on the costs and technical difficulties of cleaning up contaminated land. What was missing was an appreciation that the company had a head start in the almost certainly rapidly growing market of site decontamination.

The **CLEANER** corporation therefore needs a much greater supply of business-minded environmental scientists and technologists and of general managers with substantial environmental background and understanding. It also needs analytical techniques and methodologies to help these and others to understand the interactions between business and the natural environment. Several authors have initiated the development of these techniques and methodologies.[18] The following pages make an additional contribution by adapting the well-known value chain model of Michael Porter to provide a framework for analysing the operational changes which result from the process of becoming cleaner.

The Sustainability Octagon

Michael Porter's concept of the value chain 'disaggregates a firm into its strategically relevant activities in order to understand the behavior of costs and the existing and potential sources of differentiation'.[19] Figure 1 extends this approach to cover environmental impacts and risks and public acceptability by developing a 'sustainability octagon'. It does so by incorporating five additional strategic activities: external relations, premises, design, product disposal and risk management.

For Porter, the objective of value chain analysis and action is to increase customer satisfaction and therefore profit margins. The sustainability octagon incorporates three less tangible but very important 'margins' which need to be managed, that is, the **eco margin**, the **risk margin** and the **social margin**.

The eco margin is the ratio between an organisation's actual impacts and those impacts which are compatible with Sustainable Development. Of course, the latter is difficult to calculate, but some proxy measures might be used. In the process area, for example, it might be the ratio between the actual efficiencies and impacts of processes and those which are technically feasible. In the short to medium term, it could be the ratio between present impacts and that required by the most stringent national legislation for each category of impact. The key point is that, just as a firm cannot operate without a reasonable profit margin, so in the long term it cannot survive without a low, or minimal, eco margin.

The risk margin is the ratio of actual or potential environmental liabilities to net assets. With the development of strict liability approaches to environmental pollution in the USA and other countries, it is likely that this ratio is already greater than unity for some companies and could be for many more on pessimistic assumptions.

Every enterprise requires some degree of trust from its customers (often termed its consumer franchise) and the communities within which it operates. In the past, this trust has often resided in brands

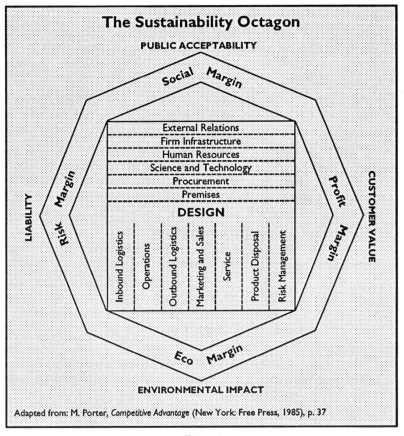

Figure 1

and strategic business units, but increased corporate visibility means that it is now necessary for the corporation as a whole. Every business therefore has a social margin, or the ratio between the minimum social acceptability which the enterprise needs to carry out its activities and that which it actually enjoys. The more that the latter exceeds the former, the more scope the corporation has to enter or expand in markets where trust is important, and to overcome adverse events such as accidents or environmental campaigns.

The advantages of high social margins are increasingly recognised by capital markets. The Body Shop, for example, has typically enjoyed twice the price/earnings ratio of other retail stocks. In mid-1991, one retail analyst noted that the rating was 50% justified by previous rapid growth in earnings per share, 25% by the company's strong consumer franchise, and 25% by the personal qualities of the company's founder and Managing Director, Anita Roddick.[20] Prominent among the latter were her high standing among green consumers and the potential this created to develop new products and enter new markets.

External Relations

Management of external relations is, of course, an important feature of any business. However, this area is especially important for environment-sensitive organisations. They are the main targets of the £200m per annum which environmental organisations spend on campaigns to influence public opinion, legislators and regulators, often with considerable success. Such campaigns are not only directed at recalcitrant companies, but also ones such as Du Pont, who have proclaimed their environmental concern and therefore, in the eyes of environmentalists, have to be judged by higher standards than others.[21]

While the most appropriate action is sometimes to accept environmentalists' demands, there will obviously be many occasions when business wants to counter their arguments. In these situations, good access to opinion formers and decision makers is crucial. This is particularly true at the European level, which is now the source of much environmental legislation, and in the UK is generally perceived to be a more sympathetic milieu for environmentalists than Whitehall. Influence in these areas can be useful, not only in blocking and softening policy proposals, but also by shaping government actions in favour of a particular company or industry.[22]

The larger companies will lobby directly, but will also work with other ones through trade associations, which are emerging as important coordinating bodies for a range of industry-wide environmental initiatives. The UK Chemical Industries Association, for example, has had a considerable influence on the chemical industry through its Responsible Care programme and other initiatives.

Business can anticipate environmentalist pressure, and to some degree protect itself against campaigns or excessive damage by them by fostering links with moderate environmental groups. McDonald's have worked with the US Environmental Defence Fund to explore ways of reducing and recycling its wastes (although radical environmental groups were sceptical about the collaboration). Linkages of this kind also mean that a company is better positioned to take advantage of environment-related business opportunities.

As The Body Shop's ratings show, such a positioning is welcomed by another important external Stakeholder, the capital markets. An estimated 10% of the British equity market is now subject to some kind of ethical screening, which will almost always have an environmental dimension.[23] Many other fund managers are also influenced by environmental factors when making investment decisions. However, investments in ethical funds had only reached a disappointing £330m by 1991. Some attribute this to poor performance but others point to the adverse effects of recession, and expect the sector to grow rapidly during the 1990s.[24]

The initial business response to heightened pressure from external Stakeholders is usually to increase public relations activities. Indeed one of the most striking differences between many British and comparable European companies is that the former assign responsibility for environmental matters to public relations departments whereas in the latter it is given to technical departments.[25] While public relations obviously has a role to play, it is difficult to avoid the conclusion that many British companies are more concerned with presentation than the concrete realities of environmental change.[26] This is certainly the view of consumers, who are increasingly suspicious of green advertising and marketing.[27]

Effective response to external Stakeholders requires credible environmental policies and a willingness to engage in dialogue. One way in which a few pioneering companies are encouraging the latter is by bringing green thinking into the boardroom through the appointment of environmentalists as non-executive directors.

A larger number are introducing new criteria for promotion, with much more emphasis on the ability to understand and communicate with the general public and environmental groups. The German chemical company Bayer, for example, have broken with their traditions by promoting a number of young managers to senior positions on the basis of their cosmopolitan background and ability to deal with green campaigners and other outsiders.

Firm Infrastructure

Activities such as general management, planning and finance coordinate and support the entire sustainability octagon. The new British Standard on Environmental Management Systems BS7750 is, like BS5750, its quality equivalent, primarily concerned with the effectiveness of this infrastructure.[28] It requires:

- An environmental policy and detailed environmental targets
- Effective documented procedures for implementing environmental policies from the boardroom to the shopfloor
- Monitoring of environmental impacts and compliance with legislation
- Effective communication channels and training

As with quality standards, such accreditation is becoming a basic requirement for suppliers of large companies. It may also become necessary for insurance cover and dealings with banks and other financial institutions.

Organisational structures are also critical. Almost all environment-sensitive companies now have separate environmental units (often with combined responsibility for health and safety) which advise and monitor operating units. However, there is a wide variation in their effectiveness, both generally and in particular areas.[29] Those which report directly to a main board director usually have much more 'clout' than those which do not.

A number of companies have also established new business units to speed the development of greener products and services. A striking international example is the German conglomerate Metallgesellschaft, who have transformed themselves by defining pollution control and waste management as their core businesses. They recently floated a minority stake in their rapidly growing recycling subsidiary, Berzelius Umwelt-Service (BUS), and expect to finance the expansion of their environmental engineering unit, Lurgi Umwelt-Beteiligungsgesellschaft (LUB), in the same way. In the UK, ICI recently established ICI Watercare to manage existing products and services and develop new ones for the rapidly growing, but relatively fragmented, market for water treatment chemicals and processes.

Information and money are the lifeblood of any organisation and central to the creation of an environmental infrastructure. Environment-relevant information in most companies is both fragmented and over-abundant. Effective systems are needed to coordinate and structure this information, particularly at senior management level. Figure 2 provides an example of the kinds of data which might figure in such an environmental information system.

The scope of financial management is being greatly expanded by the growth of environmental concern.[30] Indeed, almost every environmental conference held these days has a contingent of sober-suited accountants in pursuit of a lucrative new market for environmental accountancy and audit services. Pollution control and waste management expenditures are now a major cost category for many companies and need to be controlled in the same way as any other. The calculation of environment-related liabilities is already a common feature of US balance sheets and a necessary part of any acquisition or joint venture, and the practice is spreading to Europe. American accountants also need to calculate optimal responses to increasingly complex environ-

Information for Environmental Management

Indicator	Means	Examples of Measures
Financial	Calculate social costs of recurrent impacts	Annual social costs (compare with/deduct from profits/value added)
	Calculate medium-/long-term costs of environmental impacts	Financial provisions for medium-/long-term environmental liabilities
	Place monetary value on environmental assets	Value of environmental assets
Physical	Assess physical impacts	Quantities of emissions/land etc.
	Assess consequences of impacts.	Index of harm (e.g. biological oxygen demand)
Relational	Relate physical impacts to financial performance	Emissions per financial unit Composite impacts per financial unit Value added per emission unit
Managerial	Benchmark environmental systems/performance	Financial, physical, relational measures Percentage of senior managers whose income is linked to environmental performance
Market	Analyse market performance	Reputation amongst consumers Market share of environmentally-sensitive segments Percentage of product recycled (by value/volume)
Stakeholder	Assess perceptions of key Stakeholders	Reputation amongst environmentalists, legislators, etc. Ratings of ethical investors
Legislative	Assess compliance with present/projected	Absolute/comparative distance from present/projected legislation in California, Germany and Japan

Figure 2

mental taxes, regulations and marketable permit schemes, and this too is becoming more common in Europe.

A number of large companies have now introduced an environmental component into their budgetary procedures. Rhone Poulenc, for example, have a sophisticated waste accounting system which allocates the full costs of waste disposal to the departments responsible for its production. A smaller number also have a self-contained environmental capital budget for which individual plants or sections can make applications for environment-related capital expenditure. An innovative Dutch computer company, BSO/ORIGIN, have gone even further and drawn up a set of environmental accounts which place a monetary value on all their environmental impacts. More companies are likely to follow when the accounting associations develop a standardised approach to the subject.

Human Resources

Human resource management is central to the achievement of employee awareness and enthusiasm and effective environmental leadership. Chapter 11 notes how a good environmental image assists in the recruitment of new staff and improves the morale of existing employees. Environmentally sensitive companies have also started to make environmental understanding and performance important criteria for rewards and promotion. This is obviously facilitated by environmental training programmes, although these have until recently been thin on the ground. In the longer term, companies will have to change their recruiting patterns and develop linkages with educational institutions to provide necessary environment-related skills.[31]

A problematic area for a number of companies is union involvement in environmental issues. Historically, the union's interest in conservation has focused on that of jobs. However, the social deepening of environmental interest and the recognition that environment-based change can create jobs as well as destroy them has led to a more positive interest. The Trades Union Congress and leading unions have encouraged their members to become more involved in company environmental decision making and to seek union participation in Environmental Audits.

Many companies, while claiming a desire for substantial workforce participation, have been less keen on channelling this through the unions. However, union interest is unlikely to diminish and it seems likely that companies will have to become accustomed to environmental issues appearing on the negotiating agenda.

Science and Technology

All companies deploy a broad range of technologies, many of which need to be changed if good environmental performance is to be achieved. In the long run, this requires the development of completely redesigned clean technology, and the amount of R&D expenditure devoted to this aim—which is already considerable—can be expected to increase. More and more companies will also establish specialist environmental research centres, such as ICI's Brixham laboratory, although these will need to be closely linked with mainstream innovation activities so that these are permeated with environmental awareness.

New legislation and public pressure also require companies to demonstrate that their technology is adequate for environmental protection. In the UK, the 1990 Environmental Protection Act requires companies to adopt BATNEEC, or Best Available Technology Not Entailing Excessive Cost. Whilst there is obviously much scope for interpretation in these words, the likelihood is that British regulators will follow their American and European counterparts and err on the side of stringency in their application of the act.

Procurement

For many organisations, particularly those in service and light industries, the environmental impacts of their own activities are less important than those of their suppliers. McDonald's, for example, have been pilloried because much of their beef was allegedly grown on deforested tropical land.

The environmental performance of suppliers is therefore a central feature of large company environmental management. Even the largest suppliers are having to change in response to this concern. Xerox and Hewlett Packard, for example, were sceptical about the feasibility of using recycled paper in their equipment, but were eventually forced to find technical solutions because of pressure from their customers.

The billions of dollars which IBM spends on components and materials adds up to one of the largest procurement budgets in the world. IBM places great emphasis on environmental concern and has demanded a similar commitment from its suppliers. According to its northern Europe procurement manager, John Gillett, there are four key aspects of good, environment-influenced, buyer–supplier interaction:

- Build sound relationships with suppliers in which there is mutual respect
- Make sure your staff understand the issues and support you

- Create a vision of where you want to take your suppliers
- Create environmental awareness and communicate the issues[32]

In the long run, there is also likely to be considerable competitive advantage in integrating suppliers into the design process, so that the entire value chain can be optimised for good environmental performance.

However, there is one procurement dilemma which is likely to become more pressing over time, and that is the question of geographical sourcing. A bias towards local suppliers can greatly reduce transport impacts and facilitate cooperation over design and other areas. However, a green company will be concerned with reducing global wealth disparities and should therefore have a bias towards suppliers in less developed countries wherever possible.

Premises

A company's factories, offices and other buildings and sites have a considerable environmental impact. Their construction alters the landscape and consumes raw materials, their operation uses energy, water and other inputs, creates internal and external emissions and other impacts, and influences transport patterns. At the end of their lives, demolition affects amenity and generates waste, some of which may be hazardous. And at all times they are one of the most visible manifestations of a company's existence and therefore a major influence on its public image.

Environmentally friendlier premises management has three principal aims:

- Minimal impacts from emissions, noises, visual intrusion or other causes
- More efficient use of inputs such as energy and water
- Projection of a clean image to employees, customers and communities

These objectives are most easily achieved in the design stage, especially if this meets the standards of the Building Research Establishment's Environmental Assessment Method (BREEAM). This provides credits for such features as low energy usage, usage of CFC substitutes and natural materials, use of reclaimed land, and avoidance of indoor pollution. Accessibility to public transport is another important parameter.

However, there is much that can be done to make existing premises more environment-friendly. Substitution of CFCs and other harmful substances, repainting, screening, sound insulation and other measures can greatly ameliorate direct impacts. Improved insulation, electronic energy management systems and other measures have already reduced energy consumption—and costs—for many companies, and research demonstrates that there is still enormous potential for cost-effective measures.[33] Conservation and recycling measures offer similar potential for the increasingly expensive commodity of water.

Finally, Japanese companies have long stressed the connection between clean premises and the psychological well-being of the work-force and surrounding communities. One company who have demonstrated its truth in the UK, and extended cleanliness from their own premises to the surrounding landscape, are Stocksbridge Engineering Steels. The specialist steel-making company are halfway into a £10 million, ten-year environmental programme to reduce their air and water emissions drastically, and to landscape their site. The latter involves the planting of 100,000 new trees to return the surrounding river valley to its pre-industrial state.

Stocksbridge Managing Director, David Stone, has been delighted with the results. For him:

> Cleanliness is economically important. It is not so much that dust gets into the product, but the psychological effect on everyone. If you are trying to make something clean while surrounded by lots of rubbish you have an attitude problem from the outset.
>
> The customer then equates a clean works with clean steel. We do, of course, bring all of our customers here. They see us as a high-tech industry operating in a clean, landscaped, high-tech environment, just as impressive in its way as the modern premises in which many of them operate.[34]

Design

Many existing products and processes are inherently polluting and need to be completely redesigned. Design is therefore the engine of good environmental practice.[35] Indeed, the final stage of environmental management is characterised above all else by the existence of clean design, in which environmental concerns are pervasive among all those concerned with new product and process development. The topic is explored in greater detail in subsequent chapters.

Inbound/Outbound Logistics

Inbound and outbound logistics are often distinct sources of cost advantage or differentiation to companies, but their environmental impacts are similar. These are discussed in greater detail in Chapter 8.

Operations

For non-service companies, operations are usually the main source of all environmental impacts, and particularly of emissions to land, water and the atmosphere. Figure 3 distinguishes the five principal means of controlling these emissions and places them in approximate order of desirability.

Storage or dumping obviously does nothing to transform or prevent pollution and carries a large risk of accidental releases and unanticipated future liability. Incineration and treatment does nothing for prevention and can create actual or potential hazards. Indeed community fears over dioxin and other contamination from incinerators has also made it impossible to build them in many parts of Europe. In Northern Ireland, for example, successful opposition to a proposed toxic waste incinerator for a Du Pont facility has been one of the few issues to unite both Catholics and Protestants. External recycling usually

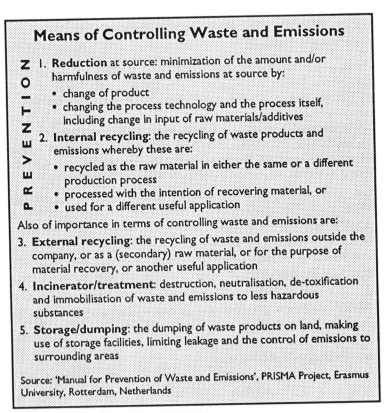

Means of Controlling Waste and Emissions

PREVENTION

1. **Reduction** at source: minimization of the amount and/or harmfulness of waste and emissions at source by:
   - change of product
   - changing the process technology and the process itself, including change in input of raw materials/additives
2. **Internal recycling:** the recycling of waste products and emissions whereby these are:
   - recycled as the raw material in either the same or a different production process
   - processed with the intention of recovering material, or
   - used for a different useful application

Also of importance in terms of controlling waste and emissions are:

3. **External recycling:** the recycling of waste and emissions outside the company, or as a (secondary) raw material, or for the purpose of material recovery, or another useful application
4. **Incinerator/treatment:** destruction, neutralisation, de-toxification and immobilisation of waste and emissions to less hazardous substances
5. **Storage/dumping:** the dumping of waste products on land, making use of storage facilities, limiting leakage and the control of emissions to surrounding areas

Source: 'Manual for Prevention of Waste and Emissions', PRISMA Project, Erasmus University, Rotterdam, Netherlands

Figure 3

carries fewer risks, but still more than internal recycling, which also avoids the additional collection and transport costs of external recycling. Best of all are changes in products or processes that actually reduce the amount of waste generated.[36] Figure 4 gives further details of the many ways in which pollution can be prevented by reduction at source and internal recycling. The opportunities are enormous, for even the best companies are still discovering new means of minimising waste. 3M has followed its 3P programme with 3P+ (Pollution Prevention Plus), which commits the company to a 90% reduction in emissions over the medium term. Successful demonstration projects in Sweden (Landskrona), the Netherlands (PRISMA) and other European countries have also demonstrated the scope for action in Europe.

Marketing and Sales

The key elements of the Greener Marketing process are discussed in other chapters. Experience suggests that success is most easily achieved, and consumer scepticism neutralised, when environmental concern permeates a company so that marketing is integrated into the sustainability chain rather than being a superficial 'add on'.

Service

The efficiency and quality of customer service provided at the point of sale, after sales and through servicing contracts will be key determinants of the success of a company's environmental policy.

Correctly explaining how a product is to be used can prolong its life and also enhance its environmental performance. Environmental awareness training will be an important method to provide customers with information about products. For example, The Body Shop places great emphasis on educating consumers about the issues behind products through informative literature and extensive employee training. Efficiently dealing with customers' enquiries and complaints will also help to improve the company's image and provide feedback for 'greener' modifications to the product.

Servicing through effective repair and reconditioning can greatly lengthen a product's life, and can improve the efficiency with which it operates. Cars which have become 'out of tune', for example, waste fuel and emit greater amounts of toxic gases; however, they can be re-tuned easily and inexpensively. Design for longevity may require the increasing use of electronics and information technology to extend the product life cycle, with consequent implications for increasing the computer literacy of service engineers.

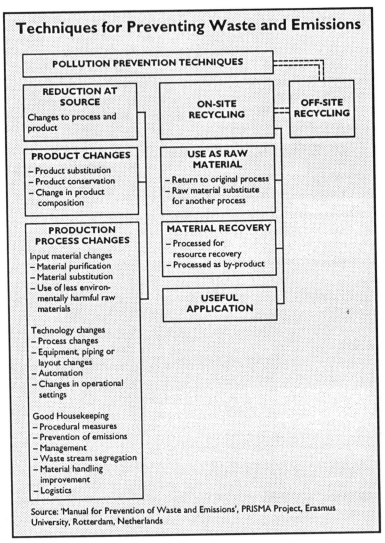

Techniques for Preventing Waste and Emissions

POLLUTION PREVENTION TECHNIQUES

REDUCTION AT SOURCE

Changes to process and product

ON-SITE RECYCLING

OFF-SITE RECYCLING

PRODUCT CHANGES
– Product substitution
– Product conservation
– Change in product composition

USE AS RAW MATERIAL
– Return to original process
– Raw material substitute for another process

PRODUCTION PROCESS CHANGES

Input material changes
– Material purification
– Material substitution
– Use of less environmentally harmful raw materials

Technology changes
– Process changes
– Equipment, piping or layout changes
– Automation
– Changes in operational settings

Good Housekeeping
– Procedural measures
– Prevention of emissions
– Management
– Waste stream segregation
– Material handling improvement
– Logistics

MATERIAL RECOVERY
– Processed for resource recovery
– Processed as by-product

USEFUL APPLICATION

Source: 'Manual for Prevention of Waste and Emissions', PRISMA Project, Erasmus University, Rotterdam, Netherlands

Figure 4

Product Disposal

The development of cradle-to-grave responsibility has been driven by the rising impacts and costs of product disposal. As other chapters demonstrate, companies have a choice between developing more effective forms of disposal (such as return for supervised disposal by the manufacturer or maximum use of biodegradable materials) or recycling for alternative use. Many companies and experts believe that, when the complete life cycle of the product is carefully analysed, well-managed disposal can be more environmentally benign than recycling. However, environmental groups and much of the general public believe that the latter is more desirable. It is likely therefore that stringent legislative targets and consumer preference will require business to design products for full recyclability and develop recycling infrastructures. Many companies will follow the aluminium industry in trying to use this trend for competitive advantage. This is particularly true of the car industry, where far-sighted manufacturers such as BMW are now designing cars with fewer, more recyclable materials, and developing car disassembly plants.

Risk Management

The 1980s saw a succession of environment-related disasters which imposed severe costs on, and in some cases threatened the very existence of, the responsible companies. The Exxon Valdez spillage cost Exxon over $3bn in clean-up costs, compensation and fines, greatly damaged its public acceptability and consumed an inordinate amount of management time. Union Carbide paid out significant compensation for the Bhopal disaster and might well have been bankrupted if the cases had been decided under American rather than Indian jurisdiction. Perrier is only one of the companies to have lost millions of dollars in sales and forfeited public trust as a result of contamination of its products.

These and other disasters have directed business attention to the extent and complexity of environment-related risks. According to Peter Schroeder, Director of Risk Engineering at Zurich Insurance:

> The fact that the Sandoz incident was an environmental catastrophe that stemmed from a fire makes people think about the interrelationships. You can't neatly separate off one risk from another.[37]

In addition, the magnitude and frequency of environment-related risks is being considerably increased by the adoption of strict liability for both future and past environmental damage in the USA, and the likelihood is that the European Community will move the same way. As a result, American business is already liable for over $100bn of clean-up costs for land that has been polluted in the past.

One response has been a drying up of liability insurance and a much greater caution by third parties such as banks and carriers about their own potential liability. These and other parties are now adding to internal pressures for companies to adopt a more systematic approach to the analysis of risks and phase out hazardous materials, introduce safety control systems and take other measures to reduce risks.[38] However, both production and marketing disasters will always happen (simultaneously in the case of Perrier, whose water was contaminated by benzene from its bottling plant) and sensible companies now have crisis management plans and training programmes to mitigate their worst effects.

The Future

The other chapters of this book confirm that the environmental shaping of production, markets and business will continue during the 1990s. Indeed a number of recent developments suggest that the pace might quicken rather than slow down. Two factors from a long list include: the heightened global awareness of environmental problems which has resulted from the Rio 'Earth Summit'; and innovation by progressive companies such as 3M or The Body Shop, which is changing public expectations of the performance of all business.

If this is so, then almost all companies will have to attain the stage of corporate responsibility, while many others will move beyond it to that of clean design. This will involve not only the changes in organisation and activity discussed above, but perhaps a more fundamental reappraisal of the nature and purpose of business. The present sense of companies as discrete entities which are relatively isolated from the broader ecological and social environment may be replaced by one which sees them as embedded in, and interdependent with, this environment. While profitability will remain a paramount objective, it may be tempered by a recognition that the company's longer-term future also depends upon the maintenance and reproduction of its environment. This may require a change in the balance between cooperative and competitive relationships, with more emphasis on partnerships with suppliers, customers and external Stakeholders.

However, the probability that business will have to pay greater attention to environmental issues in the 1990s does not mean that the agenda will be the same as in the 1980s. Past experience suggests that some problems may become less pressing, either because effective measures have been taken, initial perceptions were mistaken, or because public attention has shifted elsewhere. Environmental debates are also likely to switch from bolt-on solutions to waste minimisation and deployment of new clean technologies as the latter's advantages become more widely understood. The trade implications of environmental legislation are also a source of growing concern, as well as opportunity, for business. Finally, the development of Life Cycle Analysis and sophisticated environmental performance measurement techniques will muddy what were previously black and white issues, such as the universal desirability of recycling.[39]

These developments—and a continuing improvement in environmental performance—will allow companies to become less defensive and more self-confident and effective in challenging the Greens' intellectual and political domination of environmental debates. Their past neglect of environmental issues—and the implicit assumption that they do not warrant the attention given to them by the Greens—might be replaced by the belief that environmental issues are simply too important to be left to environmentalists. As a consequence, the environmental movement could be even more fundamentally divided than at present into those who are prepared to cooperate with—and speak the language of—business, and those who are not.

Indeed it is not too fanciful to imagine the next century as one of 'environmental capitalism' in which environmental protection and enhancement is not only a major operational issue and a substantial market, but also a central objective—and source of legitimacy—for both business as a whole and individual enterprises. In this case, the companies taking action now to anticipate environmental opportunities and pre-empt environmental threats may be developing competitive advantage on a timescale measured not merely in months or years, but also in decades or even centuries.

References

1. One survey found that half its sample of British small businesses had taken no measures to protect the environment and concluded that environmental issues have made no significant impact on the small business sector. See Cranfield Management School, 'How Green are Small Companies?' (October 1990).
2. U. Steger, 'The Greening of the Board Room' (Paper presented to 'The Greening of Industry' Conference, Noordwijk, 17th–19th November 1991).
3. Centre for the Exploitation of Science and Technology, 'Industry and the Environment: A Strategic Overview' (London, 1991).
4. J. Davis, *Greening Business: Managing for Sustainable Development* (Oxford: Basil Blackwell, 1991); International Environment Bureau, *Greening of Enterprise* (London: International Chamber of Commerce, 1992); S. Schmidheiny and the Business Council for Sustainable Development, *Changing Course* (London/Cambridge MA: The MIT Press, 1992); D. Smith (ed.), *Business and the Environment* (London: Paul Chapman, 1992); F.B. Friedman, *A Practical Guide to Environmental Management* (Washington DC: Environmental Law Institute, 1991).

5. Pettigrew has summarised these as achieving coherence, effective leadership, linking strategic and operational change, treating people as assets and effective environmental assessment. A. Pettigrew and R. Whipp, *Managing Change for Competitive Success* (Oxford: Basil Blackwell, 1991).

6. J. Hunt, 'Heseltine Attacks Business on Environment', *Financial Times*, 27 September, 1991.

7. T. Burke and J. Hill, 'Ethics, Environment and the Company' (Institute of Business Ethics, 1990).

8. R. Adams, J. Carruthers and S. Hamil, *Changing Corporate Values* (London: Kogan Page, 1991).

9. United Nations Centre on Transnational Corporations, *Benchmark Corporate Environmental Survey* (London: United Nations, London, 1991).

10. P. Marsh, 'ICI Ready to Improve its Pollution Record', *Financial Times*, 13 December 1989.

11. A. Fisher, 'Greening of the Peoples' Car', *Financial Times*, 13 September 1991.

12. DRT International/Touche Ross, 'Managers' Attitudes to the Environment' (June 1991).

13. J. Ausebel and H. Sladovich, *Technology and the Environment* (Washington DC: National Academy Press, 1989); G. Heaton, R. Repetto and R. Sobin, *Transforming Technology: An Agenda for Environmentally Sustainable Growth in the 21st Century* (Washington DC: World Resources Institute, 1991); Office of Technology Assessment, *Serious Reduction of Hazardous Waste* (Washington DC: Office of Technology Assessment, 1986).

14. J. Thornhill, 'The Trap is Set for Hidden Waste', *Financial Times*, 31 July 1991.

15. J. Hunt, 'Influence of Greens Criticised', *Financial Times*, 5 August 1991.

16. J. Elkington, *The Environmental Audit: A Green Filter for Company Policies, Plants, Processes and Products* (London: SustainAbility/World Wide Fund for Nature, 1990).

17. Quoted in J. Hunt, 'A Flight to Conserve', *Financial Times*, 17 July 1991.

18. Coopers & Lybrand Deloitte, *Your Business and the Environment: A DIY Review for Companies* (London: Legal Studies and Services, 1991); J. Elkington, P. Knight and J. Hailes, *The Green Business Guide* (London: Victor Gollancz, 1991); Smith, *Business and the Environment*, I, Part 1, pp. 11-24; Steger, 'The Greening of the Board Room', ref. 2.

19. M. Porter, *Competitive Advantage* (New York: Free Press, 1985), p. 33.

20. J. Fuller, 'Roddick's Boredom Pays Off', *Financial Times*, 8 June 1991.

21. J. Doyle, *Hold the Applause!* (Washington DC: Friends of the Earth, 1991).

22. L. Preston (ed.), *Governmental Regulation and Business Response* (Greenwich, CT: JAI Press, 1990).

23. Shelley Taylor and Associates, 'The Rewards of Virtue' (June 1991).

24. S. Daneshku, 'Funds Fail to Harvest the Growth of Greenery', *Financial Times*, Quarterly Review of Personal Finance, 25 and 26 October 1991.

25. DRT International/Touche Ross, 'Head in the Clouds or Head in the Sand?' (1990).

26. Adams *et al.*, *Changing Corporate Values*, ref. 8.
27. Mintel, 'The Green and Ethical Shopper' (1991).
28. British Standards Institute, *Specification for Environmental Management Systems BS7750* (London: BSI, 1992). See also R. Welford, 'Linking Quality and Environment', *Business Strategy and the Environment*, Vol. I, Part 1 (1992), pp. 25-34.
29. P. Groenwegen and P. Vergragt, 'Environmental Issues as Threats and Opportunities for Technological Innovation', *Technological Analysis and Strategic Management*, Vol. III, Part 1, pp. 43-45.
30. R. Gray, *The Greening of Accountancy: The Profession after Pearce* (London: ACCA, 1990); Coopers & Lybrand Deloitte, *Environment and the Finance Function* (London: Coopers & Lybrand Deloitte, 1990).
31. 'The Impact of Environmental Management on Skills and Jobs' (Birmingham: ECOTEC, 1990).
32. P. Knight, 'Green Badge of Courage', *Financial Times*, 20 November 1991.
33. Public Accounts Committee, *National Energy Efficiency, 14th Report 1989-90* (London: HMSO, 1990).
34. I. Hamilton Fazey, 'Change in the Works', *Financial Times*, 13 February 1991.
35. D. MacKenzie, *Green Design* (London: Laurence King, 1991); D. Wann, *Biologic: Environmental Protection by Design* (London: Johnson Books, 1990).
36. Environmental Protection Agency, *Waste Minimization Opportunity Assessment Manual* (Washington DC: Environmental Protection Agency, 1988); H. Freeman (ed.), *Hazardous Waste Minimisation* (New York: McGraw-Hill, 1990); Institution of Chemical Engineers, *Waste Management Guide* (Rugby: Institution of Chemical Engineers, 1992); D. Huisingh and L. Bass, 'Cleaner Production', *European Water Pollution Control*, Vol. I, Part 1 (1991), pp. 24-30; H. Dieleman and S. de Hoo, 'PRISMA: The Development of a Preventative Multi-Media Strategy for Government and Industry' (Paper presented to 'The Greening of Industry' Conference), ref. 2.
37. Quoted in R. Lapper, 'Hedging the Bets against Disaster', *Financial Times*, 31 October 1990.
38. P. Kleindorfer and H. Kunreuther (eds.), *Insuring and Managing Hazardous Risks* (New York: Springer, 1987).
39. F. Cairncross, *Costing the Earth* (London: Economist Books, 1991); P. James, 'Is the Environment Green?', *UK CEED Bulletin*, November-December 1991.

PART II

THE PRACTICAL IMPLICATIONS
OF GREENER MARKETING

Chapter 5

GREENER MARKETING STRATEGY: WHY AND HOW TO GREEN THE MIX

Martin Charter

Director, KPH Marketing

Introduction

> Greener Marketing is a holistic and responsible strategic management process that identifies, anticipates, satisfies and fulfils Stakeholder needs, for a reasonable reward, that does not adversely affect human or natural environmental well-being.

Greener Marketing takes account of the wider relationship of the organisation and its products to its surroundings. It is about a more aware, open, targeted and sensitive approach that integrates the strategic link between the company, the environment, and marketing, rather than being primarily concerned with tactical communications opportunities.

The prime emphasis is on developing relationships and satisfying separate Stakeholder needs in an environmentally and socially responsible manner (see Fig. 1).

Greener Marketing should not be looked at in isolation, as the effects of launching or re-orientating a greener product or company will have ramifications for purchasing, operations, finance and human resources. There will be a need for a coordinated approach with close involvement and communication between different parts of the organisation. After an environmental review or audit has been completed, Greener Marketing planning should be undertaken, and should include longer-term considerations which may change over time as knowledge, technology and science develop.

The 'environmental friendliness' of products and services is likely to be a secondary benefit, except in niche markets, as the product will

Key Stakeholder Needs

Stakeholder groups	Stakeholder needs
Customers	– high quality, greener products, reasonable prices
Investors	– profitability, growth, good management
Parent company	– profitability, growth, good management
Directors	– job security, corporate image, job satisfaction
Employees	– job security, corporate image, job satisfaction
The community	– social responsibility, security, open dialogue
Legislators	– social responsibility, open dialogue, over-compliance
Pressure groups	– social responsibility, open dialogue, environmental excellence
Suppliers	– secure contracts, long-term relationships, growth
The media	– good news, bad news, open dialogue

Figure 1

have to function, and be of the appropriate price and quality. Once that is proven, then the greener product will have a distinct competitive advantage. Differentiation may start to arise outside the brand through 'sounder' policies as consumers are increasingly buying not just products, but also the processes used to produce and distribute the products or services. As part of the shift, the 1990s will see a

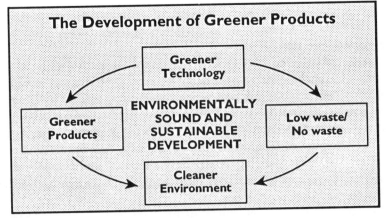

Figure 2

trend towards integrating cleaner, greener technologies into the production process (see Fig. 2), as in many cases 'end-of-pipe' environmental controls have been inadequate or incapable of preventing pollution and other environmental degradation.

The company should examine the total effect on the organisation of launching a greener product or programme, as heightened media, consumer, and pressure group attention will focus on the whole company, and then on other products and processes and related issues. The short-, medium- and longer-term implications of the provision of greener and non-green products should be considered. The key is thorough research and detailed strategic planning:

- Has the Marketing plan analysed the affect of green issues on the market?
- What effect will green issues have on profitability?
- Has the company planned for possible market shrinkage that may result from changing consumer attitudes?
- Has the company conducted market research into the probable effects of green issues on the firm?
- Can the company modify existing products? or will new investment be required?
- Is the company developing positive links with environmental groups?
- Is the company prepared for a possible backlash from environmental pressure groups?
- Do communications strategies emphasise environmental aspects and benefits?

This chapter examines the initial stages of the green market development and the problems associated with the lack of information, coupled with the increasing focus on cradle-to-grave analysis. The opportunities in a greener market will then be considered, emphasising the need for thorough research, and the development of integrated information systems. The Greener Marketing planning process will then be examined, including some strategies that have been adopted over recent years. Finally the need to align corporate, environmental and marketing strategies is discussed, coupled with the key processes involved in developing an appropriate Greener Marketing planning system.

Green Market Evolution: The Information Gap

The first phase of greening has generally seen short-term corporate responses with relatively minor adaptations to existing products and processes. The speed of environmental developments and the lack of information about the performance of products and companies has left many companies and their Stakeholders, notably consumers, confused.

In 1989 The Consumers Association conducted research into green labelling and found considerable misunderstanding.[1] Fifty-five per cent of the sample of 1,930 shoppers thought that a label making environmental claims had been officially approved; when asked who they thought had approved it, the most popular guess was the Government. Of the group that thought that goods carrying green labels did not require official approval, 83% thought that they should require it.

In May 1990 The Department of Trade and Industry (DTI) responded to the need to examine labelling requirements by establishing the National Advisory Group on Environmental Labelling (NAGEL).

A survey by Mintel, in 1991[2] indicated that the uncertainty over claims had not diminished over recent years. Sixty-three per cent of the shoppers were 'confused' about green claims and this has left many in a dilemma over responsible consumption against the ethics of manufacturers' claims.

The Consumers Association report classified inaccurate claims into four broad categories:

- Excessive claims: no manufactured product can fail to have some sort of negative impact on the environment. For example, aerosol manufacturers may avoid using the most harmful CFCs, but alternatives can still damage the ozone layer.

- Multiple claims: different forms of wording used to describe the same environmental benefit. For example, research has indicated that aerosols labelled 'ozone safe' were perceived to be greener than one labelled 'ozone friendly'.

- Claims which are not explained: due to a lack of consumer understanding, many unexplained environmental terms, such as 'no optical brighteners' and 'biodegradable' have little meaning. Products should give short and simple explanations of environmental claims.

- Meaningless claims: it is misleading to put a 'no phosphates' label on a bathroom cleaner, when you cannot buy one which does contain phosphates; products where the surfactants are

based on vegetable oils rather than petrochemicals may biode-
grade more quickly and thoroughly, but the environmental
benefits of this are still unclear.

The paucity of information has prevented many consumers from
making informed choices, and the lack of standards has enabled some
companies to jump on and off the green bandwagon for short-term
gain. In many cases, this has led to a backlash against both those companies that have taken an ethical and responsible approach and those
that have made inaccurate and unsubstantiated claims. This ill-
informed behaviour has encouraged initiatives such as Friends of the
Earth's 'Green Con of the Year Award' in the UK. The introduction
of an official EC eco-labelling scheme in Autumn 1992 is designed to
remove this consumer uncertainty and to give companies a bench-
mark of acceptability.

The rise of green issues has also left many companies perplexed by
the new set of problems and opportunities. The complexity of the
issues and lack of environmental understanding has left many directors
and managers confused. Initially, many companies felt that they had to
react to the increase in green pressures, and a number of organisations
took rather ill-considered and uncoordinated approaches. However, a
number of proactive companies are now starting to take more strategic
approaches, examining the longer-term implications of underlying
changes.

The speed and extent of national and EC legislative developments is
causing particular confusion, even in greener countries. A survey carried out for the federation of Netherlands industry indicated that some
two-thirds of Dutch companies did not know how the Government's
environmental policies would affect them, and this has led to delays in
environmental expenditure.[3] The uncertainty surrounding the implications of the UK's Environmental Protection Act is also leading to considerably lobbying, notably by the chemical industry.

The second phase of greening will see more environmentally literate
and aware Stakeholders who will require more information on products
and corporate responses. Companies will need to develop a greater
understanding of their environmental impacts if they are not to be
caught out.

Pressure groups will increasingly demand that companies supply
more information on their environmental impact, with trends in the
US serving as a useful example. In 1986, after the Bhopal disaster, the
US Congress enacted the Emergency Planning and Community Right
To Know Act, which requires considerable amounts of detailed infor-

mation about corporate environmental performance to be made available. If passed, the Corporate Safety and Environmental Information Bill[4] aims to amend the 1985 Companies Act and force businesses to add, in the Directors' report in the annual report and accounts, 'Safety and the Environment' to existing required disclosures on issues such as the disabled, political contributions and employee consultation. Another series of pressures for business will be the implementation of the EC's Directive on Freedom of Access to Environmental Information in late 1992, the promotion of the public registers of corporate environmental information, established through the Environmental Protection Act, and the arrival of the EC Eco-Auditing directive in late 1992.

Product and Market Life Cycles

Typically, a product goes through a series of stages from concept, to development and launch, then to growth, maturity and decline. Companies adapt and change the product depending on its particular circumstances and its position in the Product Life Cycle (PLC). Many companies are now starting to look at the physical life cycle of products to determine ways of reducing the harmful environmental impact of the company and its products at every stage from cradle to grave.

The increasing complexity of environmental issues will impact on the Product Life Cycle (PLC) as products and markets change even more rapidly due to tougher legislation, technological change and greater environmental awareness. This will mean that companies will have to be increasingly sensitive to the issues, and will regularly need to assess new and existing products' impact through techniques such as Life Cycle Analysis (LCA).

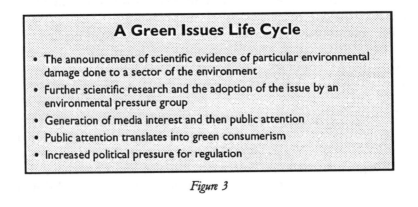

Figure 3

Proactive companies will need to monitor and analyse Stakeholder interests and concerns, especially those of scientists and pressure groups. Green issues may affect the product in different ways over the years, but as new social, legislative, technological and scientific issues arise, the effects may be rapid (see Fig. 3).[5]

The speed of market change and the emergence of specific environmental issues will provide opportunities and threats for proactive companies. For example, the aerosol market changed considerably within the space of eighteen months due to Friends of the Earth's campaign over CFCs, leading to the re-emergence of old technology pump action devices and stimulating research into substitutes. Many other marketplaces have already been affected by the advent of the green consumer and by increased pressure group activity:

- Food retailing
- Cars
- Washing powders
- Batteries
- Furniture

Strong pressures are likely to develop in a number of industry sectors and with companies which:

- Have been major pollutants, e.g. agriculture
- Use animals for product testing, e.g. cosmetics
- Are linked to major environmental issues, e.g. fridges, aerosols
- Have made strong environmental claims, e.g. oil companies
- Are competing on relative greenness, e.g. cans and batteries
- Face opportunities for differentiation based on environmental performance, e.g. food and retailing

A flexible and sensitive system will need to be established to identify the emergence of trends, and to allow products and processes to be adapted and developed as specific environmental issues arise or are forecast. Involvement of employees in the innovation process will be essential and should generate good ideas, motivation and commitment. For example, 3M developed a 'Pollution Prevention Pays' policy in the mid-1970s, which has generated thousands of new product concepts and cost-saving ideas. The programme aims to reduce pollution at source, and encourage innovation through a number of strategies:

- Product reformulation: using less polluting raw materials
- Process modification: changing from batch to continuous process to prevent the pollution control system becoming overloaded
- Equipment redesign: modifying equipment to make use of 'by-products' from another process
- Resource recovery: recycling waste products for use internally or externally

In the short term, greening may enhance corporate image and develop consumer recognition. But if the company approaches greening in a cosmetic manner, and if facts are inaccurate or inconsistent, then a number of problems may be encountered. In the medium and longer term, the generation of an honest sense of confidence will earn a competitive advantage if a consistently responsible approach has been taken.

If a company's greener stance is not professionally planned and coordinated then there may be longer-term problems in:

- Selling the product
- Keeping within the law
- Recruiting and retaining able staff
- Disposing of waste
- Share price
- Obtaining insurance
- Corporate image
- Market share
- Attracting finance
- Stakeholder relations

Greener Products: The Five Rs

To achieve objectives, existing products may need to be 'greened', or greener products developed. Greener Marketing strategies will need to incorporate recycling, re-use, reconditioning, repair and possibly re-manufacture. Repair, reconditioning and re-use are strategies to extend a greener product's life. Recycling and re-manufacture make more efficient use of waste resources, which would otherwise be discarded.

Repair

The life of a product can be extended by repairing one or more parts. Repair may represent anything from a short-term to long-term life extension for the product.

Reconditioning

Reconditioning is an option when a product is about to fail due to a number of contributory factors. It involves a complete overhaul of the product to replace worn parts. Reconditioning is a medium-term to long-term life extension for the product.

Re-use

Many products can be re-used, for instance, milk bottles. It may also be possible to design and build products which are capable of being used more than once, such as stronger plastic bags, although the full environmental costs should be considered.

Recycling

Recycling is the process of collecting and sorting used materials which are then re-processed and turned back into useable raw materials.

Greener Products: The 5 Rs

5 Rs \ WASTE	PRE-CONSUMER	POST-CONSUMER
REPAIR	✗	✔
RECONDITIONING	✗	✔
RE-USE	✗	✔
RECYCLING	✔	✔
RE-MANUFACTURE	✗	✔

Figure 4

Many materials are already being recycled, such as paper, glass and some metals. One of the problems faced by companies who try to ensure that their products are recyclable is that the recycling facilities are often poorly developed. One strategy may be for companies to sponsor recycling collection schemes.

Re-manufacture

Re-manufacture is the process of producing new products from used ones. The product is reworked so as to mend and replace the worn parts. Often a certain amount of virgin material is used to restore the product to its original form and performance criteria. An example of a company involved in this process is Onyx Associates, who re-manufacture used laser printer cartridges. A fuller account of Onyx is given in Part III, under Greener Products, page 337.

Opportunities

Greener Marketing is a proactive and creative approach to business, which aims to develop opportunities and minimise threats. Companies should be embarking on 'opportunity searches' in the environmental marketplace (see Fig. 5), and areas for consideration should include:

- Does the product or service fulfil a real customer need? Is it really greener? What specific items have been altered to ensure that the product is greener?

- What steps have been taken to ensure that the product lessens real environmental problems?

- What price or quality 'trade-offs' are consumers willing to accept for 'friendlier' products?

- Is the product likely to be still acceptable within the next three to five years? Or will it need to be adapted because of changes in legislation and consumer attitudes?

- Has thorough primary research been completed? Are marketing and Environmental Information Systems (EIS) established? And are they integrated into an overall Management Information System (MIS)?

- Are management and employees aware of the issues? Do they know how to develop greener ideas?

Opportunities will arise in a variety of areas, and appropriate strategies will need to be developed to capitalise on the emergence of new

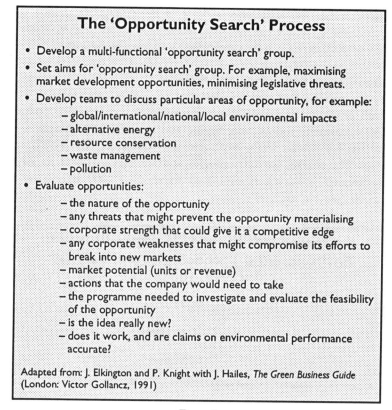

The 'Opportunity Search' Process

- Develop a multi-functional 'opportunity search' group.
- Set aims for 'opportunity search' group. For example, maximising market development opportunities, minimising legislative threats.
- Develop teams to discuss particular areas of opportunity, for example:
    - global/international/national/local environmental impacts
    - alternative energy
    - resource conservation
    - waste management
    - pollution
- Evaluate opportunities:
    - the nature of the opportunity
    - any threats that might prevent the opportunity materialising
    - corporate strength that could give it a competitive edge
    - any corporate weaknesses that might compromise its efforts to break into new markets
    - market potential (units or revenue)
    - actions that the company would need to take
    - the programme needed to investigate and evaluate the feasibility of the opportunity
    - is the idea really new?
    - does it work, and are claims on environmental performance accurate?

Adapted from: J. Elkington and P. Knight with J. Hailes, *The Green Business Guide* (London: Victor Gollancz, 1991)

Figure 5

scientific evidence, increased concern, pressure group activity and competitive inertia.

In the short, medium and longer term, considerable greener opportunities will arise in:

- Biotechnology
- Waste
- Information technology
- Environmental monitoring and control
- Clean technologies
- Water
- Organic farming
- Solar technology
- Tourism

Opportunities will arise worldwide from the emergence of new markets and the greening of existing markets. The emergent product/ market opportunities can be categorised into two broad areas.

Environmental Technology and Services
These are products or services designed to enable companies to comply with environmental regulations: consultancy; publications; pollution control equipment; monitoring; testing and analysis; water filtration and treatment; hazardous waste treatment and transport; and solid waste disposal. The market for technologies and services involved in solving environmental problems is estimated to reach £2,000 billion by the year 2000 (see Fig. 6).

Estimated UK, EC and US Expenditure on Environmental Technologies and Services (1991–2000)

UK	£140 billion
EC	£860 billion
US	£1060 billion

Source: The Centre for the Exploitation of Science And Technology, 1991

Figure 6

Greener Consumer Goods
These products incorporate ecological considerations into consumer purchases, although it is difficult to measure the exact contribution to overall product appeal; the greener consumer goods market in the US was estimated to be US$1.8 billion in 1990, and is predicted to grow to US$8.8 billion in 1995.[6]

Research and Information

The organisation should start to monitor proactively the environmental agenda for potential opportunities and threats. Greener markets will need to be properly researched and tested as issues are likely to be complex and dynamic. Research should identify the key issues as they affect the firm and provide accurate information, given the existing state of scientific knowledge.

Greener Marketing depends on reliable information on the environmental impact of both the company and its competitors. It implies that a regular flow of information is produced to support decision-making, including periodic studies such as Life Cycle Analysis (LCA) on new and existing products, Environmental Audits (EA) on existing facilities, and Environmental Impact Assessments (EIA) on new developments.

As consumers and companies increasingly buy companies' approaches as well as products, there will be greater need to have a clear picture of corporate environmental performance. This will stimulate the need for structured Environmental Information Systems (EIS) that enable managers to make informed decisions and to generate effective responses to Stakeholder information needs. Companies should develop efficient information systems that enable them to plan, monitor and evaluate performance against a set of quantified corporate, marketing and environmental objectives. The EIS will need to interface directly with the Marketing Information Systems (MKIS) and other information systems, and integrate into an overall Management Information System (MIS) (see Figs. 7 and 8).

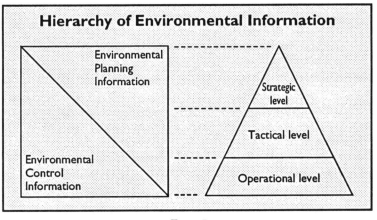

Figure 7

The proactive company will have completed an audit of Stakeholders' environmental interests and concerns, and will use a variety of information sources in planning and control. The system should be designed to support strategic, tactical and operational decision-making needs, and it is essential that decision makers have access to a central database of environmental data, and also are aware of key managers' environmental knowledge and expertise (see Fig. 9).

Environmental Planning and Control Information Characteristics

	Environmental Planning Information	Environmental Control Information
COVERAGE	Not segregated by function or department. Transcends organisational divisions.	Follows organisation divisions. Related to specific functions, department and managers.
TIMESCALE	Covers relatively long time periods and seeks to show trends.	Covers short time periods, shifts, days, weeks and months.
AMOUNT OF DETAIL	Patterns and trends more important than fine detail, particularly for long-range planning.	Detail and precision important, but trends also of importance.
ORIENTATION	Objective is to provide insights into the future.	Shows past results and activities and relates these to targets, standards and budgets.

Adapted from: T. Lucey, *Management Information Systems* (Winchester: D.P. Publications, 1976)

Figure 8

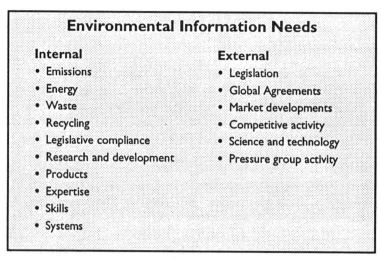

Environmental Information Needs

Internal
- Emissions
- Energy
- Waste
- Recycling
- Legislative compliance
- Research and development
- Products
- Expertise
- Skills
- Systems

External
- Legislation
- Global Agreements
- Market developments
- Competitive activity
- Science and technology
- Pressure group activity

Figure 9

Companies should also establish internal sub-systems within an EIS which provide a regular flow of data and reports on areas such as waste and energy. Leyland Daf, the truck manufacturers, examined their energy costs and produced a breakdown of costs by area. This analysis has enabled the company to identify potential emission reductions and energy savings of over £27,000 in the hot press process alone. To enable energy efficiency measures to be implemented effectively, an employee awareness and training programme has been developed that will be launched through a series of videos.[7]

External scanning systems should also be developed that cover areas such as market developments, competitive activity and law. Due to the volume and extent of UK and European environmental legislation, companies will need to become more legally literate and knowledgeable. Proactive analysis may indicate new business opportunities, and allow time for companies to lobby and/or invest in new technology and processes, rather than being caught out by the speed of developments (see Fig. 10).

Sources of External Environmental Intelligence

- National newspapers
- Environmental and professional journals
- Conferences and seminars
- Abstracting services
- On-line databases
- 'Business and environment' organisations
- Trade associations
- Local communities
- Conservation and environment groups
- Consultants
- Customers
- Suppliers
- Internal 'green champions'

Figure 10

Proactive crisis management systems should also be developed to enable companies to respond quickly and effectively to media, customer and employee concern over environmental incidents. If there are problems, companies will need to communicate environmental information rapidly to separate Stakeholder groups, and will often need to explain complex issues in a simple and concise manner, without past or present performance looking bad.

The Greener Marketing Planning Process

Companies will need to generate clearer pictures of the future to avoid the strategic myopia associated with business mission statements that are defined narrowly in product terms, i.e. we are in the business of providing information and solutions rather than in the business of manufacturing computers.

Figure 11 speculates on the possible paths that environmental awareness and concern may take in the future.

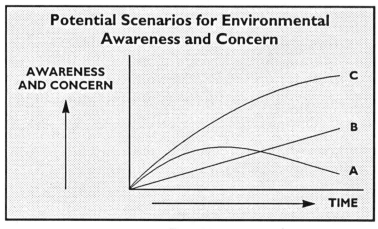

Figure 11

Scenario A suggests that recent trends are merely a short-term fad and that technology and the global system will take care of any perceived environmental problems as a matter of course. In this situation, applying Greener Marketing principles is not essential to long-term success. However, companies that do apply the Greener Marketing approach are unlikely to lose out as raised efficiency will cut costs, increased employee motivation will raise productivity, and improved environmental performance will enhance corporate image and improve Stakeholder relations.

Scenario B suggests a continued and gradual growth in awareness and concern. In this case, greening will be a long-term process and companies may be able to adapt their approach gradually with that change. Greener Marketing will evolve in the long term, but may not be essential in the short term. However, companies that adopt Greener

Marketing principles will place themselves ahead of market change and will thereby achieve competitive advantage.

Scenario C speculates that environmental problems, impending legislation and changing market standards will lead to an acceleration in environmental awareness and concern, and will therefore lead to rapid change in market conditions. In this situation, it is likely that only those companies that adopt a proactive and flexible attitude consistent with Greener Marketing principles will survive the rapid change with any degree of success. Those companies with a poor environmental performance will become more visible, and will face increasing costs and quickly lose Stakeholder loyalty. Companies with a clear record but without a positive response to greener demands may also struggle and eventually be forced out of the market by consumer, legislative or competitive pressures.

A simple summary of potential outcomes dependent upon the awareness and concern scenarios is shown in Figure 12.

Summary of Potential Greener Scenarios

GREENER MARKETING SCENARIOS	WITHOUT	WITH
A	No change	No change
B	Gradually forced to adopt greener strategy—may lose market share	Possible market gains available—strong future likely
C	Loss of market share likely and long-term survival unlikely	Secure market share—secure future likely

Figure 12

The fundamental assumption is that understanding environmental issues will become increasingly important for corporate success into the year 2000. The difficulty will be to assess the extent and speed of change.

Shell UK use scenario planning techniques to project long-term corporate strategy. Two scenarios have been used to guide the planning process:

- Scenario 1   Progressive increase in environmental awareness
- Scenario 2   Sustainable world

In the early stages of the greener nineties, much of the corporate response has been focused on short-term opportunism, rather than on a longer-term strategic approach based on a 'Sustainable world' scenario. A strategic framework has been developed by The Prospect Centre[8] that examines corporate responses to the demand for greater environmental responsibility. At present, companies are displaying a rather piecemeal and uncoordinated approach, with different stages of development within separate aspects of their corporate, business and product mixes.

The model identifies four types of organisational response. The first two types are concerned with short-term profitability and survival, and the second two are concerned with business prospering in the long term.

1. Minimising costs. The emphasis is on minimising costs of existing products in existing markets to improve short-term margins. The emphasis is on efficiency of internal operations.

2. Optimising short-term profits. Companies at this stage ensure survival by meeting customer demands while investing for short-term payback.

3. Innovation in products and marketing strategies. This approach focuses on the development of potential for the company's future profitability; effort is directed at innovation in both product and marketing strategies.

4. Positioning for the unknown. The few companies at this level look to position themselves to take advantage of the opportunities arising from discontinuities.

The majority of UK companies appear to be operating at level two, i.e. optimising short-term profits, which illustrates prevailing short-termist views, and shows that environmental awareness in business is still in its infancy. The first phase of greening has seen companies looking to satisfy greener consumers through minor product reformulation, product re-labelling and aggressive promotion of claimed product benefits, rather than through a deeper strategic response through organisational change.

The initial responses to greening can be further classified into five broad groups:

- **The greenness of a product's contents.** Companies are striving to 'de-toxify' the contents of their products for reasons of consumer and employee health and to minimise the impact of disposal.
- **The greenness of the product in its use.** Products are being formulated that reduce environmental impact. Major oil companies have developed friendlier products, such as natural gas and biofuels.
- **The recyclability of the product.** Differentiation will depend on the mix of materials and the availability of facilities for recycling.
- **The degradability of the product.** Many products are being issued with claims of bio- or photodegrability. Claims must be based on realistic assessments.
- **The greenness of the manufacturing process.** Du Pont are striving for zero emissions in the manufacture of paint; marketing acts as a channel of communications between customers and the production function, relaying the market's sensitivity to clean production.[9]

Ken Peattie of the University of Wales[10] suggests that business has developed eight different responses to Greener Marketing opportunities, with the majority falling into the short-termist category (see Fig. 13).

The Development of Greener Marketing Strategies

The corporate strategy and environmental policy will define the role of Greener Marketing. The Greener Marketeer will then become the strategic organiser of the firm's activities from cradle to grave, rather than viewing his or her primary role as that of communications. The wider perspective will mean that Greener Marketing will act as a channel between the firm and the market, and the organisation should undertake auditing and research, communicate company values and product information to Stakeholders, and feed back intelligence to decision makers.

Greener Marketing strategies are the means by which, ultimately, corporate objectives are achieved, and should relate directly to the corporate planning process, and specifically to environmental policy formulation and implementation. Companies can initially treat Greener Marketing as a separate exercise, but over time it should be integrated

Greener Marketing Strategies

Head in the Sand. The Quality Director of Addis was quoted as saying that the heavy metal cadmium is 'safe' and that 'There is no legal requirement to change yet, so I don't see why I should'. Heinz made major donations to the World Wide Fund for Nature, and sponsored Green Consumer Week, but were forced to withdraw from the event to minimise bad publicity over their subsidiary Starkist, a company involved in the destruction of dolphins through the use of drift nets for tuna fishing.

Defensive. The British Aerosol Manufacturers Association, ISC Chemicals and ICI complained to the Advertising Standards Authority over FoE's campaign on CFCs, stating that 'the conditions of the ozone layer over the Antarctic . . . were unrelated to the use of CFCs in aerosols'. Defensive strategies also came following the publication of *The Green Consumer Guide* and *The Good Wood Guide*. Companies that were criticised tended to respond by disputing or attempting to disprove the evidence in the guides. However, some retailers took a more proactive response and switched timber sourcing to managed plantations, sponsored tropical reforestation research and donated to Britain's Woodland Trust.

Lip Service. The Soap and Detergent Industry Association admitted that 'Many misleading claims are being made about the environmentally friendly nature of various Green products in order to attract the buying power of the Green Consumer . . . We are concerned that goodwill will be frittered away chasing illusory benefits claimed for some Green detergents.' This followed the rash of confusing and meaningless claims made about 'phosphate-free' washing up liquids (since none contain phosphates anyway), and the 'biodegradability' of some detergents. Another approach has been to donate to charitable causes connected with the environment while leaving products unchanged, or only slightly environmentally friendlier. This can backfire if the attention of green pressure groups is attracted.

Knee-jerk. Some companies have reacted to environmental pressures with actions rather than words, but with actions which are unplanned and aimed at defusing a particular potential environmental problem. Habitat reacted almost immediately to Green Consumer Week by announcing that they were abandoning the use of tropical hardwoods in their furniture, to the surprise of many managers.

Piecemeal. Shell has launched some very positive environmental initiatives, such as the 'Better Britain Campaign', but it continues to manufacture some of the world's most destructive chemicals.

Green-selling. A number of companies have altered their products and switched their sales pitch to highlight the new or existing environmental benefits of their products. Aerosol companies have developed a range of propellants to replace hard CFCs, and added labels such as 'ozone friendly', 'ozone friendlier', or 'ozone safe'. What many consumers do not realise is that a label saying 'ozone friendlier' tends to mean the can contains 'soft' CFCs which still damage the ozone layer, but more slowly and to a lesser extent.

Integrated Greener Marketing. In green-selling, the emphasis is about communicating the benefits of products. The degree of benefit offered to consumers, and the extent to which it matches their needs is not really considered. Developing Integrated Greener Marketing will mean looking at matching the environmental performance of products and production processes with a view to the current and future environmental concerns of consumers and other Stakeholders. This should lead to a more proactive corporate response, with a consideration of environmental issues being built into each aspect of strategic market planning.

Integrated Organisational. The desire to respond to the needs of green consumers and tougher environmental legislation will spread to all parts of the greener business. Corporate strategy, investment decisions, purchasing decisions and corporate policies should all be developed with environmental concerns in mind. There are reasonably few examples of organisations which have gone green beyond tactical marketing, but the two best examples are probably 3M and The Body Shop.

Source: K.J. Peattie, 'Painting Market Education', *Journal of Marketing Management* 6, No. 2 (1990)

Figure 13

into the corporate approach. All of the elements of the Greener Marketing mix will need to be considered when implementing the Greener Marketing strategy, but the emphasis will change, depending on the company culture and its particular circumstances.

Corporate Objectives

Greener Marketing should reflect the corporate response to the environmental agenda. It is essential that green issues are incorporated in the corporate mission statement, with corporate objectives covering environmental performance. As mentioned previously, Du Pont has pledged to remove CFCs from all operations by 2000, and this will have major implications for the company, its products and processes.

The planning process (see Figs. 14 and 16) should be based on thorough research and information, and is likely to require a multifunctional approach. The precursor should be a corporate environmental statement that is endorsed by the Chief Executive and Board of Directors. The most progressive companies are deepening their commitment through the signing of international accords such as the Business Charter for Sustainable Development and the Valdez Principles.

A number of steps should be taken before and while embarking on the Greener Marketing planning process:

- Incorporate environmental considerations into the corporate mission statement
- Develop and publish an environmental statement
- Undertake an initial environmental review of operations and products
- Undertake an Environmental Audit
- Develop and publish an environmental policy
- Prepare an action programme
- Organisation and staffing
- Allocate adequate resources
- Invest in environmental science and technology
- Monitor, audit and report
- Monitor the evolution of the green agenda
- Contribute to environmental programmes
- Build bridges between interested parties[11]

The Greener Marketing Planning Process

1. Corporate objectives
2. Greener Marketing Audit
3. Greener SWOT analysis
4. Assumptions
5. Greener marketing objectives and strategies
6. Estimate expected results
7. Identify alternative plans and mixes
8. Programmes
9. Measurement and review

Adapted from: M. MacDonald, *Marketing Plans* (London: William Heinemann, 1985)

Figure 14

Greener Marketing Audit

Once environmental commitment has been made, a Greener Marketing Audit should be undertaken. The audit should investigate the environmental implications of both internal and external factors (see Fig. 16).

Greener SWOT Analysis

The information from the Greener Marketing Audit should be analysed and key issues determined. The company's internal environmental

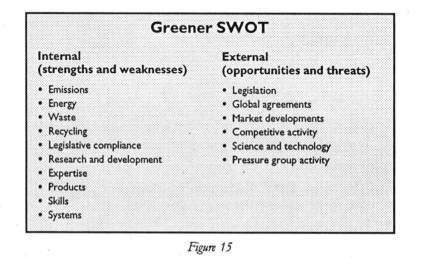

Figure 15

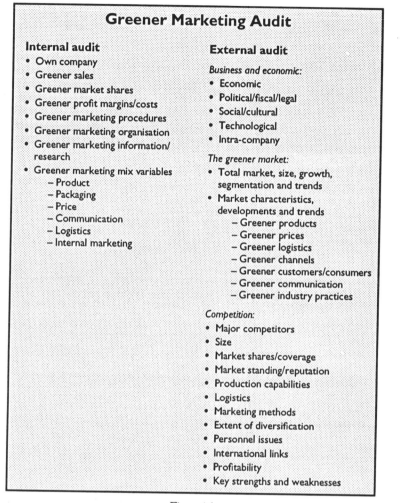

Greener Marketing Audit

Internal audit
- Own company
- Greener sales
- Greener market shares
- Greener profit margins/costs
- Greener marketing procedures
- Greener marketing organisation
- Greener marketing information/research
- Greener marketing mix variables
  - Product
  - Packaging
  - Price
  - Communication
  - Logistics
  - Internal marketing

External audit

Business and economic:
- Economic
- Political/fiscal/legal
- Social/cultural
- Technological
- Intra-company

The greener market:
- Total market, size, growth, segmentation and trends
- Market characteristics, developments and trends
  - Greener products
  - Greener prices
  - Greener logistics
  - Greener channels
  - Greener customers/consumers
  - Greener communication
  - Greener industry practices

Competition:
- Major competitors
- Size
- Market shares/coverage
- Market standing/reputation
- Production capabilities
- Logistics
- Marketing methods
- Extent of diversification
- Personnel issues
- International links
- Profitability
- Key strengths and weaknesses

Figure 16

strengths and weaknesses should be determined, to define clearly the firm's strategic capability. External opportunities and threats should then be examined to direct future corporate activities. Greener SWOT analysis should be conducted by key managers and built into the strategic planning process (see Fig. 15).

Assumptions

Companies will need to identify the key issues that will, or are likely to, affect the company and its products and markets. Change is likely to be discontinuous and unpredictable, and environmental issues may be difficult to predict, and therefore assumptions may need to be made about key determinants of success.

Greener Marketing Objectives and Strategies

Greener Marketing objectives are what you want to achieve; ideally they should be quantified and sustainable. Greener Marketing strategies are how you plan to achieve your objectives. The objectives can be broken down into four main categories (see Fig. 17):

1. Existing greener products in existing greener markets
2. New greener products in existing greener markets
3. Existing greener products in new greener markets
4. New greener products in new greener markets

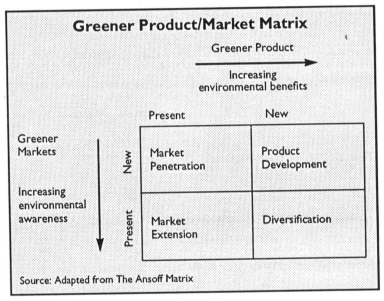

Figure 17

A number of strategies can be adopted to achieve the above objectives. Greener Marketing strategies are the means by which greener marketing objectives will be achieved and are concerned with six Ps, as follows:

The Six Ps	
Product	The general policies for product modification
Packaging	The general policies on suitability of packaging
Place	The general policies for channels and logistics
Price	The general pricing policies to be followed for product groups in market segments
Promotion	The general policies for communications
People	The general policies covering employees and internal marketing

Figure 18

Programmes

The general Greener Marketing strategies should be developed into specific sub-objectives, detailed policies and action plans designating responsibilities, timescales and budgets. The particular approach will depend on the extent to which the organisation has been 'greened', and whether the company is organised functionally, or is product-based, market-based or geographically based.

However, the most aggressive environmental Greener Marketing opportunities will arise from the decision made by the firm to make environmental responsibility a priority equivalent to, or greater than, short-term profitability.

Georg Winter[12] describes a number of areas that companies should be examining in the Greener Marketing Mix (see Fig. 19).

Conclusion

Greener Marketing will mean taking a holistic perspective that integrates with other organisational functions. The emphasis will change from only satisfying customers or investors to a broader view of satisfying interdependent Stakeholder groups.

The Chief Executive will need to define 'the environment' and 'people' as key areas and develop a coordinated plan with clear objectives, strategies and programmes. Many environmental issues affecting business are complex, and will require the involvement of multidisciplinary skills ranging from environmental services to engineering and law. Because environmental law, along with science and technology, will act as important drivers for change, the company will need to

Points to Consider in the Greener Marketing Mix

1. Product policy
   - Manufacture or offer products which minimise consumption of raw materials and which can be recycled
   - Eco-label products to draw attention to their environmentally positive features
   - Ensure that the product is used in an acceptable manner by providing aftersales and advisory services

2. Packaging
   - Devise packaging made from environmentally acceptable materials (e.g. increase re-usability)
   - Reduce the amount of packaging used

3. Communications policy
   - Embrace the trend towards increasing Stakeholder concern and reinforce it with advertising and public relations activities
   - Enhance the image and reputation of the company for expertise in environmental matters by exposing selected groups to ecological arguments and publicity
   - Make sure that all claims are honest and true and can be substantiated
   - Allay public distrust of the business world in environmental matters through broadly based activities (e.g. through trade associations)

4. Logistics policy
   - Set up marketing channels by agreement between manufacturers and distributors in order to make systems possible ('retro-distribution' channels)
   - Establish recycling centres and provide advice at the point of of distribution in order to encourage a positive response from consumers
   - Give preference to transport systems which have reduced environmental costs in terms of energy consumption and pollution

5. Price and discount policy
   - If higher prices cannot be avoided as a result of ecologically sound manufacturing processes, make it clear to distributors and consumers how the costs are calculated (e.g. price differentials based on ecological factors)
   - Consider whether the additional costs of ecologically acceptable products can be spread by combined costing

6. Internal marketing policy
   - Ensure that all levels of management are sensitive to ecological issues
   - Enhance awareness by means of information and training
   - Foster an *esprit de corps* and pride in setting an example in environmental matters

7. Management and organisation
   - Check that all individual measures form part of an integrated package, making a definite impact in environmental terms, and adjust them as necessary
   - Check and adjust marketing organisation and control (i.e. create structures and systems appropriate to the strategy pursued)
   - Ensure that the company's organisation enables the strategies to be implemented
   - Adapt the company structure
   - Appoint a person to be responsible for all environmental questions at senior management level
   - Develop monitoring and incentive systems
   - Develop arrangements for environment control by means of additional instruments to check whether environmental objectives are being attained (monitoring systems)
   - Provide incentives for achieving or surpassing the environmental targets (e.g. bonus systems)

Adapted from: G. Winter, *Business and the Environment* (Hamburg: McGraw–Hill, 1988).

Figure 19

watch developments closely, either internally or through appropriate outside experts. The marketing and environmental departments should act as conduits through which internal and external information flows. There will also need to be a considerable commitment to training and development, as every employee is a reflection of the environmental policy, and hence a potential ambassador for the company.

Business should move progressively towards a policy of environmental excellence.[13]

- Single greener product
- Greener product range
- All greener products
- Greener manufacturing
- Greener corporate activity
- Greener corporate policy
- Greener investment

The Greener Marketing mix will place a greater emphasis on environmental responsibility from cradle to grave. It will also mean investment in internal marketing, and the broader aspects of Stakeholder communications, reflecting the values of the company in both products and services. Greater consciousness of environmental issues will lead companies to recognise Greener Marketing as being a strategic management process that defines products and markets in broader terms, with the objective of satisfying Stakeholder needs.

The next six chapters discuss some of the environmental issues associated with the elements of the Greener Marketing Mix (product, packaging, logistics, price, communications and people), and give some practical guides to action.

References

1. 'Green Labelling', *Which? Magazine*, January 1990.
2. Mintel, 'The Second Green Consumer Report' (May 1991).
3. 'Companies Confused over Green Policies', *Financieele Dagblad*, 12 December 1991.
4. Andrew Jack, 'Green Tinge to Company Books', *Financial Times*, 15 January 1992.
5. K.J. Peattie, 'Painting Marketing Education (or: How to Recycle Old Ideas)', *Journal of Marketing Management* 6, No. 2 (1990).
6. The Management Institute for Environment and Business, 'Marketing and Ecology: Readings and Discussion' (June 1991).

7. 'Leyland DAF: Making Environmental Protection Pay its Way' (ENDS Report 202, November 1991).
8. The Prospect Centre, 'New Capabilities for the Green Organisation' (1990).
9. The Management Institute for Environment and Business, 'Marketing and Ecology'.
10. Peattie, 'Painting Marketing Education'.
11. J. Elkington and P. Knight with J. Hailes, *The Green Business Guide* (London: Victor Gollancz, 1991).
12. G. Winter, *Business and the Environment* (Hamburg: McGraw–Hill, 1988).
13. C. Holman, 'The First Green Year Seminar', *Media Natura*, November 1989.

Chapter 6

GREENER PRODUCTS

Ian Blair

Environmental Affairs Manager, AEG (UK) Ltd

The Challenge

To begin with, we must attempt to define what we mean by a greener product. A truly green product does not exist. No consumer product contributes to environmental health. The best only cause less harm. Man's interaction with nature to produce 'consumables' has, in the face of galloping technology and ever-increasing demand, become exploitative. The task we must now set ourselves is to reduce the harm we inflict.

Progress in this sphere over the last twenty years has been significant, both in terms of enthusiasm and achievement. Much of what we have learned has come from our German counterparts who woke up to the ecological crisis before we did, and translated rhetoric into a coherent philosophy which has guided their manufacturing progress.

The Third Dimension

The products which emerge from this new philosophy have a third dimension. Manufacturers in all areas now realise that price and quality are not the only criteria by which to judge a product. Ecological concerns now play a part, most notably in the chemical industry, energy production, car industry, white goods manufacture, paper industries, detergents, cosmetics and, to a lesser extent, food.

A Question of Values

How do we compare the relative greenness of different products? Comparing a potato (was it organically grown?) with a lipstick (has it been tested on animals?) with a washing machine (how much water/ electricity/detergent does it use?) poses problems that are continuing to plague the efforts of those EC and UK committees set up to work out an effective and fair eco-labelling scheme.

The huge range of products that must be assessed constitute only one half of this arduous task. There are also problems over the great number of environmental issues and problems which need to be taken into account, some of which may conflict, and prioritising them is always going to be controversial. Informed judgement and defining a level playing field will be increasingly important.

There are committed environmentalists who support nuclear power because it does not contribute to the greenhouse effect, yet others find its waste problems and health risk too high a price to pay. Can we call nuclear power 'greener' than fossil fuels? This will depend on how we weight the different environmental issues. Do we consider the problems of global warming more environmentally dangerous than radiation risks? More importantly perhaps, are we prepared to put global issues above national or local issues? Similarly, if one takes a more holistic perspective, there is an argument in favour of aeroplanes carrying only plastic cutlery and crockery—for first class as well as economy—on the basis that the subsequent difference in weight of the aircraft allows for a substantial saving in fuel to be made. Yet plastic utensils can only be used once, and either further energy must be consumed in recycling the cutlery, or it can be thrown away, thus adding to the solid waste stream. What are the customers' and employees' reactions to the environmental options? Is it better to keep the china and glass or not?

Environmental conundrums such as these cannot, at the end of the day, be answered by existing product alternatives and/or substitutes. New thought must be brought to bear on the problem of generating new, greener design ideas. Becoming more energy efficient is the easiest, cheapest way to ease the energy crisis, a point which has been dramatically brought home by the recent claims that if every household in the UK fitted a low energy light bulb, we could save the output of a power station the size of Hinckley Point.

Aside from energy efficient products or product adaptations, designers could change the whole conception of the product. For example, fuel consumption of aircraft may be reduced if improved telecommunications lessen the need for business air travel, thus removing rather than solving the problem of in-flight meals. This sort of approach will characterise the search for greener product/service development. Companies will have to move away from product-focused marketing strategy towards wider business perspectives. This will involve looking at the core benefit derived from the product or service and then deciding whether and how this can be provided in a greener way. Volkswagen, for instance, have changed their defined business from manufacturing cars to transport. This important strategic move leaves them free to develop greener transport options such as rail, buses and alternative cars.

Greener Product Characteristics

The difficulties of defining greener concepts will plague any company which chooses such a route to new product development. They must be overcome, or a compromise must be reached. Progress towards a definition can be made by looking more closely at what characteristics make up a greener product (see Fig. 1).

First, companies must realise that a greener product cannot be judged by what comes off the end of the production line. At one time, performance was the key environmental criterion, e.g. how much water did a washing machine use? How much petrol did a car consume? How energy efficient was a central heating boiler?

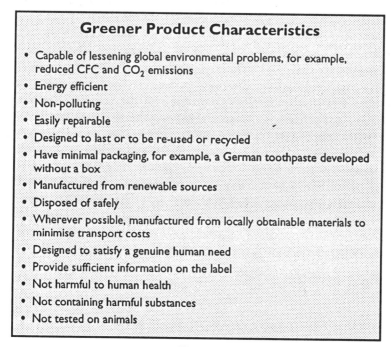

Greener Product Characteristics

- Capable of lessening global environmental problems, for example, reduced CFC and CO_2 emissions
- Energy efficient
- Non-polluting
- Easily repairable
- Designed to last or to be re-used or recycled
- Have minimal packaging, for example, a German toothpaste developed without a box
- Manufactured from renewable sources
- Disposed of safely
- Wherever possible, manufactured from locally obtainable materials to minimise transport costs
- Designed to satisfy a genuine human need
- Provide sufficient information on the label
- Not harmful to human health
- Not containing harmful substances
- Not tested on animals

Figure 1

Now performance is just one of the many elements that must be considered in the quest for ecologically sounder products. Today, environmental concerns affect every stage of a product's life cycle, from its inception right through to its final disposal.

Life Cycle Analysis

Analysing products' environmental impact from cradle to grave through techniques such as Life Cycle Analysis (LCA) will become increasingly important with the implementation of the European eco-labelling guidelines in the Autumn of 1992. When undertaking LCAs, it is important to take a holistic view, and below are a few examples of how environmental problems can accumulate in a typical manufacturing process (see also Fig. 2).

Two examples illustrate this perspective.

A water filter gives a short-term benefit to the consumer, but its manufacture makes people's water a little bit more polluted. The more polluted the water, the more people want to buy water filters, and the process continues.

Bread serves as another useful example. Wheat is taken by the fossil-fuel-driven truck made of non-renewable material to a large, centralised bakery housing numerous machines that inefficiently refine, enrich, bake and package bread. At the bakery, the wheat is refined and sometimes bleached. These processes produce white bread, but remove vital nutrients, so the flour is then enriched with niacin, iron, thiamine, and riboflavin. Next, to ensure that the bread will be able to withstand long truck journeys to stores where it will be kept on shelves for many days, or even weeks, preservative and dough conditioners are added. Then the bread is baked and placed in a cardboard box which has been printed in several colours. The box and the bread are placed within a plastic bag made of petrochemicals, which is then sealed with a plastic tie, also made from petrochemicals. The packs of bread are then loaded into a truck which takes them to a retailer. Then a car is driven to the store, and back, and then slices of bread are put into a toaster, and then spread with butter and marmalade and eventually eaten. Finally the consumer throws away the packaging which will then have to be disposed of as solid waste.[1]

Identifying a Genuine Need

A decision must be taken as to whether the proposed product responds to a genuine need. Non-essential items, however efficiently

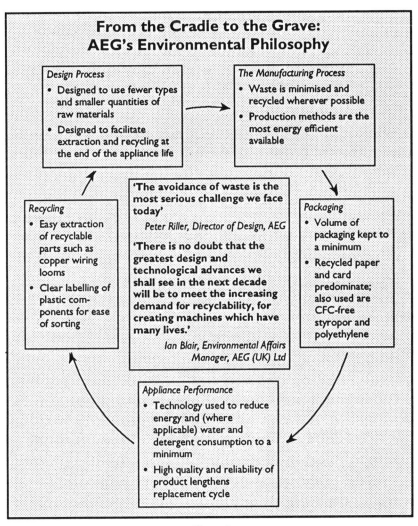

From the Cradle to the Grave: AEG's Environmental Philosophy

Design Process
- Designed to use fewer types and smaller quantities of raw materials
- Designed to facilitate extraction and recycling at the end of the appliance life

The Manufacturing Process
- Waste is minimised and recycled wherever possible
- Production methods are the most energy efficient available

Recycling
- Easy extraction of recyclable parts such as copper wiring looms
- Clear labelling of plastic components for ease of sorting

'The avoidance of waste is the most serious challenge we face today'

Peter Riller, Director of Design, AEG

'There is no doubt that the greatest design and technological advances we shall see in the next decade will be to meet the increasing demand for recyclability, for creating machines which have many lives.'

Ian Blair, Environmental Affairs Manager, AEG (UK) Ltd

Packaging
- Volume of packaging kept to a minimum
- Recycled paper and card predominate; also used are CFC-free styropor and polyethylene

Appliance Performance
- Technology used to reduce energy and (where applicable) water and detergent consumption to a minimum
- High quality and reliability of product lengthens replacement cycle

Figure 2

and sensitively they are manufactured, cannot be truly called 'green' because their production will cause avoidable impact on the environment.

But once again, we have a problem of definition. Many people cannot distinguish between need and want, as wants so often become needs. Isolating what people need becomes almost impossible. For instance a cocktail stick umbrella may be an unnecessary item to most people, but others might consider it an essential ingredient of a good cocktail. Who is right and what should the company make of the value judgement involved? First you must define what the need is for: Is it to live comfortably? Is it to live in aesthetically pleasing surroundings? Is it to live in a fairer world? There are many possible objectives.

What may well be considered essential for some is a luxury for others, and an increasing global awareness brings this home very clearly: when faced with television screens of starving children in the developing world, it is difficult to define anything other than food, fresh water and medical supplies as essential. However, we clearly consider many more products and services than those to be essential in our everyday lives.

A necessary product could be defined as something which society has come to rely on, and the sudden absence of which would pose problems to the majority of our buying public. This however, poses problems for future technological developments and products. It also avoids the issue of whether those products we rely on are in fact essential.

The car is the most obvious example of this. There is no such thing as a green car, because the car is a non-essential item in the basic need sense. To cease production overnight however, would be unthinkable in our modern world because many people have come to depend upon the car. There are also arguments that the car provides a useful social service in the case of doctors responding to emergencies, or for people who live in remote areas.

Efforts to reduce the impact of a car's performance and manu-facture must be applauded and encouraged, although in the longer run society may decide to try and phase out the excessive use of cars by placing increased emphasis on shared methods of transport, such as trains, or transport which does not have such a high impact on the environment, such as bicycles. The lower risk option for manufacturers is to adapt the existing products by adding or subtracting environmen-tal aspects. An analysis of why people use or need cars may also be useful in providing alternative solutions to the environmental problems caused by cars. For instance, if people use cars to travel to work, then teleworking from home may provide an answer. If people use the car for shopping then maybe teleshopping could be encouraged, or local shops or group shopping.

The washing machine poses similar problems. Purists would argue that it is an unnecessary product. However, it is essential for people to wash clothes and fabrics for hygiene reasons. The modern washing machine can wash clothes far more efficiently than is possible by hand, using less water and less energy. However, using Life Cycle Analysis (LCA), the washing machine may not be greener than washing by hand.

Design for the Future

Once the decision has been taken to go ahead with the manufacture of a product on the grounds of necessity, the designer must set about making it as environmentally benign as possible. It is at this stage that almost everything else is determined: efficiency, effectiveness, reliability, lifespan and recyclability (see Fig. 3).

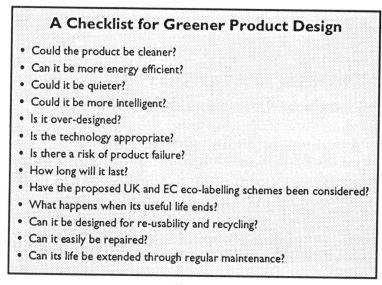

A Checklist for Greener Product Design

- Could the product be cleaner?
- Can it be more energy efficient?
- Could it be quieter?
- Could it be more intelligent?
- Is it over-designed?
- Is the technology appropriate?
- Is there a risk of product failure?
- How long will it last?
- Have the proposed UK and EC eco-labelling schemes been considered?
- What happens when its useful life ends?
- Can it be designed for re-usability and recycling?
- Can it easily be repaired?
- Can its life be extended through regular maintenance?

Figure 3

At the beginning of the design process will come the choice of raw materials. For the greener product, these must be chosen from recycled sources or renewable resources and obtained by low impact methods of extraction. Wherever possible, materials should be locally obtainable, reducing environmental damage caused by long-distance transport.

The number of different types of raw materials and the amount of each used should be reduced as far as possible. Advances in technology make this increasingly possible. The washing machine provides an example of how this has been achieved.

There is a trend in the market toward washing machines with higher spin speeds to improve performance. Higher spin speeds, however, cause more vibration and stress which in turn necessitate the use of more raw materials (concrete, steel, iron) to stabilise the machine. AEG now use a different solution, employing electronics to control the spin phasing and the distribution of the wash load. Vibration is thus greatly reduced. This system has been so effective that it has been possible to reduce the raw material mass of the washing machine by nearly 20%.

The raw material consideration of other products can be very different. For cosmetic and pharmaceutical products, for example, considerations of human safety and animal testing must also come into play. Has a raw material ingredient been tested on animals already, or is it, for instance, possible to use modern computer models or humans to test the safety of the raw material? Interestingly, cosmetics manufacturers are now starting to react to the call for products which have at no stage been tested on animals, largely because of the commercial success of companies which have already chosen this route. The commercial viability of such products is an example of how consumers can show their concern through buying power rather than 'banner power'.

In the future, we may well see pharmaceutical companies pooling animal testing results with competitors. We are likely to see an extension of already existing computer simulation models and tissue techniques in another attempt to reduce the level of animal experiments. These changes, however, are likely to be more a result of legislation and pressure group activity than of direct consumer pressure, as the consumer does not have ultimate buying power in the UK pharmaceutical market—the NHS does.

In the car industry we are already seeing a movement towards recyclability and use of alternative fuels. Thus, different raw materials will be needed if recyclability is to be guaranteed. This will even affect the way the car is made, as it will have to be designed with dismantling in mind. For example, the electronics will have to be easily removable, as will all copper and plastic components. The use of alterative fuels may require a new design for engine size and specification.

Manufacture

Keeping the manufacturing process as efficient and clean as possible must be the aim of the manufacturer of the greener product. Undertaking a thorough Environmental Audit will be a part of achieving this, as will the implementation of employee awareness and training programmes. For those manufacturers who buy in components, a thorough vetting of suppliers' environmental practice must become as standard as quality assessment. It is only in this way that environmental claims or aims of the finished product can be guaranteed.

Many large companies, such as IBM, British Gas, British Telecom, Gateway and B&Q, are already conducting supplier audits. More details are given in the relevant sections in Part III. Firms have started to send extensive questionnaires to their suppliers and some have set standard criteria which all suppliers must meet before being accepted.

Clean Up Your Act

As legislation on pollution is tightened, manufacturers will be forced to introduce new waste processing measures, and possibly even to redesign the manufacturing process to eliminate waste. The 'Duty of Care' proposals in the Environmental Protection Act 1990 ensure that a producer will be responsible for waste even when it has passed into the hands of a waste contractor.

Often it is the workforce who are best placed to suggest modifications which can make the manufacturing process both more efficient and less polluting. It has been noted by companies who have chosen the greener route to product development that one of the side-effects of such a managerial decision has been an increased sense of involvement and responsibility from workers at all levels of the production process. It is also true that those companies who already value their workforce and who treat them well will be best equipped—and most likely—to make the switch to cleaner, greener manufacturing. A participatory approach to management will encourage the generation of new ideas for both products and processes.

Industrial Revolution Mark II

Technology also has a major part to play in the greening of the manufacture of a product. New techniques are being produced all the time which can reduce energy consumption and pollution. Many may pose the 'priority problems' discussed earlier in relation to the product, and a standardised order of merit would have to be developed along the lines of eco-labelling. The BATNEEC principle (Best Available Technology Not Entailing Excessive Cost) may be one way of doing this, but industry still needs a clear guide as to how to judge BATNEEC.

An example of how new technology can ease pollution problems can be found in car and white goods manufacture, where new techniques are now being implemented to reduce pollution by solvents used in the painting process. Paint shops are increasingly being replaced by 'powder lacquering plants' where the parts which were previously painted are now electrostatically charged so that when powder is sprayed onto them, it firmly adheres. They are then fed through a station where the powder is melted at a high temperature, and burnt onto the parts. Any surplus powder falling away from the part can be vacuumed out and fed back to the initial powder container for re-use. This environmentally benign process eliminates emissions containing solvents and reduces lacquer remnants, which are expensive and difficult to dispose of, as they are classified as 'special waste'.

Performance

For the consumer, the performance phase of a product may be the time they judge the manufacturer's environmental claims. For some products, the impact of the performance phase is minimal, while for others, it constitutes the most damaging period. For instance, cosmetics produce very little environmental damage during their use, relative to their manufacture. However, cars and washing machines will use several times the amount of energy in their working lives that they use at any other time in the rest of their product life cycles.

To take the latter group of products first, it therefore becomes clear that the most important way of designing the product to be greener, must be to make it efficient and non-polluting during its use.

The greenest of washing machines will use the absolute minimum of water, electricity and detergent needed to produce the required results. The proposed EC guidelines on the environmental standards of washing machines require machines not to exceed the following criteria on the average wash:

0.43 kWh/kg	energy consumption
16.81 l/kg	water consumption
1%	mean detergent loss

A study by The Council for the Protection of Rural England in November 1991[2] indicated that only 35% of washing machines surveyed would actually pass these water and energy guidelines. Of those machines tested which were marketed as 'environmentally friendlier', only 56% would pass. As part of the extended product of a washing machine, detergent manufacturers themselves are increasingly modifying products so that less needs to be used, reducing pollution, packaging and waste.

Another appliance example is that of refrigerators, which are turned on 365 days a year, twenty-four hours a day and must run as efficiently as possible to reduce the need for electricity generation. The main environmental problem usually associated with fridges—that of CFCs and the depletion of the ozone layer—does not arise until the time comes for their disposal (and also occasionally during servicing). Alas, there is no totally satisfactory method of disposal currently available, but temporary solutions have been found. The search continues for safe and effective replacements for CFCs before the internationally agreed conditions on their use come into effect in 1998.

A different solution was found to the problem of CFCs in aerosols. Unlike refrigerators, aerosols release CFCs every time they are used. The greener alternatives that have been developed over a relatively short time period—a few years—can be divided into two categories; those products which have been repackaged using different technology so that propellants are no longer needed—such as roll-on deodorants, solid air fresheners and pump-action furniture polish—and those products which use the same spray technology, but where a less harmful gas has been found to replace the CFCs in aerosol cans—with hairsprays for example.

Reliability

Ensuring that a product is reliable has long been a concern of the manufacturer of quality products—not only to satisfy the customer, but to reduce the expense of after-care service. But the cost of raw materials, manufacture, packaging and distribution of new parts or replacement products must also be measured in environmental terms by the greener manufacturer. It is a cost which could probably be avoided.

Similarly, maximising the lifespan of a product must be a priority when considering greener performance. Built-in obsolescence has no part in the design of a greener product, and is becoming increasingly unfashionable. The emergence onto the market of energy-saving light bulbs does not result from a technical revolution: the know-how has existed for years. It has been suppressed by light bulb manufacturers who are going to sell fewer light bulbs as a result, but who must now bend to the demands of a more environmentally conscious public.

However, the arrival of the green decade may see design for modularity and longevity. For instance, products may be designed which will not become obsolete. If the product is based on electronics—as some washing machines and automatic processors are—then the software on such products could be updated whenever new models are developed, therefore upgrading the product without replacing a single bolt. This may necessitate more detailed aftersales service and increased computer literacy among service engineers, with consequent implications for training. Similarly, clear instructions must appear on all packaging material explaining the ways in which it can be recycled or re-used.

Design for Re-use/Dismantling

The final set of problems which the greener product must attempt to solve is that of disposal. Can it be re-used? Can it be modified and become something else? Can it be recycled?

While recycling has become the buzz-word for disposal of greener products, it is worth remembering that it is often less ecologically damaging to design a product that can be re-used. Milk bottles, for example, are washed and refilled, as are an increasing number of cosmetic containers, such as certain ones from The Body Shop.

Secondary uses for the waste of the western world has been successfully exploited by organisations such as Intermediate Technology, and points to a way forward with manufacturers liaising with such organisations to find ways in which their products can be designed with a secondary use in mind. In fact, the Advisory Committee on Business and the Environment (ACBE), made up of representatives of Britain's top twenty-five companies, has drawn up proposals for just such a scheme entitled 'Waste Exchange'.

The less developed countries have long been a source of ideas for recycling and re-use of waste because of shortages of raw materials and goods. Examples are the re-manufacture of light bulbs into oil lamps, the domestic production of floor polish from old polythene bags melted with paraffin and the widespread use of empty metal cans as a source of sheet metal.

Recycling of refuse is the third possibility, and for many products which cannot be re-used this remains the most viable 'greener option', as it can be used to save money, generate revenue and develop community relations. But the economics of recycling will depend first on the investment needed to set up a recycling plan, and second on the resale value of the material.

The total environmental impact of recycling will not necessarily be positive—when transport effects and energy use are taken into consideration—until we have widely available recycling facilities and a strong resale value. While it is undoubtedly the responsibility of the manufacturer to ensure that the product has been designed to make recycling as simple and cost-effective as possible, there is still much confusion about who will actually perform the recycling operation. Potential legislation in Europe is looking at making the manufacturer responsible for the cost of recycling.

Since no coherent infrastructure for recycling exists in the UK, it is difficult to attribute the ultimate responsibility for dismantling and recycling the product. Companies must liaise with local councils, local pressure groups and schools. Schemes involving private and public sector organisations have been successfully launched in Sheffield, Milton Keynes and Cardiff, and show the way forward for companies who want to substantiate their claims for an integrated environmental approach. Companies can become involved in developing recycling facilities, and many retailers have started to provide collection points. Some manufacturers, such as BMW, have started to appoint regional dismantling and re-processing centres in an effort to improve the recycling potential of their products. BMW aim to have ten such centres by the end of 1994.

One thing is certain, however: products must be designed with easy dismantling in mind. Some dismantling processes are familiar through well-established maintenance procedures; others are unique to dismantling for recycling. By studying the best processes for dismantling, the product designer can include features which make the operations as quick and easy as possible. For cars, this will mean enabling the battery, alternator and any copper material to be removed to allow the metal casing to be shredded and recycled. For other products, it will mean clearly labelling and identifying the different substances in the product. One product that is currently dismantled in large numbers is the telephone. Old-style telephones contain precious metals, and about 3.6 million are dismantled each year, with 80% of each item being recycled.

Greener Customer Service

Should a company be offering customers greener service, or offering services to greener customers? In reality, the answer is both, and the key words for such a policy must be education, training and communications. Through encouraging and educating customers, the company is likely to stay in touch with changing attitudes. A policy of openness and honesty will pay dividends, both by reducing the chances of any adverse publicity resulting from the discovery of un-green skeletons in the cupboard, and by encouraging customer confidence.

Furthermore, the attributes of many greener-designed products will need to be explained to customers. For example, many people still use the same amount of washing powder in greener machines, even though they no longer need to. Ensuring that a product is used correctly is the responsibility of the manufacturer. Clear instructions will ensure that the product is not abused and its life expectancy unnecessarily shortened. Similarly, products which may be environmentally dangerous need to be accompanied by clear instructions. ICI have developed a stewardship policy for the use of pesticides, especially for less developed countries.[3] Without education and customer service, the environmental improvements or hazards will not be taken on board by customers.

As far as providing greener customer service goes, emphasis should be placed on quality, problem solving, reliability, aftersales service, speed of delivery and courtesy. Employees should be made aware of product-specific issues and of the wider environmental impacts. Reparability should be built in at the design stage, and repair data should be collected and analysed to enable products to be modified and improved continuously.

Support for the Greener Product

The availability of expert advice and support is crucial to the success of a greener product. Without it, companies may be doing more harm than good. In the UK, the Department of Trade and Industry (DTI) is responsible for assessing the impact of environmental standards on industry and consumers, acting as a information gatherer and disseminator.

There is a need for a database containing information on the environmental performance of different raw materials. Currently, designers have no means of obtaining reliable, adequate information on the materials which have the least environmental impact. Until this information is widely available, environmental directives will be difficult to implement and eco-labelling and Life Cycle Analysis (LCA) will be problematic.

Conclusion

Greener product development will centre on making more from less. Ideas of greenness coincide with ideas of efficiency, reliability, longevity, staff and customer care—the watchwords of companies committed to quality. For those companies, the development of a greener product strategy will be comparatively straightforward, as making progress on all these factors will help to improve the greenness of their products.

Design for longevity may lead to a change in the system of product ownership. With such long lifespans, it may become more beneficial to lease equipment. In this way, when older equipment becomes obsolete, the lessee can simply lease a more up-to-date model and the owner can lease the older model to someone else. This sort of scheme already works for some photocopier manufacturers and may help to prevent premature disposal of products.

However, in the long term, products will have to be holistically designed from cradle to grave in order for their full environmental impact to be lessened. This will mean deciding on the necessity of a product, choosing the greenest materials, the cleanest, most efficient production process, and designing for re-use and easy dismantling. For many products, it will also mean designing for increased efficiency in use, as this is often where the environmental impacts of products will be realised.

References

1. Adapted from J. Pearce, 'The Big "E" ', *Green News*, Winter 1991–92, who in turn adapted from Rifkin, 'Entropy: A Brave New World'.
2. Council for the Protection of Rural England, 'New Analysis of Washing Machine Water Efficiency Illustrates Profligate Use of Water' (press release, 19 November 1991).
3. J. Elkington and P. Knight with J. Hailes, *The Green Business Guide* (London: Victor Gollancz, 1991).

Chapter 7

GREENER PACKAGING

Anne Chick

Principal Consultant
The Anne Chick Green Design Consultancy

Introduction

Packaging is at the sharp end of environmentalism: it affects and involves everyone. It can be found in everyone's shopping bag, and it ends up in everyone's dustbins. Packaging has become a symbol of our affluent, throw-away society.

Europeans generate 100 million tonnes of household waste every year, while in the USA, 140–200 million tonnes of municipal solid waste is produced annually. American packaging waste takes up over 30% of the dwindling space in landfills. Experts predict that the US will throw out an estimated sixty-three million tonnes of packaging in 1995.[1] As well as increasing in volume, the character of packaging is also changing. Fuelled by the explosion in plastics technology, packaging is becoming more high-tech, more difficult to recycle, and more toxic.

Alongside this has been the rise of the green consumer, impending environmental legislation and the increase in green pressure groups, all of which have caused companies and retailers to re-assess their use of many staple materials and chemicals used in packaging, and the damaging effect they have on the environment.

Down With Packaging

Citizens' groups were the first to mobilise protest against a packaging system based on the infinite extraction and disposal of raw materials. In Germany, for example, it is very common for shoppers to tear off excess packaging in the supermarket and demand money back from their shopping bill. Most supermarkets now supply waste bins at the checkouts where the consumer can place excess packaging. This form of protest is gaining considerable momentum in many other parts of the world.

A recent US survey into consumers' attitudes towards the environment found that a company's reputation on environmental issues had a strong effect on attitudes towards its products. It found considerable support for the use of biodegradable or recyclable packaging, with 74% saying they were more likely to purchase a product packaged this way. Seventy-eight per cent of respondents indicated they would be willing to pay more for such a packaged product, while 84% said that there should be legislation requiring manufacturers to use recyclable or biodegradable packaging.

The Rise of Legislation

Many industrial nations share a common approach to rubbish; this approach is known as 'the waste management hierarchy'. This sets out a list of management options in order of priority:

1. Source reduction (avoiding waste in the first place)
2. Direct re-use of products
3. Recycling
4. Incineration (with recovery of energy)
5. Landfilling (as a last resort)

The UN Environment Programme endorses this hierarchy, as do citizen groups, many industry leaders, and government officials from Europe, North America and Japan,[2] although a number of pressure groups still have problems with incineration.

Unfortunately, practice has run directly counter to principle. Most governments continue to focus on managing rather than reducing waste. When faced with disposal crises, they tend to fund waste management options in inverse proportion to their position on the hierarchy, usually moving one notch up the ladder, from landfilling to incineration.

EC member states have reacted very differently to the environmental issues surrounding packaging. Some have been extremely complacent (e.g. UK), while others have really taken this issue to heart and developed hard-hitting legislation (e.g. Germany). The absence of an overall European policy and legislative guidance from Brussels is only now being addressed.

Germany is by far the most active of the member states and appears likely to become the model for future EC developments. The German Government, through its controversial Waste Packaging Ordinance, intends to make producers and retailers accept greater responsibility for product packaging, even to the extent of contributing to the process of collection and recycling. Retailers will also be obliged to offer a refill service and provide more facilities for recycling, and must accept all used packaging material returned by the customer.

The most important provisions of the Waste Packaging Ordinance require that:

- From 1 December 1991 producers and retailers must accept for recycling and disposal all returned transport packaging;
- From 1 April 1992 the consumer can leave all packaging material at the point of sale;
- From 1 January 1993 retailers must accept all used packaging material returned by the consumer. To encourage the consumer, a mandatory deposit of half a mark will be levied on all drinks, detergents and paint containers.

Other European Countries

The UK has a target to recycle 25% of household waste by the year 2000; while, since January 1990, Italian law has required separate collection of glass, metal and plastics drinks containers, and recycling targets have been set to be reached by the end of 1992 (50% for glass and metals, 40% for plastics, of which 50% might be used for energy production, such as incineration).

A joint agreement between The Netherlands Government and industry aims to reduce packaging weight and increase recycling to meet a target of 90% of recyclable packaging materials by the year 2000.

A French levy on packaged goods is proposed to reimburse municipal authorities for costs of sorting collected materials for recycling and/or investing in energy recovery facilities. A target of 75% is set for valorisation—refilling, material recycling and energy recovery.[3]

Packaging Waste and the European Community

Controlling the environment will be one of the four main objectives of EC politicians during the next five years. The EC Commission produced numerous discussion documents on packaging waste during

1991 and 1992. It is on the basis of these documents that a directive will be agreed.

The packaging waste policies of individual member states have run in many different directions and the Commission recognised the need to tackle packaging waste on an EC-wide basis. The need to act is so urgent that an initial directive may be brought out soon to reduce packaging and landfill disposal. The Commission then proposes to set up systems for member states to quantify and monitor packaging waste, while a complete cradle-to-grave Life Cycle Analysis (LCA) of all packaging types is undertaken. The Commission's proposals will be broad enough to include packaging waste created by materials used for the distribution of goods, industrial packaging, agricultural products, retail and office waste, and consumer product packaging. These sectors account for an estimated fifty million tonnes of packaging waste each year in the EC as a whole.

The Commission has at present insisted on the following:

- At least 60% of all packaging waste should be recycled within five years of the directive being ratified (compared with only 19% at present)
- No more than 30% of the waste is to be incinerated within the same time period
- No more than 10% should be placed in landfills

The proposal also specifies that each packaging unit should feature markings indicating what it is made of, if it is returnable, and if it can be recycled. Ultimately, priority is placed on the reduction of packaging waste, the refill and re-use of containers, recycling, and energy conversion. Voluntary pan-European agreement between industry and public authorities is also encouraged.

The Impact of Packaging

The chief purpose of a pack is the containment and protection of contents from the time of manufacture through storage, distribution and sale, and for a period of time thereafter. Secondary functions include the provision of information and guarantees about quality and purity, e.g. through the use of 'pilfer-proof' or 'tamper-evident' rings and seals. Third, there are the marketing and promotional aspects of packaging.

While convenience, safety, hygiene, nutrition, information and marketing are claimed to be the watchwords of the packaging industry, they can be taken to extremes and cause unnecessary environmental impact. Over-packaging is the most obvious example, but there are many others, discussed below.

There will be a great balancing act between the 'conventional' benefits of packaging, mentioned above, and the environmental demands of consumers and governments. For example, how far can the source reduction of packaging be carried out without prejudicing product protection and consumer convenience? How does it square with tamper-evidence and child resistance?

A Life Cycle Analysis (LCA), sometimes called a 'cradle-to-grave analysis', takes account of all stages, including the extraction of raw materials out of the ground, production of the packaging, storage, distribution, retailing, consumer use and final disposal, and it is the only method of gauging real overall impact of any product, including its packaging.

The environmental issues surrounding packaging do not, however, make it easy or even possible, in many cases, to categorise materials into acceptable or unacceptable groups. One of the main problems has been the over-simplification of the issues by the media and sometimes by environmental groups.

Where does this situation leave the retailer or manufacturer trying to choose a greener pack; or the design, PR and advertising company trying to design or advise on greener packaging? In the following section there are some specific guidelines which will help to ease this predicament.

How to Choose or Design a Greener Pack

Specific questions and suggestions to help make the design and selection process more manageable are listed in Figure 1.

It is not advisable to claim environmental superiority for a pack, as it only invites counter-attack. No pack has a monopoly of environmental virtues. Furthermore, by solving one environmental problem, care must be taken not to cause another.

It must be emphasised that there are a number of key players who must work together if the above points can become part of an integrated strategy for waste reduction. Designers, environmental consultants, marketing and advertising departments have as important a role to play as local authorities, manufacturers, retailers, consumers and pressure groups.

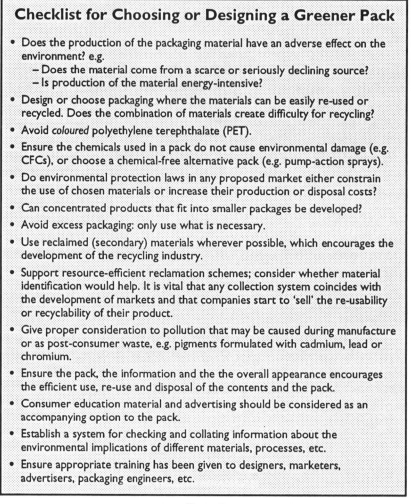

Checklist for Choosing or Designing a Greener Pack

- Does the production of the packaging material have an adverse effect on the environment? e.g.
  - Does the material come from a scarce or seriously declining source?
  - Is production of the material energy-intensive?
- Design or choose packaging where the materials can be easily re-used or recycled. Does the combination of materials create difficulty for recycling?
- Avoid *coloured* polyethylene terephthalate (PET).
- Ensure the chemicals used in a pack do not cause environmental damage (e.g. CFCs), or choose a chemical-free alternative pack (e.g. pump-action sprays).
- Do environmental protection laws in any proposed market either constrain the use of chosen materials or increase their production or disposal costs?
- Can concentrated products that fit into smaller packages be developed?
- Avoid excess packaging: only use what is necessary.
- Use reclaimed (secondary) materials wherever possible, which encourages the development of the recycling industry.
- Support resource-efficient reclamation schemes; consider whether material identification would help. It is vital that any collection system coincides with the development of markets and that companies start to 'sell' the re-usability or recyclability of their product.
- Give proper consideration to pollution that may be caused during manufacture or as post-consumer waste, e.g. pigments formulated with cadmium, lead or chromium.
- Ensure the pack, the information and the the overall appearance encourages the efficient use, re-use and disposal of the contents and the pack.
- Consumer education material and advertising should be considered as an accompanying option to the pack.
- Establish a system for checking and collating information about the environmental implications of different materials, processes, etc.
- Ensure appropriate training has been given to designers, marketers, advertisers, packaging engineers, etc.

Figure 1

Green, Greener, Greenest

The first priority is to reduce the quantity of material used in packaging, while maintaining sufficient product protection. Re-using packaging by refilling primary packs or returning them for cleaning and re-use is the next most desirable objective. Recycling should perform a secondary role, used in conjunction with reduction and re-use.

Over-packaging

One way of achieving 'friendlier' packaging is by source reduction, i.e. reducing the amount of materials used. The reasons for this are obvious: it is the only option that reduces the extraction and processing of virgin materials, the need for disposal, and even the energy and pollution of recycling. The Ferrero Rocher chocolate box has become the supreme example of over-packaging. There is no denying the expensive, luxury appeal of the packaging, but the same effect could be achieved with so much less.

Light-weighting and energy-saving techniques have long been used to improve the production costs of packaging products. Reducing energy costs and saving on raw materials have additional environmental benefits. For example, the weight of the returnable milk bottle has dropped from 540g in the 1920s to 230g in the 1990s.

After minimising environmental impact by using as few resources as possible, the next stage is to enable the pack to be recyclable. But this objective is not simple, since the two aims may be contradictory. For example, combining different materials in one pack may use less material overall, but may not be so easy to recycle. On the other hand, less packaging to transport through the distribution chain may give consequent savings in fuel. These factors, together with where the pack is sold, the function of the pack and the country's environmental legislation and recycling facilities all play a part in determining how the pack's impact can be minimised and made environment-friendlier.

Re-use, Refill and Return

The useful life of a pack can be extended by refilling or returning it, while still satisfying requirements for tamper-evidence, protection, etc. Refilling results in significant energy savings and helps to keep empty bottles, cans and cartons out of landfills and incinerators.

Repeated studies show that washing out and re-using an old bottle takes less energy than melting the same bottle and making a new one, or making a new bottle from virgin material. Nevertheless, more energy is needed initially to manufacture a refillable bottle than a non-refillable because it needs to be heavier to survive a large number of trips. On top of this must be added the energy required for the bottle washing process and the extra fuel needed to distribute refillables because of their weight. The initial investment in energy and resources required to manufacture the refillable bottle is gradually recouped as the bottle completes a number of trips; but if the bottle is lost or bro-

THE BODY SHOP APPROACH

The main product of the cosmetics industry are packaging, garbage and waste. The Body Shop chooses to go in the opposite direction...

Anita Roddick

WASTE NOT, WANT NOT.?

The Body Shop creates and sells skin and hair care products. That is what we do. What we do not do is create waste through unnecessary packaging: we do all we can to avoid it.

Packaging is a regrettable by-product of the retail industry, and in particular the cosmetics industry. Generally, the more expensive the product, the more layers of packaging you get. Packaging can mean waste. Many manufacturers and retailers (or their Marketing departments) admit that much of the packaging is there just to attract and seduce customers, convincing them that they want or need that particular product.

That is not The Body Shop's approach. So what is?

We are aware that packaging can have a potentially damaging impact on the environment (and on customers' wallets!) For The Body Shop, packaging has to work, and when designing packaging, we consider the following practical points:

- the material has to be compatible with the product.

- the container must be strong enough to contain the product from the time it is filled to the time it is empty.

- the packaging must provide an effective barrier to prevent contamination of the product; safety is of prime importance.

We choose to use minimal packaging, within the context of what is appropriate and practical. Our gift baskets are obviously more 'packaged' than our other products: they are designed to be attractive presents, but we also aim to make them as environmentally-friendly as possible.

2

PLASTICS: GOOD OR BAD?

We use plastic packaging for our products because it provides an effective barrier; it is robust, durable and light (this means it is easier on fuel when transporting products from warehouse to shop). We are phasing out glass jars for this reason and also because, if shattered, dangerous particles of glass could go unnoticed and cause damage to soft skin tissues around the eye.

Although plastics used in packaging are all based on synthetic polymers (which are derived from non-renewable oil reserves), only some 4% of oil ends up as plastic, and The Body Shop believes that we should maintain our policy of reusing plastic packaging where possible and encouraging customers to bring bottles back for refilling.

If a customer brings any Body Shop packaging back to any of our outlets we will do our best to recycle it. Most synthetic polymers can be recycled, but they need to be sorted. The fewer varieties of plastic that are used, the easier recycling will be, and this is why The Body Shop is trying to rationalise the materials for product packaging. Compatibility between product and packaging material will determine this. By the end of 1991 The Body Shop aims to identify the plastic on each of its bottles, tubes, jars, etc. by means of an abbreviated code: this will make the sorting process easier.

3

One Company's Response to the Packaging Issue:
The Body Shop's 'Refill' leaflet, designed in-house, 1990.
Reproduced courtesy The Body Shop ©.

ken before the break-even point has been reached, the overall energy impact is negative.

A study commissioned by a plastics trade group found that a 16oz glass refillable bottle used eight times was the lowest energy user of nine containers considered.[4] The key to savings is the number of times the bottle is used: eight to ten trips is a short life for a refillable, while fifty or more uses can be reached in areas where refillables dominate the market.

Refillables are still in favour in most developing nations, where nearly all beverage bottles are refillable, and in some developed countries, such as Finland, where 95% of the soft-drink, beer, wine and spirit containers are refillable.

In the US and UK, however, the market share for refillables has sunk dramatically over the last thirty years. The decline has been attributed principally to reduced competition in the beverage industry. As national brands replaced local or regional soft-drink products, beverage bottling became more centralised. The trend toward fewer bottlers with increased distribution networks increases the distance from consumers back to the plant, reducing the cost advantage of refillables over throw-aways.[5] As refillables lost their market share, consumers found it less convenient to return bottles, since there were fewer drop-off spots. Fewer uses per bottle cut the cost advantage for refillables.

A shift back to refillables is possible, but it will take strong action from government and consumers. Without support from consumers—at the polls and the checkout counter—the refillable container is unlikely to return to prominence.

A New Type of Refill

Packagers of household chemical and detergent products are now giving consumers a choice with new types of 'refill' packages and products sold in concentrated form that trade a little consumer effort for a big reduction in household waste. This also means considerable environmental and economical savings in energy and resources.

The consumers simply buy the pouch, cut off the corner and pour it into their empty bottle. Then they add water, shake it up and the result is four litres of the product and only a pouch or carton to throw away. Consumers have up to 85% less waste to dispose of than if they bought large plastic bottles. The pack not only saves on packaging waste, but also on transport costs, shelf space and money, since it costs less than the bottle. Ten pouches can be packed into a display tray, which takes up the same shelf space as three bottles.

One Company's Response to the Packaging Issue.
Till bags from The Body Shop
(Reproduced courtesy The Body Shop ©)

Refills demonstrate that creating a new pack to cut down impact on the solid waste stream can also be extremely economical for the consumer, the retailer and the manufacturer. In addition, this opens up new design and marketing opportunities, which are still not being exploited to the full.

Waste Disposal and Recycling

Early civilisations dealt with waste by burying it on the edge of their property. Later in history, it became the practice to dispose of waste on the edge of town—Athens established the first municipal dump in recorded history around 500 BC. Now waste has become an export to be shipped out of town, if not out of the country. Recycling is seen as one of the best solutions to solving the municipal solid waste problem.

High population densities in Japan and a number of countries in western Europe forced them to face the environmental faults of landfills long before the US and UK had to. These nations experienced shortages of dumping space and rising landfill costs much sooner. Their lower waste generation rates, higher levels of recycling, and greater reliance on incineration reflect this earlier awakening to landfill problems.

In contrast, the US landfilled more than 80% of its waste until the late eighties. Nearly 75% of American rubbish still ends up in landfills, with half the remainder burned and half recycled. The UK is similarly dependent on landfills, with an even lower rate of recycling.[6]

The relative worth of different types of recycling can be ranked: the most valuable is the manufacture of new products from similar, used items, e.g. making new glass containers from old ones; the least valuable is the conversion of waste materials into entirely different products for which a market has to be created. The overall aim is to reduce the amount of materials that enter and exit the economy, thus avoiding the environmental costs of extracting and processing virgin materials and of waste disposal.

The success of programmes that have received adequate funding and attention, and for which there is an end use for the collected materials, makes it difficult to argue that recycling is impractical. It is important to remember, however, that these efforts are a means, not an end. Recycling is but one element of a Greener Marketing strategy—which must also include strong efforts to reduce waste at source and directly re-use products. The most environmentally acceptable waste disposal option may not always be the cheapest in the short term. Economics should not be the only criteria by which the waste problem is viewed.

The Use of Reclaimed Materials in Packaging

In choosing recycled products, it should be ensured that they contain waste collected from consumers, not just industrial scraps that are already commonly recycled. This will support public recycling programmes and help create a market for these materials, enabling reclamation to become a more feasible first option. Consistently available markets for secondary materials are essential to successful recycling programmes.

Glass, aluminium, steel and paper are widely recycled and have strong secondary markets, but plastics have, until recently, been uneconomical to recycle. Bans on non-recyclable packaging have spurred manufacturers to undertake plastic recycling initiatives at a frenzied rate, and steps have already been taken to use reclaimed plastics in packaging. Proctor and Gamble in the US have taken the lead by producing a cleaning fluid, 'Spic and Span Pine', in a transparent container made from 100% recycled PET (polyethylene terephthalate). None of the recycled plastic is from industrial scrap: all of the material for the bottle is obtained from post-consumer recycled material.

The use of reclaimed plastics in packaging used to be restricted to non-food items. However, for the first time the use of recycled plastics for Coca-Cola has been approved in the US and in parts of Europe. This has been hailed as a significant breakthrough for the recycling industry, and soft-drinks bottles made from a blend of virgin and recycled plastic have been sold in US shops since May 1991, and in Europe from Summer 1992.

Packaging Materials

When creating a new pack, there is a need to be aware of the environmental and economic implications of packaging materials. In the following section, the advantages and disadvantages of glass, aluminium, steel and paper are considered.

Glass

Not so long ago the future for glass as a mass-produced packaging material looked bleak, as dramatic developments in lighter, less breakable materials threatened to erode its traditional markets.

While the raw materials for glass-making (sand, limestone and soda ash) are relatively cheap and easily available, much energy is needed to process them into glass, so recycling makes economic as well as environmental sense. The biggest market for waste glass is in containers.

Aluminium and Steel

Source Reduction. The creation of thinner materials that do a comparable job has been the most significant recent source reduction in metal packaging. For example, over the last twenty years the weight of a steel drinks can has been reduced by 40%.

Aluminium Recycling. Recycling aluminium containers from scrap saves over 90% of the energy required to produce the same product from alumina (processed bauxite), and demand is very strong. This is of great importance, as aluminium is the most energy-intensive material in common use. The metal can be recycled indefinitely, as re-processing does not damage its structure. The aluminium can is by far the most valuable commodity in the rubbish pile.

Steel Recycling. Steel of all types has been recycled for a long time. In modern society, recycling embraces used cars and other durable goods. Over 40% of steel produced worldwide in 1990 was recovered from recycled materials.

Magnetic separation, which is unique to the steel can, provides the key to extraction from both domestic refuse and incinerated waste. As with aluminium, there are considerable energy savings to be had from recycling steel. Every ton of steel recycled saves 2,500 pounds of iron ore, 1,000 pounds of coal, and forty pounds of limestone. Unfortunately, steel cans are harder to recycle than aluminium cans due to their tin plate coating. Nevertheless, they are still a very valuable commodity.

Paper

Paper is the largest single component of all that we throw away, making up over 41% (before recovery and recycling) in the US, and continued growth is expected. Although reducing paper usage would be a logical environmental step forward, the trend appears to be in the opposite direction. This is due largely to the growth in popularity of convenience foods, such as individual frozen meals.

Paper Recycling. Increased waste paper recycling would bring many economic and environmental gains, such as a reduction in the use of energy and raw materials, and a reduction in air and water pollution.

Paper is a good candidate for energy recovery through incineration because it has a high heat value and little ash remains after burning. But recycling is becoming the preferred environmental option due to concerns surrounding the emissions and ash resulting from incineration.

Plastics

A wide variety of plastics is available for an increasingly diverse and expanding set of applications, with packaging being the largest and fastest-growing market. Plastic has rapidly evolved into a necessity in today's society. However, it is much easier to acquire than it is to dispose of. The main problem has been the poor performance of plastic recycling compared to the other packaging materials. The incineration of plastic is an option with energy recovery potential: because they are derived from oil, plastics have a high calorific value. Unfortunately, there is the possibility that dangerous toxins can be created and, in addition, incineration means no further use of what is a valuable resource.

More traditional products could be used in place of the plastics packaging, such as cardboard and paper. However, packaging weight would quadruple, waste volume would increase by 250%, and energy consumption and cost would double. Plastic packaging actually proves greener in this account.

Consequently, many governments and environmental organisations want to promote a strong recycled plastic packaging market rather than incineration or increased production of degradable plastics.

Plastic Recycling. Although most people think of plastic as a single material having numerous applications, more than forty-six different types are in common use. A squeezable ketchup bottle, for example, is made of six layers of plastic, each engineered to do a different job, e.g. giving the bottle shape, strength, flexibility or impermeability. Few recycling processes exist at present, and fewer still can handle more than one type of plastic. Those that can mix varieties of plastics to form a much lower-grade plastic than the incoming waste products.

Environmentalists are still not convinced by plastic recycling, as a 'closed loop' has not been efficiently achieved on the little plastic that is recycled. Because the quality of recycled plastic generally drops dramatically, the result is a large amount of poor-quality plastic suitable only for things such as flowerpots. The market can only cope with so many poor-quality plastic products, leaving an increasing stock of used plastic containers for which there will be little demand.

The Issue of Degradable Plastic. For some years, interest has grown in the possibility of producing plastics which would degrade, either by biological action (biodegradable) or by the effects of sunlight (photodegradable).

With accelerating research, tomorrow's plastics are likely to be made with non-petroleum ingredients such as potato scraps, corn, molasses, beets and castor oil. Unlike their petroleum-based counterparts, these plastics will decompose completely within months—or even days. These are generally referred to as 'totally biodegradable' plastics, unlike the products that are presently on the market such as carrier bags, which misleadingly state that they are 'biodegradable'. In reality, these bags and other products are 'bio-disintegratable', i.e. they consist of petrochemical plastic 'building blocks' held together by a biodegradable 'cement' of starch, but the plastic itself does not degrade and will persist forever in the environment.

Just as mounds of rubbish keep growing in our landfill sites, criticism and questions surrounding degradable plastics keep piling up. For one, there is no conclusive evidence that degradable products degrade in oxygen-starved landfills. Moreover, consumers, believing that degradable products will simply disappear once they are thrown away, may be less likely to participate in recycling programmes and more likely to litter. There is the additional worry that degradable plastic will contaminate the recycling mix by introducing less durable materials. Perhaps most importantly, if the degradable plastics work as advertised, the plastics will break down into bits and some of these bits may include highly toxic additives such as cadmium and lead.

Conclusion

At present, information covering environmental issues and packaging processes is incomplete. However, with increasing pressure from consumers and European legislators, industry will be forced to redirect their resources to increase research on packaging if they are to avoid prosecutions and keep the greener consumer more informed.

The pressure to use new packaging types will not only lead to the reduction in the use of non-renewable resources and the quantity of resources being used, but it will also lead to increased benefits such as decreased transport costs as product packaging becomes more refined and lighter. It will be the responsibility of consumers and those companies with the foresight to have developed greener packaging alternatives to lobby for economically viable recycling facilities. Only then will recycled materials be available for product designers to produce packaging which is holistically greener. The drive towards an official EC eco-labelling scheme in Autumn 1992 and an EC database, which is being developed on products' impacts from cradle to grave, can only further this cause.

Packaging will become an increasingly important environmental issue, with consumer awareness of these issues driving industry to produce friendlier packaging. There should be positive interaction between all industry sectors to establish sound packaging. The opportunities are there for the taking, and it may only be those companies that grasp them now that will grow, or even survive to talk about them in the future.

This situation should be seen as an exciting and creative opportunity and there is great scope for new innovative solutions to these problems. This will be most successful if an overall approach is taken towards the company, its product and service as well as its packaging. Tackling this area proactively rather than reactively is the best formula, and it makes good business sense!

References

1. J.E. Young, 'Worldwatch Paper 101: Discarding the Throwaway Society' (USA: Worldwatch Institute, 1991).
2. Young, 'Worldwatch Paper 101'.
3. 'France Gets Tough over Household Packaging Waste', *Packaging Week*, Vol. 7, Issue 33 (5 February 1992).
4. Young, 'Worldwatch Paper 101'.
5. J.E. Young, 'Refillable Bottles: Return of a Good Thing', *Worldwatch*, March/April 1991.
6. 'Did You Know?', *UK Monitor*, Issue 5 (1991).

Chapter 8

GREENER LOGISTICS

Ian Jolly[1]
Institute of Logistics and Distribution Management and BRS Ltd
Martin Charter
Director, KPH Marketing

Introduction

'Logistics' is the term used to describe the management of the entire materials supply chain, from cradle to grave. Logistics covers the transport of raw materials and supplies from the point of production to the processing plant or factory, the movement of part-processed or part-finished goods from process to process within the factory, the trunking of finished goods or products to stockholding locations or warehouses, the management and operation of these locations, the distribution of the products to the buyers or consumers and the total flow of related information. Logistics management is one of the important behind-the-scenes processes that will come under scrutiny as not just products, but companies' entire approaches are bought by the consumer.

Logistics managers are beginning to realise that the environment is becoming an issue of competitive advantage. The movement of goods impacts on everybody's life, and so is highly visible. Pressure is beginning to bear on the industry to 'clean up its act' and look at the means of accomplishing this.

The importance of logistics has increased as the level of competition in the market has risen. The development of Life Cycle Analysis (LCA) is making the cradle-to-grave impacts of the logistics function more evident. Tolerance of supply chain inefficiency has been reduced and in some cases completely eliminated, resulting in a higher priority being given to this function.[2] The importance of the logistics function should not be underestimated. It has a key role in the Greener Marketing process because of its cradle-to-grave environmental impacts and its close relationship with all other departments, notably operations, human resources, finance and purchasing.

Logistics has important consequences for the environment. Vehicle emissions are a major source of pollution in the UK. Road traffic noise is experienced by 89% of the population and is cited as the worst form of noise disturbance by 16%.[3] This figure is twice as high as the next most intrusive source of noise. Transport accounts for 31% of all energy usage in the UK.[4] Heavy Goods Vehicles (HGVs) are involved in a smaller number of accidents compared to other vehicles, but these accidents are more likely to result in fatalities.[5] Warehousing has an important visual impact, and materials handling can also be a major source of noise pollution.

Particular warehousing activities, notably those involving refrigeration, can have major environmental impacts due to the use of CFCs that add to the depletion of the ozone layer and further aggravate the greenhouse effect. This gives a glimpse of the scale of the environmental problems currently facing logistics managers.

The decisions made in one area can have environmental repercussions in another, but most logistics decisions will have some impact on the environment. This chapter will look at the type of decisions that need to be made, and how these decisions can help in the 'greening' of logistics. Particular attention will be paid to road transport because of the significant environmental impacts of this form of physical distribution.

Logistics Planning

The logistics plan will vary considerably depending on the nature of the process under analysis. Traditionally, logistics decisions have been taken purely for financial reasons. However, recent and forthcoming legislation will introduce a greater need for corporate environmental responsibility. Numerous regulations and directives have been enacted by the EC on the environment, with many more currently in preparation. In the UK, the Environmental Protection Act of 1990 introduced Integrated Pollution Control (IPC) and the level of the fines introduces a whole new area for consideration. The logistics planning function must be aware of the 'Duty of Care' on waste, the standard of care currently demanded, and aware of what are likely to be the liabilities under future legislation.

EC legislation has introduced Environmental Impact Assessments (EIAs) for certain types and scales of development and proposals exist to extend greatly the use of EIAs. Companies should rigorously apply EIAs to all logistics plans, and the most obvious application of an EIA is in the planning of new depots or warehouses. It is important that all Stakeholders are defined for new developments, and that the company effectively communicates the use of an EIA to all interested parties through public exhibitions and other media. Failure to do so in the future may lead to fines and penalties, weakened community relations, and worsening corporate image. Managers will need to become more familiar with other tools for assessing environmental impacts from cradle to grave, such as Life Cycle Analysis (LCA) of new and existing products, and Environmental Auditing (EA) of existing operations. Transport, packaging and waste are areas which will benefit from close examination, as they will come under increasing legislative and public scrutiny. Including an Environmental Audit programme in the logistics plan will enable companies to assess and monitor environmental performance as plans progress.

As the green consumer matures and becomes better informed, the spotlight will move from the company's products to its processes. Logistics is only one part of the corporate system, but it too will be subject to closer examination. A failure to include logistics in the environmental programme could lead to a marketing and competitive disadvantage. Developing an environmentally conscious logistics plan will play a key role within the overall Greener Marketing strategy.

There are several ways in which logistics can affect the environment:

- Transport management
- Materials handling
- Warehousing
- Management of human resources

Developing a Greener Logistics Strategy

Companies must develop coordinated greener logistics strategies for the short, medium and longer term that are integrated into the Greener Marketing plan. The emphasis in the short term is to maximise the efficiency of the existing logistics system, while in the long term companies should plan to adopt more efficient and less environmentally damaging logistics operations as technology develops (see Fig. 1).

Companies producing significant noise and emissions from their logistics practices should recognise the importance of community relations and consider providing subsidies to reduce the impact of pollution, for example through double glazing. Particular efforts should be made to design-out and reduce noise and other nuisances at source.

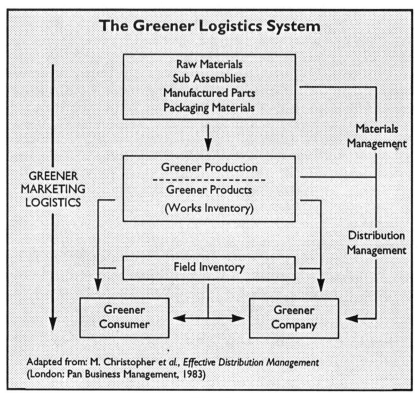

Figure 1

The short-term greener logistics strategy should:

- Carry out a full Environmental Audit of current activities
- Use Life Cycle Analysis (LCA) to determine the environmental impacts of the logistics strategy
- Develop a programme to monitor and review environmental performance of the logistics function
- Develop links with the local community to improve feedback on environmental and other social responsibility issues
- Produce a balance sheet for materials and energy used in the logistics function
- Consult the UK Institute of Logistics and Distribution Management regarding their research project, *Logistics and the Environment*

- Focus efforts on improving operations (channels and facilities) that have the worst environmental performance
- Implement a top-to-bottom environmental training programme, including courses to improve driver skills
- Develop a programme for management of hazardous or environmentally damaging substances, e.g. CFCs
- Implement a vehicle purchasing strategy with fuel efficiency and aerodynamics as key priorities, and include environmental criteria in the general purchasing strategy using the principle of BATNEEC (Best Available Technology Not Entailing Excessive Cost)
- Switch to 'environmentally friendlier' products and materials wherever possible, e.g. vehicle cleaning products

---

The Short-Term Benefits of Adopting a Greener Logistics Strategy Include:

- Improved vehicle efficiency: engine efficiency and aerodynamics
- Reduced operations pollution: noise and emissions
- Improved materials handling efficiency and safety
- Improved facility efficiency
- Improved load management, e.g. through increased 'backloading'
- New efficiency levels, maintained through an updated maintenance programme
- Improved community relations
- Increased employee commitment and motivation

Figure 2

The long-term greener logistics strategy should:

- Carry out EIAs on all future developments
- Adapt logistics strategies to land-use policies aiming to reduce the need for transport
- Lobby vehicle manufacturers to prioritise improved vehicle efficiency in fuel economy and emissions
- Develop an awareness of likely changes in legislation and plan proactively
- Develop an awareness of likely developments in the transport network

- Develop an Information Technology (IT) strategy aiding efficient inventory and load management and replacing paper documentation with Electronic Data Interchange (EDI)

The Longer-Term Benefits of Adopting a Greener Logistics Strategy Include:

- Financial savings from improved fuel efficiency
- Financial savings from reduced insurance premiums and compensation claims
- Lower maintenance costs from improved driver care
- More relaxed and better drivers leading to fewer accidents and lower absenteeism
- Improved Stakeholder relations: internal and external
- Reduced threat of fines and increased costs as legislation tightens
- Increased opportunities for contracts with new greener companies
- Increased employee commitment and motivation

Figure 3

Transport Management

The logistics manager has a variety of distribution modes at his or her disposal. Consideration of the environmental impact of transport strategies and their effect on Stakeholder relations must be integrated into the decision-making process. Where the logistics manager does not directly control transport decision making, as may be the case with the transport of raw materials or other inputs to the company, the manager should use his or her influence within the supply chain to ensure that environmental considerations are taken into account. Liaison with the purchasing department will ensure that such considerations are integrated into purchasing decision making. The Body Shop, for example, have successfully influenced the distribution chain for its products through insistence upon supplier audits. With the trend towards third-party distribution, the incorporation of environmental criteria into purchasing strategies of companies who contract distribution services is likely to grow.

Modes of Distribution

Figure 4 shows the modal split of UK distribution. Road transport dominates the distribution market, both in the amount of goods car-

Inland Freight Transport by Mode: 1989				
	Tonnes lifted		Tonne-kilometres	
	Million	%	Million	%
Road:				
Heavy Goods Vehicles[1]	1,704	82	132,100	79
Small Commercial[2]	103	5	5,300	3
All Road	1,807	87	137,400	83
Rail	143	7	2,400	1
Water[3]	68	3	17,300	10
Pipeline	71	3	9,400	6
All modes	2,089	100	166,500	10

1. Over 3.5 tonnes gross vehicle weight (i.e. those included in CSRGT)
2. Up to 3.5 tonnes gross vehicle weight
3. On rivers and inland waterways; excludes traffic at sea (provisional estimates)

Source: Department of Transport, *Continuing Survey of Road Goods Transport* (London: HMSO, 1989)

Figure 4

ried and the distances travelled. The next largest carrier is rail with less than one-tenth of the freight carried by road. The other two modes mentioned are excluded from further discussion here because of their marginal market share and specialised applications.

Transport by air causes significantly greater environmental impacts than all other modes of transport, and it is also much more expensive. For these reasons, it is only used for a few specific types of traffic, such as airmail, highly perishable goods and highly time-sensitive material.

The reasons for the dominance of road transport have been discussed in *Transport* and the *Environment* by Sharp and Jennings,[6] and have been summarised as:

- Speed
- Reliability
- Cost
- Flexibility

Which Mode is Greener?

To attempt to answer this question, we must evaluate the environmental impacts of the different modes of distribution. The benefits of rail against road are discussed at great length in *The Wrong Side of the Tracks?* produced by TEST,[7] while the disadvantages of rail are discussed by Sharp and Jennings.[8]

First, **road transport**; there are a number of environmental impacts to consider:

Emissions. There are a range of exhaust and other gases, such as CO_2 and NO_3, with differing toxicity and impact on the environment, including, for example, depletion of the ozone layer and aggravation of the greenhouse effect.

Noise and Vibration. Road transport is frequently cited as the most obtrusive source of noise and vibration experienced by people in their local communities.[9]

Accidents. HGVs are among the safest vehicles on the roads and have fewer accidents per kilometre than other road vehicles. However, when they are involved in accidents, the third party has a much higher chance of being killed or seriously injured.[10]

Road Wear. HGVs cause more damage to road surfaces than any other class of traffic.

Visual Intrusion. Many people do not like to see goods vehicles, particularly when they block a scenic or picturesque view or detract from the enjoyment of an amenity.[11]

Congestion. HGVs take up large amounts of road space and often have difficulty manoeuvring in narrow streets. Additionally, when delivering to high street shops, they can partially block the road. This worsens the effect of congestion in towns and cities.

Use of Resources. Road transport consumes huge amounts of energy. Transport consumes 31% of all energy used, and road transport consumes 80% of this, mostly in oil.[12] Alongside this is the consumption of materials used in the building of vehicles. The impact of improvements in resource efficiency and levels of demand within the transport sector, particularly road transport, is therefore very significant.

The impacts associated with **rail transport** are as follows:

Emissions. Diesel locomotives give rise to similar emissions as trucks. However, when the effect on emissions by the weight of the load is

Estimated Emissions from Various Modes of Freight Transport in the UK (grams per tonne-km)			
	ROAD	**RAIL**	
Pollutants	**Diesel**	**Diesel**	**Electric**
CO (Carbon Monoxide)	2.58	0.02	0.01
HC (Hydrocarbons)	0.39	0.09	–
NO_x (Oxides of Nitrogen)	4.68	0.72	0.17
SO_x (Oxides of Sulphur)	0.42	0.42	0.41
Aldehydes	0.03	0.02	–
Pb (Lead)	–	–	–
CO_2 (Carbon Dioxide)	275.30	28.77	40.65

Note: Converted from mg/ton-mile to gm/tonne-km using a division factor of 1635.0. These figures are indicative rather than exact.

Source: Department of Transport, *Continuing Survey of Road Goods Transport* (London: HMSO, 1989)

Figure 5

considered, as in Figure 5, the comparison becomes more revealing. Electric locomotives are substantially cleaner, and in fact emit almost nothing directly. The emissions associated with electric locomotives arise at the electricity generating station.

Noise and Vibration. At present, there is no railway noise legislation in the UK, in spite of EC proposals in 1983 and 1986. A committee looking at this subject has now reported its findings, which are currently under consideration. It is difficult to compare the relative 'noisiness' of road and rail freight because of the problems of designing an objective test. The case is similar when considering vibration. A railway locomotive produces as much noise as a truck but road noise tends to be more persistent in any one location than rail noise.

Accidents. Railways have a better safety record than that of roads. The relative death rates are shown in Figure 6. These are rates for passenger transport, not freight, but the comparison remains valid.

Track Costs. Up-to-date track costs for railways are not available since very few new railway lines have been built in recent years. TEST estimates that railway tracks designed to carry the same traffic as a three-lane motorway would require 80% less land, would use a third as much energy in their construction and maintenance and use 90% less aggregate (broken rock) in their construction.[13]

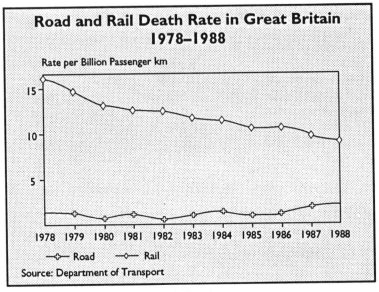

Figure 6

Visual Intrusion. Trains are generally less intrusive than trucks and in fact are often seen as picturesque.[14] Many terminus buildings and other structures are Victorian; some are listed buildings and are believed to enhance the area in which they are situated.

Congestion. The removal of freight from the roads and onto rail would have the effect of reducing vehicle mileage and the number of vehicles on the road.

Use of Resources. The main comparison here is energy required per tonne-kilometre of freight. Figure 7 shows the results of a study by the Netherlands Road Transport Institute, indicating the comparative use of energy by various modes of freight transport. The values shown in the table are relative energy use per tonne-kilometre, with rail given a value of 100 for comparison purposes.

The table demonstrates the low use of energy resources by rail transport relative to road transport. Although rail vehicles are larger and hence consume more resources, such as steel, per locomotive than a lorry, railway locomotives have a longer life and a greater load capacity.[15] This demonstrates some of the complexities involved in Life Cycle Analysis (LCA).

On the above criteria, rail transport has lower environmental impacts than road transport in each case; in some cases the impact is very

Relative Energy Use	
Mode	Relative Energy Use
Water	57
Pipeline	60
Rail	100
Trunk Roads	300
Aircraft	4,000
Source: Netherlands Road Transport Institute	

Figure 7

significantly less. However, this simplified interpretation does not take into account some of the problems that arise from the current limited development of the rail network in Britain:

Trunking. In switching to rail transport the largest part of the journey taken off the road would be trunk mileage on motorways and dual carriageways, the roads designed to accept heavy flows of traffic. The rail system has less capacity and is less flexible than the road system.

Transhipment, Collection and Delivery. The rail journey will almost certainly involve transhipment at either or both ends of the rail journey, which increases costs, transit times and the opportunity for damage and pilfering. Very few premises are adjacent to railway premises, so it is highly likely that road transport will be required. This road transport element will increase congestion in the vicinity of rail goods yards, many of which are in urban areas, thereby bringing environmental disbenefits to those areas.[16] It will, however, reduce congestion in other areas.

Any plans to use rail freight should be made bearing these points in mind, although where rail transport to Europe is involved, more developed rail systems may lessen these problems. These considerations are particularly important in short-term planning. When developing the long-term logistics strategy it is important to be informed on the likely developments in the transport networks, in order that any changes in the balance of benefits and disbenefits between road and rail transport can be understood.

Aerodynamics and Fuel Economy

Fuel is a major operating cost of road transport. Depending on the type of operation, fuel usage has been estimated at 8–23% of total vehicle costs.[17] The financial benefits of improved fuel economy and load planning are clear, as are the environmental benefits.

Improved aerodynamics reduces the effect of air resistance, particularly at higher speeds, reducing the power requirement and thus reducing fuel consumption. There are monetary incentives to reduce fuel consumption as well as the environmental benefits of less exhaust emissions.

An Energy Efficiency Office report states: 'The importance of aerodynamic efficiency and its effect on fuel economy cannot be over-emphasised. To put it into perspective, a 15% improvement in the drag coefficient is equivalent to a reduction of about 6% in the engine's specific fuel consumption which, on past experience, is the result of about ten years' engine development.'[18]

Approximately 30% of all HGV mileage in the UK is run without a load,[19] so approximately 30% of the environmental disbenefits of road transport are caused by empty vehicles. There is obvious room for considerable improvement in fuel efficiency relative to load, in addition to mileage improvements.

Materials Handling

Handling is either mechanised or manual. Manual handling will cause less environmental disbenefits, but of course has drawbacks.

1. There is a limit to the weight one person can lift
2. There can be a speed penalty for manual handling
3. Many people may be required in order to achieve a high throughput
4. Wage costs may be prohibitive

Mechanical handling is employed in most logistics operations. The environmental disbenefits caused by this will depend on:

- Method
- Power supply
- State of repair
- Materials handled

The method of handling in very many cases is the 'works truck' or variations thereof, including fork-lift trucks, mobile cranes and others. Other methods include overhead cranes, conveyor belts and pneumatic tubes. The various methods will vary principally in the amount of energy required for their operation, the materials needed for their construction, the noise created by their use and the safety level for the operators.

Commonly used power supplies for mechanical handling are:

- Petrol and diesel fuels
- Liquid Petroleum Gas (LPG)
- Electricity (mains or battery)

A major environmental impact in this area will be noise produced from both machinery and materials handling. Generally, older machinery in poorer states of repair produces more noise, and is likely to be less efficient, and possibly more dangerous. Only robust goods that do not demand careful handling will produce noise, but in some cases that noise may be considerable.

Noise and the approach that operators take to handling goods and materials are important health and safety issues. Industrial noise is a major cause of damage to hearing in the UK. Managers should consult the Health and Safety Executive (HSE) in the UK for advice on noise reduction and avoidance, as well as guidance on any expected tightening of legislation. Hearing damage is a major area for compensation claims, and any reduction in noise pollution produced by materials handling will improve employee relations, place the company ahead of tougher legislation and reduce the chances of claims.

The use of CFCs and other environmentally hazardous substances in the distribution industry is significant, in both warehousing and transport. Less harmful alternative refrigerants do exist and are continuing to be developed. Leaks from and decommissioning of refrigeration plants and vehicles are the major causes, in the logistics function, of the release of ozone-depleting gases.

To develop a strategy for greening materials handling, it will be necessary to carry out a full audit of operations, analysing inputs, outputs, transformation processes and handling. Audits should focus on environmental acceptability of inputs, waste, emissions and energy use. Having carried out the audit, objectives should be set for environmental performance improvements and a strategy developed to achieve those targets.

Consultation with the purchasing and product design department should aim to ensure that inputs and subsequent transformation processes are more environmentally friendly. If greener alternatives are not available from existing suppliers, substitutes should be sought, with pressure applied to improve the environmental performance of

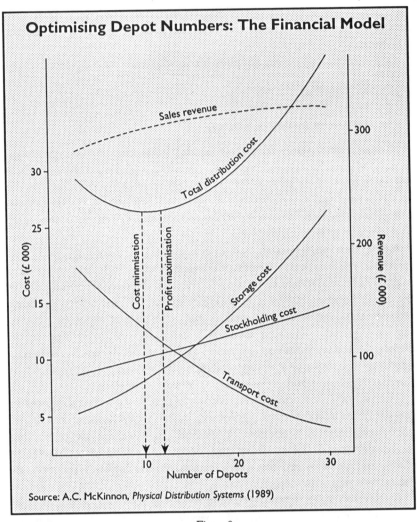

Optimising Depot Numbers: The Financial Model

Sales revenue

Total distribution cost

Cost minimisation

Profit maximisation

Storage cost

Stockholding cost

Transport cost

Cost (£ 000)

Revenue (£ 000)

Number of Depots

Source: A.C. McKinnon, *Physical Distribution Systems* (1989)

Figure 8

suppliers. Any reductions in waste and energy use will lead to direct savings. If waste cannot be reduced directly, an effective recycling strategy should be developed wherever possible. As packaging is a major contributor to the waste stream, particular attention should be paid to this. Cutting out wasteful transport packaging will reduce the inputs handled and may also reduce the weight of goods, leading to savings in fuel costs. Emissions within the handling process should also be minimised or designed-out if they are environmentally harmful.

The development of the Total Quality Management (TQM) approach will stimulate the evolution of a greener materials handling strategy, through its emphasis on the drive for zero defects, and the minimisation of waste and emissions.

Warehousing

How Many Depots?

It is possible to derive an environmental cost model from a financial cost model when considering the optimum number of distribution facilities. Figure 8 shows the relationship between storage costs and transport costs.

In the same way, it is possible to construct a model showing the change in environmental impacts against the number of distribution depots. The validity of this model depends on assigning a value to the environmental costs and benefits of vehicles and depots that will allow a variety of depot options to be compared. Figure 9 shows a theoretical application whereby an environmental optimum could be established for decisions on the number of depots required.

The environmental impact of a warehouse would be dependent on:

- Location and size of site
- Use of energy
- Generation and management of waste
- Visual intrusion
- Noise and disturbance
- Pollution, e.g. 'run-off'

Where Should the Depots Be?

The simple answer is 'close to the consumer',[20] and that is as true for environmental concerns as it is for both financial and operational reasons. The closer a depot is to the consumer the smaller the environmental impacts of its transport activities. However, few companies' customers are all in one area and so the choice of location will be a compromise or 'optimal solution'.

There are computer software packages to assist in making this decision,[21] but they are only guides and offer advice, not definitive solutions. Normally the depot should be located so that vehicle mileage is minimised, but congestion points should also be considered. In the case of most distribution operations, particularly national suppliers, demographics will play a large part as larger towns and cities will tend to exert a 'pull' with their larger demand for goods and services.[22]

Having chosen the area in which to locate the facility, the choice of site will require more detailed attention. This may require the comple-

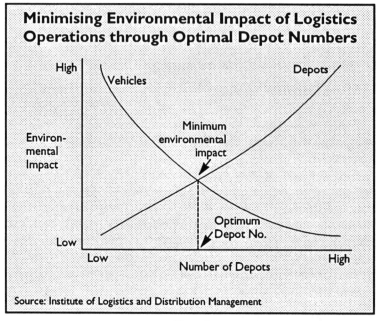

Figure 9

tion of an EIA if the development is significant. It is not likely that a logistics manager will have the skills to carry out this specialist task, and professional advice through organisations such as the Institute of Environmental Assessment will be essential in achieving greater environmental acceptability for the development.

What Design Criteria Should Be Used?

Internal layout should be considered very carefully to ensure facilities operate with maximum efficiency and minimum environmental impact arising from the handling of inputs, products and waste. Internal logistics between processes should be efficient, and drop-off and pick-up points should be congestion-free. Emissions within the factory or warehouse should be minimised, and those that are produced should be carefully monitored and controlled.

In depots requiring refrigeration plants, alternatives to CFCs and other ozone-depleting substances should be specified. Energy efficiency should be an essential element, particularly where refrigeration is involved. There should also be strict adherence to health and safety procedures.

Management of Human Resources

How Can Driver Training Benefit the Environment?

A great part of the environmental impact of a vehicle is under control of the driver. The factors which the driver can influence are:

- Road safety
- Fuel economy
- Choice of route

Road Safety. Although HGVs make up 7.5% of all traffic, they are only involved in 3.9% of accidents. However, the accidents they are involved in tend to be serious and in 1987 HGVs represented 11.8% of all vehicles involved in fatal accidents.[23]

The most obvious benefit of improved driver training in road safety is to reduce the number of fatal accidents on our roads. However, there are also internal financial savings; for example, a Birmingham haulage company saved £7,000 on their annual insurance premium through a programme of training their drivers for safety.[24]

Fuel Economy. BRS Limited have investigated this subject and have introduced driver training for fuel economy at all their driver training centres. Their experience is that savings of 5–40% can be achieved as a result of one day of training. They estimated that a 5% saving represents 375 gallons per annum based on an average annual consumption of 6,500 gallons.[25]

The course involves driving over a set route and measuring the fuel consumed. This is followed by a classroom session during which the driver's performance is discussed. The route is then retraced and the fuel consumption measured for a second time. This allows a measure of the driver's improvement. The course is designed to avoid lengthening journey times unduly, but to reduce environmental impact.

Choice of Route. Most drivers choose their own route.[26] They may be given a specific route, but many will alter this for a number of reasons, e.g. personal preference, local knowledge, traffic disruption, etc. In many cases the decision is not taken on environmental grounds.

Effective route management can minimise the impact of noise levels on the surrounding built environment by ensuring that the use of roads in residential and sensitive areas is kept to a minimum. Travelling at night may be an option to avoid traffic congestion; however, noise level restrictions already exist in Austria and are to be made considerably tougher in the EC by 1995.

In addition, by effectively routing vehicles away from congestion black spots, the overall air pollution can be kept to a minimum as the energy consumption per tonne-kilometre will be reduced. The air pollution can also be targeted away from built-up areas to minimise any possible harmful effects. Such policies will improve Stakeholder relations with the local community and reduce driver tension.

Other Employee Training

There will be benefits in the logistics function from the implementation of a greener personnel strategy with an emphasis on environmental awareness training. Employees should be encouraged to develop and contribute ideas that improve the environmental performance of the logistics function. The benefits of driver training have been discussed above. Similar benefits will be visible at all stages of input and output handling if appropriate training is developed. Health and safety regulations are likely to tighten, and with increasing compensation claims by employees for physical injury, such as hearing impairment, there will be clear benefits—in insurance for example—for companies with quieter and safer handling procedures. In many cases, this will also produce improved employee motivation.

The Future of Logistics

EC legislation is anticipated in the field of vehicle emissions, as shown in Figure 10. The Stage 1 limits are due to take effect on 1 July 1992 for new models, and on 1 October 1993 for new vehicles in existing model ranges. The corresponding dates for Stage 2 are 1 October 1995 and 1 October 1996. This EC directive has now been agreed by Ministers, who have also agreed that new limits will be determined using an existing European Test Cycle, though the test procedure may be changed at a later date.

The general approach being taken on engine efficiency is that engine manufacturers will have to meet continually more stringent requirements (as indicated above). Another good example is the so-called 'Carbon Tax', which is designed to force the price of fossil fuels up sharply. The purpose of this tax will be to discourage the use of and the pollution caused by carbon-based fuels, which currently are the dominant form of fuel for all forms of transport.

When European trade is made easier by the lifting of national trade restrictions, there could be greater flows of goods across national borders, giving buyers greater choice of products. More energy would be consumed and there would be increasing congestion on cross-border routes as length of haul increases.

The Development of Emissions Legislation			
	Current (g/kWh)	Stage 1 (g/kWh)	Stage 2 (g/kWh)
CO	11.2	4.5	4.0
HC	2.6	1.2	1.1
NO$_x$	14.4	8.0	7.0
Particulates 85 kWh or less	–	0.63	0.15
Over 85 kWh	–	0.36	0.15
Source: ENDS Report 194 (March 1991)			

Figure 10

When the Channel Tunnel opens in 1993, it will be the first fixed link between the UK and the rest of Europe. Eurotunnel plc, the owners and operators, will be offering a cross-channel service for passengers, cars, coaches and freight vehicles. Their service will be in direct competition with the operators of roll on–roll off ferries. The operational advantage of the tunnel is claimed to lie in shorter transit times.

The greatest logistics gains that the Channel Tunnel will offer are in long-distance rail transport, such as trains loaded in Glasgow that can run direct to Athens, or Bristol to Berlin. Whole days can be cut from transit times, and costs could be substantially lower than the road–ferry–road option. The Channel Tunnel should cause all transport decisions between the UK and Europe to be re-evaluated, and will mean in many circumstances that the less environmentally damaging rail option may become a practical alternative to road haulage.

Heavier trucks are due to be permitted on UK roads from 1999 in line with EC plans to harmonise vehicle dimensions across Europe. This will lead to bigger but fewer lorries on our roads. The Armitage Committee recommended forty-four-tonne vehicles as long ago as 1980.[27] This recommendation was diluted by political pressure and concern over bridge and road damage.

Already Austria has a strict eighty-decibel noise limit on night traffic, and the EC will reach these standards in 1995. While four decibels may not appear to make a great difference, it in fact equates to a 60% reduction in noise levels. The German truck manufacturers MAN have responded with their 'Silent' range of trucks and have sold around 4,000 in the Austrian market since its launch in 1989.[28]

In the long term it is likely that increased Europeanisation and environmental awareness will cause the UK to develop an integrated national transport policy, as is the case already in France and Germany.

This would improve the flexibility and performance of the transport network and provide greater opportunities for intermodal transport.

Some recent trends in industry indicate:

- A decrease in the amount of in-house or own-account transport and a growth in the use of third-party hauliers
- Increasing centralisation of stockholding as the trunk road and motorway network develops
- Increased fuel efficiency and lower emissions, driven by legislation and environmental pressure group activity
- Increasing use of Just-In-Time (JIT) delivery
- Increased emphasis on quality of products and customer service

Some of these trends conflict with improved environmental performance and will come under severe pressure as environmental awareness and legislation increase. There will also be other trends that will have significant impacts on logistics planning, especially in the longer term. Information Technology (IT) will certainly lead to increased teleworking, and may lead to significant increases in home shopping, so that delivery will be made more often from the works or depot direct to the consumer. IT will also have a significant impact through Electronic Data Interchange (EDI), which in particular will affect distribution documentation, and should considerably reduce the distribution industry's levels of paper consumption. IT will also provide opportunities for considerably improved load management and inventory control. These measures will be a part of strategies focusing on increased quality of customer service, which will also involve driver training, as drivers are seen as ambassadors of the company.

The European eco-labelling scheme and EC directives on Eco-Auditing will be implemented in the latter part of 1992, and with the growth of cradle-to-grave analysis this will drive environmental awareness forward among both companies and consumers. The eco-labelling legislation will place particular attention on manufacturers and retailers and will raise consumer awareness and concern. This concern will move down the supply chain as retailers in turn use their buying power to influence suppliers through the increasing use of supplier audits. In addition to the use of audits, supplier challenges will set environmental performance targets and will put companies under pressure to minimise their environmental impact and place an incentive on the provision of greener options.

In the short term, there is likely to be dramatic growth in greener products, and this will be particularly associated with increases in consumer prosperity. It seems likely in the long term, however, that there will be a shift from the desire to consume more to the desire to consume less, but of a higher quality. This will require the quality of logistics services to increase in parallel with the quality of goods, but will also lead to a decline in the quantity of goods handled by the logistics function. Both in the short and long term, the companies offering the best quality of service will be in the best position to compete in the more competitive market, so that if companies perform equally well on other buying criteria, those with the best environmental performance will almost certainly win the contract.

The influence of Total Quality Management (TQM) will continue to grow and Environmental Auditing and Life Cycle Analysis (LCA) will become an important tool for determining the environmental impacts of the company's products and processes. Just-In-Time (JIT) will be an important element in the drive for quality in service, but its emphasis is likely to broaden from logistics to production. The success of JIT production will depend on an efficient logistics system, which in turn will depend on well-trained and motivated staff. Logistics will also come within the scope of the British Standards Institute's new standards on Environmental Management Systems. The launch of the Engineering Council's Green Code for Engineers, and the Institute of Logistics and Distribution Management's (ILDM) manual, *Logistics and the Environment* are also likely to have an impact on logistics management.

In addition, the land-use planning system will develop policies that are designed to reduce the need for travel and, as a part of this, policies will probably also be designed to encourage localised production and distribution.

Conclusion

Goods will always need to be moved, and customers will always want to be supplied. It is likely that many new and strengthened laws will appear on the statute books to improve environmental protection. In June 1991 there were eighty-seven proposed regulations or directives in the EC policy pipeline, but legislation will be only one of the drivers of change demanding a response from the logistics function.

The logistics function plays an essential role in the economy, and has a major impact on the environment. The increasing emphasis on cradle-to-grave analysis will place greater pressure on the materials supply chain, but there is no 'quick fix' for environmental problems. This applies as much to logistics as to any other aspect of Greener Marketing.

Proactive companies will adopt responsible attitudes to the environment ahead of legislation. The green revolution in the UK has been led by the consumer, and with consumers increasingly demanding products and services which match up to their environmental expectations, retailers will demand improved environmental performance from their suppliers. The greening of logistics will need to be integrated into and coordinated within the Greener Marketing strategy if the company is to maintain or improve market position in a more socially and environmentally aware world. The green challenge has emerged and is growing, and a greener logistics strategy will help industry to meet that challenge successfully.

References

1. Ian Jolly is on secondment to the Institute of Logistics and Distribution Management from BRS Ltd, and is co-author of the ILDM's *Logistics and the Environment*, a project that was undertaken with the intention of providing a comprehensive reference manual for logistics managers. The manual covers environmental legislation, details of environmental impacts and pressure, and case studies demonstrating best practice and industry initiatives.

   The work is to be published in three volumes: Volume 1 deals with transport, Volume 2 discusses the other aspects of logistics operations, and Volume 3 is concerned with non-operational aspects of environmental performance and measurement. The volumes can be purchased as a set or singly. An updating service will be provided to keep registered users abreast of all the relevant changes.

2. A. Wasik, *Logistics Information Systems* (1991).

3. J. Morton-Williams, B. Hedges and E. Fernando, *Road Traffic and the Environment* (1978), p. 390.

4. Government Statistical Service, *Transport Statistics Great Britain, 1979–1989* (Department of Transport; London: HMSO, 1990).

5. Government Statistical Service, *Transport Statistics Great Britain, 1979–1989*.

6. C. Sharp and T. Jennings, *Transport and the Environment* (Leicester: Leicester University Press, 1976).

7. TEST, *The Wrong Side of the Tracks?* (Transport and Environment Studies, 1991).

8. Sharp and Jennings, *Transport and the Environment*.

9. Morton-Williams *et al.*, *Road Traffic and the Environment*, p. 390.

10. Government Statistical Service, *Transport Statistics Great Britain, 1979–1989*.

11. Department of Transport, *Lorries in the Community* (London: HMSO, 1990).

12. M. Walsh, *Motor Vehicles and Global Warming* (1990).

13. TEST, *The Wrong Side of the Tracks?*

14. Sharp and Jennings, *Transport and the Environment*.

15. N.H. Zeevenhooven, *The Energy Consumption of Various Transport Systems* (1990).

16. Government Statistical Service, *Transport Statistics Great Britain, 1979–1989*.

17. Institute of Logistics and Distribution Management.

18. Energy Efficiency Office, *Energy Efficiency in Road Transport* (1990).

19. Department of Transport, *Continuing Survey of Road Goods Transport* (London: HMSO, 1989).

20. K.B. Ackerman, *Warehousing* (1977).

21. Institute of Logistics and Distribution Management, *Guide to Physical Distribution Software* (ILDM, 1991).

22. A.C. McKinnon, *Physical Distribution Systems* (London: Routledge, 1989).

23. C. Mitchell, *Lorries and the Environment: Problems and Solutions* (TRRL, 1989), and Government Statistical Service, *Transport Statistics Great Britain, 1979–1989*.

24. 'On the Defensive', *Commercial Motor*, 2–8 August 1990.

25. BRS Limited.

26. Sharp and Jennings, *Transport and the Environment*.

27. G. Armitage, *Lorries, People and the Environment* (London: HMSO, 1980).

28. 'The Word is Out on Silent Trucks', *Financial Times*, 3 January 1992.

Chapter 9

GREENER PRICING

Jan Bebbington and Professor Rob Gray[1]

University of Dundee

An accountant is a man who knows the price of everything and the value of nothing.[2]

Introduction

The ubiquity of 'prices' can often obscure the complexity of the processes which produce them. A price in a final consumer market is some combination of the costs (actual and estimated) that are embedded in the product or service and of what it is judged the consumer will be willing to pay for it. Each of those costs themselves represent prices deriving from processes (or financial charges—of which more later) at earlier stages in the production of that good or service.

This rather glib statement of the obvious is necessary if we are to try and understand how price can—and cannot—be developed to reflect environmental factors and how price can—and cannot—be used to encourage more environmentally benign behaviour.

Prices are only generated when property rights are exchanged. For much of the biosphere—'the environment'—there exists no property rights which can be exchanged. Sea, air, rivers, wilderness, deserts, rain-forests, species, habitat, and their like are not, in general, 'owned', and therefore their use cannot be reflected in price. Where elements of the biosphere **are** owned, as is the case with some land, forestry and water rights for example, the 'value-in-ownership' that will be reflected in any price relates to the economic merits of the thing owned rather than to its intrinsic or environmental value. Thus land may be 'valued' for its ability to support livestock or because it contains minerals, but it is the nutrient value of the grass (for example) that the land produces or the likely financial **net** return from extracting those minerals that leads to the price in exchange—**not** the land itself.

Thus, as long as much of the biosphere remains unpriced and 'rational' decisions are taken principally upon priced data, those decisions will be made regardless of their environmental effect and must, therefore, encourage the destruction of the natural environment.

Similarly, as long as western persons are culturally predisposed to consider that while some elements of the biosphere are 'ownable', such 'ownership' can be viewed only in terms of the financial returns it can generate, it seems inevitable that 'freely' operating prices must lead to environmental degradation.[3]

Figure 1 is an attempt to illustrate both the extent of the environmental impacts that a truly 'green' price must include and the different points at which it might be possible to influence the ultimate consumer price. This figure will then provide an outline for our subsequent review of current initiatives to develop greener prices, the likely developments in the near ('light green'), future, as well as some suggestions for the sorts of prices that will be necessary if The Brundtland Report's commitment to **Sustainability** and **Sustainable Development** are to mean anything.[4]

Ultimately, all our products and services consumed draw from the finite biosphere and, ultimately, return there as waste or pollution. These impacts are not part of the cost structures of the companies and thus are no part of price. They are 'externalities' and, for price to reflect environmental factors, the 'externalities' must be made 'internalities'.

Prices which are Greener

The rapid expansion in general concern for the environment has generated a steady growth in attempts (or, often, greater publicity for those attempts) to begin the process of incorporating the environment into prices. These vary from the obvious to the more subtle.

In the UK, there are a number of more widely known instances. On the one hand, the direct intervention by the Government in the duty charged on leaded and unleaded petrol is widely quoted as an example of using markets to bring about more environmentally benign behaviour. On the other hand, the 'market' has encouraged the expansion in existing and new products. Many of these, although involving greater cost, claim less environmental impact. Furthermore, the initiatives of companies such as The Body Shop (in the wake of Traidcraft and others) to monitor the whole product life cycle and minimise its negative social and environmental impact are widely quoted as illustrations of how business and the environment can work hand-in-hand. These

The Pricing Process

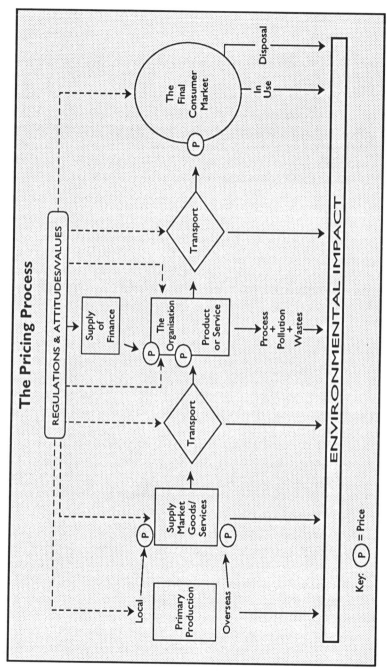

Figure 1

examples represent the two most direct ways in which price will reflect the environment:

- Conscious changing of the relative prices of green and non-green products to encourage a more environmentally benign market place; or,

- The encouragement of the 'green consumer' willing to pay a premium for the green product (which might be seen either as a form of non-price competition or as the price paid for the purchase of an additional product—whether it be 'clean environment', lifestyle or simply smugness).

These require initiative either from the consumers themselves (helped along perhaps by public relations and enterprise) or from regulatory authorities willing to directly influence consumer prices.

In more subtle ways, a wider range of pressures is now beginning to feed into price through less direct routes. Consider the stages in Figure 1 which, working from left to right, suggest a simple model of how a consumer price is built up and the stages that are compounded into it.

1. **Primary Products.** Primary commodities are not as freely wrestled from the ground as they have been. Whether it be the rising concern over the environmental effects of oil exploration and extraction (with the attendant rise in public and regulatory expectations of the oil companies), the increased incidence of required remediation of mineral exploitation sites, the declining stocks of naturally occurring resources or food sources (e.g. fished-out oceans) or the growing political disquiet about the rate and manner in which companies conduct their exploitation of the resources of lesser developed countries, the costs of primary products are rising and will continue to do so.

2. **Suppliers of Physical Goods and Services.** Suppliers, depending upon their location, are facing changing cost structures. Whether to reflect remediation costs, to reflect scarcity or to meet home-country regulatory requirements, every organisation can expect its choice of supplier to become more complicated. Furthermore, as markets become more subtle, customers (as well as other Stakeholders) will need to know the history of the contents of a product. There is little purpose in buying a CFC-free product which involves extensive use of CFCs in the manufacture of its components. This is leading to the sorts of **supplier audits** that companies such as IBM now conduct as

standard practice. Costs must be incurred in the conduct of the audit and in the supplier meeting the higher level of standards.

3. **Transport.** While there is still a considerable reluctance on the part of governments to address the effects on the environment of road and air transport, it is clear that this state of affairs will be short-lived. Whether it be through the much-mooted Carbon Tax, regulation to limit emissions (even, as in the Californian proposal, to zero emissions), rising costs of fuel, airport noise taxes or the sheer impossibility of movement on the roads, prices will begin to reflect a changing pattern of transport choices and/or charging systems.

4. **The Cost of Finance.** The terms on which finance is provided to organisations and the costs thereby included are far from trivial in either a financial or an environmental context. However, the ways in which the price of finance may become greener, or in which the provision of finance may encourage or restrict more environmentally benign behaviour, are complex. We return to this below.

5. **Organisational Change.** It is in the organisations themselves that the biggest changes are currently occurring. Changing corporate policy, tighter monitoring and penalties from the regulatory bodies, the pressing and growing demands for new investment in cleaner technologies through Best Available Technology Not Entailing Excessive Cost (BATNEEC) and Best Practical Environmental Option (BPEO), not to mention the increasing costs of waste disposal and the changing attitudes of employees, are bringing a slow but significant change in the way many organisations do business. It has taken some time, but the CBI and DTI are now willing to acknowledge that, while there may be profit for some in going green, there will certainly be costs for all. The area of organisational change with regard to the environment is a critical one, and so we also examine this in more depth in the sections below.

6. **Consumers.** The early euphoria (in 1989 and 1990 in the UK) around green consumerism promised an enlightened consumer, willing, if not actually keen, to pay more for products which did not destroy the environment. Three major changes appeared to have occurred in the green consumer market by 1991.[5] First, the recession in the UK in the early 1990s has placed pressure on consumer spending and dampened enthusiasm (and the ability) to pay 'green premiums'. Second, there has been a growing

scepticism about green claims for products.[6] The green consumer has recognised that hype is no substitute for information. Third, the complexity of environmental issues as they affect products and prices has shown that educating a green market is far from simple. Until there is a reliable and thorough means of eco-labelling that demonstrates a serious concern to minimise environmental impact, we cannot know just how far a green consumer market can move the western industrial nations towards more environmentally benign practices.[7]

But so far, this slow but inexorable incorporation of environmental sensitivity into the process that generates consumer products has yet to have an especially profound effect on consumer prices. There are four major reasons for this:

1. Organisations are changing their ways of operating and thereby absorbing many of the costs

2. It is the products and services bought, rather than the prices themselves, that are changing, and which will—in the short term at least—continue to change

3. The major impact of the changes to environmental sensitivity are only now being felt, and this process will take time to fully feed through to consumers

4. Significant though some of the changes are, they still represent only a 'light green' response to the environmental crisis, and are therefore, from an environmentalist point of view, fairly superficial

There are not yet many notable moves towards the pursuit of sustainability. It is this that will have the really profound impact throughout the systems shown in Figure 1.

We will address each of these areas briefly. The first three are related to how environmental issues are encouraging organisational change and are dealt with in the next section. We will then look briefly at the 'greening of finance' before moving on to look at the immediate future and, only then, to consider how prices might reflect sustainability.

The Greening of Organisations and their Costs

On the face of it, the last few years have brought a panoply of new costs to the organisation, and one might expect these to have found their way into prices. However, the incidence of these new cost pressures is not ubiquitous, and many organisations have still been able to ignore them.[8] In the UK, the changing supplier markets, the supplier audits, the tighter COSHH regulatory framework, the increased activity of HMIP, the use of Environmental Impact Assessments (EIA), the growing costs of waste disposal, the demands of the Duty of Care etc., etc., are only now beginning to make their presence felt.[9] These are the thin ends of what may very well become very thick wedges. The UK's Environmental Protection Act, the European Community's growing environmental legislation and the dawning realisation that even 'light green' means a substantial re-think will ensure that the pressure for change is in only one direction.[10]

The message from bodies such as CBI, DoE and DTI, however, has been that there is profit in going green.[11] There is some truth in this. The rising environmental debate has encouraged organisations to consider the adoption of Total Quality Management (TQM) strategies, to minimise all forms of waste; to examine possibilities for recycling and re-use, and, especially, to investigate energy usage. Regardless of any environmental matters, these are pointers to good business practices and are likely to save money. Therefore, in the short term, many more enlightened organisations who either recognised the environmental exigencies or were simply adopting a more rigorous and sensible attitude to business, have managed to genuinely reduce their environmental impact **and** to absorb many of these new costs.[12] This has avoided the pressure on prices so far.

It is doubtful that this capacity can be exploited indefinitely, however. Environmental pressures are forcing companies away from end-of-pipe solutions into cleaner techniques. This requires significant investment, building the environmental factors into the investment at the design stage. The recent wide publicity for ICI's considerable new investment in an attempt to design-out many of the more obvious environmental impacts is the tip of a newly emerging and growing iceberg. And whether these investment costs can be amortised and absorbed by the organisations in the normal way is questionable.

The environmental issues have brought yet another uncertainty to the business environment, and product risk has thereby risen. Equally, the environmental agenda is developing so quickly that it is far from clear that companies can rely on the goalposts staying in place for any period. This means that the period over which companies will **wish** to write off new investments will be shorter—in order to stay flexible in this highly volatile environment. This must increase periodic costs and must eventually impact on prices.

Oddly enough, there is a sad irony in this. The environment is perhaps **the** major factor which requires a long-term rather than short-term perspective. The rapidly changing regulations and consumer attitudes would seem to be encouraging a pursuit of shorter payback periods. It is difficult to estimate the ultimate effects this will have or how they can be avoided. For any company faced with a fairly inelastic consumer price and a significant environmental impact, it is difficult to imagine how it can address the serious long-term restructuring necessary without taking a long-term view. The alternative would seem to spell environmental disaster.

But organisations are not just facing changing product markets; the market for employees and for finance do appear to be slowly changing. The employee market has been considered elsewhere[13] and quite how this will affect prices is not yet clear. The financial markets, on the other hand, are already showing changes and these must not be underestimated (nor, for that matter, overestimated). This aspect deserves more detailed examination.

Can one Green the Price of Finance?

Finance deserves separate attention, because it is noticeable that most discussions of environmental matters as they affect business tend to assume that any increase in costs will end in the laps of the consumer or, possibly, the employee. An equally important place where they could end up is in the laps of the financial community.[14]

One of the major costs any organisation has to bear is that of obtaining finance. This generally consists of charges for debt (interest) and, for companies, the costs of attracting (and retaining) shareholders (dividends and capital growth of share prices). Of the other related financial costs, probably the most important is that of insurance.

These financial costs not only enter the price calculations like any other set of costs, but the provision of finance also tends to be accompanied by (actual or anticipated) covenants or restrictions upon how it is employed. The financial markets (in the widest sense) are therefore very powerful, both in principle and in practice. It seems probable that the costs and terms of the provision of finance will have a significant impact on the organisation and, in particular, on the organisation's environmental activity. However, there are, so far, only three aspects of the relationship between the financial community and environmental degradation about which we can be sure:

1.　Taken as a whole, the worldwide capital markets exhibit an awesome indifference to the social and environmental performance of the companies they own, **except in so far as such performance will affect cash returns.**[15]

2. Loan creditors in general, and the banks in particular, have only recently started to take any interest in the environmental impact of the activities to which they lend.[16] This has principally been encouraged by the USA 'Superfund' experience and by the probable development of its counterpart in Europe.[17]

   At a minimum, the lenders are undertaking Environmental Audits to assess potential liability, and this will raise the costs of finance. It is likely that the increased risk of lending will also drive up the price of finance.

3. Insurance costs related to environmental cover have risen significantly as the costs of fines, penalties and law suits related to environmental catastrophe continue to grow. Some activities are now uninsurable. Thus another financial cost is rising in the face of growing fears about financial liabilities.

Thus organisations are facing complex financial markets that will not 'reward' the organisation for environmentally sound activity that has no obvious financial benefit, but will heavily penalise the organisation for any increase in risk of exposure to environmental liability. This double-edged and blatantly self-serving sword will push up an organisation's financial costs in the short term.[18] It is more likely, however, that organisations will seek rather more understanding sources of finance, or else seek ways of reducing their financial (alongside their resource) needs.

The growth of ethical and, in particular, environmental investment funds raises interesting possibilities in this area.[19] The full potential influence of the ethical funds has yet to be explored. It seems certain that they are a positive influence in encouraging companies into more environmentally benign activities. Whether this encouragement will stretch as far as foregoing dividends and capital growth in the interests of environmental sensitivity has yet to be put to the test.[20]

The role that the providers of finance play in the governance of organisations continues to be less than crystal clear. However, it is apparent that financial costs are significant, and that financial providers are increasingly concerned about their own personal liabilities. There is urgent need for more investigation into the claims that capital markets can help organisations become greener. However, it would seem that, generally, the evidence points in the opposite direction.

The Immediate Future?

We have seen that there are three forces at work that are achieving a degree of greening of prices: direct government intervention through taxes, subsidies and duties; the willingness to pay green premiums; and the consolidation of various influences and impulses along the price-generation route, which eventually turn up (in one form or another) in the price paid by consumers (see Figure 1). In the immediate future, we believe it will be via these three routes that prices will respond to environmental issues. The pressures that we have outlined will continue and, waiting in the sidelines, there are also:

- The full manifestation of the Polluter Pays Principle
- A whole array of potential tax changes—including energy taxes
- Increased fines and penalties for breaking laws and consents
- Potential subsidies for greener technologies
- The possibility of tradable pollution permits
- The continuing possibility that the United Nations (UN) will eventually manage to control Multi-national Enterprises (MNEs) in order to prevent the degradation of environments in less developed countries and the abuse of international transfer pricing
- The serious possibilities of agreements between countries much tougher than the rather feeble but widely quoted Montreal Protocol and the North Sea Agreements
- The growing interest in arrangements such as the Per Cent Club or identification of part of a price with a donation to a particular environmental activity[21]
- The EC's growing dedication to the introduction of regulations governing environmental management and control

These, and many other, possibilities are going too slowly but will certainly change the structure of the market and the processes by which prices are generated. But it is not really the prices—**in themselves**—that are the important factors. It is the regulations, the banning of products and activities, the changing attitudes and values, consumer and other boycotts, the increased policing of standards etc., that are really going to make the difference. These factors will, of course, affect price, but the normal, and rather glib, assumption that the 'market' is capable of making all the necessary adjustments itself to protect the environment is really an empty one.

Alternatives and Ways Forward?

Everything that we have discussed above has assumed a slow and gradual change which, in general, will have no very radical effect on the ways we do business. That is, we have taken the 'light green' stance that business people throughout the world are adopting[22] and to which politicians, most notably in the UK, prefer to subscribe. Such a stance can be justified if the 'environmental crisis' is really only a fad with no real substance, or else one is unconcerned about the present obvious (and the future, less obvious but likely) consequences of environmental degradation.

However, an increasing number of commentators are beginning to recognise that environmental issues are more pressing, more ubiquitous and more complex than many of the 'light green' had originally imagined. Among the factors which have encouraged this recognition are:

- The recognition that the environmental impact of industry is a great deal more widespread than at first appreciated and the costs of correction much higher.[23]

- Recognition that the global problems (acid rain, desertification, ozone depletion, species extinction, etc.) are connected and accelerating.

- Recognition of the links between economic growth and environmental degradation. This has put the question of the pursuit of unbridled growth, at least tentatively, onto the agenda.

- Recognition of the link between aid, 'third-world' debt, MNEs, economic development, poverty, starvation and environmental crises. Thus environmental issues are not only endemic, but attempts to deal with them go the very heart of the price-generation mechanism.

- This leads to questions about the inequitable distribution of material well-being in the world.

- This in turn, raises questions about our basic economic and social institutions and structures—including commerce and industry.

It was the sum of all these factors which led the United Nations in 'The Brundtland Report' to recognise that piecemeal attempts at environmental problems must fail.[24] The central issue to concentrate on is that of sustainability.

Sustainability, at its simplest, means undertaking present activity in a way which does not reduce the options available to future generations. It is widely accepted that present, especially western, ways of life are **not** sustainable. However, beyond this, the concept of sustainability and its real implications are widely debated, and there is no total consensus. It seems to us though that consumers will have to make 'more of less'—that consumption will have to fall, not rise. That is, the activities of the green consumers are not sustainable.

But price **could** be an important issue here. It would be possible to calculate a *sustainable price*—the price which not only incorporated all the economic costs but also the costs of being sustainable. These costs of being sustainable would be the costs of putting the biosphere back into the same state **after** the consumption of the product as the state which it was in **before** the product began its long haul from primary product to consumption. For some products this would clearly be impossible—the cost of using CFCs is infinite—it removes the irreplaceable, the priceless. The sustainable price of an aerosol can with CFC propellant is therefore infinity. For many other products, the sustainable price will be more achievable but **will** be considerably greater than the price which only impounds the strict 'economic' costs. If such a price could be charged, then we **really** would see price driving environmental responsibility!

But conventional price is not the only route to environmental consumer responsibility. For example, information through greater organisational accountability can achieve a great deal by informing consumers (who are also employees, teachers, parents and voters), and thereby encouraging individuals and groups to demonstrate that values and 'quality of life' (human and non-human) are more important than price. Alternatively, communities can seek to create local systems which stand outside the national and international markets.[25]

For example, the various (very successful) experiments with local money systems, with such creations of 'green dollars' as the Local Employment and Trade Systems (LETS)[26] and with alternative barter systems of one sort or another have shown that we may have to change our conceptions of what we think of as 'price', 'consumption' and 'markets'.[27] Accustomed as we are to consider 'prices' and 'markets' as exogenous we probably forget that there are many political, social, psychological, justice and community questions tied up in them. Prices can only be truly green when they do not reflect certain types of power and do not allow insulation between environment, producer and consumer.

Conclusion

In the short term, price may be greened and may provide positive benefits to the cause of environmental protection. However, from a deeper-green perspective, relatively superficial price adjustments will not provide a substantial or long-lasting boost to more benign behaviour towards the environment. More radical concepts need to be developed to do this. These might be either notions, such as the development of sustainable prices, or concepts that question the whole economic system and process that underlies this thing we take for granted—this thing called 'price'.

References

1. Jan Bebbington is Research Fellow and Rob Gray is Mathew Professor of Accounting and Information Systems in the Department of Accounting and Business Finance, University of Dundee, Dundee, DD1 4HN, Scotland, UK. Rob Gray is the author of *The Greening of Accountancy: The Profession after Pearce* (London: ACCA, 1990). Their current research into the environmental accounting and information systems being developed by organisations on which much of this chapter is based is funded by the Chartered Association of Certified Accountants and is due for publication in 1992.

2. Oscar Wilde, as quoted in H. Pearson, *The Life of Oscar Wilde* (Harmondsworth: Penguin, 1960), p. 202. The choice of 'accountant' is added to replace 'cynic'.

3. It is worth noting that the 'First Nations'—Maori, Aborigine and Red Indian, for example—had no concept of individual, private land ownership and therefore nature was, literally, priceless: something to which price cannot be attached.

   A principal theme in environmental economics is that all nature can be valued—or is implicitly valued by our actions now. Many environmental economists would argue therefore that we should make such implicit valuation explicit. The introduction of a fee, tax or levy on environmental behaviour is an implicit pricing of environmental value. Thus the current experiments with tradable pollution licenses, for example (a futures market in these is to be opened by the Chicago Board of Trade in 1993), will suggest values. Perhaps, aesthetic issues aside, it is better to have this whole process out in the open and systematic rather than piecemeal and implicit. We have considerable difficulties in accepting the suggestion that one can (or should) put a price on nature.

4. World Commission on Environment and Development, *Our Common Future* ('The Brundtland Report'; London: Oxford University Press, 1987).

5. M. Lynn, 'Can Environment Survive the Recession?', *Accountancy*, September 1991, pp. 76-77.

6. The Friends of the Earth 'Green Con of the Year Awards' and the 'Gremlin Awards' of the *Green Magazine* illustrate how widespread this hype is.

7. The most substantial efforts in this direction are probably those of New Consumer and, in particular, *Changing Corporate Values* by R. Adams, J. Carruthers and S. Hamil (London: Kogan Page, 1991). The complexity of the issues, although collated and summarised in this book, still ensure that any consumer wanting to make socially and environmentally sound purchasing decisions would be faced with considerable difficulties.

8. In our own research we have talked to a number of UK companies to whom the whole environmental agenda remains a matter of complete indifference. Further, the recent surveys of business response to the environmental agenda have shown a widely varying degree of concern and action. For a summary, see R. Gray and D. Collison, 'Environmental Audit: Green Gauge or Whitewash?', *Managerial Auditing*, Vol. 6, No. 5 (1991), pp. 17-25.

9. But still many organisations continue to exhibit the 'EDAM' syndrome: 'Environmental Legislation Doesn't Apply to Me'. See *Integrated Environmental Management* No. 3 (October 1991).

10. See, for example, P. Ghosh, 'The Green Conundrum', *Management Today*, August 1991, p. 72.

11. See for example: Confederation of British Industry, 'The Responsibilities of the British Public Company' (London: CBI, 1973); Confederation of British Industry, 'Waking up to a Better Environment' (London: CBI/PA Consulting, 1990); Department of the Environment, *Sustaining Our Common Future* (London: DoE, 1989); Department of the Environment, *Environment in Trust* (London: DoE, 1989); Department of the Environment, *Clean Technology* (London: DoE, 1989); Department of the Environment, *Environmental Protection Bill* (London: HMSO, 1989); Department of Trade and Industry, *Your Business and the Environment* (London: DTI, 1989); Department of Trade and Industry, *Cutting Your Losses* (London: DTI, 1990).

12. The most famous examples of this are 3M's 'Pollution Prevention Pays' and Dow Chemical's 'Waste Reduction Always Pays'. For more detail, see for example: J. Elkington (with T. Burke), *The Green Capitalists: Industry's Search for Environmental Excellence* (London: Victor Gollancz, 1987); J. Elkington, *The Environmental Audit: A Green Filter for Company Policies, Plants, Processes and Products* (London: SustainAbility/World Wide Fund for Nature, 1990); J. Elkington, and J. Hailes, *The Green Consumer Guide: High Street Shopping for a Better Environment* (London: Victor Gollancz, 1988); J. Elkington, P. Knight and J. Hailes, *The Green Business Guide* (London: Victor Gollancz, 1991).

13. See, for example: M. Holdgate, 'Changes in Perception', in D.J.R. Angell, J.D. Comer and M.L.N. Wilkinson (eds.), *Sustaining Earth: Response to the Environmental Threats* (London: Macmillan, 1990), pp. 79-96; M. Charter, *Graduates: Fewer and Greener* (Alton: KPH Marketing, 1990); M. Charter, *The Greener Employee* (Alton: KPH Marketing, 1990).

14. A recent survey by PR agency Dewe Rogerson of eighty fund managers found that two-thirds considered environmental factors were important for company business, although two-thirds also thought that less than 20% of UK companies had a coherent environmental policy.

15. See: D.J. Cooper, 'A Social Analysis of Corporate Pollution Disclosures: A Comment', in M. Neimark (ed.), *Advances in Public Interest Accounting*, (Greenwich, CT: JAI Press, 1988), Vol. 2, pp. 179-86; R.H. Gray, D.L. Owen and K.T. Maunders, *Corporate Social Reporting: Accounting and Accountability* (Hemel Hempstead: Prentice Hall, 1987); M.R. Mathews, 'Social Responsibility Accounting Disclosure and Information Content for Shareholders', *British*

Accounting Review 19.2 (1987), pp. 161-68; H. Mintzberg, 'The Case for Corporate Social Responsibility', *The Journal of Business Strategy* 4.2 (1983), pp. 3-15.

16. For an especially good introduction to these issues, see: D. Sarokin and J. Shulkin, 'Environmental Concerns and the Business of Banking', *Journal of Commercial Bank Lending*, February 1991, pp. 6-19.

17. The 'Superfund' Act relates to the newly established liability in the USA to clean up contaminated land. The party responsible for the clean-up need not be the person causing the mess, but might be the owner. Where banks have taken land title as security for a loan, they might find themselves with a liability. For more detail about the USA, see: L. Specht, 'What Auditors Don't Know about Environmental Laws Can Hurt Them!', *Proceedings of the Third Interdisciplinary Perspectives on Accounting Conference* (1991), Vol. 1, pp. 1.12.1–1.12.11; and for a European perspective, see: P. Aitken, 'Environmental Pressures on Business: The Polluter Pays', *The Accountants' Magazine*, January 1991, pp. 18-20; D. Wheatley, 'Greener than Green?', *New Law Journal*, 15 February 1991, pp. 208-209.

18. It is still too early to be able to assess whether this sort of thing will encourage environmentally malign or environmentally benign activity.

19. See for example: V. Burman, 'Budding Friends of the Earth', *Money Marketing*, 24 May 1990, pp. 9-10; R. Dunham, 'Virtue Rewarded', *Accountancy*, June 1988, pp. 103-105; R. Dunham, 'Ethical Funds no Bar to Profit', *Accountancy*, June 1990, p. 111; J. Edgerton, 'Investing: Tanker from Hell', *Money*, June 1989, pp. 66-67; G. Harte, 'Ethical Investment and Corporate Reporting', *The Accountants' Magazine*, March 1988, pp. 28-29; G. Harte, L. Lewis and D.L. Owen, 'Ethical Investment and the Corporate Reporting Function', *Critical Perspectives on Accounting*, forthcoming; D.L. Owen, 'Towards a Theory of Social Investment: A Review Essay', *Accounting, Organisations and Society* 15.3 (1990), pp. 249-66.

20. Such 'investment' possibilities do exist. Both Traidcraft plc and The Centre for Alternative Technology, Machynlleth, offer shares with no promise of either dividend or capital growth.

21. A body calling themselves the Ethical Investors Group distributes 50% of their profits to designated environmental groups.

22. This is perfectly illustrated by M. Stephens, 'Pressure Turned on Green Movement', *Business Review Weekly (Australia)*, 17 August 1990, pp. 87-91.

23. See, for example, P. Ghosh, 'The Green Conundrum', *Management Today*, August 1991, p. 72.

24. World Commission on Environment and Development, *Our Common Future*.

25. See for example P. Ekins (ed), *The Living Economy: A New Economics in the Making* (London: Routledge, 1986), esp. p. 17. See also D. Weston, 'The Rules of Lucre', *Geographical Magazine*, April 1991, pp. 38-40.

26. The LETS system has been running for some time on Vancouver Island, Canada. It is called by Dauncey 'barter as a collective proposition'. Money does not change hands between members of the LETS system but their purchases and sales of goods and services are recorded locally on computer

and all are encouraged to use, supply and provide local services and goods throughout the community. See also A. Dobson, *Green Political Thought* (London: Unwin Hyman, 1990).

27. For more detail, see in particular, G. Dauncey, *After the Crash: The Emergence of the Rainbow Economy* (Basingstoke: Greenprint, 1988).

Chapter 10

GREENER COMMUNICATIONS

Rita Clifton and Nicky Buss
The Green Unit, Saatchi & Saatchi Advertising

Introduction

It can be cheaper to advertise one's green virtue than to earn it
Jonathan Porritt
Former Director of Friends of the Earth

Unfortunately, this rather caustic comment was made with some justification in the light of early 'green' promotional activity. Readers will probably recall their own favourite 'howlers', e.g. 'ozone-friendly' unleaded petrol and other 'truth economies' of the time. Consumers in research groups have long recognised and criticised the 'green bandwagon', and talked of being 'taken for a green ride'.

However, after the initial panic and stampede to be 'seen to be green', with all the hype and misunderstandings it caused, it does look now as though the issue has reached a much more mature and realistic stage of development. Initially, many companies, either through lack of knowledge or through commercial pressures to get a piece of the action, seemed to treat green issues as **just marketing** issues. There is now evidence of a widespread realisation that these issues need to be tackled at the **corporate** level of policy and strategy. Recent studies by Touche Ross have indicated that more than two-thirds of larger companies now have an environmental strategy. Also, there seems a much greater acceptance that far-reaching **internal** policy and action on environmental issues must always precede external communication if the latter is to succeed.

The key for companies is to recognise their Stakeholder audiences, understand their concerns and to communicate effectively. In fact, looking at how the green issue is developing, it seems increasingly important to question **whether** an overt, public and focused green message is right for one's business now. If it is, then the next question is how one puts the message across.

That is absolutely not to imply that one should not be highly active on environmental policy and improvements. On the contrary, inactivity is just not a tenable position any more, and there can still be real business gains made by publicising proactive, substantial and relevant environmental initiatives. The major supermarket chains are perhaps the best examples of this, battling for the 'environmental high ground', with own-label ranges of 'greener' products, information leaflets, recycling facilities, and so on.

In many product categories, a certain standard of green credentials is just a 'given', a part of the total quality mix of a product or brand—for instance, no CFCs in aerosols, recyclable or compact packaging, etc. And in this more mature phase of greening, the 'say anything to be seen to be green' philosophy is doomed to fail. Nowadays, companies need to be even more disciplined and sophisticated in planning and implementing any kind of green message—both from a consumer perception and a regulatory point of view. With the implications of 1992 and the plethora of European directives on the environment, not to mention the increasingly strict guidelines applied in the UK to green promotion, this point is becoming critical for business success, or even survival. The effect of this and of the current state of environmental issues was well described by the *Investors' Chronicle* in its article, 'A New Phase in the Green Revolution':

> There will be less hype amongst marketers and media, but there will be a greater necessity to be aware of the growing impact of the environmental legislation that is now coming on stream or being proposed.
>
> Furthermore, the present recession makes it more, not less, important for businesses to look to their 'environment-friendliness'. For while there is anecdotal evidence that companies, especially smaller ones, may be putting off compliance with green laws to protect dwindling profits, they run the risk in so doing of being killed off by the competition, or being closed down by regulators.[1]

This chapter will examine some of the issues for greener communications. It is, however, important to bear in mind that the general strategies and guidelines outlined here for communications to consumers will apply equally to communications directed at other Stakeholders, both internal and external. Areas relevant to employee communications will also be covered in Chapter 11.

Basic Disciplines of Greener Communication

Talking about greener communications to greener Stakeholders, and particularly greener consumers, might make it sound as though there is suddenly a world full of entirely changed people out there, and somehow a new and magic formula is needed for a 'style' of greener communication to reach them successfully. Worse still, it makes it sound as though green is just an ingredient one can add at whim to the marketing mix this year, just a passing fad out there in the marketplace.

There is, of course, no magic green method or style of promotion. Quite the opposite; it cannot be emphasised too strongly that greener communication should be approached in just the same way as any other communication: the basic disciplines are the same. And the same questions need to be asked, namely:

- Is there something substantial that can be said about the greenness of your product or company that will drive the business?

- Who should you be talking to (by product category)? How do they currently feel and behave?

- What can and should be said to them to encourage them to buy the product or company? Is it a major feature, or just reassurance?

- If it is a major feature, you will need single-minded communication, which will stand out and be seen, be understood, be relevant, and be true.

- If just a reassurance or a 'given', what kind of communication and promotion would be appropriate to use, and at what level?

Many companies have felt pressured by the speed of green development into just saying and doing something, or blowing small gestures towards environmental consciousness out of all proportion—only to trivialise their efforts (and the seriousness of the problem) and contribute to the inevitable consumer confusion and cynicism.

However, being an environmentally responsible corporate citizen does not stop at marketing; companies have to take a holistic approach to environmental management, especially if they are planning to communicate environmental activities to the public. Any greening process must be effected thoroughly and completely, not cosmetically and hypocritically. If a company is not prepared to go all the way, it cannot even think about trying to develop its environmental image with the public. It will not work because its vulnerabilities will far outweigh the good things it is doing to protect the environment. Companies will have to practise what they preach, as they will increasingly come under the spotlight from a more sceptical public and better-informed media.

So in summary, the principles of planning and implementing a green message are the same as any other communication, but the communicator needs to be even more scrupulous and responsible. To be successful in communications requires that an environmental policy is set to demonstrate commitment from the highest level, and is sincere.

Who is the Consumer?

If the same disciplines are going to be applied to planning and executing greener communication as they are to any other sort of communication, it will be crucial to look first at would-be greener consumers, and get to grips with how they feel and behave.

Well, of course there is nothing new about consumer concern for the environment on a local level, i.e. rubbish and litter on the streets, or concern about having a motorway in your back garden—people just did not call it the environment then. Global ecology issues, however, were very much seen as the province of intellectuals and academics, ex-hippies and radical 'greens'. What media coverage they received, if any, was limited to intellectual and scientific articles, or minority television, and referred to things happening far away, in the rainforests, or far out to sea. The issue simply did not connect with ordinary people.

Research groups formerly expressed public feelings of helplessness and people's belief that they could not effect a change:

The world is being destroyed, but there is nothing we can do.

Nothing I can do individually is going to make any difference.

For them to listen and take notice, consumers said 'you have to make environmental issues immediately relevant to **my** environment, **my** life'. And that is exactly what has happened with the green consumer revolution. After the jolt of Chernobyl, and the rush of national issues, such as the seal virus in the North Sea, there was real heightened public concern, and an acceptance that global, ecological issues could affect them personally. Now all that was needed was for acceptable personal solutions to be offered and individual actions to be encouraged. The publication of *The Green Consumer Guide*,[2] along with very focused publicity surrounding CFC-free aerosols ensured that this happened.

The result has been the emergence of the 'environmentally concerned' consumer, and today in the UK, it is difficult to find people who are not concerned about nuclear waste, the ozone layer, about pollution, rainforests, the greenhouse effect, and so on. These consumers have now been given the opportunity and encouragement to act on their concerns.

The difference now is that they have realised or have been told that they, personally, can do something that will make a difference. Recent studies indicate that at least 60% of consumers say they are prepared to withdraw their custom from companies which are exposed as polluters, and around 40% claim to have made a positive contribution through environment-friendlier purchasing decisions. Depending on which figures one looks at, and which product category, up to 25% of consumers say they were prepared to pay substantially more for these products.

How Widespread is the New Consumer?

There is of course a real danger of taking these kinds of theoretical claims at face value. Looking at these figures in the earlier stages, many companies and manufacturers were urgently motivated by a combination of panic and greed into making over-enthusiastic green claims in marketing and advertising, and being over-optimistic about the sort of price premiums they could charge. However, in practice it has been shown that the majority of consumers are radical at the research questionnaire and reactionary at the checkout. For instance, although research suggested that 50% of their customers would be willing to pay extra, Tesco are reported to have found that their cash receipts suggested that only 10% actually did.

Just because consumers had got the message about the ozone layer, and acted by choosing CFC-free aerosols, did not mean they had suddenly become broad-issue, self-motivated green consumers across everything they did. There is a limited trade-off that consumers are prepared to make in the real world. While 'theoretical willing' might be there, for the moment at least, most consumers are just not prepared to give up the things they know and the price and performance standards they have come to expect. They also like using the brands they are accustomed to, and have limited time, limited budgets and limited altruism. CFCs and aerosols required no trade-off in product, image or price terms. And the explanatory job was done so thoroughly by the media that all an advertiser had to do was to rubber-stamp his usual advertising with a reassuring sign-off.

This is just not the case yet with other issues. Although most people are aware of terms, such as 'greenhouse effect' and 'acid rain', they are often very confused about what they really mean, and particularly how these issues affect them personally, or what they in turn as individuals can do about them. After the initial rush and euphoria, scientific disagreements and bogus claims have muddied the waters. Now mainstream consumers have become confused, cynical and disillusioned with many greener products. As one consumer put it, 'you just don't know who to believe'.

Companies should not therefore jump to conclusions about consumers' understanding of, and likelihood to respond *en masse* to, broad, assumptive greener communications. Each category needs to be looked at on its own merits with consumers before effective communications can be developed. And mostly the onus will be on the marketers to educate consumers and simplify environmental issues, as well as to offer product solutions.

Finally, the end user is not the only relevant Stakeholder to be identified and understood in the context of green issues. For many companies, opinion formers, the media, politicians and environmental pressure groups are all key targets for any greener communications. Companies will almost certainly find that all Stakeholders in a business have been or can be touched in some way by environmental issues, whether from a personal or professional perspective. It might be from a schoolchild coming home and lecturing parents on environmental responsibility, or the realisation of commercial problems and opportunities from political and media coverage. Increasingly, the business-to-business communication is becoming more and more important for manufacturers and suppliers. After all, if a company (and particularly a retailer these days) is taking some kind of environmental stance, and has an environmental policy, they are going to be more demanding of the green credentials and green practices from their suppliers. Again, the major retailers are good examples of this. Gateway issued a report on packaging in 1990, which introduced a tough and proactive policy on supplier packaging. In it they promised to phase out materials that did not conform to their green standards. The report provoked considerable controversy, but is a good example of retailer policy forcing supplier compliance. More details of Gateway's Greener Packaging policy are given in Part III.

What To Say

As mentioned in the introduction, the first question here is often not what to say about your company or product in communicating a green message, but whether it is appropriate to communicate the message as a main feature. There are two reasons for this: first, communicating a one-off or less-than-thorough environmental initiative runs the risk of alienating consumers and opinion formers if the corporate environmental policy is limited or insincere. In exaggerating environmental contributions, the regulatory and media backlash could endanger the product, service or corporate integrity—even if the claim is valid in the first place. For instance, Friends of the Earth (FoE) have been operating a 'Green Con of the Year Award' over the past few years, and British Nuclear Fuels and Eastern Electricity were the unfortunate recipients in 1989 and 1990, based on promotional claims FoE deemed to be misleading. It is difficult to quantify the effect of the ensuing bad publicity, but whatever it was, it would still act against the corporate image both companies were trying to foster. The rules applying to environmental communication are now quite stringent, and with the launch of an EC eco-label in the Autumn of 1992, any cosmetic or overblown claims will certainly be exposed for what they are, while conscientious competitors will reap their rewards of retail distribution and consumer sales.

The second issue is whether a green message is appropriate for your Stakeholders and, particularly, consumers. This will depend on both how committed and educated the users of your product are, and on the competitive environment. As mentioned, in many product categories now, a certain standard of green credentials is just a 'given', a part of the total quality mix of a product or brand. A company needs to establish through research whether green is or could be a major driver of their individual markets, and whether it can offer a differential competitive advantage. If a particular green credential (e.g. recyclable packaging, non-bleached pulp, etc.) is becoming a 'given', why spend a lot of money telling your consumers you are just like everybody else? Perhaps a pack mention, or other method of reassurance would be more appropriate.

How To Say It?

There are a variety of communications tools available within a Greener Marketing mix, which will be explored more fully below. Whichever are chosen, however, in order to be effective it is important that they are used within an integrated and coordinated environmental strategy for the reasons outlined earlier, and that they should follow the disciplines of all good communication mentioned earlier, i.e. to be single-minded in one's approach, **to stand out and be seen, to be understood, to be relevant, and to be true.**

It is easy to lapse into the bland, expected and interchangeable. Consumers have been inundated with the cliched, generic imagery of greening in much of environmental communication: trees, more trees, nature, wildlife and, of course, babies, globes and dolphins. Very few of these images have been used with enough freshness or energy to break through the noise of media advertising with a compelling message. As a result, consumers have tended to remember only generic product categories, such as unleaded petrol and ozone-friendly deodorants, rather than distinct brand names. The generic and cliched imagery has also contributed to the consumer concern of companies jumping on the bandwagon.

As far as the requirement to 'be understood' is concerned, far too much communication has assumed detailed consumer knowledge or motivation across a whole range of environmental issues. Each issue or problem needs to be explained on its own account, and then the reason why the consumer should change behaviour brought to life and made directly relevant to them. For instance, why recycling is important, why buying phosphate-free detergents can be a good thing, why energy efficient appliances/organic produce seem to cost a lot more, and, specifically, what direct and noticeable benefit it will have.

The final requirement—'to be true'—is a particularly contentious issue for greener communications. There have been numerous complaints made to the advertising standards authorities, and newspaper headlines exposing bogus green claims. The risks to any marketer of either doing nothing about the environmental unfriendliness of a brand or company, or at the other extreme of making exaggerated, over-enthusiastic claims, cannot be over-emphasised. Having spent many years building good consumer loyalty and goodwill towards a brand, the last things needed are derogatory headlines in the popular press with disastrous effects on both corporate integrity and the bottom line.

There are specific guidelines for environmental claims. With regard to advertising, any generalised claim for environmental benefit will be assessed in view of its net environmental benefit, taking into account 'the complete life cycle of the product and its packaging, and any effects on the environment of its manufacture, use and disposal' (ITVA). And,

> while [extravagant language] may present the claim as forcefully as possible, it will most probably have the effect of confusing and possibly misleading. Shaking consumers' confidence in advertising and provoking cynicism is not the way forward. In the long term no advertising will be successful unless it is believable and proven to be true. Most consumers are not experts on 'the greenhouse effect', 'acid rain' or ozone layer depletion

rates, and advertisers have a special duty to ensure accuracy in an area where even the scientists are not yet absolutely certain of the facts (Advertising Standards Authority).

Any communication can and should only reflect the reality of a company or brand's green policy—it cannot drive it.

So in terms of executing communication, companies should not over-assume people's knowledge or altruism when it comes to any green issues. Neither should they under-assume how much consumers like their current brands, their lifestyles and their price and performance standards. The majority are not out to seek ways to complicate their lives, but they might take notice of a simple, compelling and explanatory story from a legitimate brand or company. And this compelling explanation will be critically important if companies are expecting them to pay a premium for what might ostensibly be seen as a less effective or less attractive product. Unfortunately, this perception is often what affects green products, and is offputting to all but the most committed. As an example of a hardening and more cynical mass-market attitude towards the green issue, a *Sun* headline in 1989 urged its readers 'Go for Green!!!' Eighteen months later the same tabloid was asking 'Green, but does it Clean?'

Many companies are failing to communicate green policies and actions to customers. A survey by David Bellamy Associates in November 1991[3] found that less than 25% of companies provide information on their green activities, although nearly 40% were considering doing so in the future. Customer information is more often produced by consumer goods companies than by 'sensitive' sectors, such as oil and chemical companies. Many companies were aware that pressure groups were ready to attack unsound approaches, and they were reticent about placing themselves in the spotlight.

The Range of Tools in the Promotional Mix

While the principles are the same across the communication and promotional spectrum, there are specific points which a company should ask itself with regard to particular elements and practical procedures. Public attitudes towards advertising claims, and copy-checking authorities for media advertising have been discussed above.

Corporate and Public Relations

- Have you done an Environmental Audit to establish exactly where your company and product stands—from a regulatory and 'selling benefit' point of view? (This should, of course, be done anyway.) Have you actioned its recommendations, and thought how you could be proactive as much as corrective? If you do say something specific about yourself, are there any other environmental issues on which you might be exposed to criticism?

- Do you know exactly what you would say in answer to enquiries about your 'green credentials'? Do you have an open and honest approach to enquiries? (If not, you had better pay attention to upcoming EC directives and commitment to access to information, as in the USA.)

- Presumably your Stakeholders will want to know what is being done—particularly in terms of their responsibility, and business liability?

- Do you ensure a good 'corporate citizen' relationship with your employees and local community?

- Perhaps PR is a good way of publicising genuine environmental projects and initiatives to more selective groups?

Lobbying

- Will your organisation be affected by the Environmental Protection Act? Do you know about the impact of the forthcoming EC directives relating to the environment, and whether they will have an impact on your business?

- Would it be a good idea for your company to be involved at the consultative stage (i.e. now) rather than have the regulations forced upon you by competitors and hostile groups?

Sponsorship

This can be a very good way of targeting support, and obviously has spin-off benefits for both the company and the environmental project/ group being supported. But this will not work if it is cynically trying to veil environmental problems. The publicity and 'poor fit' will be exposed. However, some companies choose to donate money on a private, anonymous basis, until they are more confident of public green credentials.

Ideas might include:

- Money or land for environmental projects

- Equipment, training and literature for environmental organisations and groups

- Linking purchases to donations (e.g. World Wide Fund for Nature, etc.)
- Contributing to local community/school activities

Direct Marketing

Despite the fact that direct marketing is used with success in fundraising by charitable organisations, such as The World Wildlife Fund and Greenpeace, it is still often overwhelmed by the term 'junk mail' in consumers' eyes. If a company wishes to utilise the efficiency and tight targeting possible with direct marketing, and particularly if it is to convey a green message, it is worthwhile asking the questions:

- Is the list as 'clean', efficient and up-to-date as it can be?
- Can the mailings be justified in terms of bulk and weight? Can you say it better and less often?
- Can recycled materials, and non-chlorine-bleached paper be used? Can less toxic inks be used, rather than those with heavy metals?

Personal Selling

- Do the salesforce understand the company's environmental policies? And have they been made aware of the broader issues?
- Are the salesforce developing relationships or selling one-off products?

  There is no point in developing cleaner or more energy efficient technologies and products, if they are not going to be sold at least as aggressively as their more polluting or wasteful competitors.[4]

- How carefully are the ethics of the salesforce monitored?
- Has the car fleet been converted to unleaded petrol, and are new cars fitted with catalytic converters?

Other Things to Bear in Mind

Consider the greenness of your suppliers—agencies, printers or otherwise. Do your suppliers understand the effect of green trends on your business, and are they being proactive in this area? Have they begun the greening process in their own businesses, or developed an environmental action plan? A company's agencies should be an important source of grass-roots information on the pace of greening and changing attitudes in the marketplace, and as such should be leading environmental initiatives. However, companies will need to be realistic about the effects environmental demands might have. For instance, quite often the cost of friendlier alternatives might be higher, or the product less effective. At the end of the day, all customers and suppliers want a good-quality product at a reasonable price and, particularly in service industries and communications, the customer is rarely prepared to put up with what appears to be second-best quality in a competitive environment. There needs to be understanding on both sides.

Conclusion

It should be clear by now that green is here to stay. Despite increasing consumer scepticism and an increasing realisation of the complexities and difficulties involved, the environment is still a mass-market concern. The issue now is not 'Should we?' but 'How far and how fast can we and should we go?' And 'Who is responsible for your company's environmental strategy? Have you consulted an environmental expert to carry out an audit of your company's environmental strengths, weaknesses, opportunities and threats?'

There seem to be two options on the environment: either to control your own destiny, or to have it controlled for you. Legislation will require companies to address environmental policy, so change is going to have to be made either now voluntarily, or later by forced regulation. And there is the chance to reap real business rewards by being proactive, for instance, in the way that 3M, The Body Shop, Sainsbury's and Tesco are now finding.

There is also evidence that consumers do not expect their favourite brands and favoured companies merely to hitch a ride on the green bandwagon—they expect them to be driving it. And while they might not be ready to jump yet themselves, they will expect the brands and companies to be there, offering them the choice for whenever they do—or even encouraging them.

Finally, green should be seen as only the first major symptom of changing social attitudes and a feeling of growing collective responsibility—a new humanisation, or perhaps even a new 'feminisation' in society! This means a growing consumer awareness of the need for good 'corporate citizenship' from business, and of Corporate Social Responsibility across a broad range of ethical issues, of which the environment will be a part. Social attitude surveys across Europe suggest this is a leading-edge consumer trend, particularly among the young.

And today's young activists can also be tomorrow's consumers and even management trainees.

So it would seem the ethical consumer, never mind the greener consumer, is now on his or her way, making purchasing decisions influenced by a wide range of social issues. Consumers want to know that the company behind a greener product or greener communication is environmentally and socially responsible. Companies should and will need to think more broadly about the total impact and implications of their business—and, indeed, about how to communicate and to promote this to new and discerning Stakeholders.

References

1. Gareth Jones, 'A New Phase in the Green Revolution', *Investors' Chronicle*, 20 September 1991.
2. J. Elkington and J. Hailes, *The Green Consumer Guide: High Street Shopping for a Better Environment* (London: Victor Gollancz, 1988).
3. David Bellamy Associates, 'Industry Goes Green' (November 1991).
4. Keith Brunt of Boots, quoted in J. Elkington, T. Burke and J. Hailes, *Green Pages: The Business of Saving the World* (London: Routledge, 1988).

Chapter 11

GREENER PEOPLE

Martin Charter
Director, KPH Marketing

Introduction

Society has rapidly moved through what some have coined the 'selfish seventies' and 'aggressive eighties' to arrive at the 'caring nineties' or the 'green decade'.[1] With the declining number of younger people across western Europe, this will mean a greater need to attract quality staff, and to nurture and develop existing employees.

Environmental awareness and concern is growing among managers and employees, notably within younger groups, and this is leading to the emergence of corporate environmentalists at all levels in the organisation. Employees seek a sense of purpose in their jobs, and good environmental performance may not necessarily motivate all employees to excel but, conversely, corporate negligence or tokenism may act as universal demotivating factors. On implementing Greener Marketing strategies, a key factor will be the generation of employees' support. An aware, committed and motivated workforce will be the company's best asset.

This chapter will first examine the emergence of the greener employee, and will consider some of the implications for organisational change. Next, the changing demographic trends will be analysed, coupled with the increase in environmental education among younger people. The response by companies will then be examined alongside the need to undertake internal marketing of green policies, and to develop environmental awareness and training among employees.

The Greener Employee

Employees' attitudes have been changing over the last two decades. Since the early seventies, Taylor Nelson has been monitoring the emergence of three groups, the 'Inner-Directed', the 'Outer-Directed', and the 'Sustenance-Driven'. 'Outer-Directeds' are concerned about material matters and external appearances. 'Sustenance-Driven' people tend to be reactionary and fear change. 'Inner-Directeds' as consumers and employees are more concerned with the objectives and behaviour of the firm, the nature of the product, relationships with employees, and the company's social and environmental impact. The research indicates that these individuals have a greater need for personal growth and development, and are the type of employees that companies want.[2] The largest and fastest growing proportion of 'Inner-Directeds' is in Europe (see Fig. 1).

The Spread of Inner-Directedness			
	Inner-Directed (%)	Outer-Directed (%)	Sustenance-Driven (%)
Europe	28	41	31
USA	19	49	32
Japan	10	55	35

Source: J. Elkington, T. Burke, and J. Hailes, *Green Pages: The Business of Saving the World* (London: Routledge, 1988)

Figure 1

Back in 1989, MORI conducted a survey among 200 senior business-people, covering attitudes to environmental issues. The research indicated that the UK's top business-people appeared to be greener, but they did not perceive the same level of interest among other groups in society, indicating that they were out of touch with the undercurrents developing among the rest of the population. Sixty-five per cent of the sample claimed to have raised money for environmental groups, 20% were members of green groups, and 10% had been actively involved in campaigning on an environmental issue (see Fig. 2).

In 1990, two surveys[3] indicated that environmental concern in the UK was strong and was increasing among prospective and existing managers (see Figs. 3 and 4).

Another study in 1991 by David Bellamy Associates[4] indicated that 63% of the sample of 176 managers thought the environment was very important to them personally, but only 51% thought the environment was quite important to their business and customers. It suggests that many individuals are facing a number of dilemmas, with some

Business-People's Personal Response to Environmental Issues

Activity over the past year	Business-people	General public	Business-people's estimate of public activity
	%	%	%
Choice of product actively influenced by green packaging/ advertising	65	42	27
Given/raised money for wildlife or conservation charities	65	41	20
Started using lead-free petrol	57	15	19
Membership of environmental group or charity	20	8	11
Campaigned about an environmental issue	10	5	8

Source: MORI/RSCG, 'The Greener Manager' (May 1989)

Figure 2

Change in Interest towards Corporate Environmental Matters over the past 12 Months

	Graduates	Managers
	%	%
Strongly increased	22	21
Increased	44	53
About the same	34	25
Decreased	–	–
Strongly decreased	–	1

Source: M. Charter, *Graduates: Fewer and Greener* (KPH Marketing, 1990), and M. Charter, *The Greener Employee* (KPH Marketing, 1990)

Figure 3

companies selling products and services whose environmental performance is lower than employees and customers may wish.

In a number of organisations, employees are forming 'eco-consciousness' groups as internal pressures for change. Some North

Strength of Interest in Green and Environmental Matters		
	Graduates **%**	**Managers** **%**
Very strong	22	18
Strong	38	38
Average	36	37
Little interest	3	6
No interest	2	–

Source: M. Charter, *Graduates: Fewer and Greener* (KPH Marketing, 1990), and M. Charter, *The Greener Employee* (KPH Marketing, 1990)

Figure 4

American and European companies are recognising the importance of the employee in the greening process, but overall, UK companies are being slow to adapt.

Companies whose environmental practices are relatively poor will find it increasingly difficult to recruit and retain staff, as employees, conscious of their value on the job market, begin to discriminate between employers' agendas as well as their salaries and conditions (see Fig. 5).

A survey[5] by ICM Research conducted for *The Guardian* newspaper in 1990 indicated that a number of industries have problems with their corporate image, which in some cases are being translated into difficulties in recruitment, especially among graduates (see Fig. 6).

A number of organisations are now examining where corporate values lie within the organisation. Companies must attempt to match employee needs and goals against organisational needs and goals. A key strategic issue for companies will be the nurturing of existing employees, and a number of companies are taking innovative steps towards personal development. IBM are using techniques such as guided imagery and the *I Ching*—The Chinese Book of Wisdom[6]— based on a philosophy of unceasing change, and the interconnectedness of all things. The approach is used to help employees live with the effects of change, which are putting them under increasing pressure in the workplace and at home.

The re-examination of key values and beliefs within companies may lead to significant organisational change (see Fig. 7). Oticon, a Danish hearing-aid manufacturer, is a good example of the 'new-age' thinking taking place in some companies. It is possibly Europe's first paperless

Companies or Industries Perceived to have Bad Records on Environmental Matters

	Graduates %	Managers %
Exxon	34	4
Nuclear	28	10
Oil	18	21
ICI	15	13
Petrochemical	12	7
Union Carbide	12	–
McDonald's	11	–
Engineering	–	4

Source: M. Charter, *Graduates: Fewer and Greener* (KPH Marketing, 1990), and M. Charter, *The Greener Employee* (KPH Marketing, 1990)

Figure 5

Protection of the Environment by Industry (Top Five Sectors)

	Very good	Fairly good	Fairly bad	Very bad	Don't know
Chemical industry	1%	14%	40%	29%	16%
Nuclear industry	1%	14%	29%	32%	24%
Automotive/car industry	1%	30%	38%	15%	16%
Oil/petrochemical industry	1%	19%	29%	27%	24%
Power industry	2%	28%	26%	15%	29%

Source: ICM, 1990

Figure 6

office, with incoming mail scanned into a computer system and then shredded and ejected from the office down a giant perspex tube that runs out of the offices via the works canteen. The only other paper products in the building are each employee's essential files, which are restricted to their personal trolleys. There are no desks, only terminals, and employees can not only choose where they want to sit each day, but also what job they would like to do, subject to their technical qualifications. The staff are viewed as a team, and flexibility and all-round ability are seen as essential to the company's success. Oticon is 25% owned by its 472 employees, and has achieved a 12% share of

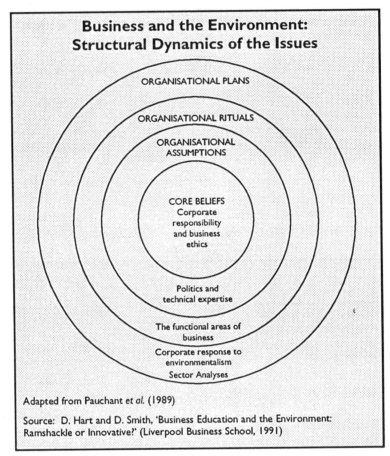

Figure 7

the world hearing-aid market. Since the company established its greener organisational plan, it claims a 15% increase in productivity in the first twelve months, and predicts a further 30% increase over the next three years.[7]

Organisations appear to be increasing the value they place on the knowledge and intelligence input of employees, with a shift in emphasis from manufacture (making by hand) towards 'mentifacture' (making by thinking). Emphasis on brain skills has implications for the relationship between employers and employees, as companies will be increasingly dependent on the information held by their employees, and on their creative and problem-solving abilities. This will enable quality employees to demand better working conditions, and more flexibility. Tomorrow's firms will be built on mental capabilities and values, and it will be these that determine success.[8]

Changing Demographics

Throughout the nineties, European companies will have to face a considerable decline in the number of young people. Human Resource strategies will need to identify requirements among target employee groups clearly, and examine opportunities to recruit from under-represented groups such as women, racial minorities, and the less able. The greener company will have to look closely at policies such as equal opportunities if it is to attract these groups. Women returners may be more likely to be attracted by a more responsible company, as research indicates that they tend to be greener than their male counterparts.

In the mid-nineties, western Europe will see a significant downturn in the number of young people (see Figs. 8 and 9). Young people are likely to be more environmentally literate, and this will mean that companies will need to take account of an increasingly critical employee and consumer audience. Germany (West) will be particularly affected by the demographic shortfall. Georg Winter, the founder of BAUM (German Environmentalist Business Management Association), has suggested that the recruitment policy should be viewed as part of a Greener Marketing strategy in that the cosmetic will not be tolerated—the corporate approach must be integrated or quality employees will not be attracted or retained.[9]

In a number of surveys, women as employees and consumers appear to be more concerned about environmental issues. The corporate image of the company aligned with the provision of childcare and training facilities may become key factors in attracting women returners.[10] A study in *The Director* magazine[11] indicated that the family were increasingly influencing directors (still tending to be males) to improve environmental performance, as children are receiving more environmental education, and women are being targeted by Greener Marketing campaigns (see Fig. 10).

Environmental Education

Environmental awareness is increasing in schools throughout Europe. In May 1988, the Council of Education Ministers of the European Community agreed 'on the need to take concrete steps for the promotion of environmental education ... throughout the community', and adopted a resolution to improve environmental education. In the UK, Environmental Studies narrowly missed being included in the national curriculum, although its importance as a cross-curricular subject is being recognised, and environmental topics are appearing on a variety of different syllabuses. Children and students are acting as important

Demographic Change among 15–19 Year-Olds			
	1990 (millions)	2000 (millions)	% change
UK	4.3	3.7	−15.1
Belgium	0.7	0.6	−14.1
Denmark	0.4	0.3	−25.5
France	4.3	3.9	−10.1
Germany (West)	4.2	3.3	−22.1
Greece	0.7	not available	−
Ireland	0.3	0.3	−11.2
Italy	4.6	3.1	−33.2
Luxembourg	0.02	0.02	−9.1
Portugal	0.9	0.7	−19.5
Spain	3.3	2.5	−22.8
The Netherlands	1.2	0.9	−23.9
Total	24.9	19.9	−20.2
Source: Eurostat, 1990			

Figure 8

Demographic Change among 20–24 Year-Olds			
	1990 (millions)	2000 (millions)	% change
UK	4.8	3.5	−27.3
Belgium	0.8	0.6	−23.0
Denmark	0.4	0.3	−22.2
France	4.3	3.6	−14.6
Germany (West)	5.3	3.2	−39.8
Greece	0.8	not available	−
Ireland	0.3	0.3	−5.5
Italy	4.9	3.7	−23.8
Luxembourg	0.03	0.02	−23.2
Portugal	0.9	0.8	−9.0
Spain	3.3	3.1	−5.5
The Netherlands	1.3	1.0	−25.2
Total	26.5	20.8	−21.3
Source: Eurostat, 1990			

Figure 9

Have You Found Yourself under any Pressure from the Following Groups to Develop an Environmental Policy?			
	All	Manufacturing (%)	Services (%)
Public opinion	49.5	51.6	49.5
Family	48.0	39.1	53.5
Employees	25.3	21.1	28.3
Customers	21.3	25.5	17.7
Suppliers	6.7	9.2	5.1

Source: Tom Nash, 'Green about the Environment', *The Director*, February 1990

Figure 10

green catalysts, raising family consciousness by reporting back what has been learned about the environment at school or college.

The key for chief executives and corporate planners is to recognise that attitudes are forming early. The younger generation will be the consumers, investors and employees of the future, and their increasing awareness through the education system and media should not be overlooked. These attitudes are likely to develop as environmental matters become increasingly integrated.

Graduates and younger people are starting to ask more questions about companies' environmental records (see Fig. 11). Individuals are looking at corporate stances, with environmental aspects being one area of investigation. Policies on nuclear armaments, animal experimentation, and less developed countries are all starting to move onto the agenda.

A recent survey[12] amongst 1,107 business studies students from Europe and North America indicated that environmental pollution controls were perceived to be a major issue for business in the nineties, with this perception significantly stronger in Scandinavia, Italy and Germany (see Fig. 12). Overall, German business students' attitudes on environmental issues appear to be considerably more developed than their counterparts. In 1984 a survey was conducted among the Association of Young German Businessmen. Seventy-seven per cent welcomed the incorporation of environmental protection into the constitution of their organisation, 75% intended to adopt a more environmentalist approach to production, while 60% were prepared to make economic sacrifices in the interests of the environment.[13]

Importance of Socially Responsible Corporate Image Perceived by Graduates when Selecting Potential Employers			
		Sex	
	Total	Male	Female
	%	%	%
Very important	30	26	33
Important	44	43	45
Average	17	15	18
Little importance	6	9	4
No importance	1	6	0

Source: M. Charter, *Graduates: Fewer and Greener* (Alton: KPH Marketing, 1990)

Figure 11

A number of new student initiatives have been established in the UK during 1991. For example, the Green Business Club was formed among MBAs at the London Business School, with over sixty members recruited out of an intake of 200, indicating considerable interest in green issues among potential 'high fliers'.

Environmental aspects are being slowly integrated into a small number of MBA management programmes, notably INSEAD in France, Limerick in Eire, and Manchester, Bristol and Canterbury in the UK. But the majority of business schools are lagging behind the speed of recent developments.

Two surveys in Britain and Scotland[14] in 1991 indicated that universities and polytechnics are also being slow to provide undergraduate courses that include input on green issues and business ethics, even though perceived student response is seen to be favourable. There is little indication that new areas such as Environmental Auditing (EA), Integrated Pollution Control (IPC), and Life Cycle Analysis (LCA) are receiving attention in syllabuses. This low uptake of green issues bodes ill for a change in the finance-based model that dominates business education. Interestingly, the British survey indicated that the prime pressures for course development came from staff and students. In response to the lack of information being provided by business educators, an increasing number of students are choosing to complete green business projects themselves.

Environmental understanding and awareness is developing in even younger age groups. The Henley Centre conducted a study for British Telecom in 1991 entitled 'Young Eyes: Children's Vision of the Future

European Business Studies Students:
Top Five Issues Regarded as Having the Most Impact on European Companies

Nationality

	Total	Belgium	Germany	UK	France	Spain	Italy	Scandi-navia	Other West Europe	Other
Environmental pollution controls	3.9	3.7	4.1	3.6	3.2	3.6	4.2	4.2	4.2	3.9
International financial instability	3.5	3.3	3.1	3.5	3.9	3.9	3.7	3.6	3.2	4.0
Trade unions	2.9	2.7	2.8	2.4	2.6	3.4	2.8	3.1	2.5	3.3
Consumer groups	3.2	3.1	3.1	2.9	2.8	3.6	3.3	3.3	3.0	3.5
Government regulation of business	3.0	3.0	2.8	2.9	3.1	3.1	2.8	2.9	2.8	3.5

Source: Profile/AIESEC, 'Tomorrow's Managers: Sheep, Horse or Wolf' (February 1989)

Figure 12

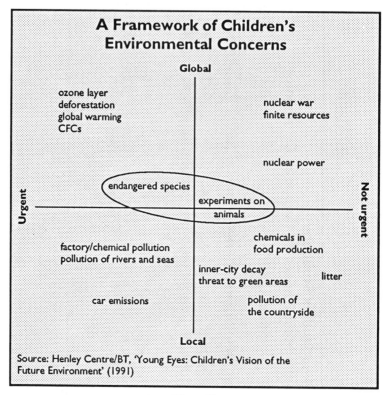

Figure 13

Environment', indicating that strong green undercurrents are starting to develop among younger groups (see Fig. 13). The survey was conducted among 450 10–14 year-olds. Levels of environmental concern were high, as most children believed environmental problems were urgent and may directly affect society in their lifetimes, and values tended to be realistic and pragmatic, as opposed to being woolly idealism.

A cynicism appears to be developing about environmental claims made on behalf of products, especially among older children. Inconsistent claims are likely to be picked up and high environmental standards will be expected from cradle to grave. They will expect manufacturers and retailers to provide easily digestible facts about products and environmental performance.

Government and industry are seen as potentially enabling society to make an effective consumer response. Expectations are that industry should be proactive in researching environmentally benign alternatives to existing products. If substitutes are provided, customers will be willing to pay more, but not at the cost of functional or aesthetic shortfalls. Government will be expected to encourage and force industry to develop environmentally benign processes, and to stimulate conscious consumerism through the market mechanisms, such as the price differential between unleaded and leaded petrol.

Other surveys among younger people have indicated that concern for environmental issues is strong and is seen as a normal common-sense reaction to the problems. An earlier survey,[15] in 1990, among 329,000 of Barclays Bank's 11–19 year-old customers indicated that concern over global environmental matters was growing, with twice as many 11–15 year-olds voting global warming and the disappearing ozone layer as their greatest concern, compared to the previous year.

Another survey[16] among 14–16 year-olds in the UK, France, Germany and Spain indicated similar concern arising throughout Europe. The UK was the most 'environmentally aware' and concerned, and issues were perceived as relatively new—the property of younger people with high commitment to action.

German children saw the issues as part of everyday life, and the property of teenagers, parents or older people. Awareness of the problems was high, with commitment to overt action less developed, but perceived to get stronger with age, typically when they reached 20–30 years. French and Spanish children's attitudes to environmental issues were not 'top of mind' and commitment was low, especially in Spain. The dominating attitude was one of helplessness and powerlessness, although teenagers felt they would become more active as they grew older.

Corporate Response

Corporate environmental policies should come from the top, and a number of companies worldwide are introducing positive initiatives aimed at increasing awareness among employees. For example, Frank Popoff, CEO of Dow Chemical, describes himself as 'one of 62,000 environmentalists in the company'.[17]

Environmental commitment should come from the Chief Executive. TransAlta Utilities Corporation in Canada recently released an Environmental Policy Statement that could be viewed as a model of what a new greener mission statement should be:

> TransAlta is committed to the protection of the environment and to sustainable development. Environmental stewardship is a vital element in our business. We strive to empower all our employees to take initiatives to

protect and enhance the environment, based on shared values and the need to satisfy the environmental concerns and expectations of customers, investors and the public.

Our commitments are to:

- report complete and accurate information on the environmental impact of our business, to meet or surpass all environmental standards, and continuously improve our environmental performance.
- advocate socially responsible environmental standards and the recognition of the economic value of environmental resources.
- implement conservation and efficiency initiatives for all resources and pursue alternative energy opportunities, both within our own operations and in partnership with others.
- seek out research opportunities and develop alliances that will improve our environmental performance and make a positive contribution to solving environmental challenges.
- consult and work cooperatively with those who may be affected by our business and respond to their environmental concerns.
- recognise and respect the relationship between environment and health in all phases of our business, and use the best knowledge available to protect the health of employees and the public.
- encourage the development of educational programmes and resources, to provide balanced public information and to foster environmentally-sensitive attitudes, knowledge and skills.
- identify and develop business ventures where value can be added to environmental solutions while providing investment opportunities for the corporation and its shareholders.[18]

Many UK companies are not recognising the link between environmental responsibility and positive corporate image. A major survey by the Confederation of British Industry (CBI) in 1990[19] indicated that nearly 40% of large companies considered public perception of their company to be a major problem, ranked fourth after effluent, gaseous emissions and wastes. This squares directly with public and employee concern over environmental issues, but contrasts sharply with the low priority accorded by many UK companies to the development of environmental policies and communications programmes.

Companies' concern for environmental matters appears to be strongly influenced by local pressures: local authorities, the local community, and local pressure groups. It is likely that this will be reinforced as concerns over community relations and changing demographic trends begin to squeeze, in both national and local recruitment markets. A number of initiatives are being taken by companies to improve and develop community relations. For example, ICI Agrochemicals in Fernhurst have established an annual open day highlighting rural and country matters.

Companies that are failing to make changes may start to demotivate and lose staff, and may have recruitment problems especially among younger people and in more 'environmentally aware' countries such as Germany and Scandinavia. Many North American and continental European companies are finding that employees feel good about making a contribution to environmentally responsible performance. The initial investment of time and effort pays dividends, as an increasing number of internal and external Stakeholders pay more attention to a company's environmental record. Employees and potential employees will increasingly make a careful appraisal of the company's credentials before committing themselves.

Two surveys in 1990[20] indicated that environmental matters are important to existing and potential managers. The most important issues for graduates and managers were records on health and safety, industrial disasters and the elimination of CFCs (see Fig. 14).

Importance of Environmental Factors when Choosing Potential Employers

	Graduates %	Managers %
Setting of environmental policy	56	60
Record on health and safety	90	85
Record on industrial disasters	84	84
Elimination of CFCs	72	83
Green product range	56	57
Green office policy	–	57
Recycling initiative	–	72

Source: M. Charter, *Graduates: Fewer and Greener* (Alton: KPH Marketing, 1990), and M. Charter, *The Greener Employee* (Alton: KPH Marketing, 1990)

Figure 14

A recent survey by Touche Ross[21] on management attitudes towards the environment sampled 250 large companies from sixteen European countries. Findings indicated that employees have a growing influence on a company's environmental performance. In nearly half the sample, employees raised concerns about environmental issues, and just over half of the companies surveyed had invited suggestions from employees on environmental issues. About 80% of the companies that invited suggestions changed their products or processes as a result, while only 54% of all respondents have made such changes. This happens not only in environmentally advanced countries such as Switzerland and Norway, but also in less aware nations such as Hungary, where employees are keen to tackle the country's considerable environmental problems. The whole company should be involved in the environmental protection process. The more staff feel part of a team effort, the more energy and creativity will be put into planning and implementing a green strategy (see Fig. 15).

Employees' Input to Environmental Issues

Questions	% of respondents
Do you invite suggestions from employees on environmental issues?	56
Have you changed any products/processes as a result of suggestions from employees?	54
Have employees raised concerns regarding your company's environmental performance?	45

Source: DRT International/Touche Ross, 'Managers' Attitudes to the Environment' (June 1991)

Figure 15

Leadership is also a vital factor in the success of a greener strategy. In 1990, AT&T's CEO, Robert Allen, published an open letter to all employees urging increased environmental awareness.

> We're selling ambitious new goals for our business ... goals that go well beyond the requirements of government agencies ... Reaching these targets will require the attention and participation of each of us ... I extend my thanks to those of you who have already applied your imagination and creativity to our environmental challenges. I urge each of you to consider how your actions, at home and at work, affect the environment.[22]

As a result an 'eco-consciousness' group, Employees in Action for the Environment, has been formed at AT&T (New Jersey). The objective of the group is to 'identify, communicate and effect actions that have a positive effect on the environment'. The formation of these groups will give employees a sense of personal accountability, and that they are doing something concrete and useful.

In 1990 Norsk Hydro, a diversified Norwegian company with over 2,000 UK employees, published the results of its Environmental

Audit, to considerable acclaim. Norsk's prime pressure came from employees.

> We believe that this environmental report breaks new ground as regards UK companies.
>
> It was prepared primarily for employees of Hydro in the UK but, as a socially responsible group, we believe that the material it contains should be widely available; hence its broader circulation to local authorities and schools, to customers and shareholders in the UK, and to all others interested in a large company's approach to matters concerning health, safety and environment for which it is responsible.[23]
>
> *Mr Torvild Aakvaag*
> *President of Norsk Hydro a.s.*
> *October 1990*

Georg Winter, the founder of BAUM, sees each employee as a 'cell' in the living corporate organism, and as such states,

> No ecology-minded firm can operate effectively unless its workers are well versed in the environmentalist outlook.[24]

Edgar Woolard, Chairman of Du Pont, goes further,

> No company can be truly innovative until everyone in the company has adopted an environmental attitude.

Employee Commitment

Many employees want to work for more environmentally responsible companies, and making a genuine corporate commitment to the environment can have other benefits that are less tangible, but equally real (see Figs. 16 and 17).

Mr Richard Robson, Group Environmental Communications Manager, ICI stated,

> Employees are our most critical audience. Our employees face much criticism from their friends and associates ... who hold them personally responsible for ICI's pollution problems.[25]

Alan Newman of Seventh Generation in the US comments:

> Your staff will see it as a fringe benefit. That may be hard for some people to believe, but that's the way the world is moving these days.[26]

The Greener Employee survey[27] indicated that people want to work for greener companies (see Fig. 18).

Women both as consumers and employees are greener, and appear to be attracted by positive environmental initiatives. The Body Shop's

---

Ten Steps to Employee Commitment

1. Make employees aware of senior management commitment to greening through an open letter to employees: talk from the top
2. Conduct an environmental audit, involve staff where possible, know exactly what your company does
3. Publish the result of the audit, provide summaries to interested parties: tell employees what you are doing
4. Establish a clear policy
5. Communicate the policy to employees
6. Give employees the opportunity to comment and ask questions: admit mistakes and quash rumours
7. Examine key environmental performance areas and incentivise individual teams, or plants
8. Prepare training material
9. Complete up-dates
10. Assess and evaluate performance

Adapted from: J. Elkington and P. Knight with J. Hailes, *The Green Business Guide* (London: Victor Gollancz, 1991)

Figure 16

Environmental Auditing and Motivation

Principle	Auditing activities	Motivation involved
Granting additional authority to employees in their activities	Giving employees the responsibility for the environmental performance of their own departments or tasks	Responsibility Achievement Recognition
Assign individuals specific or specialised tasks, enabling them to become experts	Members of the audit team developing new skills Involve as many employees as possible in the auditing and monitoring process	Responsibility Growth Advancement
Introducing new and more difficult tasks not previously handled	Use of advanced technology or testing procedures	Responsibility Growth Advancement

Source: Jacqueline M. Hill, *Environmental Auditing as an Aspect of Competitive Strategy: An Analysis* (unpublished undergraduate thesis, April 1991)

Figure 17

Would You Be Prepared to Take a Drop in Salary to Work for a More Environmentally Sound Company?

	Total %	Sex Male %	Female %
No	78	83	68
Yes	22	17	32

Source: M. Charter, *The Greener Employee* (Alton: KPH Marketing, 1990)

Figure 18

pioneering role in greener retailing appears to be well received, being mentioned by both managers and, notably, graduates well ahead of other companies on environmental responsibility (see Fig. 19).

Companies and Industries Perceived to be Environmentally Responsible

	Managers %	Graduates %
The Body Shop	7	37
Sainsbury's	–	12
Boots	–	7
ICI	3	7
Chemical companies	2	–
Tesco	2	–
High street food retailers	2	–

Source: M. Charter, *Graduates: Fewer and Greener* (Alton: KPH Marketing, 1990), and M. Charter, *The Greener Employee* (Alton: KPH Marketing, 1990)

Figure 19

A number of US companies have created 'ecology circles'[28] as an extension of quality circles to discuss green issues among employees. A company that is sensitive to employees' opinions and acts on employees' suggestions tends to be a well-managed company. Companies with cultures based on caring about employees and product quality are those that are more likely to adapt to the challenges of tackling complex environmental problems.

Wider Involvement of Employees

Personal involvement in corporate environmental activities will enable environmentally concerned employees to express their need to do something for the environment at work. One participant on an IBM personal development course recognised that he was most fulfilled when he was working evenly between work and the wider community. His core process was 'fully utilising my skills for the good of the communities in which I live and work'.

Employee volunteering is becoming a powerful and cost-effective way of improving both the motivation and morale of the workforce and the company's performance, while the local community is provided with the resources to tackle problems.

An initiative has been taken by IBM in the UK which allows their employees to demonstrate the company's commitment to the environment. The Local Environmental Action Team programme (LEAT), launched in April 1990, aims to stimulate the involvement of volunteer teams and IBM employees in local environmental projects. It is hoped this will strengthen IBM's partnerships with local and national environmental agencies and respond to the volunteer recruitment needs of the environmental organisation.

The teams have been involved in a number of schemes throughout the country, and IBM have awarded funds of anything from £100 to £15,000 for the projects. Training and advice was provided by The Volunteer Centre UK, which encouraged employees to initiate their own projects with a selected environmental group. This approach has encouraged a sense of commitment and enthusiasm to maintain and complete projects. LEAT has so far been very successful, and IBM hopes to expand the programme by developing schemes to support employee involvement, for example by allowing employees to request 10% of their time to work on community activities. This pattern of local project involvement has certainly proved to be beneficial in terms of allowing employees to express their concern for the environment.

The Body Shop takes a wider perspective. All direct employees and all employees of its franchisees are pledged to engage in local volunteer work and encouraged to spend half a day each month within the community. In the first six months of employment it is a requirement that every staff member does at least one day of voluntary activity.

The projects range from caring for the elderly, ill, dying, differently abled, or disadvantaged people, through to work carried out for conservation and pressure group activities. Over the last year The Body Shop has been involved in numerous employee volunteering activities including:

- Restoring three orphanages in Romania, with the help of over 100 Body Shop International volunteers
- Helping to teach job-related skills to prisoners at Holloway Prison
- Teaching childcare and self-confidence building skills to residents of the Richmond Fellowship (a drug rehabilitation clinic)
- Providing massage therapy to patients with the HIV virus at AIDS hospices
- Involvement in a mass tree planting with the British Trust for Conservation Volunteers in the 'Plant a Million Trees' campaign
- Leading play groups in the terminally ill children's ward of the Leeds Hospital

In 1991 The Body Shop was presented with the 'Award for Employee Volunteering' in recognition of its support for employees' activity in the community.

Internal Marketing

An integral part of Greener Marketing is to remember that 'people are the business' and employees have to implement change. Employees should be made aware of the environmental issues, should be involved in decision making, and should be given a sense of 'strategy ownership'. Internal marketing should be used to launch Environmental Audits and policies to employees. Employees can make or break relationships with other Stakeholders and can ensure that greener products meet customers' requirements. By involving employees in product and organisational development, companies will generate new ideas and potentially useful insights.

The success of any Greener Marketing strategy depends on the quality of the planning and implementation. Plans should invite the participation of directors, management and employees. Environmental suggestion schemes should be developed using a variety of incentives to encourage motivation and commitment. Easily achievable elements should be tackled first, so benefits can be achieved quickly and easily and sold to senior management. Rhetoric must be followed by action, and programmes should mirror what employees are doing at home. The most effective waste management and energy conservation programmes give employees a sense that they are making a difference.

Dr Raymond Brouzes of Alcan states:

> Our employees want to work for a clean and green company. They want to make a difference at work, as well as at home.[29]

Waste minimisation initiatives should be developed, such as the WRAP (Waste Reduction Always Pays) campaign at Dow Chemical. A key starting point might be a recycling programme (see Fig. 20).

Launching a Paper Recycling Initiative

- Make sure employees are clear as to what can be recycled and what cannot.
- Make sure that employees understand that even if materials can be recycled, it is better to avoid wasteful use.
- Re-use paper on both sides; make sure that all paper is re-used, even incoming mailshots; re-use envelopes for writing on, or for inter-departmental envelopes.
- Develop separate coloured recycling bins for different types of paper, and a bin that contains waste paper.
- Make sure you know where your local recycling unit is; talk to your local authority: do they re-sell waste paper, or is it sent to landfill, or is it incinerated? Plan your journey to ensure you are not doing more environmental harm than good.
- Can creativity be incorporated into the scheme? *The Daily Telegraph* and Friends of the Earth set up a scheme in the newspaper's office, and then produced a book.

Figure 20

Alan Newman of Seventh Generation in the US commented on employee motivation:

> I know companies that never dreamed their 'button-down' staffs would get excited about a recycling programme—but believe me, it happens.[30]

Any organisation that embarks on the process of greening may face a difficult and turbulent time. It will mean that projects will need to be looked at in different ways and inter-disciplinary skills will be required. Greener Marketing strategies and plans can be treated conceptually as products. Once the strategies have been developed, the organisation must encourage a change in attitudes and behaviour. The price will be represented by the resources required to implement the policy, the opportunity cost of sacrificing existing competing projects, and the psychological cost of adopting new key values and changing the way jobs have been traditionally done.

Once environmental policies have been established, they should be clearly communicated to staff and then to other Stakeholders. Messages and media should be designed to inform, encourage and persuade key personnel to accept the benefits of change. Strategies should be physically launched at a venue, although the development process should be ongoing by making recruitment and training programmes built into the overall strategy.[31]

Internal marketing recognises employees as sophisticated individuals, and incorporates approaches to communication, research, design, development, testing and launching. It aims to support a movement towards environmental excellence as part of the overall goal of Total Quality Management (TQM). Quality can only come from inside the organisation, whether it is best policy, best process or best practice.

Internal marketing is a fusion of marketing, human resources, and training. It aims to match the needs and objectives of the workforce with the needs and objectives of the organisation, and requires certain conditions to work effectively.

- First at board level, working with the board and senior management in creating and internally marketing 'vision, mission and values': the future goals of the leader (the vision); the way the organisation will meet those goals (the mission); and how it will treat its people on the way to getting there (the values).

- Second, internal marketing works as a strategic tool at a management level to fulfil the environmental policy. It creates a demand by internally marketing and branding processes, programmes and initiatives such as environmental excellence, recycling, cost-saving exercises, innovation, leadership, motivation, team building and communication. The organisation needs these to get where it is going.

- Third, internal marketing works at a tactical level driving forward specific initiatives and working practices that are required to allow people to get on with their job. In a lot of cases, internal policies fail because of lack of effective internal marketing.

Marketing personnel have a key part to play in the greening process, through:

- The overview of the organisation's strategy and its clout
- The understanding of customer and other Stakeholder needs
- The marketing techniques and the tools to meet those needs
- The ability to adapt techniques towards employees and other Stakeholders
- Budgets[32]

In the early stages of environmental policy development, employees should be advised that the company is researching into greening. Employees will want to know what the company plans, what new greener products have been launched, and what will be the return on green investment. Participation should be encouraged at all levels, and in all disciplines. Managers should work in various areas, to increase exposure and experience in the issues. Once employees are involved in the greening process, ideas will be generated. If employees feel that ideas are being followed up by the company they will be encouraged to act further. Regular communications on the development and implementation of the green strategy are important through newsletters and meetings, with success stories and 'good news' very important. A coordinated approach is likely to improve pride and morale in the company, and employees will be impressed that the company is concerned about other issues as well as the bottom line.

Organisations can motivate change by giving incentives to groups or individuals through rewarding good environmental performance. Financial reward or recognition should be open to all levels of staff. Ashland Oil give bonuses to operators who have demonstrated environmental initiative, and in 1990 Conoco Inc. established an environmental bonus programme, rewarding employees who initiate environmental change, and individual plants that have achieved excellent environmental performance.[33]

Implications for Human Resources

Managers and employees will need to develop different skills, knowledge and attitudes in order to implement environmental responsibility. Leading companies are starting to recognise strategic issues concerning the capability of management and the workforce to deal with environmental problems and opportunities:

- Working towards target setting and goal achievement
- Skills shortages in environmental fields, which are becoming more acute as the demand for environmental specialists increases
- Developing the competence to handle environmental issues throughout the organisation at all levels
- Organisational culture change to develop an outlook supportive of sustainable development

The Human Resource function will need to support managers in the recognition of the need for improved environmental performance, and will have some influence over taking a proactive or a reactive stance in furthering the environmental aims of the organisation.

A useful summary of the different approaches to the environment with implications for the Human Resource function has been developed by The Prospect Centre (see Fig. 21).[34] Four strategies are considered: the cost-minimising strategy, which views environmentalism purely as an additional cost driver; the short-term profit-maximising strategy, which seeks to capitalise on green consumerism in the short term; innovation in products and marketing strategies, which recognises opportunities to innovate and market new products; and the strategy of positioning for the unknown, which recognises the long-term opportunity and need for proactive response across all functions (see Fig. 22).

Environmental Awareness and Training

Environmental training is being recognised as a key strategic issue among leading companies. The International Chamber of Commerce's Business Charter for Sustainable Development launched at WICEM II in April 1991 states employee education as one of its sixteen core principles:

> To educate, train and motivate employees to conduct their activities in an environmentally responsible manner.

The 1991 Touche Ross survey indicated that just over half of the sample of 250 European companies provide employee training on environmental issues, rising to over 75% in Sweden, Switzerland and Norway, although training often relates to health and safety issues, rather than being specific to environmental matters. About a quarter of companies have an internal newsletter or publication aimed at employees, notably in The Netherlands and Switzerland. The 1990 Touche Ross survey found a third of UK companies had an environmental training programme ranging from briefing on general issues to safety and emergency training. Another UK survey in 1991,[35] among 176 companies, indicated that only 20% of respondents had undertaken staff training on green issues.

Environmental training packages should be developed to raise employees' awareness, remembering that everyone is an ambassador for the company's environmental policy. Training should be targeted at the needs of different job functions and levels in the organisation, and should be designed to support each in their awareness and decision-making needs. A variety of media, including conferences, videos, newsletters, workshops and notice boards, should be used to communicate to directors, management and staff.

280

A Checklist for Greener Organisational Development

- Organisational ambitions
  - What does the whole organisation need to learn next to show it is developing its capability for environmental excellence?
  - What achievements does the organisation need to develop to indicate that it can manage environmental issues effectively?
  - How can a consensus about environmental issues be created among senior managers?
- Management development and business education programmes
  - Do environmental issues form a part of management development and business education programmes?
- Recruitment
  - Have links been made with educational establishments that are most likely to develop students with environmental expertise?
  - Which further and higher education institutions act as prime recruitment sources, and how are their programmes changing to reflect greater concern for green issues?
  - Should the organisation indicate to educational establishments that they require potential employees with a sound environmental understanding?
  - What actions are relevant educational establishments taking to green themselves?
- Induction
  - What do newcomers learn about green issues and environmental management?
  - Is the induction process used as a means of gaining understanding about the company's attitude to environmental management?
- Job training
  - Does this include environmental awareness courses, and opportunities to develop knowledge and skills for environmental management?
- Job descriptions
  - Do these include environmental responsibilities?
- Pay and rewards
  - Should effective environmental performance be reflected in these?
- Involvement with schools and community groups
  - Are conservation and green issues on the agenda?

Adapted from: The Prospect Centre, 'New Capabilities for the Green Organisation' (1990)

Figure 21

Human Resource Responses to the Environment

Recruitment

Minimising Costs
- Hiring environmental specialists on a short-term, ad hoc basis
- Recruitment concentrates on identifying individuals with a record for achieving sales targets or reducing costs

Optimising Short-Term Profit
- Recruiting staff with expertise in green aspects of marketing and knowledge of alternative channels

Innovation in Products/Marketing Strategies
- Recruiting a broad pool of environmental expertise, both scientists and managers, who are able to work cross-functionally
- Attracting high-calibre staff as a result of corporate image

Positioning for the Unknown
- Influencing labour market supply of appropriately qualified individuals
- Recruiting individuals capable of thinking futuristically, and free of the restraints imposed by corporate norms
- Recruiting appropriately qualified staff in advance of possible discontinuities

Training and Development

Minimising Costs
- Environmental training required to meet ad hoc requirements

Optimising Short-Term Profits
- Training to make employees aware of the implications of 'green consumerism' for the company

Innovation in Products/Marketing Strategy
- Educating employees in the understanding and skills of environmental management and likely future trends
- Training employees to work in creative, innovative cross-functional teams, and with external parties, i.e. customers and suppliers, in pursuit of green product opportunities

Positioning for the Unknown
- Investing in environmental training and development that goes well beyond immediate business needs
- Providing opportunities for employees to broaden perspectives and acquire new learning

Performance

Minimising Costs
- Measuring performance against budgeted sales and costs targets
- Establishing remuneration systems to reward short-term sales/cost performance

Optimising Short-Term Profit
- Performance appraised on achieving green targets
- Reward systems for short-term profit targets

Innovation in Products/Marketing Strategies
- Appraising and rewarding individuals on their contribution to the innovative thrust of the organisation

Position for the Unknown
- Commitment to scenario planning

Employee Communications

Minimising Costs
- Communicating environmental information on an ad hoc basis

Optimising Short-Term Profits
- Making staff aware of the importance of 'green consumerism' to the firm

Innovation in Products/Marketing Strategy
- Proactively managing individual and organisational environmental learning through staff forums, postings, etc.

Positioning for the Unknown
- Extensive formal and informal communications at all levels

Source: The Prospect Centre, 'New Capabilities for the Green Organisation' (1990)

Figure 22

There may be some knowledge among employees, although views may differ greatly and key issues may be confused. The company should devise a programme utilising the knowledge and expertise that already exists within the organisation. If there is not the appropriate level of understanding and expertise, external specialists may need to be contracted. The programme should be designed to be a positive experience and highlight the interrelationship between personal commitment and corporate concern (see Fig. 23).

Environmental Awareness: Key Questions

- Do you encourage environmental awareness amongst your staff?
- Do you ensure that all your staff are properly trained?
- Are staff given environmental objectives and responsibilities?
- Are your staff encouraged to play an active role in improving the company's environmental performance?
- Do staff have sufficient information about the company's environmental performance, policies and plans?
- Has the company recognised that staff can be an important resource in raising the company's profile as 'ambassadors' for your company?
- Are all staff fully trained both for normal events and for accidents or emergencies?
- Do management and staff receive training to improve their environmental awareness?
- Do you mention your environmental policy, actions and performance in your recruitment literature?
- Are time, money or facilities available to enable employee participation in voluntary environmental activities?

Source: Business in the Environment, *Your Business and the Environment: A DIY Review for Companies* (London: Coopers & Lybrand Deloitte, 1991)

Figure 23

A workshop could be held for senior management to clarify strategic issues and relate them to the business, looking at the effects of competitive activities, new legislation and market pressures and how these can become opportunities and threats in both the short and longer term. Separate packages should be developed for other levels of staff, examining individual environmental responsibility, such as the environmental benefits of energy efficiency and waste minimisation.

The programme should be positive and regard the environment as an integral consideration among management and staff at all levels. Running an environmental awareness training programme will give staff new knowledge and a new philosophy, and will enable employees to look at products and processes afresh. The shopfloor employee who develops an energy efficiency idea and saves the company money, and the engineer who produces a more environmentally friendly design, will be considerable assets in a more environmentally conscious world.

Conclusion

Environmental issues are complex and will need to be seriously addressed by companies if they are not to be caught out by tougher environmental legislation and shifting consumer attitudes, notably among the next generation. The company should recognise that environmental responsibility begins at school, where pupils are increasingly being taught to integrate environmental consideration into all areas of their activities. With a drop in the number of young people projected for the mid-nineties, there are likely to be increasing pressures from new groups of environmentally critical customers and employees. A key enabling factor will be the ability of organisations to develop and communicate environmental commitment to potential and existing employees, and to motivate ownership of environmental policies.

Caring for employees will be an increasingly important concern for the organisation, and the Human Resource function will play an important role in facilitating the corporate response to environmental issues. Many employees may lack the necessary understanding to make environmentally responsible decisions, and will benefit from courses aimed at developing environmental awareness and skills. Environmental responsibility should be promoted at all levels of personal and professional development, education and training. Regulatory and customer pressures will have an impact on training requirements, recruitment profiles and appraisal systems. This will mean that organisations will need to develop an environmentally conscious and committed workforce, and professional internal marketing of policies will become a key factor in the success of Greener Marketing strategies.

References

1. 'Caring Sharing Consumers', *What's New in Marketing*, October 1990.
2. J. Elkington, T. Burke and J. Hailes, *Green Pages: The Business of Saving the World* (London: Routledge, 1988).
3. M. Charter, *Graduates: Fewer and Greener* (Alton, KPH Marketing, 1990), and M. Charter, *The Greener Employee* (Alton, KPH Marketing, June 1990).
4. David Bellamy Associates, 'Industry Goes Green' (November 1991).
5. Melanie Phillips, 'Must Do Better', *The Guardian*, 14 September 1990.

6. 'Management Topics', *IBM*, Issue 34 (February 1989).
7. Nick Toksvig, 'Going Down the Tubes', *The Guardian*, 3 January 1992.
8. Henley Centre/BT, 'Young Eyes: Children's Vision of the Future Environment' (1991).
9. T. Peters, 'Making Winter Green: Tool Maker Responds to Environmental Demands', *On Achieving Excellence*, Vol. 6, No. 1 (January 1991).
10. Confederation of British Industry, 'Workforce 2000: An Agenda for Action' (September 1990).
11. Tom Nash, 'Green about the Environment', *The Director*, February 1990.
12. Profile/AIESEC, 'Tomorrow's Managers: Sheep, Horse or Wolf' (February 1989).
13. G. Winter, *Business and the Environment* (Hamburg: McGraw–Hill, 1988).
14. D. Hart and D. Smith, 'Business Education and the Environment: Ramshackle or Innovative?' (Liverpool Business School, 1991), and J. MacConnell, 'Towards Environmental Competence in Scotland: Phase 1—Tertiary Education' (Glasgow Polytechnic, 1991).
15. 'Barclays Reveals Changing Attitudes' (Barclays Bank Youth Poll, 1990).
16. 'Attitudes Towards CPPs amongst Young People', *Educational Project Business*, March 1991.
17. P. Carson and J. Moulden, *Green is Gold* (Canada: Harper Business, 1991).
18. Carson and Moulden, *Green is Gold*.
19. Confederation of British Industry, 'Waking up to a Better Environment' (CBI/PA Consulting Group, March 1990).
20. Charter, *Graduates: Fewer and Greener*, and Charter, *The Greener Employee*.
21. DRT International/Touche Ross, 'Managers' Attitudes to the Environment' (June 1991).
22. Carson and Moulden, *Green is Gold*.
23. Norsk Hydro (UK) Ltd, 'Norsk Hydro UK Environmental Report' (Paragon Communications [UK] Ltd, 1990).
24. C. Moss, *Why Not to See Red When You See Green* (Unpublished MBA thesis, September 1991).
25. Moss, *Why Not to See Red When You See Green*.
26. S. Bechtel, *Keeping your Company Green* (Rodale Press US, 1990).
27. Charter, *The Greener Employee*.
28. Maxwell, 'The Rise of the Environmental Audit', *Accountancy*, June 1990.
29. Carson and Moulden, *Green is Gold*.
30. Bechtel, *Keeping your Company Green*.
31. N. Piercy and N. Morgan, 'Making Marketing Strategies Happen in the Real World', *Marketing Business*, February 1990.
32. K. Thomson, 'Internally Yours', *Marketing Business*, September 1991.
33. Carson and Moulden, *Green is Gold*.
34. The Prospect Centre, 'New Capabilities for the Green Organisation' (1990).
35. David Bellamy Associates, 'Industry Goes Green'.

PART III

CASE HISTORIES

INTRODUCTION

The aim of this section is to provide a series of case histories which will help to illustrate the topics covered in the first two sections of the book. There are twenty case histories covering a wide variety of companies and organisations which have been affected in some way by environmental issues. As far as possible, the case histories have been arranged so as to follow the order of the chapters. However, some of the cases illustrate more than one aspect of Greener Marketing.

The first two case histories provide examples of strategic issues of which companies should be aware. Friends of the Earth's 'Green Con of the Year Award' illustrates the growing influence of pressure groups, and how important it is to understand green issues and get communication right first time. The Merlin Research Unit's policy on evaluating green business provides details of the sort of questions green and ethical investors are asking. These act as good pointers to the kind of information a company should be looking for when attempting to assess its own environmental and social position.

Next, the issue of corporate response is considered. Examples of how various companies are responding to environmental pressures are provided by ICI, B&Q, Loblaw Companies Ltd (Canada) and Exel Logistics. ICI has developed an innovative environmental awareness programme for employees, and is also looking closely at the opportunities presented by greener markets. The case history of B&Q outlines the development and implementation of supplier auditing. Loblaws provide an example of a Canadian company who strove to introduce greener products amid intense criticism from environmental groups. Exel Logistics illustrate the development of a corporate environmental policy, and the detailed work that is involved in such an undertaking.

The following three cases look at Greener Marketing strategy. British Gas and McDonald's have both bowed to greener pressures, and have developed communication programmes aimed at clarifying their environmental position. Countrywide Holidays undertook a thorough Environmental Audit and pledged their financial support to conservation projects—actions which they are now using as valuable marketing tools. Traidcraft, a company working to encourage fair trade, are very aware of the environmental problems caused by the development of less industrialised countries, and have incorporated environmental issues into company policy.

New product development is considered next, and four case histories illustrate how different individuals and groups set about devising and producing greener products. The examples range from Onyx Associates, a company re-manufacturing and distributing used laser toner cartridges, to silk production in Thailand by EntoTec; from Dawes Environmental Coatings, a company producing solvent-free paint, to Natural Fact, who manufacture and distribute organic cotton clothing. These examples provide valuable insights into the research needed to launch such greener products, and the ongoing process of self-evaluation which is an essential part of the success of such projects.

Three case histories cover other important elements in the Greener Marketing mix: packaging, logistics and price. An example of Greener Packaging policy is provided by Gateway's '50% Pledge' on packaging reduction. Peter Lane Transport illustrate Greener Logistics at work and a corporate response to the environmental challenge. The record of the Ethical Investors Group serves as an example of Greener Pricing. This organisation cap the income of employees and pledge over 50% of profits to charity—and still make money.

The following two case histories look at Greener Communications strategy. The records of Hampshire County Council and The London Borough of Sutton on waste management illustrate how important it is to involve Stakeholders in green initiatives: both examples provide useful recommendations for enlisting Stakeholder interest. Eco-sponsorship is the subject of the second communications case history, which looks at the work of the Green Business Service, sponsored by BP.

The importance of employee involvement in the greening process is emphasised in the final two case histories. BT have introduced internal communications to capture the enthusiasm and commitment of their employees in their green drive. Pilkington Glass Ltd's case history looks at the launch of the internal communications programme, within their environmental care programme, entitled 'Looking to the Future'.

Strategic Issues

PRESSURE GROUP PERSPECTIVE
Friends of the Earth
'Green Con of the Year Award'

Neil Verlander
Information Officer, Friends of the Earth

Over the last few years, the environment has become a major issue. Everyone, it seems, wants to be a friend of the Earth. Nowhere has this concern been more apparent than in the rise of the so-called 'green consumer'. In September 1988, a MORI opinion poll found that 18% of those asked had 'selected one product over another because of its environmentally friendlier packaging, formulation or advertising'. By July 1990, this figure had dramatically increased to 50%. This was reinforced by a Mintel survey in May 1991, which found that nearly 60% of those questioned 'always/nearly always/tended' to buy products they perceived to be less damaging to the environment.

The green consumer is a force to be reckoned with, and a fierce battle has been waged by a number of companies to try and win the hearts, minds and money of these caring shoppers. From shampoo to champagne, companies compete to persuade us that their product is less damaging to the environment. 'Environmentally friendly', 'phosphate free', 'recyclable' . . . the supermarket shelves are laden with a bewildering collection of slogans and logos, which often confuse rather than inform. More worrying have been the all-too-many instances of products being sold using information which is at best inaccurate and at worst fallacious.

The 'Green Con of the Year'

At the Friends of the Earth Local Groups Conference in the summer of 1989, one of the topics on the agenda was the rise of green consumerism, and it became apparent that many were very concerned about the environmental claims many companies were making in order to try to take advantage of the green market. It was suggested that something be done to try to regulate these claims—perhaps by giving a special award to companies who were making the most outrageous green claims. The 'Green Con of the Year' was born.

The media were told of the competition, and soon nominations from the public came flooding through the letter box—280 in total. An independent panel of judges, including Ian Hislop (*Private Eye*) and Chris Baines (broadcaster and environmentalist) were given the task of selecting the most outrageous claims. There were plenty to choose from.

For many companies, green consumerism had merely been a convenient bandwagon to jump on in an attempt to boost sales. Truth and accuracy were often the first victims as the advertising copywriters were given a free hand to produce greener copy.

An example of a misleading advertising campaign was one run by Austin Rover who produced an advert proclaiming: 'What's more, the Surf is capable of running on unleaded petrol. This means it's as ozone-friendly as it is economical.' What the advert did not say was that lead has no effect whatsoever on the ozone layer. The judges gave Austin Rover a special Green Con award.

The winners were announced in December 1989, with first place going to British Nuclear Fuels, who, while playing on public fears about global warming, ignored the environmental hazards associated with nuclear waste, such as radiation risks. There was a host of other winners, including Higgs Furs, sellers of 'environmentally friendly' fox furs. The judges felt that the foxes in question were probably more 'environmentally friendly' before the intervention of Higgs.

The 1990 award was given to Eastern Electricity plc, which was urging customers to use 'more electricity rather than less' to combat global warming. Electricity generation, which relies mainly on the burning of fossil fuels, produces significant levels of carbon dioxide, a major contributor to global warming. Other winners included 'ozone friendly' aerosols that damaged the ozone layer, a 'recyclable' can that could not be recycled and an 'environmentally friendly' cleaning product, the manufacture of which polluted a river.

There was a mixed reaction from the recipients of the Green Con. Some tried to ignore the Green Con, while a handful admitted that perhaps they had made a mistake and would try to get it right next time. We had little sympathy for those who claimed 'ignorance', or who pointed an accusing finger at the environmental records of their rivals and claimed we were picking on them. If companies had been as rigorous at fact-checking as they were quick to take advantage of the public's concern for the planet, then they might have avoided the attention of Friends of the Earth. Hopefully the Green Con has encouraged companies to pay more attention to the facts and to the things they should be doing to help clean up the Earth.

The 'Green Con of the Year Award' has had an impact. The obviously misleading claims of 1989 are not nearly so common, though they can still be found. Instead, many companies are now making relatively sophisticated claims about the environment, which, even when accurate, can still baffle the public, most of whom know little about such things as phosphates or optical brighteners. Furthermore, there are examples of companies making sophisticated claims which give a misleading impression of their product's environmental impact.

For example, some paper and pulp companies have claimed that their activities are helping to combat global warming. The argument is based on the notion that paper companies plant lots of trees which in turn will 'suck in' carbon dioxide—thus reducing global warming.

There is a flaw in this scenario. The next stage of the paper making process is to chop down the tree, turn it into paper using all sorts of chemicals, and then finally to landfill the waste paper. Once landfilled, the paper decomposes, and all the stored carbon dioxide is released back into the atmosphere.

Unfortunately, there are still companies who have not got it right. Little wonder then that the public should start treating all claims with scepticism. Mintel reported in 1991 that 63% of those questioned were 'confused' about green claims.

Not all companies are trying to con the public about their environmental impact. Indeed many companies are genuinely concerned about their environmental impact and have taken steps to reduce it, and also want to provide their customers with clear and accurate information. The problem is that the public do not know when they are being misled.

The Trade Descriptions Act and Eco-Labelling

So what can be done? There are two important measures which Friends of the Earth has been pressing the Government to adopt.

First, companies who are making misleading green claims should be prosecuted. Unfortunately, the Trade Descriptions Act—the legislation which should deal with the issue—is weak on environmental claims and, as a result, companies have been allowed to get away with misleading the public. As long ago as January 1990, the Government acknowledged that there was a problem, but has since failed to take any action. However, a recent House of Commons Environment Select Committee investigation, to which Friends of the Earth gave evidence, called on the Government to amend the Act as soon as possible. Friends of the Earth will keep up the pressure until this happens.

Eco-labelling is another important measure which Friends of the Earth want to see introduced. At the moment consumers do not have access to reliable and independent information about a product's environmental impact. Companies act as judge and jury, assessing their own products and awarding themselves special 'green' labels.

An EC eco-labelling scheme should be running by Autumn 1992, but Friends of the Earth would like to see three important amendments to the scheme proposed by both the UK Government and the European Commission:

- The scheme should be mandatory. Once a product category has been decided upon, all products in that category should be assessed for a label.

- Products failing to meet certain basic standards of environmental performance should be withdrawn from sale.

- The scheme should be graded, not just pass or fail. This would mean that the less damaging a product was, the more green 'stars' it would receive. In this way products would compete on environmental performance as well as price.

Eco-labelling is a welcome step forward, allowing consumers to make more informed choices. However, there is a danger that people will expect more from it that it can actually deliver. Consumer power is important but it cannot solve all our problems and should be viewed as one of a number of tools that governments should introduce as part of a rigorous environmental strategy.

Environmental protection cannot be left solely to consumer preference and an unrestrained market, as has already been shown. Eco-labelling and the Trade Descriptions Act are important tools, but they must go hand in hand with other measures, such as the tightening of environmental standards, the setting of minimum environmental criteria for products and the imposition of green taxes, such as the tax differential between leaded and unleaded petrol, and a carbon tax.

Friends of the Earth is running the 'Green Con of the Year' in 1992, but hopefully its days are numbered.

Strategic Issues

EVALUATING GREEN PERFORMANCE
The Merlin Research Unit

Cerian Moss
KPH Marketing

Jupiter Tyndall Merlin (JTM)—the pioneer of green investment—is the investment management division of Jupiter Tyndall Group plc, a publicly listed investment management and banking group with funds under management and bank deposits totalling £1.3 billion.

JTM have a special interest in greening investment and promoting a wider understanding of the role of capital markets in sustainable development. In April 1988 JTM launched The Merlin Ecology Fund, and have since seen a dramatic growth in the number of green investors: the volume of investments in the green funds have grown from £250,000 in 1988 to over £43 million in 1991. This includes MIGIT (The Merlin International Green Investment Trust) which raised over £24 million, other green funds managed for UK-based and European investors, and private clients committed to green/ethical investment.

The objective of the green funds is to provide environmentally concerned investors with portfolios acceptable to their principles and to their financial targets. By screening companies from an environmental perspective, the aim is to invest in companies which make a positive contribution to protection of the environment and wise use of natural resources, and to encourage industry to improve its environmental performance.

Accurate research is of key importance to the continuing success of the green/ethical investment service. The research upon which assessments are based is carried out by The Merlin Research Unit, a small group of social and environmental scientists led by Tessa Tennant. There is also an advisory committee which guides the research approaches and priorities of the Research Unit. This group advises managers on the merits of individual companies and on the overall development of the Research Unit and environmentalism.

The Assessment Process

Stage One

The first stage of the assessment process is essentially precautionary. The decision to include a company on the approved list is often taken before a complete picture of the company has been put together. However, even at this stage, the research sources are still quite varied. They include:

- A short questionnaire sent to companies under consideration to find out whether the company has an environmental policy or conducts Environmental Audits
- Company literature such as annual reports and corporate policy statements
- Official environmental bodies including government departments and regulatory and advisory agencies
- Environmental groups
- Media coverage, both mass media and specialist publications.

The minimum requirement of the company at this stage is:

- That it is operating without excessive harm to the environment. This might be put in doubt, for example, if it is currently the subject of prosecution or litigation or has otherwise attracted adverse attention from regulatory bodies or substantiated criticism from environmentalists or the media.
- That it is producing socially useful products.

If the company has a corporate environmental policy or has conducted an environmental audit, then obviously this will count in its favour. These are not, however, prerequisites at this stage, although the company should illustrate some environmental benefit to justify inclusion on the approved list. Companies may be selected at this stage, for example, because they are producing environmentally beneficial products even though they may not (yet) apply environmental principles to their own operations.

Stage Two

Once a company is on the approved list, further investigations are carried out. The research outlined above continues but is strengthened by:

- Direct contact with the company, usually including site visits following which reports are made on the company (local experts may be used in the case of overseas locations).

- Sector studies which survey a group of companies in the same field providing comparative data. **The Merlin Sector Surveys** aim to draw out the leaders in each field and to encourage companies to review their own performance in relation to their competitors. In this way, companies are encouraged to compete on environmental performance.

- Making specific inquiries with environmental bodies to throw light on problem areas or to corroborate other findings.

At this stage, a fuller profile of the company is built up, involving assessment of management, process and product.

Management

Research is undertaken to assess the extent of enlightened and effective management.

The aspects targeted are:

- **Management quality.** General competence and integrity of management, proper management systems, whether the company is registered under the British Standards Institute BS5750 scheme for Quality in Management

- **Stance.** The seriousness and sympathy with which problems raised are treated, the involvement of the Board in environmental matters, the resources available for action

- **Corporate policies towards the environment.** Adequacy of the policies, how well they are communicated, effectiveness of implementation

- **Focus.** The level of designated responsibility for the environment, the quality of leadership and how far it is likely to sustain motivation

- **Monitoring.** How well the company monitors its own environmental performance, how often and in what manner its policy is reviewed

- **Corporate disclosure.** How open the company is to external enquiries, how fully it makes available information, especially on environmental and social matters

- **Procurement.** Whether there is a purchasing policy related to environmental and social concerns

- **Community involvement.** membership of Business in the Community, the Per Cent Club and other initiatives, level and nature of sponsorship and donations to community projects, secondment programmes

Process

Research is undertaken to find out how far the policies are borne out in practice.

The aspects targeted are:

- **Pollution.** The nature and extent of emissions to air, water and land, and noise and other nuisances, and the approach to reducing or avoiding them, including track record in meeting or improving on standards set by regulatory bodies (at present, it is not possible systematically to monitor emissions data but such information should be on stream in the near future)
- **Waste.** The efforts being made to minimise the creation of waste matter, the extent to which it is reused, the methods of disposal
- **Energy.** How diligently the company is trying to conserve energy and to switch to less polluting and more renewable sources
- **Materials.** The extent to which the use of non-renewable materials is minimised, the care taken to obtain materials from sustainable sources where possible
- **Transport.** The steps being taken to reduce the need for and the environmental impact of the movement of raw materials and products
- **Land use.** Whether new buildings or operations are designed to protect and improve the environment, and are sited to avoid places of amenity or wildlife value; whether neglected land is favoured; extent and nature of landscaping of existing sites

Products and Services

The assessment of products, covering goods and services, is made as objective and penetrating as possible. JTM do not take the welter of claims of 'greenness' at face value. Environmental data is gleaned from investigations in consumer publications, but in some areas information is not readily available. The recently announced EC eco-labelling scheme should prove helpful.

The aspects targeted are:

- **Worth.** To what extent are the goods and services produced necessary and useful?

- **R&D.** The emphasis in research and development on improving environmental performance of future products

- **Environmental impacts.** To what extent are current products energy efficient, long-lasting, not damaging on disposal, capable of being reclaimed, and so on?

- **Packaging and labelling.** Whether packaging is minimal or biodegradable or reclaimable, the information given to the consumer about contents, energy rating, correct use and disposal

- **Overseas markets.** Whether products banned in one country are marketed in others, whether standards are maintained in selling to other countries, whether due care is taken to label for users overseas

The Future

These assessment criteria are obviously very stringent. The fact that so many areas of the business are investigated reflects the belief that every part of the organisation must be greener before a business can truly be considered to be environmentally aware. As the evaluation process for green investment develops, JTM's criteria paper is being rewritten to incorporate the role of environmental information arising from eco-labelling, BS7750, the draft standard for environmental Management Systems prepared by the British Standards Institute, and the proposed EC regulation on environmental auditing—the Eco-Audit proposal.

JTM believe very strongly that the firms they invest in should also meet tough financial criteria. In practice, JTM have found that firms showing good environmental performance are often attractive propositions on ordinary investment analysis. They put this down to the fact that managers in industry who are alive to an issue such as the environment, and are making a considered and practical response to it, are likely to be performing well in other areas. Ecological concern, for example, may open up new markets, involve savings in resource costs and improve a company's image. Moreover, a firm failing to respond may lose market share or fail to establish itself in new markets. So green and conventional investment criteria will often dovetail.

JTM are now concentrating on more detailed analysis of corporate environmental performance, and in particular developing the appropriate analytical tools to evaluate the corporate response to Sustainable

Development from the investors' perspective; is it a concept the company adheres to, and if so, how do they intend to ensure their processes and products are sustainable?

In the past two years, JTM have found that institutional investors are becoming concerned about the impact of environmental concerns and legislation upon company activities. For example, do companies have hidden environmental liabilities? Are production processes rendered obsolete by tougher pollution regulations? In response to these questions, there is a growing recognition among pension funds and other investors that, as long-term investors in much of British industry, they have a responsibility to interact positively with company management and to encourage them in focusing the future direction of their business along sustainable lines.

For the forward-looking investment managers, these demands are being turned into business opportunities. JTM pension fund managers, in conjunction with The Merlin Research Unit, have designed a socially responsible investment service for the institutional investor, which has so far received the attentions of socially aware local authorities, charities and pension funds.

Corporate Response

OPPORTUNITY FROM THREAT
ICI

Martin Charter
Director, KPH Marketing

This case history briefly describes some of ICI's responses to the environmental challenge. The first section examines how the company is exploring new business opportunities, and the second, how ICI are establishing an environmental awareness programme.

Background

ICI is a multinational manufacturer and distributor of chemicals, with 126,000 staff worldwide, and as such is continuously in the public eye. The majority of ICI's manufacturing sites are based in the UK and tend to be of old design; upgrading has been seen as an increasingly important issue with the toughening of environmental legislation. Many overseas sites tend to be of newer design, and as such are not in the firing line; but they still face specific local and national environmental problems because of the global nature of the enterprise and the make-up of the company's activities. Due to an emphasis on good community relations, ICI have found through research that the company are often perceived as having a good record on Corporate Social Responsibility, but conversely as not having as good an environmental record, notably on water pollution, and the production of CFCs.

ICI take a global Stakeholder perspective to their international operations, and pay particular attention to the local communities within which they operate. In the UK, plant managers and employees are encouraged to give lectures to local communities and open dialogues with pressure groups. This approach extends overseas. In a province in Malaysia, the plant manager is chairman of a regional development zone and acts as an interface between the Government and the community on regional development issues.

Environmental Opportunities

ICI are conducting research to determine which global environmental problems will have greatest impact on their businesses. As part of the process, the company are looking to change environmental pressures into opportunities through a progressive movement towards increased environmental responsibility throughout the organisation. ICI are looking at technology that could be relevant to environmental improvement both internally and externally, with a view to the development of a long-term competitive advantage. Environmental aspects are now being built in to new product development screening, alongside efficacy, health and safety, and quality. If the product has an adverse environmental impact, at any stage, then it is unlikely to be examined.

A number of existing products have been re-orientated to 'the green market'. Biopol, a biodegradable plastic, was developed in response to the increase in petrochemical prices due to the oil crisis of 1970s. Until recently, it was considered to be an interesting research project, but as environmental awareness has grown, it has been given market potential. At present, market development is in its early stages, with the product being developed with one major customer. Aquabase, a water-based paint, was designed to reduce the health and safety risks associated with solvent emissions in finishing and re-finishing, and is now being specified by Volvo and General Motors (Canada). Water-based resins were developed for similar reasons, and interest has been re-invigorated with increased green awareness. The company are also examining opportunities arising from biotechnology, with an initial success being the development of a meat substitute, Quorn.

ICI Agrochemicals have been under the spotlight due to their production of pesticides and fertilisers. Over the last decade, strong pressure has come from the US through the Environmental Protection Agency. ICI Agrochemicals' responses have included projects such as the development of an expert system designed to advise farmers on rational use of pesticides.

Employee Environmental Awareness Programme

Environmental excellence is being seen as an integral part of a movement towards Total Quality Management (TQM). As part of the cultural movement towards heightened environmental responsibility, in early 1991 a strategic environmental briefing session was held among 'fast-track' directors and managers. The increasing emphasis means that chief executives, within each business area, are now also being judged not just on profitability, but on their corporate environmental performance. This is filtering down the organisation, with plant managers being encouraged to improve the environmental performance of factory sites. With the heightened importance of green issues and subsequent cultural change within ICI, there is likely to be an increase in the number of job descriptions using the word 'environment', as it becomes a greater part of job functions.

ICI find that one of their most critical Stakeholder audiences is their employees. Staff are often castigated on a personal level by friends and family for their association with ICI's environmental problems. This is causing problems with corporate esteem, and has become an issue of management concern. In response, initial ideas for an Employee Environmental Awareness Programme were developed in mid-1990 by a small group of ICI's environmental managers, who saw the need for improved internal environmental education and communication at all levels in the organisation. In October 1990, a proposal was developed and accepted by senior management, and between May and June 1991, a pilot study was conducted among 350 staff in nineteen locations in the US, Australia, Malaysia, Germany, Holland and the UK.

A training resource was then developed, and was test-launched in late 1991. The resource is aimed primarily at improving environmental understanding among junior staff, with the purpose of encouraging employees to be good environmental ambassadors. An interactive approach was chosen to enable employees to develop self-awareness of the issues, and to make them conscious of the environmental impact of their own decisions and behaviour. The project is being coordinated through an internal Organisation Performance Consultant. Much of his time is spent helping managers to take up the resource and apply it to their particular situations, with the plan of making the resource available to all employees on a non-compulsory basis.

Training materials are supplied as a resource, with several modules, and are designed to integrate with existing communications approaches concerned with local and community issues. The manager is left to decide how to use the materials, and to decide if they are applicable to their staff. For instance, a manager of a small plant in Bangladesh may not see that it is relevant to give employees an in-depth understanding, unless the community is particularly aware of the issues. If the manager considers the package to be relevant, then he or she selects a group of around ten staff for a workshop session. The manager then acts as the leader for the session, and shows a three-minute video entitled 'Opinions on the Environment' which airs a variety of attitudes to environmental issues. After this there is usually a discussion lasting about forty-five minutes. Employees are then encouraged to take work books home, to be completed with the involvement of their family. Following this, another session is held and a second video is shown examining personal values, waste and pollution. This is then followed by a discussion, with employees encouraged to bring forth ideas arising from both the videos and workbooks. Initial training sessions have proved to be lively, and are generating considerable commitment among staff.

Corporate Response

GREENER RETAIL AND SUPPLIER AUDITS
B&Q

Dr Alan Knight

Environmental Coordinator, B&Q

A company, by their very nature, are dedicated to a continual increase in turnover and profit. For themselves or their suppliers, this will mean an increase in production and the associated costs to the environment. Their existence, therefore, contradicts the principle held by environmentalists: companies are committed to growth and environmentalists to reducing consumption. It may seem that no company could claim true commitment to the environment unless they were prepared to cease operations.

As one of Britain's largest retailers, B&Q believe that their own responsibility lies in working within the parameters of these apparent contradictions. This means they should do their best to work towards a truly sustainable economy, both in environmental and economic terms. The company are not and should not be an environmental pressure group. But as customers themselves, they have the power to make changes to their own supply chain; and they are prepared to use that power.

B&Q have, to that end, appointed an environmental coordinator with the task of creating and implementing their environmental policy.

Using Buying Power

B&Q have put pressure directly onto their suppliers by requiring them to meet their own environmental standards. In 1990 B&Q began sending questionnaires to their suppliers aimed at evaluating the environmental impact of their products. The response indicated that many suppliers neither understood B&Q's objectives nor the consequences of poor environmental performance.

A change in approach was needed, so a new policy was created. This was revealed to 200 of B&Q's suppliers—representing the vast majority of the company's turnover—at a special conference in December 1991. Suppliers are now required to create and implement an environmental policy supported by a thorough Environmental Audit. B&Q review this policy and performance, and those who fail to show any commitment to change will be delisted.

Even those suppliers which are not themselves manufacturers will have to meet these conditions, and eventually all new suppliers and their products will undergo an environmental assessment before winning any orders from B&Q.

Softwood and Hardwood Policy

B&Q have set themselves a deadline of 1995 for selling hardwoods and softwoods from sustainable sources only, a target supported by The World Wildlife Fund.

It is the range of B&Q's tropical hardwoods that has come under the heaviest fire from environmentalists. Not without reason, when you consider one of many examples: environmentalists claim that the forests of Sarawak, in Malaysia, will disappear within eleven years.

In one sense the issue seems straightforward: stop buying wood from these countries. In another, however, as B&Q saw for themselves when visiting Indonesia, the Philippines and Malaysia in 1991 and 1992, there are no simple answers. The extent of poverty and the link between poverty and environmental degradation mean that there is a need to balance socio-economics with environmentalism. B&Q recognise that the rainforests have an ecological and economic value. As long as sufficient forests are protected for conservation, then the remaining forests should be harvested in such a way that timber is produced in a sustainable manner. Nor should the rights of indigenous populations be ignored.

B&Q have made a beginning by ordering their own suppliers of softwoods and hardwoods to remove all 'green labels' from their products. Many are misleading in either claiming or implying that their timber comes from a sustainable source. Most softwoods, such as pine, do now come from properly managed plantations in the UK and abroad. The present hardwood logging operations in producer countries have not, however, been proven to be sustainable, and legislation alone does not seem to be sufficient to ensure the long-term preservation of the rainforests.

The company is now working with environmentalists and the timber trade to come up with a single, clear method of monitoring and labelling, along with an agreed definition of sustainability.

Peat Policy

Versatile peat has always been a popular product with keen gardeners. But it is an environmentally sensitive and finite resource. Last year, B&Q sponsored a conference aimed at exploring the potential of recycling organic wastes to use as alternatives to peat. They have now stopped buying peat from Sites of Special Scientific Interest. B&Q now stock a comprehensive range of alternatives, which includes own-label peat-free coir, own-label peat-free growbags and a range of peat-free mulch.

Waste Management

B&Q have not forgotten to put their own house in order. They now recycle office paper at head office and cardboard from their stores. Bottle bank schemes which are in operation at thirty stores will be extended to most stores. B&Q have launched a packaging review, and are planning a detailed environmental audit of their head office, stores and warehouses.

Communicating the Message

Once the environmental programme of auditing suppliers is complete, B&Q intend to launch the initiative to consumers. The company are considering using direct marketing to communicate their policy. As Bill Whiting, the company Marketing Director, states, 'We will need to explain it in thirty paragraphs, not three.' The communication will need to be 'below the line', therefore, to cope with the complexity of the issues involved.

At the end of the day, consumer power is, by definition, limited. You can choose not to buy, but you cannot choose what does not exist. Manufacturers and retailers can bring about real change by producing and ordering products which have the minimum impact on the environment. By doing so they can give customers a meaningful right to choose. B&Q believe that it is the responsibility of all those involved in the supply chain to do just this.

Corporate Response

A CANADIAN RETAILER'S PERSPECTIVE
Loblaw Companies Ltd

Patrick Carson
Vice President, Loblaw Companies

Andrew Fyfe
KPH Marketing

One of the fundamental challenges facing modern-day society is to bring environmental concerns into the mainstream of our thinking and decision making. According to Canada's Environment Minister Tom McMillan, in a speech in June 1988, public opinion polls showed that 94% of Canadians believed that they must all take responsibility if planetary survival is to be secured. Other surveys showed that Canadians are prepared to pay up to 10% more for environmentally friendly products. However, if consumers are to take environmental issues into consideration when buying products, they must be well informed and understand the environmental impacts of different products. In order to aid the consumer, Canada set up an eco-labelling scheme in 1989, which was modelled on the German Blue Angel scheme.

In 1988, when few companies worldwide had made the environment a top priority, Loblaw Companies Ltd, a major Canadian retailer, started to think about launching a line of environmentally friendlier products. Loblaw Companies Ltd are one of Canada's largest food distributors and are part of George Weston Ltd, who are involved in food processing, food distribution and resource operations in North America.

Researching and Introducing the New Line

Loblaw Companies Ltd researched the possibility of introducing a new product range which consisted of either environmentally friendlier products or products which were healthier to the body. In the early stages of research, the company met with ten environmental groups in North America and Britain in order to gain feedback on which environmentally friendlier products would generate the most demand. Pollution Probe and Friends of the Earth were then approached for information on products which they felt were unacceptable, and these included diapers made from chlorinated paper, detergents with high phosphate levels, paper products made from non-recycled paper, and foods sprayed with pesticides. After identifying more than 100 potential products, an extensive research and development programme began. In some cases, turning green was a matter of merely repackaging existing products. Friends of the Earth suggested that to educate consumers, everyday baking soda, for example, should be promoted as an excellent alternative to toxic household cleaner.

After in-depth research into the manufacturing processes, packaging issues and consumer demands of green products, Pollution Probe were invited to endorse the G•R•E•E•N product range, to which they duly agreed. The first line of environmentally friendlier products was launched in June 1989 under the name President's Choice -G•R•E•E•N-. The most significant effect of the introduction of Loblaws' G•R•E•E•N product line was that it enabled shoppers, for the first time, to comprehend the real extent of their purchasing power. By 'voting at the cash register' and demonstrating support for the environment, they began to realise the potential they had to change producer behaviour. By embracing the programme, they forced manufacturing and retailing competitors to play a part in protecting the environment, and to try to produce better products.

Coping with Controversy

With the launch of the new line, a great deal of attention was focused on the company. And it was not long before controversy began. Some environmental groups angrily accused Pollution Probe of compromising its reputation by endorsing a line of consumer products. Many environmentalists were especially shocked when Pollution Probe's Executive Director Colin Isaacs appeared in G•R•E•E•N television commercials alongside David Nichol, President of Loblaw Companies Ltd, promoting disposable non-chlorine-bleached diapers.

'In the best of all worlds,' Isaacs told viewers, 'everyone would use re-usable cloth diapers. But cloth diapers aren't always convenient.' Nichol then described why G•R•E•E•N disposables were environmentally friendlier. Isaacs' next move was his most controversial. He urged shoppers, 'If you must use disposable diapers, use these non-chlorine-bleached ones.' Disposables had been singled out by some environmentalists as a major contributor to the solid waste problem. These environmentalists fell over one another to be the first to denounce Isaacs, Pollution Probe and Loblaws, and to cast aspersions on the rest of their green claims. The widely publicised controversy escalated—even Pollution Probe started to distance itself from Isaacs, stating that he had acted independently. Isaacs resigned his position and Pollution Probe asked Loblaws to stop using their name to promote the line.

Before the controversy, press coverage of the G•R•E•E•N line launch was widespread, and cautiously favourable. Manufacturers besieged Loblaws with calls, wanting to know how to produce greener products for the line; many delivered prototypes to the company's head office. Consumers responded by purchasing G•R•E•E•N as fast as the company could restock their shelves. After the controversy struck, however, suppliers stopped calling for the most part, and media coverage adopted a critical tone.

Problems with an earlier product launch had prepared Loblaws for the Pollution Probe controversy. When the company launched its all-natural fertiliser in the spring of 1989, Greenpeace held a press conference to criticise the product, claiming it contained traces of dioxins and furans. Loblaws had conducted extensive testing of the product, under the watchful eye of Pollution Probe, and the scientific facts themselves disproved these claims.

This time, by enlisting an environmental group's public endorsement of the G•R•E•E•N line, the company hoped they would pre-empt any criticism and would add credibility to its products. Patrick Carson, Vice President of Environmental Affairs, recounts, 'We believed we were taking important steps by working with an environmental group to develop greener products. The environmental pronouncements against us seemed counter-productive. We were, after all, under no illusions that this was only the first step in the journey of a thousand miles, environmentally speaking.'

Throughout the process of introducing the G•R•E•E•N line, Loblaws never claimed to be environmental experts, nor radical activists. The company's stores still carry products considered by some to be harmful to the environment. 'If we were to remove all the harmful products from the shelf, we would have nothing to sell our consumers', commented Patrick Carson.

The End Result

In the end, the new line's extensive media coverage and basic integrity won the day—G•R•E•E•N outsold projections by 50%, and is still selling well across Canada and in half a dozen other countries. Patrick Carson also commented, 'It is quite possible that no matter how thoroughly you research your product and how carefully you vet it for hidden environmental flaws, some environmental groups won't be satisfied and will attack you as loudly and as often as they can. However, you are asking for trouble if you don't complete thorough research to ensure that what you do introduce into the marketplace is really as green as you say it is.'

Loblaws' dedication to supply environmentally friendlier products to enlightened customers did serve as a model to others. The success of the G•R•E•E•N products prodded other companies into action. Perhaps the greatest environmental contribution of the G•R•E•E•N products was that they proved to one of the world's largest industries—grocery produce and product distribution—that helping the environment is not only socially responsible, it is also good business. Loblaws' market share grew by 2% between 1989 and 1991, with an expenditure on market research of just CDN$10 million. (Studies of market share show that a 1% increase normally costs CDN$110 million.)

What Loblaws have done is to demonstrate leadership by offering consumers a new option incorporating good environmental practice. Loblaw Companies Ltd addressed the two critical issues of the 1990s—health and the environment. They created awareness and sustained criticism in the process. Loblaws proved that well-researched greener products can generate profits and goodwill simultaneously. As Patrick Carson states, 'This company proves that you can do the right thing, for the right reason, and still make money!'

Corporate Response

ENVIRONMENTAL POLICY DEVELOPMENT AND IMPLEMENTATION
Exel Logistics

Ivy Penman
Head of UK Planning, Exel Logistics

Back in 1989, Exel Logistics recognised the importance of the Environment, and started a comprehensive and rigorous programme which culminated in the launch of an environmental policy in June 1991. Almost eighteen months were spent researching all the issues, determining those which were most affected by the physical distribution industry and then developing an action plan. Exel Logistics' own senior managers undertook the work, helped by companies such as Volvo—a current supplier. Consultation took place at each stage in the drafting of the policy—across all UK businesses. Fundamental to the development of Exel Logistics' Environmental Policy was a basic core value—that of social responsibility or 'good citizenship'. Exel Logistics are a division of NFC plc, previously known as National Freight Consortium. Exel Logistics' shareholder employees had already demonstrated their commitment by voting in favour of allocating resources to improve the environment.

The Key Issues

The detailed research revealed that Exel Logistics, and in turn the distribution industry, impacted the environment in four key areas:

- Vehicles
- CFCs
- Waste
- Energy

The extent of environmental damage varied considerably, the worst offenders being vehicles, followed by CFCs. Little waste is produced by the distribution industry, although transit packaging often becomes superfluous within the warehouse. Energy usage, compared to other industries, is relatively low.

One major problem is that distribution and, in turn, transport activity has increased throughout the 1980s, and this is forecast to increase, especially with the opening of the Eurotunnel. Although the consumer is delighted to have an ever-increasing choice, the downside of increased transport activity is not so welcome. This is further accentuated by the high proportion of UK road transport, relative to the more environmentally friendly rail or inland waterway traffic used to a greater extent in continental Europe.

Road transport means lorries, bringing obvious negative aspects such as visual intrusion and noise, fumes and pollution. Lorries bear the brunt of public displeasure and contribute to environmental damage, causing:

- Global warming
- Pollution
- Depletion of the ozone layer
- Depletion of resources
- Congestion
- Waste

However, it is important to point out that HGVs account for only 0.5 million of the UK's 25 million total vehicle population in 1990.

Warehousing is considerably less environmentally damaging, with the exception of CFC refrigeration equipment. Alternative refrigerants do exist and are often used, unlike vehicle refrigerants which still use CFCs—although alternatives should be available shortly.

One UK distribution trend, centralisation, as practised by the major grocery multiples, has led to considerably reduced transport levels, although the Just-In-Time (JIT) trend practised for example by the automotive industry is unfortunately increasing transport levels by saving inventory holding costs.

The Development of an Environmental Policy

Having identified the key issues, a rigorous exercise began, to identify potential improvements and environmentally friendlier initiatives within Exel Logistics. Concentrating initially on the UK, to limit the extensive scope of the exercise, attention was concentrated on the four key areas previously identified.

The Environmental Policy

Vehicles

Reducing Fuel Consumption. With 3,300 vehicles, any fuel reduction programme would have a significant impact, and would of course directly reduce emissions of carbon dioxide, a major greenhouse gas, and other pollutants. Also, by using less fuel, Exel Logistics would be helping to conserve a resource. The company has already made significant progress in reducing fuel consumption by paying close attention to the highest standards of maintenance and ensuring that vehicles are tuned to give optimum fuel economy. Careful attention is already paid to driver training, to ensure fuel-efficient driving practice. Regular 'refresher' courses will be incorporated, and disciplinary procedures for speeding reviewed. Speed limiters, already fitted to some of Exel Logistics' vehicles, will be extended throughout. Strict monitoring of all fuel consumption will continue in order to identify any areas for improvement and initiate action, such as training, to rectify inefficiencies.

In 1988 Exel Logistics pioneered UK trials of an aerodynamic vehicle. This showed fuel savings of up to 20% for high-mileage, long-distance vehicle movements. The vehicle design was subsequently introduced to the UK vehicle fleet, and a top priority will be to extend its use throughout the division whenever mileage and type of operation make it appropriate.

Exel Logistics estimate that they can save up to 15% of their fuel bill, equating to £2 million, as a result of aerodynamic kits, speed limiters and good driving practice. If adopted by the entire industry, this could save up to £400 million, thus showing that environmental concern need not just be altruistic. Fuel efficiency has always been an important criterion when purchasing vehicles. Exel Logistics will continue to attach great importance to this and monitor all new vehicle designs in order to maintain a state-of-the-art position. Similarly, vehicles will not be over-specified for a particular operation—a common fault, unfortunately, in the industry.

Although multi-modal logistics solutions are not currently appropriate to our existing UK business, Exel Logistics will consider their implementation when planning new operations. In view of the long distances, they will be highly relevant in mainland Europe.

Noise and Emissions. Exel Logistics already fit air brake silencers to vehicles and this will continue to be part of the specification. Quietness will be an important factor in vehicle purchasing criteria, and contact with suppliers will be maintained in an attempt to bring about joint improvements. Noise associated with the running of vehicle refrigeration units is recognised to be a problem. Exel Logistics have taken steps to minimise this, by ensuring that all vehicles use plug-in power points at depots. Exel Logistics have carried out a thorough investigation of existing methods for reducing vehicle emissions. Should fuel additive trials prove successful, they will be introduced to the vehicle fleet.

Particulate traps are not yet viable for commercial operations, but Exel Logistics will monitor developments. Similarly, the company will keep abreast of progress in the hope that engine and fuel technological developments will make particulate traps unnecessary.

Exel Logistics' company car policy will specify the use of unleaded petrol and the fitting of catalytic converters on all new cars.

Congestion. Exel Logistics have in-cab communication in a number of their customer fleets, and this is also a valuable tool in optimising vehicle operating efficiency. Although the company are not general hauliers, they welcome the forthcoming removal of restrictions on cabotage as a means of improving vehicle utilisation. Similarly, Exel Logistics would welcome the introduction of heavier lorries as a means of reducing numbers. Both moves will not only help to reduce congestion, but also reduce fuel consumption and pollution.

Exel Logistics further maximise vehicle utilisation by 'backloading' vehicles—collecting from suppliers wherever feasible on the return trip to any distribution facility, and information technology improves vehicle utilisation by means of optimum scheduling.

Other. Exel Logistics already recycle all used engine oil. Strict procedures are enforced to ensure that spillages are kept to a minimum.

Currently, some of the vehicle washes recycle water. All new vehicle washes will incorporate recycling.

Exel Logistics recognise the value of air suspension and will fit this where appropriate to reduce wear and tear on the roads. Exel Logistics welcome forthcoming European legislation which will allow vehicles with air suspension to operate at greater gross weights, and would welcome the early introduction of this measure to the UK.

CFCs

As major UK cold store operators, Exel Logistics are aware of the ozone-depleting potential of CFCs. Unfortunately, the negative properties of CFCs have only become known relatively recently, together with the varying impact of the different formulations. Sixty-six per cent of Exel Logistics' cold store capacity is CFC-free. As soon as the harmful nature of CFCs was proven, the company took action to use alternative refrigerants in new cold stores and to ensure minimal leaks in the five existing CFC stores. Exel Logistics always ensure safe decommissioning of refrigerated vehicles and will safely collect CFCs, ensuring that there is no discharge into the atmosphere. Wherever possible, Exel Logistics will ensure that all future cold stores use environmentally friendlier refrigerants.

Exel Logistics intend to keep abreast of all new refrigerant developments and to switch to less environmentally harmful alternatives as soon as they become viable. An environmentally friendlier refrigerated vehicle will be available shortly, and Exel Logistics will introduce this to their fleet as soon as possible.

Similarly, wherever possible, all future insulation will be CFC-free and will use no CFCs in its manufacture.

Exel Logistics will specify that, wherever possible, all fire extinguishers must use ozone-friendly propellants. The use of aerosols will be banned throughout our operations, with a similar ban imposed on cleaning contractors.

Energy

Through rigorous inspection and maintenance of refrigeration plants, warehouses and offices, Exel Logistics already ensure high standards of efficiency and energy conservation, but greater savings will be sought through an energy audit. Exel Logistics already fit electrically operated doors to minimise lost cold air from freezers and warm air from ambient facilities, but will, in their energy audit, review the installation of timed automatic doors.

Exel Logistics are extending the use of heat produced by refrigeration equipment to augment space heating of the offices. Again, further potential benefits will be examined within the energy audit.

Exel Logistics will also carry out a lighting review to ensure that they are using the most effective and energy-efficient lighting. Energy efficiency will also be a top priority in the design of new buildings.

Through an extensive training and ongoing communication programme, Exel Logistics hope to ensure that all staff become energy-conscious. This will extend from simple measures, such as always switching off lights, to the establishment of an entire energy-efficient culture, hopefully incorporated by all the 13,000 employees into their everyday lives. Such measures will be regularly monitored within a quality audit. Similarly, the company will demand high environmental standards from all suppliers. Cleaning contractors, for example, will be required to use environmentally friendlier cleaning materials, and vehicle suppliers must satisfy Exel Logistics that they have taken all economically viable steps to reduce any adverse environmental impact of the fleet.

Waste

Exel Logistics' policy is to reduce waste wherever possible and to use professional waste management contractors. Certain packaging materials from the depots are already recycled and Exel Logistics will continually review the purchase of such equipment. Exel Logistics will use recycled paper where appropriate, and will endeavour to save paper by means of staff education, restrictions on photocopying and the use of both sides of paper, whenever possible. Investment in Information Technology has resulted in paperless distribution operations—one is currently in place, and the company hope to extend this further through joint cooperation with customers.

Policy Implementation

Exel Logistics have issued an Environmental Policy in the form of a handbook to all employees outlining the points presented here. In addition, a more detailed manual has been sent to each operating centre. This is primarily used as a reference guide and specifies individual action for office staff, warehousemen and drivers at all facilities. The aim is to promote concern for the environment as a way of life for all 13,000 employees. The principles inherent in switching off lights, recycling paper and reducing waste can be even more effective when practised twenty-four hours a day, at home as well as work!

Exel Logistics launched the environmental policy in the UK in June 1991. An Environmental Director has been appointed and champions elected at all levels. Already, the company are seeing a wide and varied number of initiatives from the workforce. These range from a new bottle collection service for customers, to clearing out a polluted lake, subsequently stocked with fish by the Local Authority. Bottle banks and can and paper recycling facilities are appearing at UK operating centres. Exel Logistics are very encouraged by the enthusiasm displayed by management and employees.

On the formal side, Environmental Audits will be carried out within the quality programme. The policy will need continuous updating—Exel Logistics recognise that they constantly need to search for improvement. Exel Logistics hope to be able to play their part in slowing down the rate of environmental damage, and possibly to redress the balance in favour of a greener future.

Greener Marketing Strategy

OPEN COMMUNICATIONS
British Gas and McDonald's

Nick Hawkins
Senior Lecturer in Marketing, Liverpool Business School

Environmentalism is a word which is becoming increasingly used and understood at all levels of society. Environmentalists argue that the physical environment has to be taken into account if firms are to pursue strategies that are ethical and credible to consumers. Increasing consumer awareness of green issues has put pressure on manufacturers to respond. An important adjunct to this process is provided by voluntary schemes such as the embryonic EC Eco-Auditing regulation, which aims to encourage firms to undertake regular audits of their environmental policy. Firms already have to take account of the Environmental Protection Act. The outcome of this is that firms are having to reposition not just products, but their whole business entity to ensure that they are not perceived as laggards in the move to environmentally friendlier marketing practices.

This is not to say that there are clear differences in emphasis from different parties interested in the issues. Steve Robinson, Chief Executive of the Environment Council, has pointed out that, 'In future, companies will not be able to promote products as environmentally friendly, because it will be assumed that they will be.'[1]

Associate Director of Proctor and Gamble, Peter Hindle, has said, 'To address green issues we need further technology that will allow us to continue to develop while preserving the environment.'[2]

It is clear, however, that whether marketing is placed before or after environmentalism in the corporate list of priorities, no business that ignores green issues can contemplate a long-term profitable future. Firms can either move, or be driven by, consumer power, competition and legal regulations.

With the above points in mind, it is possible to examine some companies who have taken a stance on environmental issues.

British Gas used a full-page press advertisement as a vehicle to establish their green credentials. The company hoped to gain a certain amount of credibility by releasing control of the communication to various experts who would write in an informed manner on subjects such as the ozone layer, deforestation and global warming. By clipping a coupon at the bottom of the page, an interested reader could send for a copy of the information in leaflet form. Having built up a collection of leaflets, the interested reader was then sent a copy of the British Gas environmental booklet.

British Gas are in a difficult position on the subject of the environment. The product is naturally less damaging to the environment than other fossil fuels, with regards to the production of greenhouse gases such as carbon dioxide. Yet the use and production of gas, as well as gas exploration, are still detrimental to the environment. The key for British Gas is to position themselves as satisfying an acceptable compromise—they need to ensure that society perceives that the benefits of gas have not been gained at too high an environmental cost. The precise quantification of the environmental cost will remain a very difficult calculation.

Richard Cassidy, the Business Issues Manager of British Gas, pointed out that 'British Gas does not want to overplay the environmental hand because we know we are not perfect.' Two years ago, for example, British Gas was criticised by the Advertising Standards Authority (ASA) for the wording of its 'Burning Greener' campaign. The ASA insisted that instead of being the 'earth's cleanest fuel', gas should be called the 'cleanest fossil fuel'.

The 'expert' press campaign was aimed to coincide with the Government White Paper on the Environment in September 1990. British Gas wanted to contribute to the environmental debate at a time of heightened awareness of the topic. The advertisements were targeted at an ABC1 audience in the quality press, and the company received over 30,000 responses for one or more of the fourteen specially produced booklets. British Gas eventually used this database of environmentally concerned ABC1 readers to send out copies of the 'Gas and the Environment' booklet. Over 75,000 copies of this booklet have been distributed so far. The main target audiences the company hope to influence are:

- Schools: teachers and children who are future consumers and potential employees
- Property developers: the company hopes to establish the 'green credentials' of gas through trade shows and exhibitions
- Environmentally aware members of the general public

British Gas realise that they have to be seen to be acting in an ethical manner towards the physical environment if they are to achieve their global corporate objectives. For example, exploration concessions frequently depend upon a company's previously established record on the environment. Also, in a worldwide consultancy capacity, their green credibility is a key issue. British Gas have links with Turkey, where they are advising the Government on the introduction of natural gas to Ankara. They have recently acted in an advisory capacity to the Greek Government over reducing air pollution.

British Gas have had setbacks on the environmental front. They bought oil drilling rights in central and southern Ecuador from Tenaco who operated under stringent United States standards. However, in northern Ecuador, unscrupulous oil exploration had left rich areas of natural rainforest irreparably damaged. The company felt the backlash of being seen to be opportunistic at the cost of the environment, even though they were not unscrupulous operators. The company are no longer involved in Ecuador.

In the UK, British Gas have constantly tried to prove that they can operate in an acceptable manner in environmentally sensitive areas. For example, the Wytch Farm oilfield set in the Dorset heathland, which British Gas operated in 1982–83, was subject to intense environmental scrutiny because the site was of internationally recognised importance. The company was instructed to sell their interest in Wytch Farm prior to privatisation, and it is now run by BP.

In the New Forest and Morecambe Bay, the company constantly monitor the environmental impact of their operations—knowing that they are under intense scrutiny from government bodies, environmental groups and an increasingly environmentally aware public.

British Gas have undergone a test eco-audit, and a full study is now being undertaken by independent environmental consultants to ensure impartiality. The results will be made public via the annual report as part of the 'openness' policy on this issue. The company clearly hope to be perceived as early adopters on the issue of environmental concern.

Richard Cassidy summed up the British Gas position on the environment: 'The price, reliability and security of our products are of paramount concern to our consumers. Environmental strategy is not the most important part of our marketing strategy, but it comes very high up on our secondary list. Nobody wants to feel that they work for an environmentally dirty company, so there is an internal as well as an external environmental push. The company is committed to environmental awareness.'

McDonald's provide another example of a company which had to think hard about their marketing strategy in view of the environmental debate. The company had to combat two very serious claims from environmentalists before they could be considered to have established a measure of green credibility. First, there was the claim that CFCs in packaging were contributing to the depletion in the ozone layer. McDonald's decided to remove CFCs from their packaging.

Second, there was the perception that the fast-food hamburger companies are actively supporting the destruction of the Amazonian rainforest by providing a market for cheap Brazilian beef from deforested areas such as Rondonia. There is a vicious cycle to this process. The cleared rainforest is used to graze beef herds which eventually leads to the land becoming desert. More rainforest has to be cleared to allow the process to begin afresh, and so the cycle goes on. Ultimately, there is only wasteland. Clearly McDonald's could not allow such a perception to remain unchallenged, as to do so would implicitly give the claim validity.

McDonald's chose to put out an informative two-page newspaper advertisement which showed pictures of rainforest creatures, such as the pangolin, and stated that as no beef was imported from former rainforest areas, the company were in no way responsible for the destruction of the Amazonian ecosystem.

Both the British Gas and McDonald's examples illustrate attempts to minimise the negative perceptions of the company in order that the corporate communications, both in controlled advertising messages and in publicity terms, will be assigned a higher environmental credibility. When such credibility has been established, consumers will give the messages more attention. The importance of this process is clear, given that consumers are more aware and informed than ever before, and will increasingly review the corporations in a holistic sense before trusting them with long-term loyalty and support.

As Bob Reid, Chairman of British Rail, has argued, 'No business has a secure future unless it is environmentally acceptable.'[3] Companies that are environmentally 'hostile' will find it hard to market their products with a premium price and quality strategy. Equally, they will find it increasingly difficult to recruit well-educated, environmentally aware young graduates. In short, they could become a corporate underclass, ignoring long-term strategy and relying on crude short-term tactics to survive. The future is bleak given such a scenario, and this explains the contextual importance of communicating exactly how the firm has achieved environmental targets. It is only then that consumers will assign credibility to the organisation and its messages.

One firm which successfully followed such a policy were the German battery manufacturers, Varta. Their decision to be the first to market mercury-free batteries in the UK coincided with a rise in market share from 2% to 13% in the late 1980s. The company received favourable editorial comment for its pro-environmental stance and made its environmental commitment the subject of a full-page press advertisement.

Other industries which are adapting to meet the challenges and opportunities of becoming greener include the soap powder industry, with an emphasis on lower-temperature washes, less phosphates and less packaging. Ecover, manufacturers of environmentally friendlier washing powders and detergents, sold approximately £10 million worth of goods in 1989, against £1 million in 1988.

The pharmaceutical, chemical and integrated 'cosmeceutical' companies have been affected by environmentalism in areas such as depletion of non-renewable resources, use of CFCs, production of toxic wastes and animal testing. Given that the global market is estimated at $60 billion[4] and the UK industry is estimated at £1.7 billion,[5] it will be very important to pay attention to such issues if these companies are to continue to be successful.

In a strategic sense, it is clear that the pharmaceutical and chemical businesses will never be considered environmentally friendly. The quest for credibility will revolve around individual firms removing the perception that profits are going to be achieved whatever the environmental cost. The problem for high-profile chemical companies such as ICI is that 'mistakes', such as toxic waste pollution of waterways, receive a great deal of adverse media attention. This creates a climate of opinion in which their real environmental achievements, such as their award-winning clean ammonia synthesis technique, and expert systems to advise farmers on safe use of pesticides and agrochemicals, are harder to publicise effectively, because a barrier of scepticism has been established.

It is clear, having examined some of the corporate strategy issues which environmentalism raises, that the subject is at the heart of current marketing thinking. Whatever the specific response of individual companies, it is apparent that no business can afford to ignore the key issues. Environmental credibility, a key tenet of corporate credibility, can only be achieved by showing hard evidence to aware consumers to back up claims.

In 1989 The Henley Centre made a prediction: 'In the future, for many, environmental friendliness will be a prerequisite for purchase, and those that do not address these issues will find their products increasingly rejected.' In addition, it might be said that firms which fail to address the crucial issues and develop synergistic solutions will find themselves spiralling to corporate oblivion due to environmental and strategic myopia.

References

1. D. Snow, 'Green Marketing: A Passing Fad?', *Marketing Business*, October 1990, pp. 2-3.
2. Snow, 'Green Marketing: A Passing Fad?', pp. 2-3.
3. 'Marketing Trends: Putting the Price on being Green', *Marketing Business*, December 1989.
4. C. Brady, 'Cosmetics Consolidation Characterises a Moderately Paced Market', *Chemical Week*, Vol. 145 (1989), pp. 20-21.
5. National Westminster Bank, 'Cosmetics and Toiletries Industry Brief, Market Intelligence Department, August 1990' (1990).

Greener Marketing Strategy

BALANCING ECOLOGY AND ECONOMICS
Countrywide Holidays

Cerian Moss
KPH Marketing

This year, Countrywide Holidays (CHA) celebrated 100 years of walking. As a travel company with such long traditions of countryside appreciation and use, it was not surprising that they should be one of the first to introduce a wide range of green policies.

The Aims of CHA

• To provide reasonably priced holidays with a special emphasis on walking and enjoying the countryside

• To provide an informed appreciation of the countryside and its heritage

• To provide and maintain holiday accommodation to facilitate these aims

---

Figure 1

Simon Bradford, CHA's former Chief Executive, is a very keen conservationist and the green drive at CHA can be largely attributed to his belief that, 'tourism must not be allowed to destroy the countryside'. It was Simon Bradford who decided to take full heed of the Countryside Commission's Report, 'Visitors to the Countryside', which recommended that tourism companies should:

- Create opportunities for local conservation groups to meet tourists and explain their concerns and work

- Find ways to channel income from tourism into practical conservation projects

- Use marketing resources to stimulate a greater sense of care for and understanding of the countryside

At the Green Flag International (GFI) Conference in November 1991, CHA announced the launch of their Environmental Improvement Fund (see Fig. 2). The aim of the fund is to donate money to conservation projects in the local communities surrounding CHA Houses. As was explained, 'The countryside is our main resource, why shouldn't we pay for it just as we do other resources like gas and water? We decorate our guest houses so why shouldn't we also contribute to the upkeep of the countryside by repairing paths and planting trees? We have to realise that to preserve the countryside we have to start paying for it. After all it is where we earn our living, we wouldn't have a future without it.'

CHA Environmental Improvement Fund

- Pledged £1 per guest week
- Total contribution of over £17,000 predicted for 1992
- Coordinated by the Countryside Commission
- Local support from National Parks, National Trust and Wildlife Trusts

---

Figure 2

CHA have always attempted to educate visitors about the environmental issues of the areas they visit. They have, however, introduced special interest holidays in Britain, including 'Countryside Appreciation' at Grasmere in the Lake District, Kinfauns in Perthshire and Grantown in the Scottish Highlands. All of these holidays will offer expert guidance. Other 'Green Holidays' include 'Enjoy the Countryside', 'The Flora of Yorkshire' and the 'Natural History of Norfolk'. At Grasmere a proactive management trainee has even been developing the idea of running joint packages with the British Trust for Conservation Volunteers (BTCV).

There has been another new development in CHA holidays: CHA have decided to launch a new holiday concept, 'CHA One World Tours'. The tours will travel to less industrialised countries such as Nepal, India or Peru, with the emphasis on understanding the environmental and developmental issues of the places visited. CHA will organise visits to small development projects which give the local people a chance to improve their own situation and protect their environment at the same time. Typically, they will visit charity-funded projects so that guests can see what can be achieved with relatively small sums of money. Contributions will also be made, on the visitors' behalf, to local development projects.

In addition to these greener developments, CHA also asked GFI to conduct an audit of CHA guest houses. This audit, one of the first of its kind in the British tourist industry, was sponsored by the Countryside Commission.

'We wanted to find out if we really were green, or if we were just kidding ourselves', states CHA. The auditors visited four CHA houses in the Lake District and looked at every aspect of the company's operations. The main areas covered were:

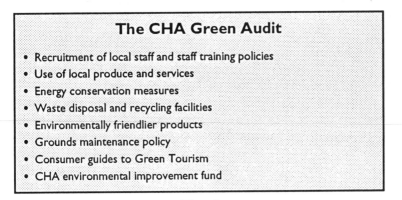

The CHA Green Audit

- Recruitment of local staff and staff training policies
- Use of local produce and services
- Energy conservation measures
- Waste disposal and recycling facilities
- Environmentally friendlier products
- Grounds maintenance policy
- Consumer guides to Green Tourism
- CHA environmental improvement fund

Figure 3

Although some of the recommendations were relatively easy to implement, CHA have encountered problems in some areas. For instance, using environmentally friendlier products is not as simple as it sounds.

'As we supply catering services we have to conform to very stringent health and safety requirements, and we have to be prepared for regular visits by environmental health officers. Therefore our cleaning materials have to be capable of performing to certain quality standards for disinfection and hygiene. In addition, the materials have to be packed in a form for industrial use—in other words, large packs—and finally all materials must list contents for safety reasons.' Products which meet all these quality, quantity and information criteria and are environmentally sounder are not yet available. CHA have contacted several of their suppliers, but as yet no real progress has been made.

The Chief Executive added, 'We do want to be greener, but in many cases we don't necessarily know what this would mean. We can contact our suppliers and say we want greener products—but as we don't have sufficient awareness of what this means in terms of paper, or cleaning materials or food for instance, we would not necessarily be able to ask the right questions—or even understand the answers.'

CHA is actively seeking the help of groups like Friends of the Earth, who can advise on the greenest products available.

After the audit, a pilot greening scheme was launched at Grasmere in 1990. Apart from trials of 'friendlier' products, the staff were encouraged to come up with greener ideas. This process has proved successful and now the scheme is being extended to all homes and holidays and is being communicated to guests.

The motivations behind the green move were explained: 'It's not only the right thing to do, it's also a useful tool to give CHA a marketing edge. We feel it's important for CHA to be confidently green. Being one of the first groups in the tourism industry to develop a greener initiative, we feel we are almost a pressure group within the industry. It will be important therefore to keep up the pressure and the marketing edge—we can, after all, always do better.'

In the future, CHA hope to develop schemes whereby visitors will actually see where their money is going, and they also intend to undertake regular audits. As far as the tourism industry goes, CHA are convinced that the tourist of the future will want to feel that he or she is not taking anything away from the place they are visiting—they will want to feel that they are actually contributing to the greening process. This is why the concept of 'One World Tours' was developed. CHA are also involved in developing an industry-wide Green Tourism Charter, as they realise that there will be a need for regulation and coordination of greener tourism development. The industry will need to change its view of tourism. According to CHA, they will have to learn to balance the use of the environment with caring for the resource.

CHA are keen supporters of GFI and Tourism Concern and through these bodies they hope that a higher international profile for tourism and environmental issues will be developed.

In the words of the Countryside Commission:

Tourism and the Environment: Maintaining the Balance

Principles of Sustainable Tourism

- The environment has an intrinsic value which outweighs its value as a tourism asset. Its enjoyment by future generations and its long-term survival must not be prejudiced by short-term considerations.
- Tourism must not be allowed to damage the resource, prejudice its future enjoyment or bring unacceptable impacts.

Figure 4

Greener Marketing Strategy

TRADING FOR A FAIRER WORLD
Traidcraft

Richard Evans
External Affairs Director, Traidcraft plc

When Traidcraft started in business in 1979, its major products were jute handicrafts, cane baskets from Bangladesh and instant coffee from Tanzania. Its initiators were a group of Christians who, recognising the plight of millions of fellow humans in the so-called 'third world' countries, who lived at or below subsistence level, believed they could do something about one of the major causes: unfair trading.

If the huge net flows of wealth from the south to the north, which are currently running at around $50 billion a year, were to be reversed, the changes in the way we deal with the countries and people of the less industrialised world would have to be radical, sustained and massive. Traidcraft was set up not just to provide a marketing channel for poor producers in less developed countries to sell the output of income-generating projects, but to attack the structural causes of poverty in the international trading system.

The product range grew, to include a wide variety of handicrafts, household textiles and more commodities, and so did the volume of trade. This created increasing demands for working capital which were exacerbated by the seasonal nature of the business. This need made Traidcraft think increasingly about how to finance the business in the long term. Whose business was it anyway?

Traidcraft had always differed from a conventional business in that their primary objective is not 'to make profits for the owners'. Traidcraft have always seen their objective as maximising the opportunities for trade, and the benefits of trading for their producers in the poorer countries.

From the growing interest in the company, it became apparent that customers and supporters felt this objective was worth investing in.

For Traidcraft's rapidly expanding network of voluntary sales reps, the investment was in the first place one of time and cash to buy stock for resale. Others were looking for ways of investing their savings that matched their own ethical principles and objectives. In 1984 the company converted to a public limited company and offered the public 300,000 non-voting shares at £1 each. James Erlichman wrote in *The Guardian*:

> A Gateshead company called Traidcraft urgently needs a £300,000 cash injection from new shareholders—but it is offering them in return only 'love, justice and equity'. And equity to Traidcraft means putting a higher value on sharing the world's resources fairly than on its own share certificates. Investors must prefer goodness to greed, and should never expect 'personal gain or profit' the prospectus warns.

The first issue was over-subscribed by 60%.

This may seem to have little to do with 'green issues' in the sense of protecting the biological systems on which life on earth depends, but that is not the case. The 1984 prospectus set a monetary value on sharing the world's resources more fairly. It also made an explicit commitment to prioritising the needs of poor people in the less industrialised world in the policies and practices of a British public limited company.

The links between economic needs and environmental damage are now more clearly understood by the public. We recognise that people, driven to the very limits of subsistence, are likely to seek survival in short-term methods of cultivation and poorly planned and poorly managed extraction of resources from their surroundings, which often result in long-term degradation of the environment. The public is, however, less aware of the extent to which our own need for foods, luxuries, security, physical comfort and a good return on investments, may result in unacceptable, but cost-saving, practices by industries in our own countries, and in widespread destruction of important ecosystems in other parts of the world, where minerals and timber are extracted or cash crops cultivated.

It is not without significance that in the same year the company became a public limited company—1984—Traidcraft launched its first recycled paper catalogue and promoted the use of recycled paper tissues for toilet and kitchen rolls. For five years the company had traded exclusively in products from community-based producers in the 'third world'. The maximum value of UK or European products sold was limited to 5% of total turnover. Because the Company Articles committed it to buying and selling products that promoted justice in trading with the 'third world', the board of directors took a considerable time to agree to the management's proposals to sell recycled paper products manufactured in the UK. In the end they agreed, not because selling recycled paper would save the tropical rainforests, or even save the British and Scandinavian softwood plantations, but in recognition of the fact that we all have responsibility for the planet, in terms of conserving energy and resources, and reducing pollution, which cannot be separated from our concern for the people with whom we want to share its resources more fairly.

Traidcraft's customers clearly found the message carried by the paper products entirely consistent with the company's established objectives, and especially the use of unbleached post-consumer waste. As a result, the sales of the paper division grew to 25% of turnover between 1984 and 1989. Although Traidcraft's sales of recycled toilet and kitchen tissues have declined in the last two years as similar products have become widely available in the supermarkets, the directors are happy to have encouraged a more caring trend in consumer behaviour.

Traidcraft's purchasing policy combines the same sensitivity to the need of the people who grow and make the products and the need to conserve the environment in which they live.

- Products should not exploit, or endanger the health of people involved in their production
- Production methods should take account of the need to protect the natural environment
- The product and production methods used should be appropriate to the economy and ecology of the country of origin
- Locally available raw materials and technology should be used wherever possible
- With food products, Traidcraft avoid trading which encourages competition for land between essential subsistence farming and exports, and trading in staple crops where peoples' diets are deficient

It is not always possible in all circumstances to achieve these ideals. Traidcraft's overriding priority is to provide opportunities for people at the bottom end of the economic spectrum to develop, by finding markets for the products of their skills and resources.

The company work closely with their associated charity, The Traidcraft Exchange. Apart from owning the voting shares, the Exchange develops educational materials focusing on the issues of injustice in trading, the role of small enterprises and trade development in less industrialised countries, and case studies of the impact on communities and the environment of both good and bad trading practice. The Exchange's educational theme materials, 'FOR PEOPLE AND PLANET' are referred to below.

Its Overseas Business Development Service (OBDS), provides a range of hands-on advisory services to small businesses in the less industrialised world, which want to enter, or develop, their overseas trading activities. OBDS can help producers to change to more environmentally sensitive production methods, to use greater efficiency in the use of natural resources and energy, or even to change to more appropriate activities. As an independent organisation, the Exchange can also alert the company, and other traders, to potentially damaging products in their portfolio.

It has been observed that people in developing countries, who are marginalised economically and socially, are often more sensitive to the need to preserve the environment and its resources. Perhaps this is because they are used to scarcity, unpredictable climatic conditions and managing to survive on very little. This is more often the case in rural communities with their traditionally conservative value systems, hence a particular focus on rural craft and food producers in Traidcraft's product selection.

If the economic benefits of sensitively managed rural production are enhanced, there is less likelihood of rural communities disintegrating as people move to the cities in search of work.

Poor people, though not the poorest and most desperate, are often, of necessity, better at environmental management, at least in some respects and on the micro scale. Chemical fertilisers and pesticides are expensive, as are the high-yield hybrid seeds that require them. Farmers who cannot afford these may get lower yields, but are more likely to use animal manure and non-chemical pest-control methods. Alternative traders in mainland Europe are moving increasingly to organic food and commodity production with their less industrialised world partners. While the motivation for consumers may have more to do with their own health than concern for the environment in which the producers live, the trend is to be encouraged and the task of educating the public about the larger benefits undertaken. However, effective and sustainable management of organic crop production does have higher costs, which consumers must accept in higher prices if this sort of market force is not to result in greater poverty for the producers.

Goods are sold through a range of seasonal catalogues and through Traidcraft's own network of 2,000 voluntary reps. Direct retailing is limited to four shops owned by the company, and wholesaling to 15% of total turnover. Wholesale methods are seen as limiting Traidcraft's ability to communicate with customers. The catalogue was chosen as a method which assured the company of direct communication with customers. Traidcraft believe that it is just as important to get their message across as to sell the product. In this way they will build up customer loyalty and awareness.

Very little has been spent on advertising. Traidcraft prefer to rely on editorial coverage which generates good PR. Most customers contact Traidcraft themselves, having learned about the company through church groups, Christian Aid, Cafod or the press.

The postal system is used to transport about half of Traidcraft's goods. The company also use road hauliers for bulk deliveries to shops and reps. Packaging is kept to a minimum and plastic packaging has been significantly reduced over the years largely due to pressure from one large customer: Greenpeace.

In Spring 1987, Traidcraft introduced their first collection of ready-made garments. All were produced by cooperatives and cottage industry groups, often in quite remote villages, in India, Bangladesh, Nepal, Thailand, Kenya and Peru. In design terms, Traidcraft set out to develop a unique synthesis of fashion with the traditional hand skills and cultural identity of the many producers with whom Traidcraft works. Technically, the company committed itself to natural fibres: cotton, silk, wool, and alpaca; low-energy production methods: spinning, hand-weaving and non-industrial garment-making techniques where appropriate; and, in the limited number of situations where the knowledge and skills still existed, the use of natural dyes.

India, Bangladesh and Thailand are major exporters of industrially manufactured ready-made garments to the UK, Europe and the USA. In most cases, these countries are favoured for their low labour costs and absence of effective textile workers' unions. Fabrics and other requirements are imported by multinational traders who re-export the finished products. This results in low earnings for the countries concerned, which often suffer further restrictions on their earning capacity because of discriminatory trading rules like the Multi Fibre Arrangement.

Traidcraft recognise that the textile and garment industries often represent the first steps towards industrialisation and the ability of an economy to add value to its raw material resources rather than export them for processing elsewhere. All their garments are made from locally produced fabrics, and, where necessary, they will substitute imported items such as plastic buttons with locally made bone, shell or coconut buttons. Clothing groups have responded enthusiastically to ideas for using local renewable resources as an alternative to expensive imports, and more are prepared to learn new techniques such as non-chlorine bleaching and vegetable dyeing.

Traidcraft did find that the marketing of fashion garments had to be more targeted than their other product ranges. 'We had to first define our target group and then design and promote the products accordingly. Advertising has been used, in the form of coupons in women's fashion magazines. We hope this more proactive marketing style will develop the market size.'

Customer reaction to garments, where a certain degree of variability was inherent in the production philosophy, and where greater care was required in use and washing than with our modern high-performance, low-care fabrics, was mixed at first. Explaining to customers how the garments are made and why these production policies had been adopted enabled them to adjust their expectations and to embrace the company's approach with enthusiasm.

Even in the area of wood-carving in India, governed by the centuries-old rules of caste and family tradition, moves are being made towards a more sustainable future for the industry. Traidcraft charge their customers a 10% levy on the price of all wood products. This money is being used to support tree nurseries and good conservation practice. One partner in the north Indian city of Saharanpur, the traditional centre for shesham wood carving, has worked with 200 wood-carving families to establish a tree nursery in the middle of an industrial estate. His concern goes beyond his own small efforts to sustain natural resources:

> The West must realise how much it influences the expectations and aspirations of other countries. If people in India and China take some of the West's consumer attitudes, think of the impact it would have on the world. If everyone in India and China used just one extra piece of paper each, then any saving made in the West could be wiped out.
>
> The West can also help in sharing information and expertise on environmental issues. We would like access to seed banks. It is difficult for us to get access to hardwood seeds, as at present hardwood growing is controlled by the Government. We would also like to share what you have learned about recycling as well.

The case of the woodcarvers in Saharanpur, and the pleas of Rakesh Kaushal, quoted above, have been used in a series of educational materials produced by the Traidcraft Exchange based around the theme, 'FOR PEOPLE AND PLANET'. The short introduction to the theme material is a good summary of Traidcraft's approach to environmental issues, and a fitting conclusion to this case history:

Traidcraft is working for fair trade—trade that sustains both people and the planet. International trade often damages the environment and ignores the needs of the people who produce the goods. Traidcraft offers an alternative:

- It gives the producers a fair deal. With greater resources, they can care for the environment on which their future depends.
- It offers the customer the power to change things.

Greener Products

A NICHE IN RE-MANUFACTURING
Onyx Associates Ltd

Paul O'Carroll

Director, Onyx Associates Ltd

Formed in April 1990, Onyx introduced a new service for the greener office. By completely re-manufacturing EP-S laser printer toner cartridges, the company intend to go some way to reducing Britain's plastic waste mountain.

Worldwide, some 300,000 tonnes of laser printer toner cartridges end up on scrapheaps each year, complete with a residue of toxic powder. In Britain alone, 1.44 million individual cartridges join the rubbish heap each year. Research has indicated that between 75% and 85% of these cartridges could be re-manufactured and re-used, as all Canon-engineered laser printers, such as Olivetti, Apple, Hewlett-Packard, Brother and Wang, use the EP-S cartridge system.

The laser printer increased in popularity as design studio printing became available to companies across industry. The accessibility of desk-top publishing further increased the growth of the laser printer market, and by the close of 1989, over one million Canon-engineered models had been sold in the UK. The toner cartridge also created a storm: it became the largest plastic consumable an office would use. This prompted environmentalists to search for solutions to curb this growth in plastic waste. In the UK, research by Onyx indicated that discarded cartridges add 2,880 tonnes of plastic waste to existing mountains each year. One answer to the waste problem was to re-manufacture the cartridge, an approach being taken elsewhere in Europe and America.

Onyx was the brainchild of Andrew Hughes, who had been working for a computer systems house. He was researching business opportunities in the greener market, when he came across this industry which was flourishing in North America. He was joined by Paul O'Carroll who was working for an international recruitment company and had a strong background in sales and marketing.

The company conducted research into the market, which produced four main findings. First, the office consumables business appeared to be relatively unaffected by economic recession, since a company must continue to send out letters and information. Second, the fact that there was no established competition in the UK re-manufactured toner cartridge market indicated that there was an accessible business opportunity. Third, the growing desire of companies to be seen to be environmentally conscious and the emergence of Environmental Audits were likely to create a strong demand for greener office supplies. Finally, the growth in laser printer use established a considerable potential market.

Due to the economic climate, the banks were very loath to lend money to the project. However, the directors were so convinced that the project would be a success that they decided to establish Onyx with their own finances. In September 1990 trading began and growth was phenomenal. At the close of the first month turnover stood at £19,441; at the end of the year it reached £636,664.

Developing the Process

Concentration on consumer satisfaction has been a key element in the company's success. In the early stages the company had many problems with quality, as the re-manufacturing process was not sophisticated enough to guarantee standards. It was soon realised, however, that quality was essential to the company's survival. With this in mind, Ralph Palombo, who had twenty-five years' experience in manufacturing, was recruited to manage production and quality, aiming for a zero-defect target.

Essentially, a cartridge works very simply: toner is passed from a reservoir onto a drum where it is charged and passed onto paper. Any residue toner remaining on the drum is then collected in a secondary reservoir. The process of cleaning and refilling the cartridge was relatively easy. However, the drum posed a more difficult problem. The drum deteriorates with age, as its photosensitive coating is eroded by the rigours of time. This problem was solved by re-coating the drum with specific chemicals. Components used in the process are imported from Germany and the US.

This process, which gave Onyx the ability to re-coat the photosensitive drums to the standard found in an original new cartridge, was revolutionary in the UK market. It meant that quality could be guaranteed.

The collection of used laser toner cartridges was another important issue. Onyx decided to supply free disposal bins to companies across the country who wished to save their empty cartridges. There was an added benefit for those who took part in the scheme: Onyx paid for every empty unit collected.

The Market

In addition to the environmental benefits of the product, the re-manufactured cartridge has been instrumental in reducing the market price of cartridges. The re-manufactured cartridge has proved to be cheaper than the new one, by about 25%. The emergence of re-manufactured laser cartridges proved such a competitor to new laser cartridges that the market price for new cartridges has fallen considerably.

Onyx market their product through direct sales. They have a small team of sales staff who make about 300–400 cold calls a day to potential customers. Records of laser printer owners are then kept on a database. In the early days Onyx mainly targeted small companies as Onyx did not have the resources to provide very big contracts or to offer favourable terms. However, as the company has grown, larger companies have been targeted.

The markets for re-manufactured cartridges in other countries are much larger than in the UK. In Germany, for instance, where it is illegal to throw away cartridges, re-manufactured items account for over 70% of all sales.

Onyx are very aware that more advanced legislation in other countries helps their overseas competitors; in particular it allows the German manufacturers to negotiate better rates on raw material supplies, such as toner. Onyx hope that through determined marketing and continued lobbying, the UK may be able to develop a similar policy on the greener office.

At present there is little in the way of legislation to further the development of environmentally friendly products in the UK, either in terms of minimum recycling requirements or eco-labelling. However, when the EC eco-labelling scheme is introduced in Autumn 1992, this may change. Brussels is continuing to pass numerous directives, and the UK Government will undoubtedly implement these if it wishes to improve the international competitiveness of its industry.

Onyx was launched by entrepreneurs who identified a need for greener office products in the UK. Their concentration on quality and marketing has enabled them to raise the image of re-manufactured cartridges and to encourage the use of greener office products. As a company committed to environmental improvement, Onyx is intending to undertake a full Environmental Audit in the near future. Packaging is also under review. In the future, the company hopes to attain the BS5750 quality standard to illustrate their commitment to quality. They have already been endorsed as a registered carrier of waste. Onyx's main hope at the moment is that legal conditions will be set that will guide the disposal of waste office products so that the company could increase its turnover and contribute a bigger reduction in waste plastic mountains.

Greener Products

SUPPORTING SUSTAINABLE DEVELOPMENT
Issan Mori

Dr Ashley Morton
EntoTec

Cerian Moss
KPH Marketing

EntoTec is a biological research and consultancy group which develops technical, economic and management solutions to the problems of rural under-employment and low incomes. The income generated is used to fund research into environmentally sound, appropriate technologies for rural development and to provide seed money for pilot rural development projects. The solutions which EntoTec develop concentrate on projects which make the most of local traditions and skills, are labour intensive, and do not require large inputs of capital and machinery. EntoTec particularly favour projects which are directed towards 'added-value' export markets, as these are most likely to be self-sustaining after EntoTec's support.

The research group is directed by Dr Ashley Morton, an ecologist who has worked on international consultancy projects for over twelve years.

EntoTec's venture into the fashion market came about through a project in Issan, northeast Thailand. Issan is an impoverished area where farming is difficult because of poor sandy soils and low rainfall. Issan Mori—Mori being the scientific name for silkworm—was set up in 1990 and is an excellent example of the new approach to sustainable development: a silk farm.

Silk is a completely natural product and probably the only fabric which can be produced without significant adverse environmental and social impacts. EntoTec have three specific criteria which projects must meet: environmental responsibility, quality, and social responsibility.

Environmental Responsibility

EntoTec believe it is crucial to Sustainable Development that a project does not impoverish the environmental characteristics of the areas in which it is involved. Issan Mori is an example of good environmental management.

- Traditionally, silk is produced from land that is too poor for food production. Therefore it provides an excellent way of generating much-needed income from marginal land. Issan Mori maintains this tradition and has deliberately avoided trying to establish highly productive mulberry plantations supported by fertiliser inputs and irrigation, or using land that could be put to productive agricultural food use.

- Silk, unlike other natural fibres, especially cotton, is produced using no insecticides, which means that the whole process is much kinder to the natural environment and the wildlife in the area.

Quality Criteria

EntoTec also believe that for developing countries to compete internationally, they must adhere to strict quality standards and use these criteria to give them a competitive edge in the market. Instead of concentrating on making cheap imitations of foreign goods, they must develop their own comparative advantages on quality issues in order to maintain long-term success. Issan Mori encourages just such an approach, and by concentrating on traditional silk reeling and weaving techniques the superior quality of the silk can be maintained.

- Unlike modern silks, Issan Mori silk is made from yarn that has been hand reeled in the traditional manner. This method conserves fuel and reduces pollution because the yarn is not exposed to the harsh chemicals and high temperatures used in the modern factory reeling of silk. It also guarantees that the yarn emerges from the process undamaged, thus ensuring that the exquisite lustre—so rarely seen in mass produced silks—for which Thailand is so well known, is captured in Issan Mori products. The hand reeling of the yarn also imparts a characteristic texture and weight to Issan Mori fabrics.

- All Issan Mori silk is entirely hand woven on traditional looms in the weavers' homes. In addition to plain and shot taffeta silks, fully reversible patterned fabrics (Mudmee) are produced using traditional weft ikat techniques. This ensures that a greater variety and quality of silk is produced.

Social Responsibility

It is very important to EntoTec to ensure that the local people involved in their projects are treated fairly and that the project as a whole enhances the social conditions of the area. At Issan Mori this responsibility to the local people has been made a priority.

- Silk reeling and weaving are skilled crafts and this work is mainly performed by young mothers and older women who are no longer able to earn a living from labouring. The work is carried out in their own homes so that the women can work on flexible time-scales, therefore not neglecting their children or other responsibilities. Unlike some sectors of the silk industry in Asia, Issan Mori prohibits the use of child labour.

- Workers are contracted to produce specified designs for a guaranteed market, subject to quality standards. They are given an advance so that they do not need access to credit.

- Issan Mori also attempts to encourage a more equitable distribution of profits between Thai fabric producer and the foreign fashion designers and traders, by ensuring that Issan Mori fabric cannot be purchased outright. Instead its use is licensed to designers and other end-users in return for a royalty based on the sales of the finished articles.

- EntoTec support Issan Mori through the provision of better varieties of mulberry, healthier silk worms, simple equipment and advice on rearing silkworms. They also provide the necessary design and marketing inputs for the production of fabrics and fashion goods for high added-value export markets. It is hoped in the longer term that through training and development the participants will learn to produce and finish silk goods to the highest international standards themselves.

The pilot phase of Issan Mori was completed in the Autumn of 1991 with the public exhibition of some completed fashion garments in the UK as part of the test-marketing of the final product. The garments received an enthusiastic reception. The production of fabrics for the expansion phase is currently under way, and it is hoped that products will enter the retail markets in the 1993/94 season. The search is now on for a major sponsor of the project as it expands, and it is hoped that the project might be taken on by the United Nations.

The main risk facing the Issan Mori project is the fickle nature of the international fashion markets. At the moment, natural fabrics, especially silk, are popular with both designers and customers, but this situation could change. The vast majority of consumers have always purchased fashion items on the basis of fashion, design, colour and care characteristics. However, this may not be the case in the future. The rise of the greener consumer has already been noted. The backbone of this group is made up of young female consumers, often with money to spare. The outcry caused by revelations of working conditions for many women in the fashion industry in less developed countries might indicate how successful a correctly marketed greener fashion industry could be. Many designers, including Katherine Hamnett, have already started looking at unbleached cotton fabrics for their designs. For these reasons EntoTec are planning to emphasise the greener nature of their garments—they are even planning to include information on the village and individual seamstresses on the garments, adding consumer interest and humanising the product. In the longer term however, Issan Mori believes success will come from a sustained quality advantage, supported by its socially responsible approach to business.

Greener Products

DEVELOPING GREENER SUBSTITUTES
Dawes Environmental Coatings

Dr Malcolm McIntosh

Independent Environmental Consultant

Dawes Environmental Coatings are a small company researching, manufacturing and selling water-based coatings for metallic surfaces, masonry and wood. The company was established in 1987 by Dr Michael Dawes with the intention of finding a niche market for environmentally friendlier products. He is now the chairman and his son, Michael Dawes junior, is the Managing Director.

At present, although they are in the research and development stage, their products are already selling on a global basis. Their turnover in 1990/91 was £100,000.

The father-and-son team always had a long-term plan to set up a chemicals company with the specific intention of developing environmentally sounder chemical products. To this end, Dawes Senior became the UK distributor for a range of Italian rust-converting materials in order to gain practical marketing and sales experience in the business. At the same time, Dawes junior was training in chemistry and accountancy. After establishing the company, an export director, Nugmais ul-Rashid, was recruited, whose background was in economics and languages. The Dawes team now have an enormous range of skills—indeed Nugmais is often asked to speak locally on such issues as eco-labelling.

As a medical practitioner, Dr Dawes was aware of the physical effects of chemicals, such as solvents, on the human body. This provided a motivation to develop safer, greener alternatives. While most weather-resistant coatings contain high levels of solvents, Dawes coatings have only 1.5%. This means that they are safer to transport, safer and easier to apply, they are odourless and the handlers do not have to wear breathing or safety apparatus. They do, however, have the same durability as solvent-based coatings. This concentration on safety will be valuable as the regulations on safety at work are tightened. While the company are waiting to be put on the list of products for use on United Nations development programmes, they are very close to becoming one of the first UK companies to be allowed to carry the German Blue Angel eco-label.

As well as being detrimental to health, solvents are also destructive environmentally. The main problem associated with such volatile organic compounds (VOCs) is that in sunlight they contribute to the formation of secondary pollutants such as ozone and peroxyacetyl nitrates. These cause damage to crops and forests and can cause lung irritation.

An official study undertaken in France shows the breakdown of that country's solvent emissions by source (see Fig. 1).

Solvent Emissions by Source		
Source	Solvent emissions thousand tonnes	%
Paints	256.4	54.5
Metal degreasing	46.5	9.9
Perfumes and cosmetics	32.0	6.8
Household products	29.3	6.2
Printing	25.8	5.5
Others	70.6	17.1
Total	470.6	100
Source: ENDS Report 172 (May 1989)		

Figure 1

The figures, which exclude emissions from the chemical industry, indicate that paints account for over half of solvent emissions. Regulatory pressures for a reduction in solvent content of paints and other products are set to increase. The UN Economic Commission for Europe's Volatile Organic Compounds protocol, which, in November 1991, agreed a 30% cut in some VOCs by 1999 set no firm standards on solvents used in paints, adhesives and inks. However, a recent draft proposal recommended using product substitutes and add-on technology to cut emissions from these sources.

Paints and varnishes are likely to be one of the first products to be included in the EC eco-labelling scheme to be launched in Autumn

1992, as they are one of the four products on which pilot studies are being carried out.

Dawes have some large competitors, some of whom could have similar products on the market in the near future, but none of whom are as committed to the environment. Dawes stress that they are the only company specialising specifically in water-based products. They hope to carve out a market for themselves through the quality of their product and the quality of their distribution and support.

What really singles out Dawes from many other companies, let alone chemical companies, is their commitment to environmental issues. This sense of social responsibility is enshrined in their mission statement which says:

- The primary objective is to reward the shareholders (Dawes Senior and Dawes Junior).

- The secondary objective is to secure a significant proportion of the world coating market so that they can reduce the level of harmful emissions into the air globally.

- Their tertiary objective is to improve the infrastructure of less fortunate peoples and by so doing minimise the impact of inefficient and polluting industry. Further they want to ensure the long-term survival of the planet, balanced with short-term economic needs.

- Most importantly, 'the primary objective will not be secured at the expense of the secondary and tertiary objectives'.

Dawes have also had an independent Environmental Audit carried out. This was undertaken for three reasons. Dr Dawes commented that: 'We wanted to satisfy ourselves that we were environmentally friendly, we wanted to see if there were cost savings in terms of energy use, waste minimisation and recycling that we could make, and we wanted to be able to tell our users that we had had an independent Environmental Audit done—and be able to show them a certificate.' The audit was carried out on both the company's products and the processes, even the office itself.

Dawes believe they will succeed not only because they have an excellent product which meets the highest possible environmental criteria, but also because other businesses are making commitments to social responsibility and the planet and, as purchasers, will welcome both the Dawes product and their statement of intent.

At present Dawes are marketing the quality of their product rather than their environmental concerns, trying to show that the increased cost of their product is offset by increased safety and usability factors. Dawes insist that they are 'not just another company with an environmental stamp' and that 'a lot of companies say they are environmentally friendly—but we really are!'

In marketing terms Dawes underwent a re-positioning in 1991. They realised that their commitment to the environment gave them a marketing edge and so decided to change their name from Dawes Coatings to Dawes Environmental Coatings. This was, after all, a descriptive term not a marketing gimmick.

The future for Dawes will be in facing up to the giants in the chemical industry where global trade in over 70,000 chemicals produces profits in excess of $500 billion a year. If Dawes can maintain their environmental edge on their competitors, then they will be able to succeed in their niche markets.

Greener Products

THE IMPORTANCE OF RESEARCH
Natural Fact

Christopher Gates
Managing Director, Natural Fact

Natural Fact is a company committed to producing natural clothing in the most environmentally conscious manner.

In the production cycle of conventional cotton clothing, there is widespread use of chemicals, ranging from agrochemicals—pesticides, herbicides and artificial fertilisers—to corrosive scours and bleaches, and dyestuffs and finishes used in fabric processing.

Environmental damage extends in some cases from chemical poisoning of farm workers, through to the destruction of river life when chemical effluent from dyeplants is flushed straight into natural water systems.

While legislation is beginning to curb the worst excesses, little progress has been made in addressing the problems created by the textile industry.

Since 1989 it has been Natural Fact's objective to design attractive and comfortable leisure clothes that consumers will enjoy wearing, and to make them in a manner less harmful to the environment. Natural Fact have achieved this objective primarily by investing in research to identify those areas of textile and garment production, and the distribution chain, which create environmental pollution, and/or waste valuable natural resources. Having defined the environmental problem areas, the company then sought alternative methods of production which avoided these processes and the wasteful use of materials.

Natural Fact Research

Natural Fact conducted research which led to the conclusion that, in both consumer perception and in environmental terms, cotton was the most suitable fibre from which the Natural Fact range should be made. The public perceive cotton to be the most natural fibre available, and it has been shown that cotton production is more energy efficient than any man-made fibre.

While it is accepted that chemical-intensive farming may produce progressively higher yields, there is great concern about the impact of agrochemicals, which has extended to consumer level. This concern has turned organic farming from an eccentric pursuit to a serious commercial proposition. Yields may be lower, but the public are willing to pay higher prices for produce that has not been grown using chemicals. One interesting finding from the research was that the use of chemicals in agriculture has not significantly affected the rate of loss to pests. Now, as has always been the case, about a third of all crops are lost to pests.

The Development of Natural Fact Clothing

Having selected cotton as the medium, Natural Fact produced a range of leisure clothes made almost entirely without the use of chemicals. The company opted to make all their garments in the UK, which enabled them to monitor closely production processes and standards and the working environments in which fabric and clothes were made. Exploitation of both adult and child labour is common throughout the textile industry outside Europe and the USA—and even within some parts of Europe, such as Portugal. Natural Fact wanted to ensure that this did not happen in their plants and were, as a result, willing to accept the cost premiums which 'Made in the UK' demanded.

Natural Fact manufacture garments from raw cotton yarn using high-quality combed cotton for softness, and have the fabric knitted and finished to given specifications. They avoid the use of bleaches, abrasive scours, dyes, chemical fixes, and finishing agents.

The garments are sewn together using undyed and unbleached cotton thread, and the only decoration is the Natural Fact brand name, embroidered in the same unbleached and undyed yarn. Trimmings and labels used in some garments are all derived from natural state cotton. Packaging is kept to a minimum, and all cardboard boxes are recycled.

The process produces a rich, natural coloured, cream clothing which because it is neither bleached or dyed, is kinder for the skin. It was instantly accepted, by both the green and the non-green consumer, and has been quickly approved by consumers with skin allergies as ideal casual clothing.

Natural Fact clothing offers the environmentally conscious consumer a natural alternative. It claims to be 'Better for you, and better for your world'. The clothing has subsequently been adopted by all the major environmental charities. Natural Fact design and produce clothing for Friends of the Earth, The World Wildlife Fund and Greenpeace.

Natural Fact clothing is not widely available in the retail sector. The garments are primarily distributed by mail order. This allows the company to dictate how the garment is presented and packaged. Every garment carries their distinctive recycled swing tag, which details the key points of the philosophy and manufacturing processes.

Organically Grown Cotton

In the early days, it was recognised that, as a small company, Natural Fact could not dictate standards of cotton production to the marketplace. This meant they were forced to buy cotton yarn on the world market, without being able to select the source of that cotton. At the beginning they therefore chose to follow a strategy which gave as much control over the manufacturing process as possible.

Natural Fact were, however, from the start always deeply concerned about the farming methods used to produce the cotton they used. They therefore set themselves the objective of sourcing cotton which was grown in an environmentally responsible way. Cotton is normally grown using chemical-intensive farming methods. As a crop it uses huge amounts of water, and little attention is paid to the well-being of the immediate environment, or of the farm workers. Much of the world's supply of cotton comes from less industrialised countries which rely upon the crop as a valuable source of foreign currency. For this reason, it is often deemed to be more important than basic food crops.

In meeting the objective of sourcing organic cotton, Natural Fact therefore had to address a number of issues. Research led them to one simple solution: the company would avoid using cotton from any less industrialised country. This was not seen as an easy option. Natural Fact simply did not have the resources, or indeed, the production requirement, to persuade suppliers to produce cotton in a more environmentally responsible manner. However, in the longer term the company would like to be in position to develop such a source of cotton, perhaps in a cooperative venture with other European businesses.

The reasons for avoiding such sources of cotton were that it was felt farming practices in developed countries could be more effectively investigated, and there would be some degree of certainty that government standards had removed the most environmentally damaging practices. Labour conditions could also be carefully monitored.

Research was centred on the USA. The need to pay a premium was again accepted, but this time for both the labour and the raw material. A few organic farmers were willing to experiment with new crops, and through associates in the US, Natural Fact managed to source limited supplies of organic cotton. Reassurance that the cotton bought is organic is provided by independent certification of both the crop and the soil upon which it is grown: the land must have been chemical-free for a minimum of three years to be acceptable. Affidavits are also obtained at every link through the manufacturing chain to ensure that the cotton is not, at any stage, contaminated with chemicals, or mixed with non-organic crop. The only non-organic chemical used is a benign lubricating wax used in the spinning process, and even here the company is experimenting with natural waxes.

The End Result

The new organic garments really are one of the most environmentally responsible forms of cotton clothing available. Natural Fact have achieved their objective by research, and by persistence in the belief that there are virtually always environmentally sounder alternatives to conventional methods. They found, in the early stages, that it may be necessary to accept some form of compromise in the development of a greener product. Yet by ensuring that products carried clear information about the company's objectives and told consumers why they had to accept different standards, Natural Fact have been able to build up support and trust.

They have also, in the long run, managed to reach their objective of providing cotton clothes which are grown, processed, manufactured and distributed in a environmentally responsible way.

Their efforts at effective communication have also made a contribution to the environmental debate—every consumer who buys one of the products becomes better informed about the problems involved in greener textile production and manufacture; every consumer who wears one of the products is making a small statement that they do care about what is happening to our world.

Natural Fact would like to see the large textile retailers and producers using their market power to encourage farmers and manufacturers to allocate time and resources to greener methods. Of course, if the larger companies do not respond they may find themselves losing out to small, innovative companies like Natural Fact.

GREENER PACKAGING POLICY
Gateway

Carol Charlton

Business and Communications Director,
Landbank Environmental Research and Consulting

The major supermarkets were the first commercial organisations to respond to what has come to be known as 'green consumerism'. In 1989, when Gateway began to formulate its environmental programme, it was determined not to just climb on the green bandwagon for short-term advantage, but to make a commitment to genuine, long-term changes that would bring real environmental benefits and business.

In 1989 Gateway and Landbank entered into an 'environmental partnership' with the objective of, in the words of the Gateway Chief Executive Mr Bob Willett, 'looking for real solutions to real problems, even if this means taking a long-term approach to difficult issues'.

Under the directorship of Bryn Jones, an experienced environmentalist and former chairman of Greenpeace, the 'partnership' commits the company to a long-term environmental strategy aimed at addressing the environmental problems associated with the food-retailing business and developing genuine environmentally responsible policies within a commercially viable context. This approach is unique in that it aims to ground the Gateway environmental policies on a comprehensive analysis rather than a reactive and superficial product greening.

Packaging was chosen as the first issue to be addressed by the environmental 'partnership', because packaging has become a major problem for food retailers. Each year in Britain we throw away around six million tonnes of valuable glass, paper, laminates, plastics, tinplate and aluminium. It is an amount that would fill the city of London to the height of 100 yards deep and almost bury St Paul's Cathedral every year!

Packaging is Not a Load of Rubbish

The cost of packaging to the consumers is around £10.5 billion a year—or roughly £500 for each household. But the environmental costs of packaging are equally unacceptable. It is a highly visible manifestation of a wasteful and unnecessary use of fossil-fuel energy with its subsequent production of greenhouse gases. Generating this energy from coal, oil and gas throws out huge amounts of polluting gases, such as sulphur dioxide or carbon dioxide, which result in acid rain and global warming. In addition, most of Britain's rubbish is dumped into landfill sites, squandering potentially valuable resources of raw materials. A tonne of aluminium for example, could be worth as much as £700. Paper, glass, plastics and steel are also valuable materials and could be re-used.

The Landbank team spent eight months researching packaging materials and drawing up a greener packaging plan for Gateway. It was these findings and subsequent recommendations which were published in the report, 'Packaging: An Environmental Perspective'. Gateway launched the report and programme for action to the public in February 1991 with the message: 'Packaging is not a load of rubbish, so reduce, re-use and recycle if you want to choose for the environment'.

Packaging: An Environmental Perspective

The controversial Gateway cradle-to-grave report on packaging has been highly criticised by some and used as a bible by others. But whatever people think, it served to reveal the scale of the problems connected with waste management and the environment in this country, and in particular with domestic waste, of which packaging accounts for one-third. It further serves to establish a basic hierarchy of conservation principles for Gateway buyers and technicians. These are:

- Choose for the environment
- Use less
- Design for re-use
- Recycle

The Gateway packaging report describes the materials used in packaging and attempts to assess their impact on the natural world—from the moment they are extracted, quarried or harvested, all the way through manufacture, distribution, use and ultimately to disposal. Although hard facts and information can be used when carrying out this type of analysis, a number of value judgements have to be made about the importance, and relative importance, of natural forests, pure rivers, unpolluted oceans and clean air.

The shortcomings of such an approach will be obvious. In all categories except energy consumption and recycling rates, an element of personal (or collective) value judgement is required which cannot be fully backed up by hard data. A striking example of this is the discharge of organochlorine compounds from papermills into river systems and oceans. Clearly (there is no debate about this), these discharges are highly damaging to the environment.

Since we cannot assign a precise mathematical value to what can only be 'guestimated', the safest course would be to ignore it. Yet not to penalise paper producers for their polluting discharges would be to ignore the most destructive environmental effects of paper manufacture, and so to render pointless the whole exercise of an environmental assessment of packaging.

Such a broad environmental evaluation of packaging was not an easy undertaking. There are few simple guidelines which can be applied equally to all materials and difficult decisions were needed. The central concern was with energy use, because of the contribution made by burning fossil fuels—coal, oil and gas—to global warming. Great weight was also given to such issues as the damage done to the natural world by mining, quarrying or drilling for raw materials, loss of forests and pollution. As was to be expected, the industrial critics bewailed the lack of scientific rigour and criticised the methodology employed. However, Gateway judged that the benefits to be obtained from the analysis were so great and the packaging issues involved so urgent that they outweighed these issues.

The 50% Pledge

As a result of the findings in the packaging study, Gateway committed themselves to reducing the energy used in the production and transport of all packaging through its stores by 50% over the next five years.

The 50% target was not an arbitrary figure. The consensus of opinion in the scientific community is that if we merely stabilise emissions of greenhouse gases at 1990 levels, as is proposed, then this will do no more than slow the rate at which global warming occurs. It will not prevent it. So Gateway's 50% commitment focuses attention on the importance of reducing emissions from fossil-fuel energy generation.

Making it Work

Having established its 50% commitment, Gateway worked with the Landbank team to prepare a plan of action to meet this target by devising ways to create the changes required and also to monitor the progress being made by measuring these changes at regular intervals.

Two software systems were developed. The first enables Gateway buyers and technicians to see the energy consumption in the production of each piece of packaging and so provide them with a basis for dialogue with the suppliers about how energy savings can be made.

The second system—'PakTrak'—enables these savings to be monitored, and so measures the success of the various initiatives towards achieving the 50% reduction. PakTrak is a packaging database—the first established by any retailer in Britain. It enables Gateway to track the amounts and types of packaging passing through their stores and also to measure the changes achieved by the energy conservation programme at regular three-monthly intervals over the five years.

Suppliers

Gateway recognise that their conservation programme will be difficult to achieve without the cooperation of its suppliers. Accordingly, all Gateway suppliers were informed of the packaging initiative and in September 1991 the company held a series of seminars which were attended by more than 400 major suppliers. Following the seminars, four study groups were set up with selected suppliers, each chaired by a member of Gateway's board of directors, with the intention of investigating ways to achieve the 50% target.

A study group was set up for each broad category in the food-retailing business, that is to say:

- Processed foods
- Drinks
- Fresh foods
- Non-foods

Each group was asked to come up with an action plan and report back to a full suppliers' conference after one year. The suppliers responded enthusiastically to the idea of setting up study groups on packaging, as finding solutions to the problems raised by the 50% target will also help them to comply with forthcoming UK and European legislation.

The overall objective of each study group in this first stage is to investigate ways to achieve a 50% reduction over a five-year period in the energy component of all packaging passing through Gateway stores. The 50% target may be achieved in the following ways:

- By 'light-weighting' or by a simple reduction in the volume of packaging material
- By designing new forms of packaging
- By incorporating recycled material into the production processes
- By developing new delivery or collection systems
- By switching to re-usable or returnable containers
- By promoting recycling or waste management schemes
- By a combination of the above

Environmental problems are complex and must be addressed by society as a whole. However, Gateway's approach is based on genuine environmentalism and will, it is hoped, encourage others—retailers, manufacturers and the public alike—to follow suit.

Without a national strategy designed to reduce waste and encourage re-use and recycling, it will not be easy for Gateway to achieve the objectives it has set itself. Nor incidentally for any retailer, wholesaler or manufacturer who will together share the responsibility for achieving the targets being set by the European Commission's draft directive on packaging, which requires that by the year 2000 all packaging sold within the Community must be either re-usable or recyclable.

However, Gateway's decision to make a bold commitment on packaging will do much to focus public attention on what can be accomplished in this field.

Greener Logistics

INTEGRATING ENVIRONMENTAL POLICY
The Lane Group

Dr Malcolm McIntosh
Independent Environmental Consultant

The bulk of the Lane Group's income is derived from their logistics division, Peter Lane Transport, based in Bristol. In support of this business they also run a driver-training scheme, Training Force. It was established in 1964, and by 1991 Peter Lane Transport employed 286 people and operated 150 trucks.

The founder of the company, Peter Lane, has taken up farming in Devon and the company is now run by Rebecca Jenkins. Under her direction, turnover is up from £4 million in 1985/86 to £12.6 million in 1990/91. She and the company have collected a string of awards which include the 'Motor Transport Environmental Award' in 1986 and Jenkins being named as 'West of England Businesswoman of the Year' by the Institute of Directors in 1990. In 1991 they were awarded BS5750, further recognition of a well-managed company. Their main contracts are with The Body Shop International, Freemans, Castle Cement, Redland, GKN Axles, Australian Canned Fruit, the National Health Education Authority, and Sharwoods.

In a business dominated by men, Peter Lane Transport is exceptional in having three women in senior management—Rebecca Jenkins is Managing Director, Di Farrell is Projects Manager and Jo Abrahams is head of the driver-training division. What also makes the company different is their approach to business and the community, which is based on interactive and proactive principles.

They have developed close relationships with two local schools, in one case hosting frequent visits from classes of children and in the other working with teachers to build a better understanding of the way business works, and in particular the way the logistics business is evolving.

On environmental matters they have faced the fact that the transport industry has a poor public image. There is a proliferation of vehicles of all types on the roads of Europe and mounting public concern about the state of the planet. This is particularly true in the UK where road transport has received considerably more financial and governmental support over the last decade then rail transport. England, one of the most densely populated areas of Europe, does not have an integrated transport policy, unlike France and Germany.

Public concern is moving ahead of business and government on environmental issues, and a business such as transport, which can be dirty, dangerous and seemingly uncaring, needs to be aware of the necessity for good public relations—particularly on environmental issues. Any logistics business is bound to come into close contact with the general public.

Peter Lane are not unaware of the Greener Marketing opportunities. As Rebecca Jenkins puts it: 'Pressure is mounting against the transport industry to take positive steps towards environmental harmony. It is now possible that introducing environmental measures could mean the difference between winning and losing a contract.'

The company is keen to increase its business in continental Europe and has established a division specifically for this purpose, which is called Eurolane and is based in Birmingham. An awareness of the opportunities and the threats posed by the Single Market has not been missed by this company, a fact which may also mark them out from some other British businesses.

So how 'green' is the company? And what business benefits can they cite for being as environmentally friendly as a transport company can ever be? Can a transport company ever be environmentally friendlier? Taking responsibility for the planet fits into a wider understanding of business's overall social responsibility. The company accepts that perhaps the movement of goods and people in the UK could be differently and better organised at a governmental level, but in the meantime they are in the logistics business to stay—and make it as safe and clean as possible. Their strategic and managerial policies can be divided into seven areas:

- Company policy decided at boardroom level, which includes a commitment to TQM, included in which is environmental care. In line with the Valdez Principles and other guidelines for responsible business, the environment is a boardroom issue and a director has responsibility for this area.

- Procurement, waste management and Life Cycle Analysis systems which operate throughout the company from the purchase of office paper to vehicles and components.

- Employee training from top to bottom on environmental issues, which includes employee-led initiatives on non-smoking and recycling policies.

- Vehicle maintenance criteria that require drivers to be personally responsible for running their vehicles to the highest possible standards.

- Driver training that includes defensive driving, minimising fuel consumption and the need for road care.

- In advance of the law, fitting speed limiters of 60 mph to all vehicles.

- Community involvement with local schools and Bristol University.

It is worthwhile looking at some specific changes in policy within the company as a result of boardroom and employee commitment to the environment:

- Procuring hardwood floors for trucks from sustainable sources.

- Changing to biodegradable soap for the truck wash.

- Siting all depots outside town centres.

- Purchasing more expensive but cleaner trucks from a Scandinavian manufacturer.

- The introduction of non-smoking areas within offices.

- The development with other companies of aerodynamic trucks that are more fuel-efficient and reduce the drag on other vehicles.

- The monitoring of the disposal of waste oil and worn tyres. The gains to the company have been significant.

- Lower truck maintenance costs through greater driver care.

- Less tense drivers, therefore fewer accidents and less absenteeism.

- Lower fuel costs through careful driving.

- Greater employee commitment at all levels and in all branches.

- The maintenance of continuing customer contracts through following customer guidelines on environmental care.

- Winning new contracts through commitment to TQM including environmental care.

In an endeavour to provide a greener transport service, Peter Lane have had three Environmental Audits carried out in the last three years—two by independent environmental consultants and the third by their major customer, The Body Shop. Even though Rebecca Jenkins insists that Peter Lane Transport were environmentally responsible before they won the prestigious Body Shop contract, this customer certainly likes to keep all contractors on their environmental toes. The Body Shop audit is instructive, it praises the company for many environmental matters and the instigation of teamwork sessions. No doubt greener customers may force other transport companies to face the environmental challenge.

In a business which is bound to grow through the establishment of the Single Market in Europe and the growth of 'Just-In-Time' management, Peter Lane transport are being proactive in their approach to the environment, and winning contracts and being profitable. In this business there are questions that have to be asked about the future of road transport, and about investment both by private enterprise and government in improved rail and freight systems. But at the end of the line, goods still have to be taken from terminal to shop, home or factory, and this must be done in a socially responsible manner, in harmony with both the local and global environment. For the logistics business there are some real challenges in the future. Peter Lane Transport have made a start.

Greener Pricing

SOCIALLY RESPONSIBLE PROFITS
The Ethical Investors Group

Lee Coates
Director, Ethical Investors Group
Cerian Moss
KPH Marketing

In 1989 Lee Coates applied for agency status within Friends Provident. He set up as a financial advisor, tied to Friends Provident, to advise solely on ethical investments. The agency status allowed Lee to define his own objectives and to develop a greener code on pricing and profits. To this end, he capped his salary to the top rate of basic income tax and he pledged at least 50% of profits to charity. In 1991 Lee took the courageous decision to become an independent financial advisor. He explains, 'In 1989 there really were no funds which competed significantly with Friends Provident ethical funds, either on a financial performance or screening basis. However, by 1991 many other existing funds and new funds were performing well. They were also sticking closely to their criteria and some even had stricter criteria than Friends Provident.' It therefore made sense for him to go independent, as he would then be free to choose between a wider range of ethical and green trusts, and could therefore be more responsible to individual clients' needs. The Ethical Investors Group now provides independent financial advice to individuals and groups who care about their world and its preservation, and who wish to extend their caring philosophy to all areas of their lives and businesses.

Ethical Investors Group formed an Advisory Committee with participants from FoE, CND, Animal Aid, the Social Investment Forum and KPH Marketing, an independent green consultancy. This committee advise on the appropriateness of companies included in the portfolio list.

EIG hope to enable people to use their finances to encourage industry to become more socially responsible by giving personalised advice and arranging such financial services as pensions, life assurances, mortgage endowments, savings plans, lump sum and unit trust investments, additional voluntary contributions and personal equity plans. All of these contracts are linked to an ethical or green fund and therefore allow clients to avoid investing in companies whose activities they find distasteful, and/or to make a positive statement with their capital.

EIG make every effort to ensure that the ethical or green policy that each client enters into matches the individual's ethical or green criteria. One person's view may not be that of another. For example, some clients may consider animal experimentation abhorrent, while others consider it a necessary evil. Clients are specifically asked about their particular beliefs and values in order that the correct advice and policy may be provided for them.

The Group stress that their commitment to both the ethical issues and the groups involved is not profit-motivated. As with all banks, building societies and other financial advisors, EIG earn commission from insurance companies on the contracts arranged for clients. This commission forms the Group's income. Fifty per cent of this profit is pledged to charities nominated by EIG clients.

Each client who effects a policy with EIG has a vote as to which charity they want to receive their share of the profits. At the end of the year, the votes are totted up and the profit distributed in accordance with the clients' voting patterns. At the end of the first year, £8,000 was available to be shared out to charity. A press conference was held at the London Ecology Centre which was attended by over forty journalists. The EIG story was mentioned in several daily newspapers including *The Times* and *The Independent*. At the end of the second year, £12,005 more had been donated to charity, making the total over £20,000 in two years.

The Group's services are also marketed in a greener way. Lee devised a way of marketing the Group which would prove beneficial to charities. EIG pointed out to such organisations that if EIG could advertise in membership circulars, and members or employees consequently took up policies, then the charity would benefit as such clients would obviously nominate them to receive their proportion of the profit share-out. Many charities saw the benefit such a scheme could bring as a new and effective way of increasing their funds. EIG particularly targeted groups they saw as dedicated campaign groups: they believed people who were committed enough to join such groups were probably more likely to be prepared to invest solely on ethical grounds. In the early years, this commitment was essential as no one knew how such trusts would perform. However, since then it has been proved that ethical trusts can, on average, perform better than non-ethical trusts, so the commitment is not quite as crucial. In the early days, EIG contacted such groups as CND, the Henry Doubleday Research Association, New Consumer and Animal Aid. Most of EIG's clients have and still do come from CND, and the largest beneficiary of EIG's charitable donations is therefore CND.

EIG have also performed a study of the occupations of their clients, to see if any patterns emerge which might be useful for marketing. Interestingly, 20% of clients are advice workers, such as Citizens Advice Bureau advisors or counsellors. Another 15% come from the caring professions: teaching, healthcare, and local government.

It is believed that the marketing of EIG's unique features puts them at the forefront of independent financial advice on ethical and green investment. In three particular areas the service offered is thought to be unique:

- Advice is only given to those clients who require ethical investment. For many clients, this is the main attraction of the service offered. However, EIG also endeavour to ensure that the financial returns of investments do not compromise the ethical commitments of their clients.

- In addition to the specialist nature of the advice, the Group are committed to raising substantial sums for charities and socially responsible groups as specified by their clients. The group would like to see the percentage distribution increase from the current 50% to 90% or even 95% as turnover and profits grow.

- EIG state that no employee will earn enough to put them in the top income tax bracket.

The Group's philosophy is very simple: the greater the distribution made each year, the more clients will want to effect their policies through EIG, to help the groups they support. This in turn will increase the ability of green and ethical investment trusts to change the way business behaves.

Greener Communications

INVOLVING THE STAKEHOLDERS
Hampshire County Council
and Sutton Borough Council

Cerian Moss
KPH Marketing

This case history outlines two accounts of waste management initiatives undertaken by Hampshire County Council (HCC) and the London Borough of Sutton (LBS). HCC have developed a Waste Management Strategy, an essential part of which is an internal waste management plan. Its success has centred on internal Stakeholder involvement. LBS have a longer history of waste management and have developed a number of innovative external waste initiatives which have relied upon harnessing external Stakeholder enthusiasm. A review of both provides a good idea of how to go about setting up waste management and involving different Stakeholder groups—vital to any greening policy—whatever the organisation.

Launching a Plan: Hampshire County Council

In 1989 when the Council adopted its Waste Management Plan, HCC decided to review their internal waste management policy. As one of the largest 'businesses' in Hampshire, and therefore one of the largest waste producers, the council realised that waste management was becoming more of an issue, and to implement a countywide strategy effectively they had to be seen to practise what they preached. To demonstrate their commitment to waste management, they decided to create the position of Recycling Officer. Maryanne Hawes was appointed in 1990, and a review of waste was initiated. An Environmental Committee was set up which looked at Environmental Audits and environmental policy development, and the Committee was given the full support of the Chief Executive's office. Questionnaires were then sent to ninety-four premises out of a total of 1,400 waste-producing offices which came under the Council's jurisdiction, in an attempt to sample the current production of and policies on waste. Plans were then drawn up for a pilot scheme on waste management. The aim was to avoid waste, to re-use and recycle as much as possible, to recover resources from waste and to landfill only where necessary. The first type of waste targeted was paper, and a pilot scheme was launched in the Council Headquarters offices of The Castle, Winchester. Once the plans had been finalised, companies were invited to tender for the collection of the waste paper. The plan was launched in November 1990.

Maryanne Hawes and her assistant, Lucy Mayer, were made responsible for publicising the scheme to those involved. A letter was sent from the Chief Executive Officer to every individual involved in the pilot scheme. Then the recycling officers went in person to each department involved, introducing green bags and explaining what the policy meant. They explained which paper could be recycled and where it should go. The initiative met with some criticism at first from a small number of staff who saw it as yet another thing for them to do. However, generally the scheme was accepted very quickly and was running smoothly within a few weeks of its implementation, with the separation of paper becoming second nature.

Although the pilot scheme was not publicised extensively throughout HCC—except on electronic mail—a measure of its success has been the steady flow of requests for involvement from outlying departments, as well as other departments at The Castle, including the Surveyors Department. These departments were allocated green bags for paper collection and are allowed to store their waste paper with the sacks from The Castle—ready for collection by the recycling company, Maybank. The operation of the scheme within outlying departments has not been constrained by its dependence on the willingness of staff to bring sacks to central collection points on a voluntary basis. So far, over seventy tonnes of paper have been reclaimed, with collection now averaging over four tonnes a month.

Since the paper scheme was launched, there has been a marked change in the attitudes of staff involved. At the regular departmental meetings, staff started to call for other waste management schemes. A bottle bank was called for, which was installed in the car park. After this, staff requested a can bank which was installed in August 1991. Next came calls to recycle laser cartridges. In addition to these recycling initiatives, staff also called for energy efficiency schemes and bicycle spaces. Other projects under consideration or trial are composting, plastics recycling and re-use of construction material waste.

The paper scheme has been running for over a year now in The Castle. In October 1991 a review of the scheme in the Surveyors Department was initiated by Stephen Tribe, a management trainee working with the Waste Disposal Authority. He found it very difficult at first to estimate the effect of the policy on paper consumption accurately, as no record of paper use by the department is kept— although £30,000 worth of paper is consumed every year. However, initial analysis of the effect of the 'Green Copier Code'—which is displayed on all photocopying machines advising on mistake minimisation and double-sided copying—shows that the number of photocopies may have fallen by as much as 10 or 20%.

The Surveyors Department seem to be very enthusiastic about controlling waste. The Graduate Engineers Group, within the Surveyors Department, have produced proactive documents on 'Suggested Methods of Waste Avoidance' which include many interesting recommendations:

- That the true cost of computer print-outs should be displayed on screen each time a hard copy of a computer file is taken.
- A recommendation should be made to central government to introduce legislation making it compulsory for the cost of packaging to be displayed on all packaged goods with the aim of discouraging excessive packaging.
- There should be an agreement by the Council to buy back all recycled paper.

The Surveyors Department are also currently looking closely at ways to reduce construction waste. Seventy per cent of all waste landfilled in Hampshire is inert construction waste. The opportunities outlined by the group, which emphasise the need for environmental considerations to be incorporated at the design stage and standards to be developed for re-usable materials, could lead to huge savings in construction waste.

The initial success of HCC's waste management policy is very difficult to measure until the results of the audit are known. The fact that people use the facilities is taken as proof by the Waste Disposal Authority (WDA) that the scheme is successful. The WDA has earned enough money from paper recycling to fund the schemes, but as yet no one knows the full environmental impact the policy has had. A survey of public opinion in the county also revealed that very few people were aware of the waste facilities available, or what initiatives the Council were taking.

HCC provide an example of an organisation which has some good ideas on waste management. They managed to minimise initial problems by publicising the scheme in advance, encouraging participation and provision of information. Perseverance and personal contact are recommended for any unforeseen problems. They found that the staff quickly accepted the changes and indeed started to come up with new initiatives themselves. HCC are now deciding how to launch the scheme countywide, not only in their own departments but also to the general public.

Involving the Community: The London Borough of Sutton

The London Borough of Sutton Council (LBS) have a history of committed environmental activity, largely due to the enthusiasm of Helmut Lusser, Assistant Chief Planner, and 'the green team'.

Sutton introduced their first major step towards recycling in May 1988. This scheme was introduced boroughwide and consisted of a 'Bring' scheme, growing from nineteen to thirty-four local recycling sites. Individuals were encouraged to bring initially waste paper, glass, and, since 1990, rags, cans and batteries, to special banks. Over 100 containers have been launched across the borough and 4,000 tonnes of waste collected in 1990/91. The success of this campaign can be put down largely to good Stakeholder communications. The Council had already published an environmental statement, so they were already seen by the press as innovative. The launch of the 'Bring' scheme therefore received much media coverage, especially locally. Second, and perhaps more importantly, LBS hit upon the idea of encouraging local groups to 'adopt' banks.

These groups—such as local green groups, rotary clubs, scout clubs and so on—became responsible for the upkeep and publicity of the bank. In this way, the banks became the property of the local groups and hence the local communities—a very effective way of capturing individual involvement and enthusiasm.

The second waste management scheme was launched in January 1990. This was the 'Collect' scheme. The Council collects specially separated waste from the kerbside outside people's homes. Three quarters of all households are involved in the scheme—totalling 50,000 homes in August 1991. In March 1990 LBS set itself the target of 50% waste recycling. It is hoped that the kerbside collection scheme will make this target possible—already 3,000 tonnes of paper have been collected for recycling.

The Council are now looking at other waste management possibilities. A decision has been made to launch a pilot scheme to 15,000 homes on composting organic waste—2,000 free or subsidised containers will be distributed to the community. Other areas of particular interest include wood recycling, rubble re-use—even tyre recycling. The Council are also looking into plastic recycling.

The overall lesson to be learned from the LBS experience of waste management is that if such schemes are to succeed, local people must be involved. LBS developed some innovative ways of generating local group interest in their waste management scheme. These local groups then communicated the vision to the local communities, which instilled a sense of ownership of the scheme. The fact that local people had become sensitive to waste management issues then left the way open for more involvement in waste management trials. LBS are seen by many to be a model of waste management practice. They have regular requests for advice on greening, and in 1991 received thirty delegations from other organisations. While the main benefits of the scheme have been environmental, involvement in waste management has also benefited corporate image tremendously, as the Council is now seen as a responsible local authority. The Council are now starting to get involved in projects with business in an attempt to spread the message of environmental concern even further into the community.

Greener Communications

ECO-SPONSORSHIP
The Green Business Service

Tim Selman

Development Officer, Thornham Field Centre
(former Project Officer, The Green Business Service)

Since the late eighties, there has been a considerable shift in environmental awareness. Companies have realised that by demonstrating environmental responsibility they can become more socially acceptable. One method of doing this is through corporate sponsorship of environmental projects. This has been especially important for companies involved in sensitive sectors, such as nuclear, chemical and heavy industries.

One of the most well-known and respected examples of eco-sponsorship is Shell's 'Better Britain' scheme. Shell's involvement is primarily for public relations reasons. The scheme has been running since 1969, offering small grants of less than £500 to conservation groups, and in 1988 it helped 366 different groups. Donations have been made to these causes without necessarily altering Shell's corporate environmental strategy. This type of eco-sponsorship has always created problems for environmentalists who on the one hand chastise the company for the inherent un-greenness of their business and on the other rely on sponsorship to fund projects.

Another example of how a small eco-sponsorship budget can generate good community relations, and media coverage for the sponsor, is The Green Business Service. In 1989 The Green Business Service was established from a donation of £32,000 from BP. The Green Business Service was set up within Eastleigh Borough Council with the brief of helping local businesses in a practical way to address environmental issues. BP's motives in supporting The Green Business Service lay in the strategic importance of Eastleigh Borough's Hamble Oil Terminal, especially as BP were undertaking major development work linking

Hamble by pipeline to Wytch Farm in Dorset. Like many large companies, BP have tended to support causes around their active sites as a community relations exercise. The service is unique within local authorities in the UK, although the concept is more common in more environmentally aware countries, such as Germany and Holland. During its first eighteen months, The Green Business Service gave help and advice to around 120 businesses. The different requirements, expectations and demands of local and regional companies resulted in a wide range of projects being completed, from tree planting and habitat management to organising conferences, Environmental Auditing and policy formulation. Research and development work also included studies into a variety of new greener technologies, including innovative treatments for organic wastes.

The Green Business Service started by undertaking a wide variety of practical projects. This included a considerable amount of work with marine-related businesses along the River Hamble, amounting to £60,000 worth of practical improvements. This was achieved from a small works budget of £2,000, supplemented by grant aid and contributions from industry. The work included a project from Marina Developments Ltd who own three large prestigious marina sites on the river. The Green Business Service drew up plans and specifications, applied for and secured grant aid, liaised with contractors and oversaw the work. This included successfully reclaiming contaminated land, woodland management, and removing rubbish from two hectares of salt marsh and tidal creeks.

The value of this type of sponsorship approach is clear. However, it has become clear that companies can no longer simply sponsor environmental projects in an attempt to become greener. They must, if they are to secure public approval, start to look at their own operations and attempt to improve their environmental performance. Thus the emphasis of The Green Business Service was changed to help companies incorporate environmental management into company policy.

The Green Business Service adopted an innovative project management approach, and a good example is displayed in the hotel and tourism industry. Botley Park Country Club were proactively approached about the business benefits of taking a greener approach. The Green Business Service then completed a full Environmental Audit and conservation management plan of their grounds and golf course. This was translated into a long-term action plan and company policy statement. The project generated considerable commitment and motivation amongst all members of staff. As a result, the hotel has received considerable press, radio and TV coverage, and the practical business benefits are starting to feed through. Research among hotel customers indicates that the greener approach is likely to influence further bookings positively, and two green business conferences have been organised at the hotel as a result of their environmental initiatives.

Botley Park is a part of the Rank Hotel Group. The Group have seen the business opportunity that lies in a greener approach, and have started to examine the environmental issues as they affect Rank hotels throughout the UK. This has resulted in the development of a corporate stance on environmental issues with the publication of a Corporate Environmental Statement in early December 1991. Thus from a small beginning, a large international company has developed an environmental position.

Many local authorities have looked upon The Green Business Service as a model, and it is clear that there is a demand from industry for such a service, especially among small companies. This will grow as legislation increases and as more consumers demand greener products and services. Without this kind of support throughout the country, British industry is likely to become less competitive in the global market. The DTI, DoE, CBI and many other organisations recognise this, but no one as yet has developed the most effective method of addressing the problem, since neither local authorities, central government nor industry have the resources to tackle the problem on their own.

Greener People

PROMOTING ORGANISATIONAL CHANGE
British Telecom

Cerian Moss
KPH Marketing

British Telecom provide a good example of proactive corporate environmental policy development. Although the company are not perceived to be particularly environmentally damaging (see Fig. 1), BT found that employees, in particular, wanted green issues to be given a greater priority.

Perceived Level of Environmental Damage				
Industry	Major/Fair	Some	Virtually None	Don't Knows
Chemical	32%	22%	5%	41%
Oil	52%	31%	4%	13%
Hotel/restaurant	6%	20%	42%	32%
BT	8%	29%	44%	19%
Source: MORI, 1991				

Figure 1

Written memos from employees and feedback from team briefings indicated the level of environmental concern to management. A survey carried out by the internal newsletter, *BT Today*, in 1990 discovered that 24% of readers wanted more information on the environment. This was second only to more local BT news.

In addition, in the late eighties, peer group pressure began to assume greater importance for BT Directors. BT's Deputy Chairman, as a member of the Business in the Environment Target Team of Business in the Community, became aware of the initiatives being taken by peer group companies. The association was influential in increasing awareness of environmental issues at main board level.

There were other pressures to go green: for instance, BT had been receiving an increasing number of questionnaires from green and ethical trusts, and in addition, shareholders were starting to ask more questions about BT's environmental performance. Customers had also started to pressurise BT into looking at its environmental performance.

As a result of these pressures, BT undertook a 'scoping study' in 1990 carried out by an independent environmental consultancy. The scoping study made five recommendations:

- Set a corporate environmental policy that is endorsed by the Board
- Create the position of an Environmental Issues Manager
- Nominate a main Board member with responsibility for the environment
- Managers should have environmental responsibility designated within their job descriptions
- Establish a high-level steering group

All of these recommendations have since been implemented with the exception of the environmental responsibility designated within all manager job descriptions. After researching the area, BT found that some parts of the company had much higher environmental impacts than others: for instance, Building Services. BT are therefore currently introducing environmental performance into certain relevant job descriptions and investigating ways of integrating environmental requirements into the company's formal management systems.

People Involvement

The steering group found that many groups within BT were already drawing up their own greener proposals, so there was a potential duplication of effort. It was recognised that in order to avoid this the environmental policy had to be coordinated effectively. This is not an easy task for a business employing around 220,000 people (1992 figures).

To launch their increased commitment, BT are incorporating environmental matters into their Total Quality Management campaign entitled 'Involving Everyone', with the aims of increasing environmental awareness and starting to initiate change in employee behaviour. 'Involving Everyone' aims to do just that. It aims to show employees what they can do—such as turning off lights and producing less waste, especially paper. It is hoped that the campaign will enthuse staff about the issues, get them involved and encourage them to work on their own initiative. To this end, the campaign is being tailored in such a way as to encourage employees to appreciate what can be done within the scope of their own job.

Dr Tuppen, the recently appointed Environmental Issues Manager, stressed how important it is to get the communication right first time. 'If you don't get it right it can switch people off. Timing is critical and it is very important to get the environmental benefits over.' With this in mind, energy efficiency has been communicated as a way of saving the planet from global warming and pollution such as acid rain, rather than as a money-saving device, which it is also expected to be in the long run.

Most communication is currently delivered through the medium of *BT Today*—which is delivered to all present and past BT employees and therefore has a readership of well over 250,000. *BT Today* has always had regular articles on the environment, but January 1992 saw the launch of a special annual supplement. The environmental supplement aims to be part educational, part motivational and, in line with BT's strategy, most importantly a good read. A new copy style has even been devised to deal with environmental issues in a way which will encourage employees to get involved.

BT sees environmental excellence as part of the whole TQM concept, and this concept is already being communicated to senior management. In addition to senior staff training, non-managerial employees will attend a one-day workshop on TQM and the environment over 1992/93.

BT are also looking at how key people would benefit from increased awareness of environmental issues. 'In a large, non-manufacturing organisation it can be difficult to pinpoint those specific people who need more environmental knowledge', states Dr Tuppen. Nevertheless, BT are constantly researching ways to develop employee awareness of the environment.

Conclusion

BT believe that the environment will become an increasingly competitive issue for business. They also believe that environmental responsibility is an important aspect of TQM and Corporate Social Responsibility. BT have realised that the involvement and participation of all employees will be crucial to the success of BT's greening policy. Only by getting everyone involved will they be able to respond to the threats and opportunities presented by the environment. It is for this reason that BT are working so hard to communicate the environmental message to their employees.

Greener People

THE IMPORTANCE OF INTERNAL MARKETING
Pilkington Glass Ltd

Andy McDowell
Environment Officer, PGL

Pilkington Glass Limited (PGL) began its formal green thinking in mid-1989. A senior manager discussed a green topic with the Chief Executive to research and report for his part-time MBA programme. As a result of this, one of the directors was asked to accept responsibility for green issues from October of that year. The following month, a PGL Green Panel was formed. The Panel looked into all aspects of PGL's activities with respect to the environment, and drafted a policy for the Company. The PGL Environmental Policy was approved by the Board in March 1990, establishing a clear and comprehensive framework for the many environmental activities of PGL.

Environmental representatives were appointed at each PGL location. These managers, responsible for each location's environmental activities, produced environmental audits for every PGL location.

In order to communicate green issues throughout the whole of PGL, the Pilkington Glass Environmental Care Programme was launched under the title, 'Looking to the Future'. A Green Conference was held in April 1991, and was attended by over 100 PGL directors, works managers, senior managers and staff. This conference formed an integral part of the communication plan with the objective to educate and motivate works managers and 'movers and shapers' at PGL sites to tackle environmental issues sensibly.

Another element of this communication plan is the Green Video. This was launched at the Green Conference and was produced with two aims in mind. First, to put into action the statement in the PGL Environmental Policy: 'To sustain and protect the environment we will promote and undertake educational programmes and discussion on green issues for employees.' Second, to communicate to all PGL employees the positive environmental characteristics of PGL business, while recognising that our activities do have an effect on the local, national and global environment. PGL employees must be amenable to environmental initiatives and make independent suggestions. But, most importantly, to communicate the genuine commitment of senior personnel that in the future, green issues will take an increasingly important role in PGL decision making.

After the initial viewing at the Green Conference, the video was shown to all the employees at each of the PGL sites in the UK. It was recommended that discussion groups were formed at the sites to deal with any queries or suggestions resulting from the video. Employee participation was encouraged and help was provided where necessary.

Children feature throughout the video, the message being that while satisfying the needs of today's society, we must not jeopardise the ability of our children to meet their needs in the future.

Although a professional presenter was used, the bulk of the video contains children, employees and the general public.

The video emphasises the message that children are the best people to judge the present generation (as it is their future), and incorporates a simple checklist. As each issue is addressed, the children cross the issue off their checklist.

The video opens with comments from schoolchildren and the public on subjects such as pollution, recycling, transport, litter and the ozone threat. Comments such as, 'time is short', 'all have to get involved', 'we are responsible', 'start putting it right', are made to raise a feeling of urgency and responsibility amongst the viewers. Issues then addressed are as follows:

- What are PGL doing about saving energy? Environmental Audits were completed recently which included energy use at each site. This served to highlight areas which should be worked on. In the past twenty years, energy consumption by PGL has been cut by 40%, and a further 10% cut is planned in the next two to three years.

- What are PGL doing about recycling? Recycling of broken glass (cullet) within PGL sites is over 99% efficient. To help recover waste glass from scrap vehicles and demolition of houses, PGL commissioned management consultants, PE International, to look at sources of recycled window glass.

- Better pollution control. Since 1974, PGL has reduced pollution from its sites by the following levels:

$$NO_x \quad - \quad 30\% \text{ cut}$$
$$CO_2 \quad - \quad 40\% \text{ cut}$$
$$SO_x \quad - \quad 55\% \text{ cut}$$

- Greener offices. A committee has been set up in PGL to deal specifically with office-related green issues. Work has been done on recycling paper and aluminium cans, and also on energy-efficient lighting. The committee encourages the use of electronic mail and double-sided photocopying.

- What about PGL's products? Pilkington K Glass used in double glazing increases solar gain, reduces heat loss and therefore cuts energy use. This is important, as energy use in buildings is one of the biggest causes of global warming. If all the single-glazed windows in the UK were double-glazed with Pilkington K Glass, energy worth £850 million would be saved. This energy is equal to three times the output of a large modern power station, and would reduce CO_2 emissions by ten million tonnes a year.

The video ends with a keynote address from the then PGL Environmental Director asking for ideas and encouraging support from all employees on green issues. This 'internal marketing' of green issues to the employees of PGL has continued since the launch of the environmental care programme, with activities on sites concentrating on pollution control, energy efficiency, waste reduction and recycling. Office activities have broadened with the Green Office Committee now looking at other issues, including the performance of company vehicles.

The final statement of the video summarises PGL's continued commitment to the environment: 'Looking and working for a better future'.

FURTHER READING

Adams, R., J. Carruthers and C. Fisher, *Shopping for a Better World* (London: Kogan Page, 1991).

Adams, R., J. Carruthers and S. Hamil, *Changing Corporate Values* (London: Kogan Page, 1991).

Angell, D.J.R., J.D. Comer and M.L.N. Wilkinson (eds), *Sustaining Earth: Response to the Environmental Threats* (London: Macmillan, 1990).

Arnold, M., F. Long and P. Choi, *Marketing and Ecology: Readings and Discussion* (Washington DC: The Management Institute for Environment and Business, 1991).

Bernstein, D., *In the Company of Green* (London: ISBA, 1992).

Burke, T., N. Robins and A. Trisoglio (eds.), *Environment Strategy Europe 1991* (London: Camden Publishing, 1991).

Button, J., *How To Be Green* (London: Century Hutchinson, 1989).

Cairncross, F., *Costing the Earth* (London: Economist Books, 1991).

Callenbach, E., F. Capra and S. Marburg, *The Elmwood Guide to Eco-Auditing and Ecologically Conscious Management* (Berkeley, CA: The Elmwood Institute, 1990).

Carson, P. and J. Moulden, *Green is Gold* (Toronto: Harper Business, 1991).

Charter, M., *Graduates: Fewer and Greener* (Alton: KPH Marketing, 1990).

—*The Greener Employee* (Alton: KPH Marketing, 1990).

—*Greener Marketing* (Alton: KPH Marketing, 1990).

Clutterbuck, D., and D. Snow, *Working with the Community: A Guide to Corporate Social Responsibility* (London: Weidenfeld and Nicolson, 1990).

Dauncey, G., *After the Crash: The Emergence of the Rainbow Economy* (Basingstoke: Greenprint, 1988).

Davis, D.P., *Gearing Up for the Environment* (Basingstoke: IBM, 1991).

Davis, J., *Greening Business: Managing for Sustainable Development* (Oxford: Basil Blackwell, 1991).

Elkington, J. (with T. Burke), *The Green Capitalists: Industry's Search for Environmental Excellence* (London: Victor Gollancz, 1987).

Elkington J., T. Burke and J. Hailes, *Green Pages: The Business of Saving the World* (London: Routledge, 1988).

Elkington, J., and J. Hailes, *The Green Consumer Guide: High Street Shopping for a Better Environment* (London: Victor Gollancz, 1988).

Elkington, J., and J. Hailes, *The Green Consumer's Supermarket Shopping Guide* (London: Victor Gollancz, 1989).

Elkington, J., *The Environmental Audit: A Green Filter for Company Policies, Plants, Processes and Products* (London: SustainAbility/World Wide Fund for Nature, 1990).

Elkington, J., P. Knight and J. Hailes, *The Green Business Guide* (London: Victor Gollancz, 1991).

Elkington, J., and A. Dimnock, *The Corporate Environmentalists* (London: Sustain-Ability, 1991).

Forrester, S., *Business and Environmental Groups: A Natural Partnership?* (London: Directory of Social Change, 1990).

Gray, R.H., *The Greening of Accountancy: The Profession after Pearce* (London: ACCA, 1990).

International Institute for Sustainable Development, *Business Strategy for Sustainable Development* (Winnipeg, Canada: IISD, 1992).

Lloyd, T., *The 'Nice' Company: Why 'Nice' Companies Make More Profits* (London: Bloomsbury, 1990).

Pearce, D., A. Markandya and E.B. Barbier, *Blueprint for a Green Economy* (London: Earthscan, 1989).

Peatty, E., *Green Marketing* (London: Pitmans, 1992).

Plant, C., and J. Plant, *Green Business: Hope or Hoax?* (Bideford: Green Books, 1991).

Prospect Centre, The, 'New Capabilities for the Green Organisation' (Kingston-upon-Thames: The Prospect Centre, 1990).

Ralston, K., and C. Church, *Working Greener* (London: Greenprint, 1991).

Schmidheiny, S. and The Business Council for Sustainable Development, *Changing Course: A Global Perspective on Development and the Environment* (London/ Cambridge, MA: The MIT Press, 1992).

Taylor, S., 'The Rewards of Virtue' (London: Shelley Taylor and Associates, 1991).

Winter, G., *Business and the Environment* (Hamburg: McGraw–Hill, 1988).

SOME USEFUL ADDRESSES

Advisory Committee on Business and the Environment (ACBE)
Department of the Environment, Room A304, Romney House, 43 Marsham
Street, London SW1P 3PY. Telephone: 071 276 3000

Bundesdeutscher Arbeitskreis für umweltbewußtes Management e.V. (BAUM)
Christian Forster-Str 19, 2000 Hamburg 20, Germany. Telephone: (49) 40 810101

British Institute of Management
Management House, Cottingham Road, Corby, North Hampshire, NN17 1TT.
Telephone: 0536 204222

British Library Environmental Information Service
25 Southampton Buildings, London, WC2A 1AW. Telephone: 071 323 7955

Business and Environment Programme
The Environment Council, 80 York Way, London, N1 9AG.
Telephone: 071 278 4736

Business Council for Sustainable Development
World Trade Centre Building, 3rd Floor, Route de l'Aeroport 10, Geneva,
Switzerland. Telephone: (41) 22 788 32 02

Business Network
PO Box 4DL, 7A Livonia Street, London, W1A 4DL. Telephone: 071 734 8139

Chartered Institute of Marketing
Moor Hall, Cookham, Maidenhead, Berkshire, SL6 9QH.
Telephone: 06285 24922

Commission of the European Communities
London Office, 8 Storey's Gate, London, SW1P 3AT. Telephone: 071 973 1992

Confederation of British Industry Environment Management Unit
Centre Point, 103 New Oxford Street, London, WC1A 1DU.
Telephone: 071 379 7400

Conservation Trust
National Environmental Education Centre, George Palmer Site, Northumberland
Avenue, Reading, Berks, RG2 7PW. Telephone: 0734 868442

Department of Energy
1 Palace Street, London, SW1E 5HE. Telephone: 071 238 3000

Department of the Environment
Romney House, 43 Marsham Street, London, SW1P 3PY.
Telephone: 071 276 3000

Earthscan
3 Endsleigh Street, London, WC1H 0DD. Telephone: 071 388 2117

Environmental Business Association
1150 Connecticut Avenue, NW, 9th Floor, Connecticut Building,
Washington DC 20036. Telephone: (202) 862 4363

European Parliament (London Office)
2 Queen Anne's Gate, London, SW1H 9AA. Telephone: 071 222 0411

Friends of the Earth
26-28 Underwood Street, London, N1 7JQ. Telephone: 071 490 1555

Global Environmental Management Initiative (GEMI)
1828 L Street, NW Suite 711, Washington DC 20036, USA.
Telephone: (202) 296 7449

Green Alliance
49 Wellington Street, London, WC2E 7BN. Telephone: 071 836 0341

Green Business Network
c/o Nottingham Business School, Chaucer Street, Nottingham, NG1 4BU.
Telephone: 0602 418418

Greener Management International
Greenleaf Publishing, Exchange Works, Sidney Street, Sheffield, S1 3QF.
Telephone: 0742 739721

Green Flag International
PO Box 396, Linton, Cambridge, CB1 6UL. Telephone: 0223 893587

Green Magazine
Northern and Shell plc, Northern and Shell Building, PO Box 381, Millharbour,
London, E14 9TW. Telephone: 071 987 5090

Green Net
23 Bevenden Street, London, N1 6BH. Telephone: 071 608 3040

Greenpeace
Cannonbury Villas, London, N1 2PN. Telephone: 071 354 5100

**Information Technology Centre for Educational Research, Development
and Training in the Environmental Sciences (IT CERES)**
School of Education, Southampton University, Highfield, Southampton,
SO9 5NH. Telephone: 0703 592385

Industry Council for Packaging and the Environment (ICPEN)
Premier House, 10 Greycoat Place, London, SW1P 1SB.
Telephone: 071 222 8866

International Association for Clean Technology
Metternichgasse 10, A-1030 Vienna, Austria. Telephone: (0222) 712 04 14/11

International Chamber of Commerce (United Kingdom)
14-15 Belgrave Square, London, SW1X 8PS. Telephone: 071 823 2811

International Network for Environmental Management (INEM)
Hellgrund 92, W-2000 Wedel, Holstein, Germany. Telephone: (49) 4103 84019

Institute of Environmental Assessment
The Old Malthouse, Spring Gardens, Grantham, Lincolnshire, NG31 6JP.
Telephone: 0476 68100

International Institute for Environment and Development (IIED)
3 Endsleigh Street, London, WC1H 0DD. Telephone: 071 388 2117

Institute of Ecology and Environmental Management
36 Kingfisher Court, Hambridge Road, Newbury, Berkshire, RG14 5SJ.
Telephone: 0635 37715

Sheffield Green Business Club
c/o Department of Animal and Plant Sciences, University of Sheffield,
PO Box 601, Sheffield, S10 2UQ. Telephone: 0742 768555

Solent Industry Environment Association (SIENA)
Civic Offices, Leigh Road, Eastleigh, Hampshire, SO5 4YN.
Telephone: 0703 614646

Technology, Research, Enterprise and the Environment (TREE)
PO Box 199, Coventry, CV2 4SJ. Telephone: 0203 692946

United Kingdom Centre for Economic and Environmental Development
12 Upper Belgrave Street, London, SW1X 8BA. Telephone: 071 245 6440

United Kingdom Environmental Law Association (UKELA)
c/o Linklaters & Paines, Mitre House, 160 Aldersgate Street, London, EC1A 4LP.
Telephone: 071 606 7080

United Nations Information Desk
20 Buckingham Gate, London, SW1 E6LB. Telephone: 071 630 1981

United Nations Environment Programme
Tour Mirabeau, 39-43 Quai André Citroën, 75739 Paris, Cedex 15.
Telephone: (331) 4058 8850

World Action for Recycling Materials and Energy from Rubbish (WARMER)
83 Mount Ephraim, Tunbridge Wells, Kent, TN4 8BS. Telephone: 0892 524626

World Resources Institute (WRI)
1735 New York Avenue NW, Washington DC 20006, USA.
Telephone: (202) 638 6300

Worldwatch Institute
1776 Massachusetts Avenue NW, Washington DC 20036, USA.
Telephone: (202) 452 1999

World Wide Fund for Nature
Panda House, Weyside Park, Cattershall Lane, Godalming, Surrey, GU7 1XR.
Telephone 0483 426444

INDEX